Ptolemy I

Ptolemy I

King and Pharaoh of Egypt

IAN WORTHINGTON

OXFORD
UNIVERSITY PRESS

OXFORD
UNIVERSITY PRESS

Oxford University Press is a department of the University of Oxford. It furthers
the University's objective of excellence in research, scholarship, and education
by publishing worldwide. Oxford is a registered trade mark of Oxford University
Press in the UK and certain other countries.

Published in the United States of America by Oxford University Press
198 Madison Avenue, New York, NY 10016, United States of America.

Library of Congress Cataloging-in-Publication Data
Names: Worthington, Ian, author.
Title: Ptolemy I : king and pharaoh of Egypt / Ian Worthington.
Description: New York : Oxford University Press, 2016. | Includes
bibliographical references and index.
Identifiers: LCCN 2016006550 (print) | LCCN 2016007840 (ebook) |
ISBN 9780190202330 (hardback) | ISBN 9780190202347 (ebook) |
ISBN 9780190202354 (ebook)
Subjects: LCSH: Ptolemy I Soter, King of Egypt, –283 B.C. | Egypt—Kings and
rulers—Biography. | Pharaohs—Biography. |
Generals—Macedonia—Biography. | Alexander, the Great, 356 B.C.–323 B.C.—
Friends and associates—Biography. | Egypt—History—332–30 B.C.
Classification: LCC DT92 .W67 2016 (print) | LCC DT92 (ebook) |
DDC 932/.021092 [B]—dc 3
LC record available at https://lccn.loc.gov/2016006550

CONTENTS

LIST OF MAPS AND FIGURES

Maps

Figures

PREFACE

Cleopatra, Queen of Egypt, is a household name, largely because of how she was said to have seduced the world's most powerful men, Julius Caesar and Mark Antony, in the dying years of the Roman Republic to keep Rome from annexing her kingdom. In the end, her grand strategy was thwarted when she and Antony were defeated at the battle of Actium in 31 BC. The following year, they committed suicide, and Octavian, the future Emperor Augustus, made Egypt part of the Roman Empire.

The story of Cleopatra, last of the Ptolemaic dynasty, is famous. Less so is that of her ancestor, who first established the dynasty from which she came almost 300 years before her own time. His name was Ptolemy. He was from rugged Macedonia, north of Mount Olympus on the Greek mainland. He marched with Alexander the Great when he invaded the Persian Empire, and fought alongside him in his epic battles and sieges, which toppled that empire. He became one of the king's elite handpicked bodyguards, but he was never entrusted with more than minor troop commands. As such, he seemed destined to be one of the peripheral figures in Alexander's invasion. But the king's death in Babylon in 323 BC changed all that. As his former commanders divided up the vast Macedonian Empire from Greece to India among themselves, Ptolemy was quick to assert himself in their negotiations, and to take over Egypt. It was a deliberate choice, showing a surprising cunning and ambition, which often cost his former comrades dearly.

Ptolemy was now 44 years old. He had opted for a country well away from what would be the major hotspots of the wars that he knew were inevitable between Alexander's Successors, as his surviving senior staff are commonly called. Sure enough, the Successors were soon waging a series of bloody wars against each other, lasting for four decades. Ptolemy played his part in these wars, slowly but surely building up his power base in Egypt, introducing administrative and economic reforms to make him one of the wealthiest individuals of the time, and founding the great Library and Museum at Alexandria to make that city the intellectual center of the entire Hellenistic age. He remained ruler of Egypt, first as satrap and then as its king and Pharaoh, until he was in his early eighties, dying in 283 BC. He established an Egyptian Empire, and even launched an ambitious attempt to capture what all the Successors saw as the jewel in the crown of possessions: Greece and Macedonia. He did not realize his ambition to become another Alexander, but he proved to be as ruthless as any of his opponents, while demonstrating a shrewdness and especially patience that they lacked. As a king, soldier, statesman, and intellectual, he was one of a kind, but even as king of Egypt, he remained a Macedonian through and through. From being one of Alexander's boyhood friends and rising only to the rank of bodyguard, Ptolemy surprised everyone by fighting off invasions, invading opponents' territories, and, against the odds, establishing the longest lived of the Hellenistic dynasties, which fell with Cleopatra's death in 30 BC. His achievements helped to shape not only Egypt's history but also that of the early Hellenistic world. Now it is time to bring him center stage in that history.

Ian Worthington
University of Missouri
May 2016

ACKNOWLEDGMENTS

It is a great pleasure once again to thank Stefan Vranka, my editor, for his willingness to take on this project, his support throughout, and his comments on the manuscript. I am still amazed he hasn't severed ties with me yet. I also thank everyone at Oxford University Press, especially Sarah Svendsen, who helped guide the book through the production process.

To the anonymous referee who pointed out flaws but still said publish it: thank you.

Joseph Roisman read the whole book in draft without grumbling too much. My heartfelt thanks go to him for his many suggestions and catches, and also to him and Hanna Roisman for their friendship and support over the years, which mean a lot.

I am also very grateful to Christelle Fischer-Bovet for her comments on the chapter to do with Ptolemy and Egypt (11); only she and I know how much she improved it, and I'm hoping she stays quiet.

My thanks go also to Aidan Dodson for supplying the photograph of the Satrap Stele (fig. 7.3).

Finally, to my long suffering family, who still won't accept that sitting in front of a computer seven days a week writing this stuff is work: thank you for letting me do what I do without complaining more than half the time.

ANCIENT WORKS AND ABBREVIATIONS

Quotations from Ptolemy's *History* (as quoted and paraphrased by later writers), Diodorus, and Justin are taken from these translations (those of other ancient writers are by me or are referenced in the notes):

Ptolemy, *History*

C. A. Robinson, *The History of Alexander the Great*, vol. 1 (Providence, RI: 1953).

Diodorus

R. M. Geer, *Diodorus Siculus 18 and 19.1–65*, Loeb Classical Library, vol. 9 (Cambridge, MA: 1947).

R. M. Geer, *Diodorus Siculus 19.66–110 and 20*, Loeb Classical Library, vol. 10 (Cambridge, MA: 1954).

F. R. Walton, *Diodorus Siculus 21–32*, Loeb Classical Library, vol. 11 (Cambridge, MA: 1957).

Justin

R. Develin and W. Heckel, *Justin: Epitome of the Philippic History of Pompeius Trogus* (Atlanta, GA: 1994).

The following modern works are abbreviated in the notes to reduce repetition of bibliographical information:

Austin   M. M. Austin, *The Hellenistic World from Alexander to the Roman Conquest: A Selection of Ancient Sources in Translation* (Cambridge: 1981).

BNJ   Ian Worthington (editor-in-chief), *Brill's New Jacoby* (Leiden: 2007–).

FGrH   F. Jacoby, *Die Fragmente der griechischen Historiker* (Berlin/ Leiden: 1926–).

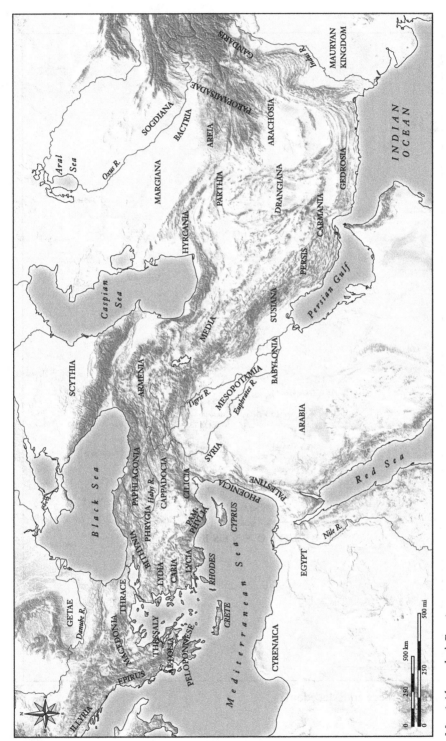

Map 1 Alexander's Empire

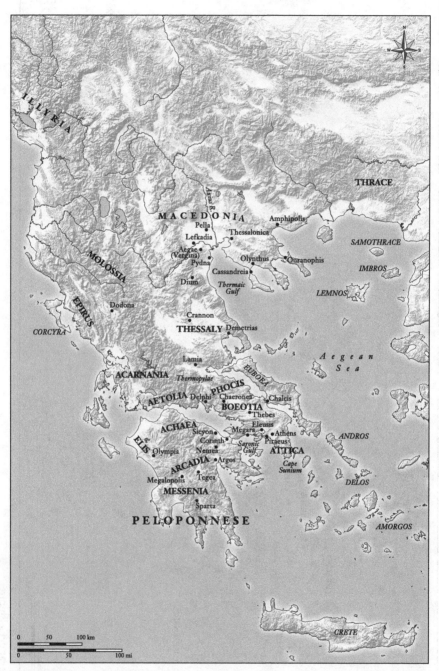

Map 2 Greece and Macedonia

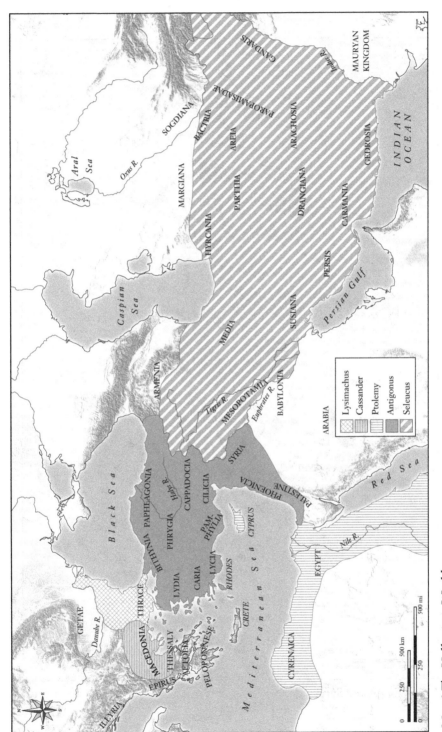

Map 3 The Hellenistic World

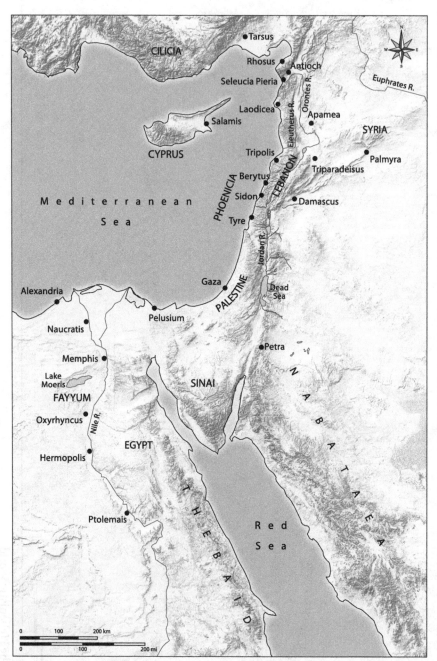

Map 4 Egypt and Syria

Ptolemy I

Ptolemy I

Introduction

From Cleopatra to Ptolemy

For her own person,
It beggared all description: she did lie
In her pavilion, cloth-of-gold of tissue,
O'erpicturing that Venus where we see
The fancy outwork nature.

So Shakespeare describes the most famous of the Egyptian queens, Cleopatra (VII), in his *Antony and Cleopatra* (II.2.198–202). His image of her is continued in the many movies and TV series in which she features: a femme fatale, supposedly drop-dead gorgeous, who ruled Egypt from 55 to 30 BC, a turbulent time when Rome had annexed almost all of the Mediterranean and Near East into its empire, leaving Egypt dangerously isolated. The Egypt she ruled was wealthy, powerful, exotic, corrupt, and an intellectual jewel in the ancient world thanks to the great Library and Museum at Alexandria. Cleopatra was more than just Queen of Egypt, though: she *was* Egypt—thus at the end of the play Octavian tells a kneeling Cleopatra, "I pray you, rise; rise, Egypt" (V.2.138).[1]

Cleopatra used her charms, the play leads us to believe, to seduce the two most powerful men of the late Roman Republic, Julius Caesar and Mark Antony. She had sons by them, and she and Antony even married and ruled Egypt together from Alexandria. There they lived a life of luxury and sexual debauchery. All that came to an end in 31 with the defeat of the Egyptian fleet at the famous battle of Actium. The following year Octavian (the future emperor Augustus) marched on Alexandria. To prevent capture, Antony committed

---

[1] The bibliography on Cleopatra is enormous: see, for example, Rice 1999; Walker and Higgs 2001; Burstein 2004; Ashton 2008; Roller 2010; more popular studies include Schiff 2010 and Fletcher 2011.

suicide, as did Cleopatra, succumbing, it was said, to the bite of a poisonous asp smuggled to her by one of her ladies in waiting. Thus died two of history's greatest lovers, and the country became the Roman province Aegyptus, the personal property of the emperor.

Reality was different. Shakespeare's *Antony and Cleopatra* is most responsible for projecting the romantic image we have of Cleopatra and her relationship with Antony. Busts of her show that she hardly surpassed Venus in looks, and she was not the promiscuous seductress of legend. She used what nature had generously given her to protect Egypt and its people from Rome and to maintain the centuries-long Ptolemaic dynasty. That was why at age eighteen she became pregnant by Julius Caesar (then 53 years old) and had his son, Ptolemy Caesar, who became her co-ruler of Egypt. Likewise her marriage to Antony, which also produced sons, ensured the continuity of Ptolemaic rule. She certainly did not need a husband, because she followed the Ptolemaic practice of incestuous marriages, having married her brothers and co-rulers Ptolemy XIII and Ptolemy XIV before assuming sole control of Egypt.

Love of her country and its people—shown by her being the only Ptolemaic ruler to learn Egyptian—and a determined stance to resist the tide of Roman imperialism were at the heart of Cleopatra's actions, both sexual and political, making her one of her country's greatest rulers.

In the end, her clever Machiavellian scheming did not succeed. Cleopatra's death brought with it the collapse of the Ptolemaic dynasty and the end of Egyptian autonomy. We all know the story. But if that is how Ptolemaic Egypt collapsed, how and why did it begin? Who founded this great, long-lived dynasty, and how different was Egypt in its early years from the splendor, power, and corruption personified by the likes of Antony and Cleopatra? And even, how did a dynasty that began with male rulers who had queens at their beck and call evolve into one with queens as rulers, especially queens as powerful and charismatic as Cleopatra?

To answer these questions, we go back almost 300 years from the battle of Actium to the last half of the fourth century, with the rise and especially fall of the Macedonian Empire under Philip II and Alexander the Great.[2] At its zenith that empire stretched from Greece to India, including Syria and Egypt. This was a remarkable achievement, given that before Philip came to the throne in 359 the kingdom was a backwater on the periphery of the Greek world. Situated north of Mount Olympus, Macedonia was disunited, economically weak, victim to invasion by the tribes on its borders, and prey to the meddling

---

[2] Most recently, see Worthington 2014.

of Greek cities such as Athens and Thebes in its domestic politics. In a reign of 23 years, Philip united the country; centralized the capital at Pella; created an army that was second to none; stabilized his borders; exploited the natural resources as never before; and embarked on an expansionist policy, which laid the foundations for the great empire under Alexander. Philip was assassinated in 336, at which time Macedonia controlled all Greece and Thrace as far as the Hellespont; Macedonia was the superpower of the Classical world, and was poised to put into action Philip's grand plan of invading Asia.

After Philip's death, his son Alexander came to power, and in 334 the new king invaded Asia. When he died in Babylon in 323, his great empire was distributed among his various officers, whom we call Successors (*Diadochoi*). They governed their areas as satraps, nominally loyal to the two kings who followed Alexander, Philip III and Alexander IV. The Successors, however, were soon at war with each other, always striving for a greater slice of the old empire and more prestige, and they remained at war for almost forty years. During this time Philip III and Alexander IV were ruthlessly executed, and those of the Successors who had survived this long changed from satraps to actual kings.

Enter Ptolemy, a Macedonian who befriended Alexander in his youth, served on campaign with him in Asia, and was promoted to the exclusive royal bodyguard, a hand-picked body of seven men, who protected the king at all times.[3] After Alexander's death in Babylon in 323, Ptolemy, then about 44 years old, found himself suddenly pitted against Alexander's generals and satraps when crucial decisions had to be made about the future of the empire. He had largely remained on the periphery of the king's retinue in Asia, but if the senior staff thought little of him because of his status they were mistaken. In a clear sign of his ambition, he immediately asserted himself as a significant player in the negotiations at Babylon over Alexander's successor and the empire. In the resulting settlement, he was appointed satrap of Egypt, eventually turning that office into a personal kingship. He established the Ptolemaic dynasty, which ended with Cleopatra 300 years later, and he enabled Egypt to become one of the great powers of the Greek world during those centuries. He helped Alexandria, his capital, become the foremost city and intellectual center of the Hellenistic period, thanks to the Library and the Museum he founded. The Egypt he forged really did stand "at the crossroads of Egyptian and Hellenistic history."[4]

[3] On the royal bodyguard ("the seven"), see Heckel 1978, 1986, and 1992, pp. 237–246, 257–259.
[4] Vandorpe 2010, p. 160.

Ptolemy's story is not one of rags to riches, nor is it one of single-minded ambition from an early age. He was ambitious, but he bided his time because he knew from experience that Alexander's generals hated each other and would not be satisfied with the territories they received at Babylon. They had carried out Alexander's orders faithfully, but they were held together only by the sheer force of his personality. Once he was dead, their dislike of each other was unchecked, and sure enough, as Ptolemy had expected, their personalities and aspirations led to their downfalls. Ptolemy, who had chosen Egypt because of its location and security, was clever and shrewd in how he went about ruling that country. He introduced policies that benefited the economy, his army, and especially his own coffers, and carefully negotiated the hazardous and treacherous sea of the Successors' diplomatic and military relations. Only when he felt sufficiently secure did he show himself to be no different from the others in wanting a greater share of empire.

Unfortunately, there is much we do not know about the man or his rule, thanks to the paucity of the ancient evidence (Appendix 2).[5] We are reasonably well informed about the Macedonian invasion of Asia because Alexander the Great captivated ancient writers. Indeed, Ptolemy himself wrote a history of Alexander, which was used by ancient writers long after Alexander was dead (see Appendix 1). The history of the Successors— and of Ptolemy—is less well served. Our principal narrative account, written by Diodorus of Sicily in the later first century BC, gives us good details down to the pivotal battle of Ipsus in 301; after that, his narrative is fragmented. Other major sources, such as Justin, do not focus wholly on Ptolemy, and deal cursorily with his later reign. We have no life of Ptolemy by Plutarch, a biographer of the first and second centuries AD, who wrote a series of lives of prominent Greeks and Romans, including Alexander and some other individuals of our period, such as Demetrius Poliorcetes ("the besieger") or Pyrrhus of Epirus. There are, then, big gaps in Ptolemy's life—his background and youth; what his relationship was like with his wives and children; how he viewed himself; exactly why he stole Alexander's corpse or founded the Museum and the Library in Alexandria; how he set out to bridge the divide between his Egyptian, Greek, and Macedonian subjects; the extent to which he allowed himself to be influenced by Alexander; and even what happened during the last two or three years of his reign, to name only some.

---

[5] The sources on Ptolemy are cited and discussed by Seibert 1969, pp. 52–83; most of his book is anchored in a very careful analysis of the ancient sources.

Nevertheless, we can still bring him out of the shadows of Alexander's retinue and into the spotlight of ancient history. Although other Successors carved kingdoms that were larger than that of Ptolemy, none had the longevity of the Ptolemaic dynasty. Nor, thanks to Cleopatra's relations with Julius Caesar and Mark Antony, did any other Hellenistic power so polarize Roman society, and play a role in the wars of the second triumvirate that ended the Roman Republic and ushered in rule by emperor. And Ptolemy started it all.

Ptolemy's rise to power was part of the complex and lengthy Wars of the Successors, which broke out soon after Alexander's death in 323 and did not end until 281. A lot happened in those forty years. While I discuss these wars as they pertain to Ptolemy and his dealings with the individuals who intersected with him, this book is not a history of the Successors, nor should it be. Those who want to read about these wars in detail should consult the works I cite in the notes.

Throughout this book I use the term "Hellenistic" to talk about the world after the death of Alexander, but a word of caution on the term is needed. Alexander's death in 323 brought to an end the Classical period in Greek history (478–323) and ushered in a new era, the so-called Hellenistic age. This lasted for a little under 300 years until 30, when the Romans annexed Egypt, and so completed their absorption of the entire eastern Mediterranean world into their empire. Alexander's death really was a turning point in ancient history; his conquests had shown the Greeks that they belonged to a world far larger than the Mediterranean, and he opened up all manner of contacts between West and East, which increased in this new world.

The phrase "Hellenistic period" was not used by those who lived at the time, but is a modern one, first coined by the German historian Johann Gustav Droysen in his *Geschichte der Diadochen* (*History of the Successors*), which was published in 1836; it had become accepted by the time of his *Geschichte der Hellenismus* (*History of Hellenism*) in 1877. Droysen took the name from the Greek verbs *hellenizo* ("I am Greek") and *hellenizontes* ("going Greek") because of the spread of Greek language and culture—Hellenism—as far east as India, which he believed was the inherent defining feature of those three centuries.

Droysen's definition, and hence the term, has been challenged because there were other important and defining features of this period (not least in the intellectual and cultural spheres), not to mention that focusing on regions that adopted Greek excludes the people who were a major driving force: the Greeks themselves. Instead of "Hellenistic period," the term "Macedonian Centuries" has been suggested, given that it was Alexander's invasion of Asia

and the ensuing reigns of his generals cum kings and their dynasties that lay at
the heart of all the changes and events.[6] This is an attractive suggestion, but also
not without its problems. There really is no one term that properly encapsulates
everything that went on during these complex three centuries, so for the sake of
convenience I use "Hellenistic."

All dates are BC except where indicated.

---

[6] For a discussion of the term, citing bibliography, see for example Green 1990, pp. 312–332;
Shipley 2000, pp. 1–5; Bugh 2006; cf. Errington 2008, pp. 1–9 (the phrase "Macedonian Centuries"
on p. 8). See also the interesting piece by Samuel 1989, pp. 1–12 ("Modern Views of the Period after
Alexander"), on the reception of Droysen's views about the spread of Greekness from West to East
and the concept of a Hellenistic period and culture over the past 150 years.

1

The Young Ptolemy

"A member of Alexander's bodyguard and a first-rate soldier, Ptolemy was even more talented at, and better known for, the civilian rather than military skills. His manner was modest and unassuming, and he was superlatively generous and approachable, having assumed none of the pride of royalty."[1]

"[Ptolemy] was a man of insight, but he was not a man of charisma. He did not excite the mass of men the way that Alexander the Great did or even Demetrius Poliorcetes. But he was shrewd. He understood what neither of these men did nor any of the other leaders of that generation. He understood, at some level, consciously or unconsciously, that Alexander's empire would not survive as an entity."[2]

These two assessments—the first by an ancient writer, and the second by a modern scholar—unquestionably praise Ptolemy, ruler of Egypt, as a man, a soldier, a politician, and later a king. Ptolemy lived much of his early adulthood in the larger-than-life shadow of Alexander the Great. When Alexander died in 323, his empire stretched from Greece to India (Map 1). However, he left no heir, but only a dynastic nightmare. Ptolemy, as well as Alexander's generals and senior officials, faced the problem of what to do with this enormous empire. Only Ptolemy seemed to have grasped that the days of a single vast empire, held together by the charisma of one king, were no more. He and the others, commonly called Alexander's Successors (*Diadochoi*), sliced up that empire, becoming, as we shall see, first satraps and then kings in their own right of the various parts. In the process they waged war against each other until the late 280s, when only three of the original Successors were left standing—Ptolemy being one.

The quotations at the start of this chapter do Ptolemy some justice, but as we shall see, when called to take the battlefield his military skills were certainly on a par with his civilian ones. What these quotations do not show is

[1] Curtius 9.8.23, trans. Yardley 1984, *ad loc.*
[2] Ellis 1994, p. ix.

what made Ptolemy tick and how he viewed himself: he was a survivor, he was ambitious, he was ruthless, and he was, like the other Successors, an imperialist who felt worthy of following in Alexander's footsteps. In the way he ruled Egypt and how he negotiated his dealings with the other Successors, Ptolemy carefully but actively expanded his realm and personal power. Whereas the others showed their cards from the outset, Ptolemy patiently and cunningly held his close to his chest, expanding his territories only when he felt the time was ripe.

It has long been the consensus that Ptolemy pursued a policy of "defensive imperialism"—in other words, he was content to rule Egypt and involve himself in foreign affairs only when he felt his country was at risk—or even a separatist policy, by which he intended to secede from the greater empire and, left to his own devices, rule an independent Egypt.[3] These views are wrong: the thesis of my book is that far from isolating himself in Egypt, Ptolemy had the same imperialistic goals as the other Successors; he had no plans to secede, but to rule more of the empire.[4] Even ancient writers lumped all of these men together as ambitious, without singling out Ptolemy as any different from the others.[5] His Egypt would not be an African power, as under the Pharaohs, but a Mediterranean one, which is why he was not interested in involving himself further south in Africa.

Ptolemy ultimately failed in some of his grand plans overseas, but not at home. Ptolemaic Egypt stood "at the crossroads of Egyptian and Hellenistic history," and was "the first multi-cultural society where East [met] West."[6] The period was also one of the most decisive ones for Egypt and its people, arguably more so than the Roman or Byzantine ones that followed it until the Arab conquest of AD 642.[7] Moreover, the Ptolemaic dynasty that Ptolemy founded survived the longest of not only all the Hellenistic dynasties but also of those of Pharaonic Egypt.[8]

---

[3] The defensive imperialism of the Ptolemies was first propounded by Will 1966, pp. 153–208; cf. Walbank 1993, pp. 100–103, based greatly on Polybius 5.34.2–4, who crticizes Ptolemy IV for not giving priority to Egypt's defenses unlike his predecessors.

[4] Cf. Seibert 1969, for example pp. 19–20, 187; Bosworth 2000; Huss 2001, p. 169; Braund 2003, p. 28; Caroli 2007, pp. 70–71 and 99–104 on his foreign policy; Grabowski 2008. See more recently the detailed treatments of Hauben 2014 and Meeus 2014; cf. Strootman 2014a. All these works provide bibliography and analysis of scholars on the defensive and separatist theories.

[5] Meeus 2014, pp. 265–270.

[6] Vandorpe 2010, p. 160.

[7] Bowman 1986.

[8] Ptolemaic Egypt: Mahaffy 1898; Bouché-Leclercq 1903–1907; Bevan 1927; Elgood 1938; Rostovtzeff 1941, vol. 1, pp. 255–422, and 1954, pp. 109–154; Tarn and Griffith 1952, pp. 177–209; Bagnall 1976; Turner 1984; Bowman 1986; Samuel 1989 and 1993; Hölbl 2001; Huss 2001; Thompson 2003; Bingen 2007; Manning 2010; Vandorpe 2010; Lloyd 2010; see also Grant 1982, pp. 37–48; Walbank 1993, pp. 100–122, Shipley 2000, pp. 192–234; Errington 2008, pp. 143–161, 165–171,

Who Was Ptolemy?

For someone who came to play a significant role in early Hellenistic history, and had so much impact on Egypt, we know next to nothing about Ptolemy's birth, family, upbringing, and early life. In fact, even though he was on campaign in Asia with Alexander for a decade, there are only a few occasions, albeit important ones, that we know involved Ptolemy.[9] It was not until he became satrap of Egypt after Alexander's death in 323 that he stepped from the wings onto center stage; had Alexander lived longer, and had his son succeeded him as king, we might know of Ptolemy only as one of the many members of Alexander's retinue.[10]

Ptolemy was said to be the son of a Macedonian named Lagus,[11] hence the alternative (and actually more correct) name for the Ptolemaic dynasty was the Lagidae, evoking Lagus' name. Lagus was apparently a member of a humble family.[12] If this information is true, then Lagus' standing must have increased when he married Arsinoe, who was connected to the Argead ruling dynasty, and may have been a cousin of Philip II (r. 359–336).[13] Lagus and Arsinoe lived in Eordaea,[14] a canton in Macedonia's west, but later may have moved to the Macedonian capital, Pella, where their son Ptolemy was educated.[15]

An alternative tradition claims that Ptolemy was an illegitimate son of Philip, which would have made him a half-brother of Alexander the Great.[16] Apparently Arsinoe was one of Philip's courtesans; she was either already married to Lagus, or when she became pregnant by the king was given in marriage to Lagus.[17] When she gave birth, Lagus exposed the baby boy to die at the hands of the elements, but an eagle (the bird of Zeus) swooped him up and saved him. Ptolemy would adopt the eagle as the symbol of his family and put it on his coinage, thereby emphasizing his association with Alexander and the Argeads.[18] To remove the taint of Ptolemy being a bastard (if this story is true),

290–308; and the papers in Van 'T Dack, van Dessel, and van Gucht 1983. See Chapter 5 n. 86 for bibliography on Ptolemy I's rule.

[9] The ancient sources on Ptolemy are cited and discussed by Seibert 1969, pp. 52–83.

[10] Bouché-Leclercq 1903, pp. 1–3; Seibert 1983, pp. 222–232; Heckel 1992, pp. 222–227; Caroli 2007, pp. 9–16.

[11] Arrian 2.11.8, 3.6.5, with Seibert 1969, pp. 8–9.

[12] Plutarch, *Moralia* 458a–b.

[13] Porphyry, *BNJ* 260 F 2, 2; Theocritus 17.26; Curtius 9.8.22.

[14] Arrian 6.28.4, *Indica* 18.5, to be preferred over Stephanus of Byzantium, s.v. *Oristia*, that they lived in Orestis.

[15] Bouché-Leclercq 1903, p. 3.

[16] Pausanias 1.6.2 (noting also the relationship with Lagus); Curtius 9.8.22; *Suda*, s.v. Lagos.

[17] Pausanias 1.6.2; Porphyry, *BNJ* 260 F 2, 2; Satyrus, *BNJ* 631 F 1.

[18] Coin iconography and its political significance: Lianou 2010, pp. 129–130.

it is argued that much later, between 282 and 275, Ptolemy II (Ptolemy's son) introduced the belief that Lagus was the father.[19]

The first account—that Ptolemy's real father was Lagus—is generally regarded as the more accurate one.[20] Among other things, Philip lived life to the full and had many dalliances with courtesans and the like. It is difficult to imagine that only Arsinoe fell pregnant to him and gave birth to a son. If Philip had had more than one illegitimate son, it seems odd that we never hear of any other receiving the same attention at court or playing a role in the army, as did Ptolemy (see further below)—or even associating himself with the Argead ruling family to claim part of Alexander's empire. We also have to wonder what Alexander would have made of a bastard half-brother foisted on him.[21] If he had accepted him, we might expect Ptolemy to have risen quickly through the ranks; if he had detested him, then why he even took Ptolemy to Asia, let alone promoted him to personal bodyguard, is hard to fathom.

Alexander was fiercely protective of his mother Olympias' honor and contemptuous of his father toward the end of the latter's reign. For example, when Philip married his seventh wife (Cleopatra) in 337, the bride's guardian, a Macedonian nobleman named Attalus, toasted the newly-weds, but then prayed that Macedonia might finally have a legitimate heir.[22] This was a slur on Alexander and his mother (who came from Epirus). A furious altercation between Alexander and Attalus ensued, in which Philip, who had little love for Olympias, took Attalus' side. He ordered his son to apologize to Attalus, but Alexander refused, and in disgust he and Olympias left the Macedonian court for a time. Given Alexander's attitude toward his parents, it is likely that he would have disregarded any offspring from an extramarital affair, rather than promoting him to a position of authority in his retinue. Ptolemy's career with Alexander in Asia has a slowly rising trajectory, which was more in keeping with a competent boyhood friend than a family member. As we shall see, Ptolemy likely put out the story of Philip as his father himself. He did so at a crucial time for him in the Wars of the Successors as he prepared to take over Greece and Macedonia and add them to his territory (Chapter 9).

Ptolemy (in the Greek Ptolemaios, from *ptolemos*, the epic form of the word *polemos*, meaning "war") became one of the friends and confidants of the heir to the throne, Alexander. The latter was born in 356, and a common assumption is that Ptolemy and Alexander were roughly the same age for them to

[19] Collins 1997, especially pp. 461–473.
[20] Green 1990, p. 104, Heckel 1992, p. 222, for example; sources: Collins 1997, pp. 439–440, 448–450.
[21] Attitudes toward illegitimacy: Collins 1997, pp. 453–457.
[22] Worthington 2014, pp. 109–110.

have been friends since Alexander's boyhood. That would put Ptolemy's birth year in the 350s. The problem is a passage in one ancient writer that states that Ptolemy was 84 years old when he died in Alexandria in 283/282.[23] If true, then Ptolemy was born in 367/366, a decade before Alexander, and would have been in his mid-forties when Alexander died at age thirty-two in 323.

It does not follow that Ptolemy and Alexander had to have been the same age. In 337 a furious Philip II expelled Ptolemy and four other friends of Alexander (Harpalus, Nearchus, Erigyius, and his brother Laomedon) for advising the heir to offer himself in marriage to the daughter of Pixodarus, the satrap of Caria (in southern Anatolia).[24] Erigyius was older than Alexander, and certainly older than his brother Laomedon.[25] All of these men in fact were likely older than Alexander, and were not just friends but advisers to him, which explains why they and not Alexander were banished for their advice.[26] If these men were older than Alexander, then so could Ptolemy. Therefore, we should not reject the passage that speaks of an octogenarian Ptolemy at death, in which case he was born in in 367/366 and died at about age eighty-four in 283.

Of Ptolemy's siblings, we know of only one brother, Menelaus, who was a general on Cyprus, an island of great strategic importance for all the Ptolemies.[27] Menelaus was still stationed there in 306 when the island was lost to Ptolemy, but since he was among the captives who were set free after the island fell, he returned to Egypt.[28] After that, a papyrus fragment of 284 shows that Menelaus became a priest of the eponymous cult to Alexander, which Ptolemy instituted in Alexandria.[29] When Menelaus died is unknown.

What did Ptolemy look like? We have no heads of him, as we do for Philip II and Alexander (Figures 1.4 and 1.6), forcing us to rely first and foremost on his coinage (Figures 1.1 and 7.2). The face we see on his coins is not an idealized one (as so often with Alexander), but a naturalistic representation: it shows him to have a large nose, which was crooked and even looks broken, very similar to "the beak of the eagle who appears on the other side of the coin."[30] He

---

[23] Pseudo-Lucian, *Macrob.* 12.

[24] Plutarch, *Alexander* 10.4; Arrian 3.6.5, with Worthington 2014, pp. 110–111.

[25] Cf. Curtius 7.4.34.

[26] Heckel 1992, pp. 205–208.

[27] Bagnall 1976, pp. 40–42.

[28] Diodorus 19.62, 79, 20.21.47–53; Plutarch, *Demetrius* 17.1; Justin 15.7.

[29] Athenaeus 12.55; Aelian, *Varia Historia* 9.3, with Thompson 2003, pp. 113–114, quoting a papyrus text (*P. Eleph.* 2) from Egypt referring to Menelaus as Priest ("in the reign of Ptolemy, in the priesthood of Menelaos, son of Lagos, for the fifth year"); cf. Hazzard 2000, p. 105 n. 16. Date of 284: Samuel 1962, p. 12.

[30] Ellis 1994, p. 58.

Figure 1.1 Head of Ptolemy. © HIP / Art Resource, New York

also had a broad forehead, prominent chin, which jutted upward toward his nose (Punch and Judy style), a big, fleshy mouth, and what looked like sad, even tired, eyes. He was not the handsomest of men, but there is a certain distinction and air of authority about him.

We also have images of Ptolemy depicted on temple reliefs. These are highly stylized, as for example one at Sharuna, in which Ptolemy appears to have female breasts (Figure 1.2). Equally stylized is the fragment of a black basalt Egyptian statue of him, which is now in the British Museum (Figure 1.3). The full-size statue is lost; only its head, shoulders, and upper chest remain. The head sports a headdress (*nemes*) with a *uraeus* (an asp, symbolizing the power of gods and kings, and so showing him as ruler), which is missing its head. He has a large nose and chin, as in his coin portrait, as well as big ears, but the chin does not jut upward. The forced smile on his face is characteristic of early Ptolemaic portraiture, which was still heavily influenced by Egyptian styles, especially of the Thirtieth Dynasty (first half of the fourth century).[31]

---

[31] See further, Ashton 2010, pp. 971–977.

Figure 1.2 Temple relief of Ptolemy at Sharuna. © Album / Art Resource, New York

We do not know Ptolemy's height or build. He was probably average in both areas, as often ancient writers commented on height, build, age, or features that were considered unusual or that set a person apart from another—thus Pyrrhus, the famous king of Epirus, had very few teeth and his upper jaw was one continuous bone, and Demetrius Poliorcetes ("the besieger") "had a face so rare and beautiful that no painter or sculptor could ever do him justice."[32] Demetrius' father, one of the period's principal protagonists and arguably Ptolemy's greatest adversary, Antigonus, was nicknamed Monophthalmus because of having only one eye; he was further described as tall and fat, with a loud laugh.[33] No such remarks were made about Ptolemy, although we have some glimpses into his character. For example, when someone once mocked his humble background, he refused to rise to the bait but said it was important to have a sense of humor.[34] He was also a very frugal person; he did not live an ostentatious lifestyle, often dressing in a regular soldier's cloak, eating plain

[32] Pyrrhus: Plutarch, *Pyrrhus* 3.4; Demetrius: Plutarch, *Demetrius* 2.2.
[33] Plutarch, *Demetrius* 19.3.
[34] Plutarch, *Moralia* 458b.

Figure 1.3 Head of Ptolemy. © The Trustees of the British Museum / Art Resource, New York

meals, such as a dish of lentils and tripe stewed in vinegar, and was supposed to have said that it was more kingly to enrich than be rich.[35]

Ptolemy's Background

Ptolemy was in all likelihood one of the royal pages (*basilikoi paides*) at the Macedonian court.[36] If so, he likely moved to Pella in 353 when he was

[35] Cloak: Curtius 9.8.23; meals: Athenaeus 3.58; saying: Plutarch, *Moralia* 181f.
[36] Bouché-Leclercq 1903, p. 3.

fourteen. The pages were young noble boys aged fourteen to eighteen who had various duties, which included attending the king and serving on campaign with him in their final year.[37] Philip may have introduced the system of the pages not only as a way of training the next generation of military leadership but also as a means of ensuring the loyalty of their families. If Lagus' family was a humble one, then his sons would not necessarily be thought of as page material, but the marriage to Arsinoe (Philip's cousin?) elevated the family's social status considerably, making Ptolemy a likely candidate for training as a page in the royal capital.

Assuming the preceding scenario has some accuracy to it, Ptolemy would have begun his training as a page when Alexander was 3 years old, and completed his instruction in 349 or 348 when Alexander was about seven. In his final year of training, Ptolemy most likely took part in Philip's invasion (and subsequent annexation) of the Chalcidice in 349–348.[38] He would have attracted Philip's attention and evidently discharged his duties well for the king to have selected him as a companion (*hetairos*) for his young heir.

As a boy Ptolemy would have been taught to ride, fight, and hunt—skills that were part and parcel of growing up in Macedonia (see below)—and he would also have learned to read and write Greek. All these things continued during his internship as a page. But in 342 Philip hired Aristotle to tutor Alexander, then aged fourteen, at Mieza in the foothills of Olympus.[39] Ptolemy was at the time about 25 years old, but we do not know if he (or any other of Alexander's friends) also studied with Alexander under Aristotle, especially as the period of tutorship lasted three years until 340. It is tempting to connect Ptolemy's founding of the Museum and the Library at Alexandria (Chapter 8) to an intellectual and artistic bent inspired by Aristotle, but we should guard against temptation. Ptolemy's motives for these institutions were as political as much as they were academic; it does not follow that Aristotle inspired anything in him.

This is not to say that Ptolemy had no intellectual qualities. As king of Egypt he patronized the mathematician Euclid, who wrote his *Elements of Geometry* in Alexandria (Chapter 8). He may even have selected his younger son to succeed him rather than his eldest one because he had provided the former with the best tutors of the day and wanted the next king to be both a man of action and thought (Chapter 12). Moreover, after his expulsion from Athens in 307, Demetrius of Phalerum, one of the leading philosophers of the day, fled to Egypt. There he befriended Ptolemy, wrote important philosophical and

[37] Hammond, 1990, pp. 261–290; Carney 2008, pp. 145–164.
[38] Worthington 2008, pp. 74–82, and 2014, pp. 59–61.
[39] See Worthington 2014, pp. 95–97.

literary works, and helped to organize the Museum and the Library. He even advised Ptolemy to read various philosophical treatises on kingship, including one he wrote for him, in which Demetrius spoke of the need to be just and pious, to listen to his subjects, and to be a good military leader.[40]

Ptolemy was also interested in history and writing about it. He composed a *History of Alexander,* which was the chief source for the later narrative of Alexander's reign by Arrian (see Appendix 1). In his account Ptolemy took pains to embellish his role in Alexander's invasion of Asia at the expense of others, and also depicted himself as a closer confidant to the king than he likely was. The veracity of his *History* is thus compromised, and in any case only excerpts of it exist, quoted or paraphrased in later writers.[41] I quote several of its more substantial fragments in the following chapters as examples of Ptolemy's projection of himself in affairs, and I should make it plain here that I believe that he was present at the events he describes. He did not write about events after Alexander's death or of his own rule in Egypt.

Macedonia

Ptolemy was a product of the rugged, militaristic society of Macedonia, a kingdom situated north of the home of the gods, Mount Olympus (Map 2).[42] His experiences served him well fighting with Alexander in Asia and in the Wars of the Successors.

While males from society's middle and upper strata in Greece, south of Mount Olympus, enjoyed intellectual and more highbrow pursuits, those in Macedonia from the earliest of ages had a far tougher upbringing. No one was spared this lifestyle, not even members of the ruling family. Boys from an early age were taught to hunt (wild boar, foxes, birds, and even lions), ride, and fight, and Macedonian society had various initiation rites, such as no man being allowed to recline at a banquet until he had speared and killed one of the ferocious wild boars that roamed Macedonia without using a net to trap it.

That the Macedonians lived and drank hard is without question, and it set them apart from the Greeks. A Greek symposium (drinking party) began with the participants discussing literature, philosophy, or public affairs while they ate and drank wine mixed with water (the ratio is not known, but the point is that the wine was diluted). Dancing girls entertained them, but only later

---

[40] Plutarch, *Moralia* 189d.

[41] Ptolemy, *FGrH* 138.

[42] See Worthington 2014, pp. 14–22, for the following, citing bibliography. On ancient Macedonia, see especially the essays in Roisman and Worthington 2010.

would the whole party dissolve into an orgy. At a Macedonian symposium, which a king and his courtiers routinely attended, the emphasis was on drinking wine neat or "unmixed" (*akratos*), and the only talk was about the participants' military or fighting exploits. As a result they were drunk "while they were still being served the first course and could not enjoy their food,"[43] and Alexander, it was said, "would sleep without waking up for two days and two nights" after some of his drinking contests.[44] Several of these parties proved dangerous. During the argument between Philip and Alexander at the former's wedding banquet in 337 (see above), Philip actually drew his sword on his son, but drunkenly fell over a table as he lunged at him.[45] In 328, a drinking party at Maracanda turned deadly when Alexander and his general Cleitus the Black got into an alcohol-fueled argument that led to Alexander running him through with a spear, killing him on the spot (see pp. 48–49).

The Macedonian kings also practiced polygamy, marrying for diplomatic and military reasons. Philip married seven times without ever divorcing a wife, and Alexander three times. Ptolemy likewise was a polygamist, marrying four times (pp. 112–115). To the Greeks, this custom was abhorrent. They also referred to the Macedonians as "barbarians," which had nothing to do with any lack of culture, but was a term used when they could not understand the language a person was speaking. The Macedonians, though, were Greek speaking, for we never hear of the need for interpreters, for example, when envoys from Greece or Macedonia visited each other. Most likely, given the various tribes on their borders, the Macedonians spoke a dialect the Greeks could not understand, not a different language (as the Persians or Illyrians did), which was foreign to Greeks.

Away from their public image, at least as the Greeks saw it, the Macedonians were a highly cultured people.[46] King Archelaus (r. 413–399), who had founded the new capital of Pella in 399, wanted his court to be a cultural one. He had invited Socrates and the Athenian tragic playwrights Agathon and Euripides to move there, and Euripides did so, writing the *Bacchae* and the (now fragmentary) *Archelaus* there. Macedonian gold, silver, and bronze artwork, tomb paintings, and jewelry were of the very highest quality, as were mosaics. The recently discovered tomb at Amphipolis boasts a magnificent mosaic of Hades abducting Persephone (there is a painting of this myth on the north wall of Tomb I at Vergina).[47] Indeed, as will be shown, Greek art and culture continued to flourish even during the Wars of Alexander's Successors.

---

[43] Ephippus, *FGrH* 126 F 1 = Athenaeus 3.120e.

[44] *Ephemerides, FGrH* 117 F 2b = Athenaeus 10.434b.

[45] Worthington 2014, pp. 109–110.

[46] Worthington 2008, pp. 8–11, and 2014, pp. 20–21.

[47] Andronikos 1983; Hardiman 2010, pp. 505–521. On cities in Macedonia and material culture, see also the essays in Lane Fox 2011.

Ptolemy grew up in this society. Its simplicity perhaps explains his own austerity even when he was king of Egypt. More than that, however, he grew up in a Macedonia that emerged from being a backwater on the periphery of the Greek world into an imperial power thanks to its king, Philip II. Experiencing firsthand what life was like in those times must have affected and benefited him (and the other Successors) in how they ruled their respective territories and in their relations with each other.

Macedonia before Philip had abundant natural resources (especially mines and timber), but they were poorly exploited. It was prone to incursions by the various tribes living on its borders (especially the Illyrians to the northwest and the Paeonians to the north), and various Greek cities often interfered in its internal affairs. Of these, Athens and Thebes were the most meddlesome. Macedonia could not boast an army; instead, its conscript soldiers, usually small farmers, were poorly trained and lacked proper arms and armor, and so could do little to prevent the plundering raids carried out by the neighboring tribes. Also to its detriment, the kingdom was split into two parts: Upper and Lower. The capital, Pella, was in Lower Macedonia (which was the eastern part of the kingdom running to the Thermaic Gulf), but the Upper and Lower parts were never united. The semi-nomadic tribes, ruled by individual chieftains, who lived in Upper (western) Macedonia felt no loyalty to the king in Pella, but had a greater affinity with their Illyrian and Paeonian neighbors.

In 359, King Perdiccas III and 4,000 troops were killed during an Illyrian invasion. The Illyrians prepared to penetrate deeper into Macedonia, while at the same time the Paeonians mobilized to invade. On top of all that, the Athenians and the king of Western Thrace (on Macedonia's eastern border) each supported pretenders to the throne. Because of these four external threats and the fact that the next in line to the throne, Perdiccas' son Amyntas, was only a boy, Philip (the dead king's brother) was declared king. He turned Macedonia into a superpower.[48] He was a warrior king *par excellence*; like Alexander, he always led from the front and was always to be found in the thick of the fighting. He lost his right eye to an arrow during a siege, broke several bones over the years, and suffered a dreadful wound to one of his legs that made him limp for the rest of his life—but he never slowed down. The reconstructed face from the skull fragments found in what is almost certainly his tomb show the life he led and the sort of man he was (Figure 1.4).

[48] Philip's reign in detail: Ellis 1976; Cawkwell 1978; Hammond and Griffith 1979, pp. 203–698; Hammond 1994; Worthington 2008 and 2014 (also comparing and contrasting him to Alexander). Focusing on Philip as general and tactician: Gabriel 2010. See too Müller 2010.

Figure 1.4 Reconstructed face of Philip II. Courtesy of the Whitworth Art Gallery, The University of Manchester

Philip neutralized all of the crises facing Macedonia at this time brilliantly and within weeks by a combination of deceit, bribery, and diplomacy, which set a pattern for the rest of his reign. He also embarked on a radical transformation of the army.[49] Macedonians were already tough and fierce fighters—a soldier had to wear a sash around his waist until he had killed his first man in battle—but Philip's military reforms created a professional fighting force of superbly trained, well-equipped full-time soldiers. Among other things, he introduced new tactics, especially that of shock and awe, by sending in cavalry and not infantry into attack first (the reverse of standard Greek tactics), as well as new weaponry, such as the fearsome sarissa (a massive 14-foot-long cornel wood pike with a one-foot sharp pointed iron head), which impaled the enemy combatants while keeping the Macedonian infantryman out of harm's way

[49] Hammond and Griffith 1979, pp. 405–449; Fuller 1960, pp. 39–54; Worthington 2008, pp. 26–32, and 2014, pp. 32–38; Gabriel 2010, pp. 62–92. On the Macedonian army, see too Sekunda 2010.

(Figure 1.5). As a result, the Macedonian army became the most feared, most successful, and most battle-ready of antiquity before the Roman army.

It was Philip's army that Alexander took with him to Asia, and enabled him to achieve the successes he did. Even the torsion catapult, the death knell for any town that resisted him, was conceived and created by his father's engineering corps.

Philip united both parts of Macedonia for the first time in its history, centralized the capital of Pella, and embarked on an ambitious economic policy, which transformed Macedonia into a prosperous kingdom. More than that, he secured its borders from the plague of invasion by hostile neighbors, again for the first time in its history, and slowly but surely expanded his realm in all directions, eventually conquering Thrace and Greece. The Greeks, who had enjoyed centuries of autonomy, fell under Macedonian rule at the pivotal battle of Chaeronea (in Boeotia) in 338. As the contemporary Athenian orator Lycurgus remarked, "with the corpses of those who died here the freedom of the Greeks was also buried."[50] The following year Philip ordered the Greeks to Corinth, where they swore an oath of allegiance to each other as well as to him and his descendants, in what was known as a "Common Peace." However, he knew that it would be only a matter of time before the Greek states reverted to their customary fighting, and so he used his military might to enforce this peace. Further, he created a council (*synedrion*), presided over by a *hegemon* or leader, to which each state would send representatives to discuss all issues affecting the Greeks.[51] Although Macedonia was not a member of this *synedrion*, the Greeks elected Philip—as he had anticipated—*hegemon*. Philip's Common Peace, of course, did not allow the Greeks their autonomy, as Macedonia remained firmly in control of their fate. This administrative arrangement—called by modern scholars the League of Corinth—was the means by which Macedonia ruled Greece; later, some of the Successors including Ptolemy would take a leaf out of Philip's book by trying to resurrect the league and proclaim Greek freedom.

Philip then announced his next grand plan: the invasion of Asia. But it was not to be. One year later, in 336, as he was poised to lead an army across the Hellespont, the stretch of water that divided Europe from Asia (as it still does today), he was assassinated the day after his daughter's wedding at Aegae, the former capital and venue for royal weddings and burials. One of his generals, Antipater, immediately proclaimed Alexander king to calm the people, and in this way Alexander the Great assumed the throne (r. 336–323).

---

[50] Lycurgus 1, *Against Leocrates* 50.
[51] Background: Worthington 2008, pp. 158–171, to which add Dmitriev 2011, pp. 67–90.

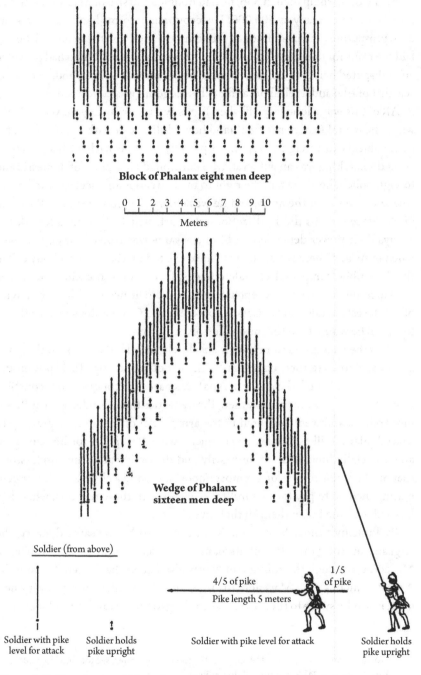

Block of Phalanx eight men deep

0 1 2 3 4 5 6 7 8 9 10
Meters

**Wedge of Phalanx
sixteen men deep**

Soldier (from above)

1/5
of pike

4/5 of pike

Pike length 5 meters

Soldier with pike   Soldier holds   Soldier with pike level for attack   Soldier holds
level for attack   pike upright   pike upright

Figure 1.5 Macedonian phalanx formation carrying sarissas. © N. G. L. Hammond,
1994, *Alexander the Great: King, Commander, and Statesman*, Bristol: Bristol Classical
Press, an imprint of Bloomsbury Publishing Plc.

By the time Philip died in 336, he had doubled the size of Macedonia and its population to as many as 500,000. His economic reforms had made the kingdom prosperous, and in addition to founding an empire on the mainland, he had laid the plans for the invasion of Asia. Even more important, Philip had provided an undisputed heir to the throne. In sum, his legacy was brilliant and, as we shall see, that of Alexander fell short as far as his kingdom was concerned.[52]

All of this was a long way off when Ptolemy as a young boy moved to Pella, where he would experience first hand how Philip dealt with people, from his own subjects to foreign ones, and especially how he wielded his power. A Macedonian king was an autocrat, who controlled all aspects of domestic and foreign policy; he alone had the right to make treaties and declare war, he was sole commander of the army, and he was chief priest in the state.[53] Powerful noble Macedonians did lead factions at court, which the king allowed, but always their power depended on him; the same was true of Alexander, even when in Asia.[54] There is also likely to have existed in Macedonia a body called the Assembly, comprised of male citizens, from whom the king could seek guidance, but he need not accept its views. Nor did he need to follow the advice of his closest friends and advisers, who were called Companions (hetairoi), and to whom he would turn the most when on campaign.

All of the Successors came to rule absolutely, aided by "friends," rather than factions, who were their courtiers.[55] This is not surprising. Their power and position (like that of Alexander in Asia) was based on conquest, not constitutionality, for they were military men; the dynasties they founded were military monarchies, and were anchored in the army.[56] All of these rulers grew up in Macedonia; all, like Ptolemy, experienced what Philip did for his kingdom, and especially how he did it, militarily and diplomatically. They understood that military control was of foremost importance, and a close second was generating income to pay for that military machine. In these respects, what they learned remained with them all their lives.

By Ptolemy's time, Macedonia had been ruled by the same dynasty, the Argead, for 300 years. It took its name supposedly from an Argeas, son of Macedon, although the ruling family was also called the Temenids, from the Argive Temenus. The Macedonians took an oath of allegiance to every new king, just as he swore to them to rule according to the law, and this subject-ruler

[52] Worthington 2014, pp. 115–119; cf. pp. 302–309 on Alexander; see too Squillace 2015.

[53] King 2010, pp. 374–391, citing bibliography.

[54] Heckel 2003a; see too Weber 2009.

[55] On "friend" as an official title and its subdivisions ("first friends," etc.), see Thompson 2003, p. 113.

[56] Billows 1995, pp. 20–24, and passim; see too Strootman 2014a, pp. 307–322.

loyalty was taken very seriously. When Alexander died in 323 and left no heir (his wife Roxane was still pregnant) there was little doubt in anyone's mind that the Argead dynasty had to continue in some way. And when in 310 the last Argead king, Alexander IV, was put to death, the Successors, including Ptolemy, waited half a decade before calling themselves kings. This was not due to any slowness on their part, but, I suspect, the realization that the dynasty they had known all their lives, and which had ruled Macedonia for three centuries, was no more—and because of their own doing. It was a new world, and they needed time to adjust.

Macedonia—its history, monarchy, and way of life—always remained with Ptolemy and the other Successors. In their wars, the Macedonian throne was seen as the crown jewel, the ultimate propaganda tool, and most of them attempted to seize it, Ptolemy included. His story, which began under Philip, continued under Alexander, and accelerated dramatically after the latter's death, can now be told.

Ptolemy's Early Exploits

In 338, when Ptolemy was about twenty-nine, Philip and the Greeks fought the decisive battle of Chaeronea.[57] Alexander, then aged eighteen, commanded the Macedonian left flank, and distinguished himself by defeating the Boeotian troops and annihilating the famous Theban Sacred Band (the elite infantry corps) on the Greek right. Ptolemy must have fought in this battle, given its importance and his by then.[58] Where he was stationed we do not know. One ancient source speaks of Alexander being supported by Philip's "most seasoned generals," which is usually taken to mean Parmenion and Antipater.[59] Ptolemy was not in their league, and even under Alexander was never a general, but it is possible that because of his relationship with Alexander, Philip had him on the Macedonian left wing with the young heir.

By the time he was thirty, Ptolemy had seen active service in at least two campaigns that we know about, and he was clearly trusted by Philip and Alexander. His future looked promising. But then came the Pixodarus episode, in which Alexander had flouted Philip's authority by offering himself in marriage to the satrap's daughter. Ptolemy's friendship with Alexander cost him dearly, as Philip banished him from Macedonia. We do not know where

[57] Plutarch, *Camillus* 19.5, 8. Battle: Hammond 1973; Hammond and Griffith 1979, pp. 596–603; Worthington 2008, pp. 149–151, and 2014, pp. 85–89; Gabriel 2010, pp. 214–222; cf. Ma 2008.

[58] Ellis 1994, p. 4.

[59] Diodorus 16.86.1.

Ptolemy went. It has been suggested that after Alexander and his mother Olympias stormed out of Pella following the quarrel at Philip's wedding banquet in 337 they went to Epirus, and Ptolemy joined them there, and that after Philip's assassination in 336 Alexander recalled him.[60]

There is the statement in our sources that when Philip was murdered in the theater at Aegae pandemonium broke out, and Alexander's friends armed themselves in case he too was attacked, especially given the discontent by some of the peoples whom Philip had conquered.[61] Who were these friends? Alexander must have had more friends than the five that Philip expelled in 337, but it is possible, given his fierce loyalty to his friends as his reign progressed, that when Philip ordered his son back to Pella, Alexander insisted that these men, including Ptolemy, return with him. Certainly Ptolemy was back at court by 335, when Alexander campaigned in the north (see below).

Alexander was only twenty when he became king in 336 (Figure 1.6). He was immediately faced with a revolt of Greece, which he quickly subdued, and at Corinth he resurrected the League of Corinth.[62] He proclaimed his intention of invading Asia, as his father had planned, and the Greeks had little choice but to support him. In the same year he began a series of purges to rid himself of possible opponents—including Attalus. In 335 he undertook a campaign against the Triballi (a tribe by the Danube) and the Illyrians.[63] It is likely that Ptolemy served with him, for he wrote of these events in his *History*.[64] During the Illyrian campaign, word reached Alexander that the city of Thebes in Boeotia had revolted. He marched south immediately with 30,000 infantry and 300 cavalry to besiege the rebel city.[65] Again, Ptolemy's firsthand account of that siege indicates that he was present at it.

Arrian, drawing on Ptolemy's *History*, says that after the Thebans refused to surrender, Alexander was preparing an attack when Perdiccas impetuously preempted him: "Ptolemy, son of Lagus, tells us that Perdiccas, who had been posted in the advanced guard of the camp with his own brigade, and was not far from the enemy's stockade, did not wait for the signal from Alexander to commence the battle; but of his own accord was the first to assault the stockade, and, having made a breach in it, fell upon the advanced guard of the Thebans."[66]

---

[60] Ellis 1994, p. 5.

[61] Arrian 1.25.1–2; Curtius 6.9.17, 10.24; Plutarch, *Moralia* 327c; cf. Justin 11.1.1–2. Discontent: Worthington 2008, pp. 187–188.

[62] Diodorus 17.3.6–4.9; Arrian 1.1.2–3, with Worthington 2014, pp. 126–127.

[63] Worthington 2014, pp. 128–130.

[64] Ptolemy, *FGrH* 138 F 1 = Arrian 1.2–3, 4; F 2 = Strabo 7.3.8.

[65] Austin, no. 2, pp. 9–11 (= Plutarch, *Alexander* 10.6–11; Diodorus 17.14), with Worthington 2014, pp. 131–135.

[66] Ptolemy, *FGrH* 138 F 3 = Arrian 1.8.

Figure 1.6 Head of Alexander the Great (Pella). © Ian Worthington, Pella Museum, Amman, Jordan

Perdiccas' action prompted another general (Amyntas) to follow suit, leaving Alexander with no choice but to follow them. In doing so, many of the attackers became trapped in the space between two palisades, which the defenders had set up; seventy of them were killed, and many others were wounded, including Perdiccas. Alexander managed to rescue his men, and as he got the upper hand over the defenders a group of them tried to retreat into the city. They jammed open the gates, and so signed their death warrants. Taking advantage of the disarray and opened gates, Alexander and his men rushed into the city. After brutal hand-to-hand fighting in the streets, the Thebans surrendered: 6,000 of their number had been killed, 30,000 were taken prisoner and sold into slavery, and the city treasury was confiscated. The Macedonians and their Greek allies had lost about 500 men. Worse was to come. In one of the darkest episodes of Alexander's early reign, he had Thebes razed to the ground, leaving intact only the temples and houses belonging to the lyric poet Pindar and his descendants. Thebes would not be rebuilt until 316.

There is inconsistency in our ancient sources about Perdiccas' role in the siege of Thebes. Diodorus is clear that he never jumped the gun, and thus did not disobey Alexander and cause the loss of so many of his comrades, and

Curtius does not mention him in this regard at all.[67] Only Ptolemy so denigrates him, but we should be skeptical. Many of Alexander's commanders did not get on with each other during and after the invasion of Asia; relations between Ptolemy and Perdiccas grew so strained that Perdiccas invaded Egypt in 320 to topple Ptolemy from power. It is therefore plausible that when Ptolemy wrote his *History* he set out to denigrate Perdiccas whenever he could in it— falsely accusing Perdiccas of recklessness at Thebes is one such instance.[68]

After seeing Thebes destroyed, Alexander returned to Pella, where he made the final preparations for the invasion of Asia the following spring. He appointed Antipater as guardian (*epitropos*) of Greece and deputy *hegemon* of the League of Corinth in his absence, entrusting him with a force of 12,000 infantry and 1,500 cavalry.[69] Then, in the spring of 334, Alexander, not quite 22 years old, marched to Sestus on the Hellespont (Dardenelles), and from there he set sail for Asia. He had with him an army of at least 30,000 Macedonian and allied infantry and 5,000 cavalry, perhaps even as high as 43,000 infantry and 5,500 cavalry, together with non-military personnel such as cooks, doctors, blacksmiths, and carpenters, and a fleet of over 160 warships and transport vessels.[70]

Before he actually jumped ashore, Alexander symbolically threw a spear into the enemy soil, signifying that he regarded all of Asia as his "spear won" territory.[71] He was going to fight to conquer all of it, and claim it as his. That same belief governed the actions of his Successors, who also saw their slices of empire as spear won; these men were determined to hold on to their territories at any cost, and to extend them. They shared Alexander's vision about empire, Ptolemy included.

Even though Philip and to a far greater extent Alexander dominate the history of the Macedonian Empire, with Ptolemy playing a subordinate role to them, it is with Alexander's invasion of Asia that the story of Ptolemy begins. Against the background of that invasion, we will trace Ptolemy's exploits as an infantryman, and eventually a royal bodyguard in the next three chapters, before turning the spotlight on him, first as satrap of Egypt, and then as its king.

---

[67] Diodorus 17.12.3; it is worth pointing out, though, that we do not have the first two books of Curtius.

[68] On the presentation of Perdiccas in the siege of Thebes, linked to the date and rationale of the *History*, see Errington 1969, pp. 236–237, but note the caution of Roisman 1984, pp. 374–376; cf. Ellis 1994, pp. 20–22, and Appendix 1.

[69] Diodorus 17.17.3, 5. On Antipater, see Baynham 1994; Gilley and Worthington 2010, pp. 199–205.

[70] Numbers: Austin, no. 3, pp. 11–12 (Plutarch, *Alexander* 15; Diodorus 17.17.3–4), with Worthington 2014, pp. 139–140, citing bibliography.

[71] Diodorus 17.17.2.

2

Invading Persia with Alexander

After disembarking on foreign soil, Alexander took a small party of men with him to Troy, where he sacrificed at the tomb of his hero (and ancestor on his mother's side) Achilles, after which he and Hephaestion were said to have run naked around it. Alexander—already seeing himself as a young Achilles—swapped his own shield for that of the famed Homeric warrior, said to be hanging in the Temple to Athena in Troy, and then rejoined the rest of his men after they had completed their crossing of the Hellespont. He also rendezvoused with Parmenion and the advance force of 10,000 troops that Philip had sent to Asia Minor in 336, and after securing a number of towns in the region, prepared to do battle with a Persian army.

Ptolemy did not play a prominent role in the Persian campaign and did not start to come to the fore until the Macedonians were in Bactria and India.[1] More senior men, such as Craterus, Perdiccas, Coenus, Meleager, and Parmenion's son Philotas, commanded the various units of the army; Ptolemy was in one of the infantry battalions, and while he took part in the three hard-fought battles against the Persians, we do not know what his position was and how he personally fared.

Taking on Persia

The Persian Empire stretched east as far as what the Greeks called India (Pakistan and Kashmir today) and southward through Syria and the Levant to Egypt. Its enormous size had led the Great King Darius I in 513 to divide it into twenty satrapies, or regions, each of which was controlled by a satrap, who was tasked with raising taxes and levying troops for the Great King. Although

---

[1] Seibert 1969, pp. 1–26. A useful survey of Ptolemy's role, compared to that of other commanders, in Alexander's Asian campaign is given by Welles 1963. On Alexander's invasion of Persia, see in detail Worthington 2014, pp. 140–211, citing ancient sources and modern bibliography throughout. I give references mostly to this book in this chapter to avoid repetition.

subservient to him, the satraps were largely free to conduct their affairs as they wished in their satrapies, and they grew very wealthy and powerful as a result.[2]

In the satrapy of Hellespontine Phrygia, Alexander faced a hastily-levied Persian army at the Granicus River, on the plain of Adrasteia, close to the town of Zelea (Sarikoy). The Great King Darius III had not been able to march from Babylon in time to lead the Persian army himself, so it fell to the satrap, Arsites, to turn back the invaders. Arsites deployed his infantry on a superior position on the heights of the eastern bank of the river and his cavalry slightly back from the water's edge, so as Alexander crossed the river, enemy missiles would shower his men from above and the massed Persian cavalry would be facing him.[3] The Granicus River was only about three feet deep, but the entire bed was eighty feet wide, and the banks on either side of it were steep. Undaunted, Alexander led 13,000 infantry and 5,100 cavalry down his western bank, but instead of risking heavy casualties by charging the enemy frontally, he ordered Amyntas and a small strike force of fast cavalry (*prodromoi*) on the right flank to cross the river first, to draw enemy fire, while the Macedonian right flank (with Alexander), the center, and the left flank (commanded by Parmenion) marched diagonally across the fast flowing river. This pawn sacrifice worked, and the invaders crossed over with minimal losses.[4] Alexander's line—about one mile in length—then regrouped into a straight one that rushed up the opposite bank and engaged the enemy of 30,000 infantry and 16,000 cavalry head-on.

The Persian cavalry collapsed as the Macedonians bore down on it, and the infantry fight on the upper banks became a blood bath as Arsites and his men (armed only with light javelins) were cut to pieces by the deadly sarissas. At one point Alexander was almost killed when a Persian soldier sheared off his helmet and another (Spithridates, the satrap of Ionia) raised his sword to strike at his bare head. The quick thinking of Cleitus the Black, a cavalry commander, saved the king: Cleitus swung his sword and lopped off the attacker's arm. The sources talk of 20,000 enemy infantry and 2,500 cavalry killed to Alexander's 34 dead, including 9 infantry, but these are likely exaggerated to magnify the Macedonian victory. Arsites managed to escape, but shortly after he committed suicide, horrified that he had not defeated Alexander.

The battle was an example of Alexander's tactical genius, audacity, and daredevil courage.[5] It also exposed his love of fighting for the sake of fighting. He had almost been killed in the first battle on Asian soil. His death would

---

[2] Duties of the Great King and his relationship to his satraps and people: Worthington 2014, pp. 142–143. On the Persian Empire, see for example Briant 2002; Waters 2014.

[3] Battle: Worthington 2014, pp. 144–150.

[4] Devine 1988.

[5] Alexander's generalship: Fuller 1960; Burn 1965; Devine 1989a; Cartledge 2003, pp. 157–188, 219–266; Strauss 2003; Gilley and Worthington 2010; cf. Worthington 2014, pp. 140–309.

have caused a dynastic crisis back home, as he was unmarried and had no heir. Macedonian kings were expected to lead from the front in battle, and Alexander, like his father, was a wonderful example of a warrior king. But as the campaign progressed and thousands of miles separated the invaders from Greece, Alexander often took personal risks and nearly died, to the consternation of his men.

Still, Alexander's first victory over the enemy sounded the death knell for the Achaemenid ruling dynasty of Persia, founded by Cyrus II two centuries earlier. After the battle, Alexander marched his men down the coast of Asia Minor, winning over key cities that previously had been under Persian rule, and also capturing Sardis, capital of Lydia and the most western of the Great King's capitals. Alexander's strategy was to control the whole of Asia Minor, especially the coastline, to protect his lines of communication before he marched deeper into the heart of Persia, while at the same time the tribute that the cities had previously paid to Persia now flowed into his coffers. As he marched south, he was faced with opposition from Miletus, which quickly fell to him, and Halicarnassus (Bodrum) in Caria, which also capitulated after a fierce siege lasting two weeks.[6]

In the early months of 333, Alexander won over Lycia, Pamphylia, and Pisidia.[7] His rapid rate of success obviously alarmed Darius, who began levying an enormous army in Babylon. Well aware of what his adversary was up to, Alexander made a special trip that summer (333) to Gordium, home of the famous Gordian knot. Whether Ptolemy was with him is not known. Legend had it that whoever untied that knot would rule Asia. The knot was made of cornel wood, and it fastened the yoke to the wagon that Gordius reputedly used when in the eighth century he traveled from Macedonia to Gordium, where he had founded the Phrygian dynasty. Many men had tried and failed over the centuries to undo the knot, but Alexander succeeded, perhaps by simply slashing it with his sword.[8] The psychological impact of his action on the Persians would have been tremendous, as he intended.[9]

In the meantime, Darius had set out to face the invader personally. From Gordium the invaders marched to Tarsus, where Alexander almost died.[10] Rather than heed the warnings of the locals about swimming in the freezing waters of the river Cydnus (which flowed from the Taurus mountains), in the searing heat of summer, Alexander leapt into the water, developed violent

[6] Siege: Worthington 2014, pp. 154–156.

[7] Worthington 2014, pp. 157–159.

[8] Aristobulus, *FGrH* 139 F 7 = Arrian 2.3.7; Plutarch, *Alexander* 18.4; see too Curtius 3.1.16; Justin 11.7.16.

[9] Fredricksmeyer 1961.

[10] Worthington 2014, pp. 163–164.

cramps, and had to be hauled out. He was soon bed-ridden with a nasty tropi-
cal fever for over a week, allowing Darius to advance further than Alexander
expected.

Eventually the two sides came together at Issus.[11] The battlefield was probably on the two-mile wide plain between the Mediterranean Sea and the
Amanus range, most likely around the Kuru Çay River. Today the river is nothing more than a stream, but in antiquity it must have been wider and deeper,
as each army set up its camp on opposite sides of it. In his *History*, Ptolemy
presents us with a vivid account of the aftermath of the battle, making it likely
that he took part in the fighting.

We do not know where Ptolemy was stationed in the Macedonian line, or
if he was given any command. The first instance of an actual command is at
the Persian Gates in 331, so it is likely that at Issus he fought under orders.
Alexander's line had the Thessalian and allied cavalry, commanded by
Parmenion, on its left flank, next to the Gulf of Iskenderun. In the center stood
the various battalions of the phalanx, each under its own commander, and on
the right flank, by the Amanus Mountains, were the Macedonians and the
rest of the allied cavalry, together with a contingent of archers and mercenaries. Alexander fielded about 40,000 troops, including 5,800 cavalry, whereas
Darius' army, according to the ancient sources, numbered 600,000 (Arrian
and Plutarch), or 400,000 infantry and 100,000 cavalry (Diodorus and Justin),
or 250,000 infantry and 62,200 cavalry (Curtius).[12] These numbers are again
exaggerated; more plausibly, the Persian army numbered 100,000 to 150,000,
which still far outnumbered Alexander's army.

Well aware that he could not defeat his enemy in a pitched fight, Alexander
resorted to psychological warfare, something that became his trademark. He
intended to capture or kill Darius as quickly as possible, which he calculated
would demoralize the Persian troops and end the battle soon after it had begun.
Darius had taken up position in the center of his line, as was the Persian custom
for safety reasons and to communicate efficiently with both flanks. As soon as
the Macedonians charged the Persians, Alexander and some of his cavalry galloped only at Darius. Despite the problems his men were facing in the fighting,
Alexander maintained his focus. When he caught up to the Great King a fierce
fight occurred, and as more of Darius' royal bodyguard died around him, he fled
the battlefield. The news of his flight provoked exactly the reaction Alexander
had anticipated. The enemy lost heart: first the infantry fled, and then the cavalry.

Ptolemy wrote that Alexander ordered his men to pursue the retreating
enemy and to show no mercy. Much of their bloody task had already been

---

[11] Lead up and battle: Worthington 2014, pp. 164–169.
[12] Diodorus 17.31.2; Arrian 2.8.8; Curtius 3.2.4–9; Justin 11.9.1; Plutarch, *Alexander* 18.6.

done, however, for the enemy cavalry fled after the infantry, and in doing so rode over and killed hundreds of them. The survivors were forced to move slowly because of their sheer number, and the Macedonians killed thousands of them—more, it was said, than in the actual battle: coming to a ravine, claims Ptolemy, the men "passed over it upon the corpses."[13] The claim is sensational; the area around the battlefield would hardly have had anything as deep as a ravine, but a river bed, for example, would have slowed the fleeing enemy down and made them sitting ducks. If enough of them fell victim to the enemy onslaught, their corpses might easily have piled up and allowed the pursuers to run over them.

After the battle, Alexander began to call himself King of Asia, thereby emphasizing his, and not Darius', rule over Persia.[14] He also subtly took on the role of protector of the Great King's family, who had accompanied Darius to the battleground and had been captured, by treating them with respect, promising to find husbands for the royal princesses when they came of age, and arranging their education. Darius had sent his baggage train to Damascus for safekeeping before the battle, and Alexander now ordered Parmenion to go there to seize it. The wealth of the Persian Empire was the stuff of legend, allowing Alexander to start to accumulate hoards of coin and treasure. But Parmenion found something else in Damascus, and that was a Persian noblewoman named Barsine, the daughter of the satrap of Hellespontine Phrygia, Artabazus. He and his family had lived at Philip's court in Pella in the 350s, where Barsine would have made Alexander's acquaintance. Parmenion sent her to Alexander; supposedly the king lost his virginity to her, a story that may well be true, as he had showed little interest in females during his youth. Alexander and Barsine had a de facto relationship, which produced a son, Heracles, in the same year (327) as Alexander married his more famous wife, Roxane.

Alexander was determined to conquer the entire eastern Mediterranean coastline in order to neutralize the Persian fleet. He marched into Syria, receiving the surrender of all the towns along his path, such as Byblos and Sidon, but it was a different story at Tyre, an important port city between Cilicia and Egypt. In antiquity, Tyre was an island about half a mile offshore, and its two natural harbors afforded anchorage to the Persian navy. The potential disruption to Alexander's entire lines of communication meant that he could not allow Tyre to remain independent. At first its king, Azemilk, promised his friendship to Alexander, but the Tyrians baulked at Alexander's request to sacrifice to the god Melqart, a local equivalent of Heracles, in Tyre's main temple.

---

[13] Ptolemy, *FGrH* 138 F 6 = Arrian 2.11.8.
[14] Fredricksmeyer 2000.

Alexander probably understood that the Tyrians saw his sacrifice as sacrilegious, but their refusal rubbed him the wrong way. He demanded their surrender, and when the Tyrians defied him, laid siege to their city.[15]

This was Alexander's longest siege, lasting six months, from winter 332 to early summer 331. He ordered that a mole be built from the mainland to Tyre, over which he would march his men to attack the city frontally, but the Tyrian defenders valiantly fought off his attacks. At one point the Tyrians launched fire ships at the mole and destroyed it and the siege towers on it in a giant fireball. Undaunted, Alexander ordered that another mole be built, protecting it with siege towers mounted on ships that sailed next to it while battering rams deployed on ships pounded Tyre's walls—these innovations in naval siegecraft stand as a testament to his inventive genius.[16]

Eventually the city capitulated, and a frustrated Alexander allowed his men to go on a rampage—between 6,000 to 8,000 Tyrians were slaughtered and 30,000 enslaved. The Macedonian casualty numbers of only 400 are clearly rhetorical.[17] Alexander was now master of the Levant, but to send out a warning to anyone who might resist him on his route, he had 2,000 Tyrian survivors crucified and their corpses displayed along the Syrian coast. Yet his grisly message did not succeed: close to the Egyptian border, the old Philistine city of Gaza resisted him. Alexander ordered its siege, and two months later it capitulated amidst a slaughter of all military personnel.[18] Egypt was next.

Son of Zeus

One week after Alexander's army left Gaza, it had crossed the 130 miles of Sinai Desert to arrive at the Egyptian border town of Pelusium (Port Said).[19] Egypt at the time was a province of the Persian Empire, under the control of the satrap Mazaces.[20] Given the hatred that the native Egyptians felt for the Persians, Mazaces knew that resisting Alexander was futile. Therefore at Memphis, Egypt's 3,000-year old capital (south of present-day Cairo), Mazaces surrendered the country to Alexander.[21] Except for a few brief periods

[15] Siege: Worthington 2014, pp. 173–178.
[16] Murray 2012, pp. 95–100.
[17] Arrian 2.24.4.
[18] Siege: Worthington 2014, pp. 178–179.
[19] Alexander in Egypt: Worthington 2014, pp. 179–184; see too Caroli 2007, pp. 20–24, Bowden 2014.
[20] Egypt under Persian occupation: Perdu 2010, pp. 149–158; Lloyd 2010.
[21] Arrian 3.1.1–3; Curtius 4.7.4.

of independence, foreign powers had dominated Egypt for six centuries, including Libyans, Ethiopians, Assyrians, and (since 525) the Persians. Now the country became part of the Macedonian Empire.

Ptolemy must have accompanied Alexander to Egypt, given that Arrian cites him for certain details that suggest a firsthand account.[22] The Persians had treated the Egyptians with contempt, among other things killing their sacred bulls in a blatant disregard of native religion. Alexander went out of his way to show that he was different, deliberately sacrificing to the native god Apis (who was in the form of a bull) in the precinct of the temple of Ptah at Memphis, and helping to restore some of Egypt's most ancient temples, including part of the temple of Amun-Re at Thebes and the great temple of Thoth at Hermopolis.[23] While he was not actually crowned Pharaoh, he took on the attributes of this position, all of which endeared himself to the people and the priests, who were a powerful stratum of society.[24] The Egyptians' attitude to Mazaces and Alexander's deliberate actions to win over the native people influenced Ptolemy when he took control of Egypt—since he faced threats from some of the other Successors, he had no desire to end up being disregarded like Mazaces.

The Macedonians spent close to a year in Egypt, during which time Alexander traveled from Memphis to visit the Oracle of Zeus Ammon (a Greek form of the Egyptian Amen-Ra, whom the Greeks equated with their Zeus) at the Oasis of Siwah in the Libyan Desert. Ammon (Amun), the principal deity of Thebes (in Egypt), had been an important member of the Egyptian pantheon since the start of the Middle Kingdom (2050 BC). He was associated with Zeus in Greek religion, and there were temples to Zeus Ammon in the Piraeus and at Aphytis in the Chalcidice. Alexander wanted to consult the god to find out about his own divinity. During a visit to Didyma shortly after he landed in Asia, the priestess at the Oracle of Apollo there had told Alexander that Zeus was his real father. Alexander had received the formal titles of the Pharaohs, making him Horus, god on earth. On top of all that, he was still only 25 years old, and had already conquered a large swath of the Persian Empire. It is easy to understand why he had begun to think of himself as superhuman, and his visit to the Oracle of Zeus Ammon became a turning point in his pretensions to personal divinity.[25]

The 500-mile journey to Siwah was a hazardous one, and since Ptolemy recorded the hardships that the men faced, he likely was one of those whom

[22] Ellis 1994, p. 5; cf. Errington 2008, p. 145.

[23] Ladynin 2014.

[24] Not crowned: Burstein 1991; *contra* Bowden 2014, pp. 40–43, but Burstein is compelling.

[25] Visit: Worthington 2014, pp. 180–183, Bowden, 2014, pp. 43–53; on Alexander's divinity, see Worthington 2014, pp. 265–269.

Alexander personally picked to accompany him.[26] Their route took the men from Memphis to coastal Lake Mareotis, which was connected by a narrow isthmus to the Mediterranean, opposite the island of Pharos. Alexander was said to have seen the potential of the area for trade and commerce, since it was only forty miles from the old Greek trading colony of Naucratis, and would also provide easy access to the Mediterranean for warships. He therefore founded a city and named it after himself—Alexandria. Ptolemy later made it his capital.

From Lake Mareotis, Alexander and his force took the 180-mile trek westward (passing through what is today El Alamein) to the coastal border town of Paraetonium (Marsa Matruh), from where began the 150-mile march southward through the searing heat and harsh conditions of the Libyan Desert. Ptolemy in his *History*, and other contemporary writers in their works, speak of the men taking two weeks instead of the usual one that the Bedouins took to make the journey, of them losing their way because of sandstorms and sudden torrential downpours that obliterated landmarks and tracks, and the hunger and thirst they endured before finally they followed some birds flying overhead to the oasis.[27] Arrian noted that the contemporary sources disagreed on several aspects of this march. For example, when the men got lost, Critobulus and Callisthenes said that they were led to safety by ravens, but Ptolemy claimed "that two serpents went in front of the army, uttering a voice, and Alexander ordered the guides to follow them trusting in the divine portent."[28] Ptolemy may have decided to use snakes, which are connected to Zeus, to make a greater association with the cult of Ammon, given the purpose of Alexander's visit.

Alexander met with the priest of the Oracle in a private sanctuary before emerging to tell his men the good news—he was the son of Zeus, and Philip had merely been his mortal father. Whether the priest actually did tell Alexander this news is uncertain, especially as Ptolemy wrote that Alexander "heard what was agreeable to his wishes."[29] His claims to divinity, which intensified during his reign, would not sit well with his men.[30] Their reaction Ptolemy witnessed firsthand, which explains why he allowed others such as the Rhodians after 304 to have a cult to him, but was careful to avoid any pretense to divinity in his own kingdom.

[26] Austin, no. 8, pp. 18–20 (Arrian 3.3–4 abr.); cf. Hölbl 2001, p. 11.

[27] Ptolemy, *FGrH* 138 F 8 = Arrian 3.3.5; Aristobulus, *BNJ* 139 FF 13–15 = Arrian 3.3; Callisthenes, *FGrH* 124 F 14b = Plutarch, *Alexander* 27.3–4.

[28] Ptolemy, *FGrH* 138 F 8 = Arrian 3.3.5.

[29] Ptolemy, *FGrH* 138 F 9 = Arrian 3.4.5; cf. Aristobulus, *BNJ* 139 FF 13–15 = Arrian 3.3–4. On the episode, see now Collins 2014, arguing that Callisthenes is the most reliable of the sources for the visit to Siwah.

[30] Worthington 2014, pp. 265–269.

Alexander returned to Memphis by a more direct route across the Nitrian Desert, according to Ptolemy.[31] It was now late April or early May 331, and he prepared to leave Egypt, having spent less than a year in it. To administer the country, given its size and diversity, Alexander appointed two Egyptians, and personally picked commanders to be in charge of garrisons at Pelusium and Memphis (in all about 4,000 troops), while the entire army was placed under the control of Peucestas and Balacrus. Further, a Greek named Cleomenes from Naucratis was to collect the taxes from all of Egypt, ensure they were paid to the king, and oversee the construction of Alexandria. Cleomenes quickly exploited his position, and in 325 Alexander made him actual satrap of Egypt.[32] This division of labor in administering Egypt was, in effect, a system of checks and balances, which Ptolemy inherited when he took control of the country in 323 or 322 (Chapter 11).

Alexander would have known by now that Darius had mustered another large army, which included cavalry provided by Bessus, the satrap of Bactria and Sogdiana (between the Hindu Kush and the Oxus River, now in parts of northern Afghanistan, Tajikstan, and Uzbekistan). The Bactrian cavalry was a match for the Macedonian in strength and ability. Thus the scene was set for the final battle for the Persian Empire. The Persian and Macedonian armies met at Gaugamela (Tell Gomel), probably close to the modern Mosul, between the Khazir River and the ruins of Nineveh. It was late September 331. There, on a wide plain between the river Bumelus (Gomel) and the Jabel Maqlub hills, between the Tigris and the foothills of the Zagros Mountains, both sides prepared to do battle.[33]

The Fall of the Persian Empire

Alexander was again faced by a Persian army that far outnumbered his own, although the figures in our sources are grossly exaggerated: Arrian claimed that it consisted of 40,000 cavalry and one million infantry; Diodorus and Plutarch have one million, with Diodorus breaking it down into 200,000 cavalry and 800,000 infantry; and Curtius has 45,000 cavalry and 200,000 infantry.[34] More plausibly, Darius had 100,000 troops under him, which was still

[31] Ptolemy, *FGrH* 138 F 9 = Arrian 3.3.1 (Aristobulus says by the same way). Howe 2014, pp. 78–79, connects the different route to Alexander's founding of Alexandria and need to divorce the two events (founding and consultation), but this is not compelling.

[32] Burstein 2008a. On Cleomenes referred to as satrap on an ostrakon from Memphis (in demotic), see Smith 1988. See also the works on Cleomenes cited in Chapter 5 n.56.

[33] Battle: Worthington 2014, pp. 188–193.

[34] Arrian 3.8.6; Diodorus 17.39.4; Curtius 4.12.13; Plutarch, *Alexander* 31.1.

double Alexander's 7,000 cavalry and 40,000 infantry.[35] Somewhere in the Macedonian line was Ptolemy.[36]

Despite the threat posed by the Bactrian cavalry, on top of which was the further danger of 200 Persian scythed chariots, with razor-sharp scythes attached to their wheels, chassis, and yoke poles, Alexander won the day. He followed the same strategy as at Issus, to kill or capture Darius, and again the Great King fell for it. Alexander forced Darius to deploy his left wing earlier than he planned under Bessus against the Macedonian right, which then went into a feigned retreat. Bessus' action opened a gap in the Persian line, as Alexander had anticipated, and he galloped through it toward the Great King. Darius hurriedly tried to plug the gap with more troops, but to no avail. As he scrambled to try to keep Alexander at bay, he delayed his scythed chariot charge, and when finally he did launch it, the Macedonian infantry phalanx was ready. As the deadly chariots rushed toward the enemy, a prearranged trumpet signal rang out shrill and loud above the noise of the battle; at once the Agrianian archers and javelin-men opened fire on the horses pulling the chariots, while the Macedonian infantrymen with split-second timing moved to their left or right—as the chariots were ridden through these sudden gaps in the line, the Macedonians shot the charioteers in their backs.

Once behind the enemy line, Alexander bore down on Darius, who realized that all was lost and fled the battlefield to Arbela, about 70 miles away. Bessus and his men soon followed him. Alexander chased his defeated enemy for some miles, but then returned to help Parmenion on the left flank, where a ferocious onslaught by Mazaeus, commander of the Persian right wing, had pushed Parmenion's men back. But the news that Darius had fled and that Alexander was fast returning proved too much for Mazaeus. As he wavered, Parmenion rallied his own men and attacked, forcing Mazaeus and his men to turn tail and flee. The battle, in which the Persians may well have lost as many as 40,000 men to the Macedonians' 1,200, signaled the downfall of the Achaemenid dynasty.[37] Darius and Bessus fled eastward into the Zagros Mountains and Mazaeus south to Babylon. Their escape did not alter the fact that victory at Gaugamela gave Alexander the Persian Empire and marked the end of the Achaemenid dynasty. Alexander now set his sights on capturing the great Persian capitals of Babylon, Susa, and Persepolis.

Three weeks later, on October 24 or 25, the Macedonians had marched the 300 miles southward along the Royal Road through Babylonia to Babylon,

[35] Arrian 3.12.5.
[36] Ptolemy, *FGrH* 138 F 11: Ptolemy was an eyewitness to the battle.
[37] Curtius 4.16.26, with Hammond 1989a, p. 149.

on the junction of the Tigris and Euphrates rivers.[38] The satrap of Babylonia, Mazaeus (the commander of the Persian right at Gaugamela), personally met Alexander and, no doubt to save his own life, surrendered the city (and its vast treasury) to the young conqueror. Alexander entered the city through the Ishtar Gate, to the cheers of the people, and took up residence in the great palace of Nebuchadnezzar, overlooking the fabled Hanging Gardens. Again, in an effort to distance himself from the oppressive practices of the Persians, he promised to rebuild the temple of the city's patrol deity, Marduk, which was known as Egasila. His care in respecting local religious customs was followed by the men who later ruled the various parts of his empire in appealing to their multicultural subjects.

One month later, Alexander left Babylon. Before he did so, he introduced a major change to his imperial administration. He had retained the Persian system of satrapies as the most effective way of administering the vast Persian Empire, but until then he had appointed his own men as satraps. Now he began to use natives as satraps, and appointed Mazaeus satrap of Babylonia. Alexander made this change for political and practical reasons: the Iranian aristocracy knew the customs, languages, and religion of the areas he was moving into, and he also wanted these men to reconcile the natives to his rule.[39] At the same time, in order to keep his native satraps in check, he muzzled the extent of their power by appointing Macedonians to command the treasuries and armies of the satrapies. The successes and failures of Alexander's administration had a great influence on the way Ptolemy governed Egypt and his relations with his own multicultural subject population, as we shall see in Chapter 11.

The next royal capital, Susa (Shush), lay 200 miles southeast, on the border of Iraq and Iran.[40] Alexander arrived there in December 331, receiving Susa's surrender from its satrap Abulites. Again Alexander netted a huge haul of money and treasure, but even more significant for the purposes of the invasion was that in one of the palace rooms he found the artworks that Xerxes had stolen from Athens during the Persian Wars. These he sent back to the Athenians.

Alexander was becoming increasingly uneasy that Darius was still on the loose. Therefore, even though it was midwinter, he prepared to cross the 15,000-foot-high Zagros Mountains, even though their passes would have been covered in snow, and seize the last great capital, Parsa—what the Greeks called Persepolis, the symbolic heart of the Persian Empire, in Persis. On the border with Persis—perhaps modern Fahlian—he divided his men into two

---

[38] Babylon: Worthington 2014, pp. 193–196.

[39] Worthington 2014, p. 196 (Mazaeus), pp. 196–201 (administration).

[40] Susa: Worthington 2014, pp. 201–202.

groups. One, led by Parmenion, would take the slower-moving baggage train by an easier but less direct route via Kazerun and Shiraz to Persepolis. Alexander led the other group of 20,000 troops, who would move faster over the Zagros Mountains via the Persian Gates to take Persepolis before Parmenion arrived. However, within days Alexander would be forced into a lengthy standoff at the Persian Gates, a narrow gorge six miles long and passable only by foot. Here Ptolemy would be appointed to his first independent command.[41]

Ptolemy and the Battle at the Persian Gates

Ariobarzanes, the satrap of Persis, blocked Alexander's march through the Persian Gates with as many as 40,000 infantry and 7,000 cavalry, which he deployed on both sides of the gorge.[42] Ariobarzanes' plan was to hold off Alexander for as long as he could so that Darius had the time to levy another army and defend Persepolis. Without hesitation, Alexander attacked Ariobarzanes' troops, but he acted prematurely for once. As his men forced their way into the gorge, they were bombarded with boulders and rocks and shot at by arrows from the enemy troops on both heights. It was a trap, and unusually, Alexander had fallen for it. He gave the order to retreat, but because his men at the front had problems turning around in the narrow defile, while those in the rear kept pushing into it, oblivious to what was going on ahead of them, there was total chaos. Eventually Alexander's men escaped, but he had to leave his dead and dying behind, something that Greeks considered a major failing on a general's part.

For one entire month Ariobarzanes kept Alexander at bay. Then a local shepherd apparently told him about a rugged, 12-mile path over the Boloru Pass, which would take him behind Ariobarzanes' position. That very night Alexander ordered Philotas and 3,000 men to follow an adjacent path until they reached a point roughly halfway along the enemy line, while Alexander led other troops over the Boloru Pass. He left behind Craterus with the remaining two battalions of infantry and 500 cavalry with orders to burn extra fires at night and to make as much noise by day as they could so as to fool Ariobarzanes into thinking the Macedonians were still stuck in their position.

It took Alexander and his men the rest of that night and all of the following day and night to make their way over the pass because of all the rocks and intense heat, but eventually they came out behind Ariobarzanes. At that point,

---

[41] Seibert 1969, pp. 8–10.
[42] Battle: Worthington 2014, pp. 202–204.

Alexander ordered a trumpet blast, a prearranged signal for Craterus to attack from the front, Philotas from the middle, and Alexander from behind. Ptolemy was ordered to take a position a little further distant from the rear of the pass to kill any of the enemy who managed to escape. The result of the Macedonian onslaught was a massacre of the Persians. There is confusion in the sources as to whether Ariobarzanes died in the battle or managed to escape to Persepolis, where Alexander caught up with him and killed him. Whichever is the case does not matter: Alexander was able to breach the Persian Gates, but his rate of progress had been severely impacted.

In his *History*, Ptolemy wrote that he, not Philotas, was in charge of the 3,000 troops who were to attack the Persians from the middle. Yet Arrian has it that Alexander ordered him to the rear of the pass to cut down any escapees, and Curtius, whose account agrees with that of Arrian, says nothing of Ptolemy's role.[43] Since we know Alexander did not tap Ptolemy for any other command before this one, it is unlikely that the king would entrust him with several thousand troops for such a vital role in the attack on Ariobarzanes. Moreover, we are told that when Alexander made Ptolemy one of his hand-picked personal bodyguards in 330, he promoted him "from the ranks," which suggests that he had not held a command before.[44] Thus we see an instance of Ptolemy picked for what he evidently considered was a low-key mopping-up operation, but making himself out to be more important and trustworthy in Alexander's eyes than he actually was at that time.[45]

By the end of January 330, Alexander had entered Persepolis, just in time to greet Parmenion and the baggage train.[46] He took up residence in the royal palace, the former home of Xerxes, which was located outside the city walls (probably at Istakhr). He also took control of Persepolis' treasury, perhaps as many as 120,000 gold talents, much of which he sent for safekeeping to Susa and Ecbatana.[47] Persepolis was the ceremonial religious center and the traditional heart of the Persian Empire; the Greeks called it "the most hated city in Asia."[48] Now Alexander, in accordance with the mandate of the League of Corinth, and in revenge for what the Persians had inflicted on the Greeks 150 years earlier, ordered his men to act as they saw fit. For a whole day the Macedonians killed military and civilian men in the city indiscriminately and

---

[43] Arrian 3.18.9.

[44] Justin 13.4.10 (*ex gregario milite*).

[45] Cf. Welles 1963, pp. 107–108; Bosworth 1980a, p. 328; though against this to an extent is Seibert 1969, pp. 4–10. On Ptolemy's *History*, see Appendix 1.

[46] Persepolis: Worthington 2014, pp. 204–206.

[47] Diodorus 17.71.1; Curtius 5.6.11.

[48] Diodorus 17.70.1.

raped the women before enslaving them, together with their children—many
of them committed suicide to escape the horror.

The Macedonians spent three months in Persepolis. Not long before
they left, the palace burned to the ground.[49] One explanation was that after
Alexander and some of his men had been drinking heavily, an Athenian courtesan named Thais urged them to set fire to the palace in revenge for what the
Persians had done to her city. Thais later became one of Ptolemy's wives and
bore him three children, though it is no surprise that Ptolemy does not mention his wife in this context. Another, more plausible, explanation is probably
based on Ptolemy's own account in his *History*: Alexander ordered the destruction of the palace in retaliation for Xerxes' burning of Athens in 480 and
to proclaim the end of the Achaemenid dynasty and the dawn of a new age.

The Death of Darius

Persepolis' fate was a blow to Darius, who had fled eastward with a mere 3,000
cavalry and 7,000 infantry into Afghanistan. From Persepolis, Alexander sent
Parmenion and the baggage train to Ecbatana (Hamadan), and with 22,000
troops set off after the Great King. He forced his men to endure marches in
the scorching heat of the Great Salt Desert, and covered 200 miles in only 10
days. Still, Darius managed to evade them by the Caspian Gates. Then his luck
changed, and with it the end of his life.[50] A week later, when the Macedonians
reached the oasis of Thara (Semnan), two deserters from Darius' cause informed Alexander that Bessus, Nabarzanes (the Persian *chiliarch*, or second-
in-command), and Barsaentes, the satrap of Drangiana and Arachosia (an area
south of Areia that comprises much of modern Afghanistan), had deposed
Darius and had bound him in chains. This startling turn of events followed
Nabarzanes' suggestion that to reignite support against Alexander, Darius
should stand down as king and bestow his title on Bessus, who actually had
blood ties to the Achaemenids.[51] When Darius refused they seized him, and
Bessus declared himself Great King, naming himself Artaxerxes V.

Alexander immediately selected 500 of his fittest men and set off across the
forbidding Dasht-i-Kavir salt desert. Reports reached him that Darius and his
treacherous captors were at Hecatompylus (Qumis), the capital of Parthia, and
two days later (resting only by day and marching nonstop by night) Alexander

---

[49] Austin, no. 9, pp. 20–21 (= Diodorus 17.70–72 abr.).
[50] Worthington 2014, pp. 209–211.
[51] Arrian 3.21.5, 3.30.4.

arrived there. His astonishing pace and the fear that the rest of his men were not far behind him had panicked the new Great King and his cronies. Bessus fled into Bactria and Nabarzanes to Hyrcania; Satibarzanes, the satrap of Areia, and Barsaentes followed suit into their own satrapies—but not before these last two individuals had stabbed Darius to death. Out of respect for the Great King, Alexander gave orders that his body was to be buried with full pomp and ceremony in Persepolis.

The Macedonian Empire now extended from Greece to Parthia, including Syria and Egypt—and all this within a mere four years since Alexander had first thrown his spear into Asian soil. Still, Alexander could not rest on his laurels, given Bessus' usurpation of royal power. Although the men now made preparations to return home, thinking that the invasion was over as it had met its objectives, Alexander knew that Bessus posed a threat to the empire's security. Therefore he persuaded his reluctant troops to hunt down Bessus in Bactria. In doing so, he took the invasion of Asia into an entirely new phase, one that furthered his own military reputation and personal glory. In this new war, we see the rise of Ptolemy from the ranks.

3

The Campaign in Afghanistan

Ptolemy's role in the Asian campaign intensified during Alexander's invasion of Bactria and Sogdiana (present-day northern Afghanistan).[1] Although Alexander had targeted the threat from Bessus as his reason for invading Bactria, personal reasons were also at play: he wanted to march as far eastward as he could, toward what he took to be the edge of civilization, the land of India.[2] Thus the Macedonians set off north from Hecatompylus to Zadracarta (Sari), the capital of Hyrcania, where according to legend Thalestris the Amazon queen came to meet Alexander so she could have a child by him.[3] Any feelings she may have had in advance of their encounter were doubtless cooled when she saw how short he was and commented that he did not live up to his illustrious record![4]

Ptolemy the Bodyguard

Still in the winter of 330, the army reached Phrada (Farah), the capital of Drangiana, where Alexander rested his army. But discontent against him was starting to grow. He was faced with a conspiracy over his increasing orientalism (which manifested itself in his wearing of the Persian upright tiara and items of Persian clothing), pretensions to personal divinity, and his continued march eastward.[5] One of his companions, Dimnus, plotted to assassinate him. The plot was betrayed to Philotas, who for some reason did not tell Alexander immediately; eventually another man who was aware of the plot warned the

---

[1] On Alexander's campaign in Afghanistan, see in detail Worthington 2014, pp. 211–230, citing ancient sources and modern bibliography. I give references mostly to this book in this chapter to avoid repetition.

[2] Heckel 2003b.

[3] Plutarch, *Alexander* 46.

[4] Curtius 6.5.29.

[5] Orientalism: Worthington 2014, pp. 214–216; Philotas affair: Worthington 2014, pp. 216–220.

king. Dimnus immediately committed suicide, but Alexander rounded up the other conspirators, who included one of his royal bodyguards, Demetrius.[6] Then, unexpectedly, he accused Philotas of complicity in the plot. The unfortunate Philotas was tortured, put on trial, and executed for treason. At the same time Alexander gave orders for Philotas' father, Parmenion, who was then 800 miles away in Ecbatana, to be put to death, as under Macedonian law the family of a traitor was also executed.

The Philotas affair, as this conspiracy is often dubbed, is controversial. Philotas was very unlikely to have been part of any plot—his defense at his trial was that he had investigated the allegation but had found there was no substance to it, so he had not bothered to tell Alexander about it. His failure to do so was certainly a mistake, but surely not one that warranted death. There is no compelling reason to explain Alexander's actions against Philotas and Parmenion, other than personal motives. For some time both men had been criticizing Alexander's favoring of Persian customs, and, as we have seen in the case of the Thebans in 335 and the Tyrians in 332, once anyone crossed Alexander, redemption was out of the question. Indeed, Philotas had first clashed with Alexander in 337 when he had told Philip II that Alexander was planning to marry the daughter of Pixodarus, and Alexander had a long memory. He now took advantage of this conspiracy to get rid of of two vocal critics, despite their seniority and military prowess.

The whole episode is seedy, and an example of Alexander's growing paranoia, something that Ptolemy and the generals were witnessing firsthand. Alexander split Philotas' previous position, commander of the Companion Cavalry, between his boyhood friend Hephaestion (his first major command) and Cleitus the Black, who had saved his life at the battle of the Granicus River. Perhaps in return for Ptolemy's friendship, especially the loyalty he had shown in the Pixodarus affair, Alexander promoted Ptolemy "from the ranks" to Demetrius' elite position of *somatophylax* ("personal bodyguard").[7] Ptolemy now had complete access to Alexander at all times; his position was a high-ranking one, which also opened the door to further elevation in the military hierarchy.[8] It has been suggested that it was strange that Ptolemy took so long to be promoted.[9] This does not follow. Alexander had to try to keep both the

---

[6] Curtius 6.7.15: Peucolaus, Nicanor, Aphobetus, Iolaus, Dioxenus, Archepolis, Amyntas, Demetrius, and Calis (the last two at 6.2.37).

[7] Justin 13.4.10; loyalty: Arrian 3.6.6. Justin's comment does not imply that Ptolemy was not nobly born, as for example Collins 1997, p. 474, would claim, but merely that he was promoted from the rank and file.

[8] Heckel 1986.

[9] Ellis 1994, p. 10, who also wonders whether Alexander and Ptolemy had been estranged (p. 86 n. 36). He bases his belief on Arrian 3.6.6 that Alexander chose Ptolemy as *somatophylax*

Old Guard personnel he had inherited from his father and the next generation of soldiers (among them his boyhood friends) working side by side, which
meant a reliance on the former. But the removal of Parmenion and Philotas
was a game changer in that Alexander now began, slowly but surely, promoting
his friends to senior positions, thereby surrounding himself with those more in
tune with his grand aspirations. Hephaestion and Ptolemy are two examples of
the next generation coming to prominence. Ptolemy's star was now certainly
on the rise.

Taking on Bessus

It was time to hunt down Bessus. From Phrada the army marched to the Hindu
Kush (which the Greeks called the Caucasus). They took the 11,000-foot-high
Khawak Pass, the highest and most eastern pass of the Hindu Kush, in the
depths of the winter of 330–329, despite the deep snow and freezing tempera-
tures. The crossing was brutal. The men suffered frostbite, and a lack of provisions forced them to eat their pack animals raw. Throughout all the hardships,
Alexander suffered like the others; in doing so, he displayed the great leadership qualities and empathy with his men that made him a legendary general.
His was the military role model that his Successors emulated.

Eventually the army emerged from the pass only 80 miles west of Bessus,
who was at Aornus (Tashkurgan) with 7,000 men. To say that Bessus was
surprised that his opponents had crossed the pass in winter is an understate-
ment. He and his commanders, Spitamenes and Oxyartes (father of Roxane,
whom Alexander would later marry), immediately fled across the river Oxus
(Amu Darya) into Sogdiana (Bokhara and Turkestan), the most northeasterly
province of the Persian Empire. Alexander thus had a clear run to Drapsaca
(Kundunz), from where he issued an appeal: he would bestow his friendship
on anyone who surrendered Bessus to him. It would not be too long before his
message did the trick.

Alexander's impressive march continued via Bactra (Balkh), capital of
Bactria, to the Oxus River, which he reached in the early summer of 329. There,
at least some of his men had had enough, and he had no choice but to grant them
honorable discharges and replace them with local troops. Bessus had cunningly
destroyed all the boats that Alexander needed to cross the river, but the king

in 336, shortly after Philip's death, and thus if he was made one then, and yet again in 330, this
shows a demotion. This suggests why so little is heard of Ptolemy during the early days of the
Asian campaign until he worked his way slowly back into Alexander's favor and was reappointed
as *somatophylax* in 330. But the same passage could simply mean that Ptolemy was recalled in 336
and eventually became a *somatophylax*; cf. Bosworth 1980, p. 283.

did not miss a beat. He ordered his men to cobble together anything that would float, and one week later they crossed the three-quarter-mile-wide river on a motley variety of rafts made of skins and grass. Their refusal to give up in the face of adversity proved too much for Spitamenes and another Sogdian chieftain, Dataphernes. They seized Bessus and, with Alexander's offer of friendship in mind, sent word to the king that they would hand Bessus over to him.

Alexander could not allow his archenemy to evade his reach again. Even though there was always the danger that Spitamenes and Dataphernes might renege on their offer, or even that it was a trap to capture some of the Macedonians, Alexander had no choice but to take them at their word. He therefore tasked Ptolemy to do the job, and gave him 4,000 infantry and 1,600 cavalry.[10] This was Ptolemy's first real command, and the size of the force and the importance of the mission show that Alexander must have trusted him.

In his *History*, Ptolemy of course has much to say about his role in taking Bessus into custody.[11] For example, he claims that Spitamenes and Dataphernes originally intended to hand over Bessus in a village of their choosing, but then either changed their minds or lost heart, forcing Ptolemy to surround the village and persuade the inhabitants that if they surrendered Bessus they would not be harmed. The villagers bowed to his diplomatic entreaty, and Spitamenes and Dataphernes beat a hasty retreat.[12] However, no other ancient writer claims that Ptolemy was forced to take this military action, or that he had to rely on his diplomatic prowess.[13] At the same time, it must be acknowledged that this was a tense and dangerous mission. Spitamenes and Dataphernes were untrustworthy. Their offer might well have been a trick to capture and kill whomever Alexander sent for Bessus and so demoralize the invading army. Alexander would have known all this. Possibly his choice of Ptolemy might have been because Alexander thought he was expendable, unlike his other senior officers, but more likely, given the importance of Bessus, it acknowledged his trust and his appreciation of Ptolemy's military skills. Nevertheless, that does not excuse Ptolemy's embellishment of his role.

Alexander had ordered that Bessus be brought to him bound in a wooden collar and stripped naked. Then, in keeping with the punishment for regicide, Alexander had Bessus whipped and sent to Bactra, where his nose and ears

---

[10] Diodorus 17.83.7–9; Arrian 3.29.6–30.5; Curtius 7.5.19 ff., with Worthington 2014, p. 222. Justin 12.5.10–11 has no mention of Ptolemy on this mission. On sources, cf. Seibert 1969, pp. 10–16.

[11] Ptolemy, *FGrH* 138 F 14 = Arrian 3.29.6–30.5.

[12] Arrian 3.30.1–2.

[13] Aristobulus, who relates that Spitamenes and Dataphernes handed over Bessus without incident, was clearly favored by our later ancient writers; cf. Welles 1963, pp. 109–110. On Ptolemy's *History*, see Appendix 1.

were sliced off. The following year Bessus was put to death by ritual impalement in Ecbatana.

Revolt

Spitamenes and Dataphernes soon showed that they had no desire to ingratiate themselves with Alexander, for they orchestrated a widespread and ferocious revolt of Bactria and Sogdiana.[14] Alexander heard this news en route to Maracanda (Samarkand, in Uzbekistan), capital of Sogdiana. For the next two years the Macedonians were faced with brutal guerrilla warfare, a style of fighting unknown to them. They had to adapt quickly, but still succumbed to the enemy. For example, shortly after crossing the river Jaxartes (Syr-Darya), on the extreme northeastern border of the Persian Empire, they fell victim to an attack by the Sacae people of the area. The Sacan cavalry was renowned for its deadly tactic of galloping around and around their foe while firing off arrows into its midst. Taken by surprise, Alexander had to order a retreat when as many as 1,000 of his men were killed. Although he was able to regroup and defeat the Sacans, killing 1,000 and capturing 150, the earlier loss was a substantial blow and encouraged the locals to maintain their resistance.

While Alexander was occupied with the Sacans, Spitamenes had besieged Maracanda and had massacred a Macedonian relief force of 2,000 infantry and 300 cavalry, at which point the entire Zeravshan valley joined with him against the invaders. A furious Alexander put half of his army through three days of forced marches to return to save Maracanda. Spitamenes fled, and in retaliation Alexander spent the rest of the summer of 329 burning crops, razing towns, and massacring perhaps as many as 120,000 Sogdians in the valley for supporting him. From this point, the level of violence and lack of mercy that the Macedonians showed to any natives who defied them—in Afghanistan and later India—intensified dramatically. At times entire peoples were wiped out—men, women, and children. It was genocide.

The best part of a year passed, with no end in sight to Spitamenes' relentless guerrilla attacks on the Macedonians, and the continued defiance of the locals. Alexander called on Ptolemy even more, appointing him as commander of a contingent of troops working in tandem with other squadrons and commanders throughout Sogdiana.[15] The frustration that Alexander was feeling manifested itself in terrible fashion at his headquarters in the palace of Maracanda the following summer (of 328), when he killed the tried and trusted old

---

[14] Worthington 2014, pp. 223–228.
[15] Arrian 4.16.2–3.

general Cleitus, co-commander of the Companion Cavalry.[16] The episode also involved Ptolemy.

During one of the drinking parties, which were being held more frequently, Alexander and Cleitus got into a furious argument. Cleitus was dismayed at the effusive praise that was being heaped on Alexander by various sycophants present, and he grew incensed when they mocked the leader of their fallen comrades at Maracanda. All of the men had been drinking heavily, which may have been why Cleitus stood up and berated everyone for their mockery, and then tore into Alexander for his orientalism and divine pretensions. He finished by lifting up his right hand and saying, "This is the hand that saved you at that time, Alexander!"—a reference to saving the king's life at the Granicus River in 334.[17]

Alexander angrily threw the first thing that came to hand at him—an apple—and then rushed Cleitus to fight him. At that point Ptolemy, as a member of the royal bodyguard, grabbed Cleitus and bundled him out of the room to defuse the situation.[18] Ptolemy was said by one ancient writer to have tried to restrain Alexander, but it is more likely that a bodyguard would remove the threat to the person he was protecting.[19] Ptolemy's quick action would have saved the day had not Alexander continued to shout after Cleitus. The latter broke free of Ptolemy, and ran back into the room. He and Alexander resumed their confrontation, and Alexander lost all reason, giving in to alcohol-fueled emotion: he grabbed a spear from one of his bodyguards (the only men allowed to carry arms at symposia), and ran it through the unarmed Cleitus, killing him on the spot. Alexander was remorseful, but his action sent another ominous warning to any of his men who felt like opposing him on anything. Moreover, at this point in the campaign, against so relentless an enemy, killing Cleitus was a grave error when Alexander needed all the experienced men he could get. It was hardly the act of a great general or king: the personal honor that had driven his campaigns, and which he expected of others, had long since evaporated.[20]

Ptolemy, as far as we know, did not write about the Cleitus episode in his *History*, which is why Arrian used Aristobulus as his source for it. One explanation is that Ptolemy did not want to draw attention to Alexander's ignoble action, which may have some truth to it.[21] But if Ptolemy were writing his

---

[16] Worthington 2014, pp. 225–227.

[17] Arrian 4.8.5.

[18] Arrian 4.8.8–9; Curtius 8.1.45, 48.

[19] Curtius 8.1.45, 48.

[20] Roisman 2003; on the Cleitus incident, see his pp. 288, 319–320.

[21] Seibert 1969, pp. 18–19; cf. Errington 1969, pp. 238–239, but note Roisman 1984, pp. 377–378.

account toward the end of his life, long after he had become king (in 306), he had no need to whitewash the deceased conqueror (see Appendix 1). We have already noted occasions when Ptolemy embellished his own role in the Asian campaign; likewise, he would not have wanted to draw attention to his failures. As a royal bodyguard he had technically failed in his duty by not preventing a threat to his king from taking place—Cleitus had broken free of him, dashed back to Alexander, and could have harmed him. This was not a situation to which Ptolemy would want to draw attention if he were out to amplify his role in the Macedonian invasion; hence he omitted it. We see another plausible instance of Ptolemy's silence to mask his inability to protect Alexander at the siege of Malli in India in 326 (p. 62).

By the end of 328 or possibly early 327, the conquest of Bactria and Sogdiana was in sight.[22] Spitamenes was killed and beheaded by the Massagetae people after Macedonian troops under Coenus wiped out 3,000 of their cavalry at Gabae in late 328 or early 327. Spitamenes' head was sent to Alexander. What remained now was mopping up operations against any locals who refused to yield to the invaders and who had taken refuge in the various rock fortresses in the southeast of the province (modern Tajikistan). Here Alexander waged some of his more spectacular sieges.

One of these sieges took place at the so-called Sogdian Rock in the winter of 328–327.[23] This fortress, controlled by a nobleman named Ariamazes, lay atop a high, sheer cliff. When Alexander demanded his surrender, Ariamazes refused, taunting Alexander that he would need "winged soldiers" to capture him from his lofty perch. Despite the icy, wintry conditions, 300 Macedonian troops volunteered to scale the rear of the cliff under cover of darkness, driving iron tent pegs into the rock face to help them. Thirty of them fell to their deaths during the night climb, but the survivors signaled their success to Alexander at daybreak with white linen flags. Ariamazes had not protected his rear, believing that no one would try the suicidal climb, a blunder that Alexander had noticed and quickly exploited. The king had gambled that the psychological effect of Ariamazes finding himself trapped between hostile forces would dishearten him, and he was right. He surrendered, and Alexander sarcastically boasted that he had found his winged soldiers after all. He crucified many of the defenders, and put the rest to work in his new cities in the region.[24]

The final siege in the area involved Ptolemy. It was conducted against a rock fortress in Nautaca, home of a local ruler named Sisimithres, who also went

[22] The chronology of these months is controversial: Bosworth 1981.

[23] Worthington 2014, pp. 228–229.

[24] On how Alexander's cities in Bactria helped to spread Hellenism, see the remarks of Waterfield 2011, pp. 32–36.

by the name of Chorienes, after whom the rock was named.[25] The so-called
Rock of Chorienes was built on the far side of a deep ravine, which ruled out a
frontal attack, and Sisimithres' proximity to local provisions and water meant
that he could withstand a siege. Alexander decided to use the same stratagem
as at Tyre in 332, but instead of a mole across water, he would build a bridge
over the ravine. His workers took to the task day and night, driving wooden
stakes into the sides of the ravine, and attaching to them a criss-cross foundation of wooden struts, covered by packed earth, over which the men would
attack Sisimithres. Ptolemy and two other royal bodyguards, Perdiccas and
Leonnatus, were put in charge of the night operations.[26] Despite suffering
heavy casualties from enemy arrows, the bridge was built, and Alexander
wheeled his giant siege engines into it. At the very sight of them, Sisimithres,
as Alexander had gambled, had had enough. Taken aback at what Alexander
had accomplished in so short a time, he lost heart and surrendered.

Thus Alexander brought to an end the widespread revolt of Bactria and
Sogdiana. He could now think about other things, not least the invasion of
India. Before that, however, he faced another conspiracy and more opposition
to his belief that he was a god on earth.

Roxane

In the spring of 327, toward the end of his stay at Maracanda, Alexander married Roxane (Roshanak, "Beautiful Star"), the sixteen-year-old daughter of
Oxyartes of Bactria.[27] Where he first met her is not known, but it was either
after he captured the Sogdian rock or the Rock of Chorienes (see above). He
married her in Macedonian fashion, slicing a loaf of bread with his sword and
sharing it with Oxyartes, but his men were unimpressed because they had
wanted their king to take a Macedonian wife. Although Curtius claims that
the "intermarriage of Persians and Macedonians would serve to consolidate
his empire," Alexander, as in everything he did, had a pragmatic reason for
marrying Roxane: he needed Oxyartes' help to ensure the passivity of Bactria
and Sogdiana. Alexander was now intent on invading India, and so could not
afford a revolt of Bactria to his rear. He believed Oxyartes, a Bactrian baron,
would prevent any problems. The marriage was thus a political one, reminiscent of those of his father Philip.

---

[25] Worthington 2014, pp. 229–230.
[26] Arrian 4.21.4.
[27] Worthington 2014, pp. 231–232. On Roxane, see Ogden 1999, pp. 43–44, and 2011,
pp. 124–133.

Roxane is one of the most tragic figures of the period. She was made to marry Alexander, who was still living with Barsine, his mistress since 333. To add insult to injury, Barsine was pregnant by him, at the time, and they had a son, Heracles (named after the mythical founder of the Argead dynasty). When Alexander died in 323, Roxane was pregnant with his child, and gave birth to a son (Alexander IV). However, the Successors never treated her with the dignity and respect that she, as Alexander's widow and the Queen Mother, deserved, and Alexander IV was merely used as a a pawn in their wars. Both Alexander IV and his mother were put to death in 310, thereby bringing to an end the Argead ruling dynasty of Macedonia.

Prostration and Conspiracy

From Maracanda the army marched to Bactra (modern Balkh in northern Afghanistan). Here, Alexander attempted to have his men perform the Asian custom of *proskynesis* (genuflection) but failed miserably, thanks to the defiance of Callisthenes.[28] The Persians routinely prostrated themselves before their Great King, and may also have blown him a kiss; the Greeks and Macedonians believed that the gesture was tantamount to worship of the living ruler, and so blasphemous. Alexander would have been well aware of their attitude toward the ritual, which raises the question of why he would try to make his own people do it. It seems unlikely that he was using the custom as a form of common greeting for all his subjects, as is sometimes suggested, otherwise we might have expected him to insist that his Persian subjects merely salute him as the Macedonians did. The most plausible explanation is that he believed he was a god, and *proskynesis* was a way that his men could worship him. However, one night at a banquet, Callisthenes, the court historian, left without blowing him a kiss. When Alexander ordered him to do so, Callisthenes refused; his defiance spurred the others to follow suit, and Alexander was forced to abandon the attempt. As we shall see, Ptolemy was careful to maintain a distance from any semblance of divinity when he was ruler of Egypt, given the army's reaction to Alexander.

More serious for Alexander, while still in Maracanda, was the attempt on his life by some of the royal pages, led by a certain Hermolaus.[29] During a recent hunt, Alexander was about to spear a wild boar, when Hermolaus killed the animal; he was flogged for denying the king the traditional right of first kill.

---

[28] Austin, no. 11, pp. 22–25 (= Arrian 4.10.5–12.5), with Worthington 2014, pp. 233–234.
[29] Worthington 2014, pp. 234–235.

Even though he was in the wrong, Hermolaus apparently persuaded several other pages to help him murder the king one night while he slept. Alexander unknowingly foiled the plot by unexpectedly drinking for the entire night with his friends, but the next day one of the pages, Eurylochus, confessed the plot to Ptolemy. Remembering what had happened to Philotas, Ptolemy immediately informed the king. Alexander had all the pages tortured for information.

Hermolaus supposedly attributed a political motive to the attempt, claiming that "we plotted to kill you [Alexander] because you have begun to act not as a king with his free-born subjects but as a master with his slaves."[30] But then Alexander went on to accuse Callisthenes of complicity, although various ancient writers insist that no page had given up his name. Ptolemy and Aristobulus had a different take on the matter, however: "Aristobulus says that the youths asserted it was Callisthenes who instigated them to make the daring attempt; and Ptolemy says the same. Most writers, however, do not agree with this, but represent that Alexander readily believed the worst about Callisthenes, from the hatred which he already felt towards him."[31] We cannot overlook the possibility that Alexander exploited the conspiracy to get rid of Callisthenes, the man who had foiled his recent *proskynesis* attempt.[32] The pages conspiracy has affinities with the Philotas conspiracy, in which Alexander may have deliberately implicated an adversary to remove him.

In his *History*, Ptolemy claims that Eurylochus came to see only him.[33] Curtius, on the other hand, states that Eurylochus approached Ptolemy and another bodyguard, Leonnatus, and that both men warned Alexander.[34] It is impossible to say which of these versions is correct, although Ptolemy's account would have him alone alerting Alexander, hence this time (unlike in the Cleitus episode) doing his job of keeping the king safe. We might therefore be justified in suspecting his story.[35]

Feeling that he now controlled Bactria and Sogdiana, Alexander could finally turn to India. His campaign there would be the zenith of his invasion of Asia, and it sees Ptolemy emerge more into the limelight.

[30] Curtius 8.6.7, trans. Heckel and Yardley 2003, p. 253.
[31] Aristobulus, *BNJ* 139 F 31; Ptolemy, *FGrH* 138 F 16 = Arrian 4.14.1.
[32] Golan 1988.
[33] Arrian 4.13.7.
[34] Curtius 8.6.22.
[35] Cf. Errington 1969, p. 234.

4

To India and Back

In the late spring of 327, Alexander and 70,000 troops marched into what the Greeks called India, but what is today Pakistan and Kashmir after the separation of 1947.[1] The Greeks did not know a lot about India, and in Alexander's time the country was only nominally part of the Persian Empire, given its great distance from the Persian capitals and the independence of the Indian tribes in the Swat, Bajaur, and Buner regions of the northwest frontier. Alexander's reasons for invading India were many: revenge for Indians fighting with Xerxes against the Greeks in 480; revenge for the Indians of the Kabul Valley sending troops and fifteen elephants to Darius at Gaugamela; the chance to follow in the footsteps of his ancestors the god Dionysus (who was said to have traveled through India on his way to Greece) and Heracles (whose daughter had a son who founded an Indian dynasty); the desire for the Indians to accept him as a god; to reach the Southern (Indian) Ocean, and so discover whether Aristotle was right to believe that India was a small promontory jutting out into the Southern Ocean; and his personal desire simply to reach the edge of the inhabited world and outdo previous rulers, like Cyrus the Great, who had also invaded India.[2]

To the Indus

Alexander intended the first leg of his invasion to reach the Indus River. He divided his army into two: one half, under Hephaestion and Perdiccas, was to follow the Cophen (Kabul) River via the Khyber Pass, the main road into India; the other half, under Alexander and Craterus, would march along the

---

[1] On Alexander's campaign in India and his return, see in detail Worthington 2014, pp. 235–290, citing ancient sources and modern bibliography. I give references mostly to this book in this chapter to avoid repetition.

[2] Motives: Worthington 2014, pp. 235–236.

Choaspes (Kunar) River and the northerly Bajaur and Swat regions. Both halves of the army were to meet up at the Indus. Ptolemy naturally served with Alexander, given that he was one of his bodyguards.[3]

Alexander suspected he would face more opposition on his route than Hephaestion and Perdiccas on theirs, and he was right. In the Swat Valley, along the Choes River, the Aspasian peoples occupied various fortresses to block his advance, forcing him to besiege each one in turn. In the first siege an arrow penetrated his breastplate, and Leonnatus and Ptolemy were also wounded.[4] However, on the second day the Macedonians were gaining the upper hand when the defenders rushed them and then fled into the mountains. Those who were captured were killed on the spot, and Alexander's men gave chase to the others. Here Ptolemy had a tough and deadly encounter with the Aspasians' chieftain, at least according to his *History*:[5]

> Ptolemy, son of Lagus, observing that the leader himself of the Indians of that district was on a certain hill, and that he had some of his shield-bearing guards around him, though he had with himself far fewer men, yet he still continued to pursue him on horseback. But as the hill was difficult for his horse to run up, he left it there, handing it over to one of the shield-bearing guards to lead. He then followed the Indian on foot without any delay. When the latter observed Ptolemy approaching, he turned round, and so did the shield-bearing guards with him. The Indians at close quarters struck Ptolemy on the chest through the breastplate with a long spear, but the breastplate checked the violence of the blow. Then Ptolemy, smiting right through the Indian's thigh, overthrew him, and stripped him of his arms. When the men saw their leader lying dead, they stood their ground no longer; but the men on the mountains, seeing their chieftain's corpse being carried off by the enemy, were seized with indignation, and running down engaged in a desperate conflict over him on the hill. For Alexander himself was now on the hill with the infantry who had dismounted from the horses. These, falling upon the Indians, drove them away to the mountains after a hard struggle, and remained in possession of the corpse.

[3] Seibert 1969, pp. 19–21.
[4] Arrian 4.23.
[5] Ptolemy, *FGrH* 138 F 18 = Arrian 4.24.3–4.

Ptolemy's self-glorification shines out from this account, assuming the veracity of it, as the struggle between him and the Indian chieftain reminds his readers of the sorts of fierce fights read about in Homer. [6] Then again, his account of his clash may not be far-fetched, as he displayed the same Homeric bravery while defending a fort against Perdiccas in 320 (Chapter 6). At the same time, if the details are factual, we can criticize Ptolemy for actually complicating the situation facing the Macedonians because he refused to relinquish the corpse, and so provoked the Indians into more fighting for it.

Alexander was eager to deal with as many of the natives as he could. After he reached a town named Arigaeum, he sent Ptolemy on a foraging expedition. [7] Ptolemy came back with the unwelcome news that he had seen many more campfires than there were in Alexander's camp, meaning that the number of natives was far greater than Alexander had anticipated. The king at first was skeptical, and divided his army into three parts, each under an individual commander—himself, Leonnatus, and Ptolemy (whose troops included cavalry and the elite hypaspists). [8] They all made their way to the native camp on a hillside, and in bitter fighting, in which Ptolemy and Leonnatus distinguished themselves, defeated them. Over 40,000 Indians were captured, along with 230,000 oxen. [9] Ptolemy, not unexpectedly, makes his particular battle the hardest fought against the toughest opponent, and describes the successes of Alexander and Leonnatus in a mere few words: [10]

> A sharp contest ensued; but Alexander won the victory with ease. . . .
> Leonnatus had the same success with the third division of the army; for his men also defeated those opposed to him. . . . [Ptolemy formed] his battalions into columns, [leading] them to the point where the hill seemed most easily assailable, not surrounding it entirely, but leaving room for the barbarians to flee if they were inclined to do so. A hard contest also ensued with these men, both from the difficult nature of the ground, and because the Indians are not like the other barbarians of this district, but are far stronger than their neighbors. These men also were driven away from the mountain by the Macedonians.

---

[6] On Ptolemy's account of the Indian campaign, see Howe 2008. On his *History*, see Appendix 1.

[7] Ptolemy, *FGrH* 138 F 18 = Arrian 4.24.8.

[8] Ptolemy, *FGrH* 138 F 18 = Arrian 4.24.10.

[9] Ptolemy, *FGrH* 138 F 18 = Arrian 4.25.1–3.

[10] Ptolemy, *FGrH* 138 F 18 = Arrian 4.25.1–2.

When Alexander reached Nysa in the Kunar Valley, an embassy from the town came to him pleading for mercy, and claiming that the townspeople's ancestors had traveled with Dionysus and named their town after his nurse.[11] This tale need not be as fanciful as it first sounds, for Dionysus was believed to have made his way through India en route to Greece, and Alexander was identifying himself less these days with Heracles and more with Dionysus. When he saw what looked like ivy, Dionysus' symbol, growing there, he accepted their story and spared them. He remained at Nysa for ten days, during which time he and his men, wearing ivy crowns, went on wild, drunken romps through the woods and mountainsides. That the Nysans most likely made up their connection to Dionysus in order to be spared mattered little, given his growing association with that god.

Further fighting soon followed in the Lower Swat Valley, near the foothills of the Himalayas, against the Assaceni peoples who occupied several mud-brick and stone fortresses. Alexander first besieged Massaga, at the northern end of the Katgala Pass, where the Assaceni's king and 7,000 Indian mercenaries had taken refuge. Ptolemy would have taken part in this siege as well. After four days of assault, the king was killed and the queen, Cleophis, agreed to Alexander's terms of surrender and that the Indian mercenaries join his army. However, as the latter filed out of the city and onto a nearby hill, Alexander slaughtered every single one of them. When their wives—or rather, widows—saw what had happened, they ran out and heroically fought Alexander's men, until they too were massacred. Alexander was condemned for his treachery even by ancient writers.[12] His action and the courage of those at Massaga encouraged the Assaceni in the other fortresses to resist him all the more. Many abandoned their positions and escaped via the Shang-la Pass to occupy a fortress on the eastern summit of the rock of Aornus (Bar-sar ib Pir-Sar), which reared 10,000 feet above ground, a few miles west of the Indus River.

Alexander had to take Aornus to gain control of the entire Cophen Valley, but surpassing that strategic reason was a personal one: the chance to eclipse Heracles (whose local equivalent was Krishna), who had failed to take the rock during his Twelve Labors. Alexander turned to Ptolemy, ordering him to take troops up to the western summit (opposite the fortress) and establish a base there.[13] The king was hoping that when the Assaceni realized that they were trapped between the two enemy positions they would surrender, just as Ariamazes had at the Sogdian Rock the previous year. This psychological tactic did not work, however, so Alexander led more troops to Ptolemy's camp. There

---

[11] Worthington 2014, pp. 237–238.
[12] Diodorus 17.84; Arrian 4.27.3–4; Plutarch, *Alexander* 59.3–4.
[13] Siege: Worthington 2014, pp. 241–242. See Seibert 1969, pp. 21–23, on Ptolemy in the siege.

they decided on a bold plan: Alexander, along with the Agrianians and 200 companions, would climb a high ridge that overlooked the 800-foot Burimar-Kandao ravine, beyond which was the citadel of Aornus, while Ptolemy would stay in command of the summit camp to keep the pressure on the defenders.

Alexander and his men took two days to reach their position. Then they began to build a bridge across the gulf that separated them from Pir-Sar, on which they would set up their siege engines to bombard the citadel with stones, while other troops would attack the defenders frontally. Four days later, enough of the bridge was built for the siege engines to be positioned on it. At that point the defenders realized that all was lost and asked for terms. When darkness fell, they began to flee down the mountainside, fearing that Alexander would massacre them regardless of what he said, as he had done their comrades at Massaga. Alexander was expecting some sort of escape attempt, though, and he and his men dashed across the bridge and took the citadel. Some of the Assaceni escaped across the Indus to Abisares of Hazara (in what is now Kashmir); the rest were captured and enslaved. Although ultimately Alexander was responsible for the success of the siege, Ptolemy's role in it cannot be overlooked.[14]

With the Cophen Valley now under his control, Alexander set off to meet Hephaestion and Perdiccas and their troops, perhaps at Ohind (Udabhandapura). The two commanders had faced none of the problems that Alexander had encountered, other than a revolt by the prince of Peucelaotis (Charsadda), who had surrendered his city to them, but reneged as soon as they had left. The city capitulated after a siege of 30 days, during which time the prince was killed. As the army approached the Indus, Taxiles, the ruler of Taxila (Takshashila), 20 miles northwest of Islamabad, and the largest city between the Indus and Hydaspes (Jhelum) rivers, sent provisions as a goodwill gesture. Alexander and his men arrived at Taxila in about April 326. Remarkably, given the distance from Greece, it had been only eight years since the army first landed on Asian soil, and Alexander was not yet 30 years old.

Any hopes that the men had of enjoying a well-deserved period of rest in Taxila were dashed when news arrived that a neighboring prince, Porus, the ruler of Paurava, the area of the Punjab between the rivers Hydaspes, a tributary of the Indus, and Acesines (Chenab), had led an army to his side of the Hydaspes River to block Alexander's march. To make matters worse, the torrential monsoon rains had begun. Nevertheless, Alexander immediately marched the one hundred miles across the Salt Range to the Nandana

---

[14] Arrian 4.29.1–6, presumably from Ptolemy; note that Curtius 8.11.5 names not Ptolemy but Myllinas, though this cannot be corroborated.

Pass, which overlooked the Hydaspes River at Haranpur. After almost five years of guerrilla and siege warfare, the Macedonian army prepared for a battlefield again.

Battle and Mutiny

Alexander had with him probably 34,000 infantry and 7,000 cavalry; Porus probably fielded 25,000 infantry, 4,000 cavalry, 300 six-man chariots, and as many as 200 war elephants.[15] The infantry and cavalry were almost evenly matched, but the major worry for Alexander was the elephants, which were alien to the invaders. Yet within three decades elephants had become an integral part of Hellenistic armies thanks to Alexander's experiences with them in India.

Alexander led his men to Haranpur, but the Indian army was deployed on the opposite bank in a line that ran anything from three-quarters of a mile to one and a half miles long, with the elephants positioned every 50 feet apart along it. Added to Alexander's concern was the river's increased depth and speed because of the melting snow from the Himalayas and the monsoons. Nevertheless, he had no desire to wait until September, when the rains would abate, but gave orders to find another suitable crossing place. To fool the enemy, he made his present location his main base camp, keeping his men active in storing provisions, so that it looked like he was going to sit out the monsoons.

About eighteen miles upstream, his men found a wooded headland (of the Great Salt Range), which was out of Porus' sight. They built a number of makeshift boats of varying sizes, and when a particularly strong storm occurred one night, Alexander used it for cover. He took 6,000 infantry and 5,000 cavalry to the headland and set off across the river. To make sure Porus thought nothing was afoot, Alexander used a double at the base camp as if he was actually there. His plan was to take Porus by surprise from one side, while Craterus and the rest of the men at the base camp crossed the river and attacked him head-on. Porus would thus be trapped between these two offensive fronts. Ptolemy must have been with Alexander, as he writes of the conflict when they finally crossed the river.[16]

---

[15] The ancient sources provide differing figures for Porus' army: 30,000 infantry, 4,000 cavalry, 300 six-man chariots, and 200 war elephants (Arrian 5.15.4); the same numbers but only 85 elephants (Curtius 8.13.6); 50,000 infantry, 3,000 cavalry, 1,000 chariots, and 130 elephants (Diodorus 17.87.2); 20,000 infantry and 2,000 cavalry (Plutarch, *Alexander* 62.2). Battle: Worthington 2014, pp. 243–250.

[16] Ptolemy, *FGrH* 138 F 20 = Arrian 5.14.5–15.2.

Alexander's plan was brilliantly simple, and in keeping with what we would expect from such an outstanding strategist. Nevertheless, things went wrong. The wide Hydaspes River had a number of small islands in it; one of these lay offshore from the hidden departure point, but as Alexander sailed quietly past it, he realized that what he had thought was the opposite bank of the river was another island. The men therefore had to make their way over another difficult stretch of the river, and as they did so the storm ended and the moon came out, robbing them of their cover. In fact, dawn was breaking by the time they got to the actual opposite bank, and enemy scouts led by one of Porus' sons spotted them. Gone was Alexander's surprise, on which he had staked his strategy to defeat Porus.

The troops managed to struggle ashore and faced the enemy scouts, who included 2,000 cavalry and 120 six-man chariots. Fortunately for the invaders, the Indian chariots became bogged in the wet ground, but still the fight was a bitter one—400 Indians, including Porus' son, were killed. The survivors fled back to Porus, but wrongly told him that the entire Macedonian army was crossing, so Porus was left with no choice but to move his position to meet Alexander.

Although both sides had time to deploy their lines, Alexander was put under considerable pressure. His men were exhausted after battling the river for much of the night, and then the recent fight with the enemy scouts. Moreover, the Indian elephants were an intimidating sight for the men and their horses. Porus himself sat atop his elephant, in full view of the enemy, to exhort his men all the more. Still, Alexander had a plan to neutralize the huge beasts. He attacked first, ordering his right flank against the Indian left to scatter the cavalry there and force Porus to reinforce it with the cavalry from his right flank. As Porus did so, Coenus and his cavalry (who had crossed the river) broke through the Indian line to trap it between the two offensive Macedonian fronts. Porus had no choice but to unleash his elephants earlier than he had planned, at which point Alexander put the next stage of his plan into effect. As with the scythed chariots at Gaugamela, a prearranged trumpet blast had his infantrymen moving to their left and right to open up gaps in their line. The elephants stomped toward these gaps, and as they did so the sarissas dislodged their mahouts, while other troops slashed at the animals' eyes, genitals, and trunks with their swords. In agony and out of control, the elephants turned back to escape and ran over their own line, trampling many Indians underfoot.

The battle became a rout. Arrian states that Porus lost 20,000 infantry and 3,000 cavalry to the Macedonians' 280 infantry and 35 cavalry, while Diodorus claims that the Indians lost 12,000 men to the Macedonians' 700 infantry and 280 cavalry.[17] Despite the rhetorical embellishment of these numbers, it was a

---

[17] Diodorus 17.89.1–3; Arrian 5.18.2–3.

momentous victory for Alexander, arguably his most brilliant against a numer-
ically superior foe whose leader had not fled the battlefield. A wounded Porus
refused to bow to Alexander; when he was brought before the conqueror and
asked how he wanted to be treated, he replied "like a king." His dignity im-
pressed Alexander, who, to the consternation of his troops, made Porus his
vassal.

After the battle, Alexander founded two new cities, Nicaea (on its site; perhaps Jalalpur) and Bucephala (modern Jhelum), after his horse Bucephalas,
who had died of wounds suffered. He also minted two commemorative medallions. One of these was a decadrachm (10 drachma coin), with what is believed to be Alexander on Bucephalas attacking an Indian (presumably Porus)
on an elephant on the obverse; on the reverse is the goddess Nike (Victory)
crowning Alexander, who wears a diadem and clasps a pike and thunderbolt.
The iconography of these issues symbolically turned Alexander's victory over
Porus into one over India.[18] This was the sort of propaganda that Alexander's
successors, not least Ptolemy, learned from and exploited when they became
rulers in their own right.

The battle of the Hydaspes River was the high point of Alexander's invasion
of India. After it, the king continued to push his men further eastward, where
they were met with fierce opposition. In the siege of Sangala (near Lahore), for
example, in which Ptolemy fought valiantly against many defenders who tried
to flee, some 1,200 Macedonians suffered wounds. In retaliation, Alexander
gave orders to put 17,000 defenders to death, take 70,000 prisoner, and raze
Sangala to the ground.[19]

By the summer of 326, the army reached the Hyphasis (Beas) River. There,
the men's long absence from their homes, along with many other factors—the
impact of fighting unknown people in a very alien country; the years of guerrilla warfare and sieges, when they were used to fighting a pitched battle that
was over in a short space of time; the dysentery, deadly snake bites, trench foot,
and other things they suffered; Alexander's continued plans to keep marching
east; the psychological effect of their disintegrating armor; and the nonstop
torrential monsoon rains that left them continually soaked—proved too much.
In a nutshell, their whole experience of war and battle was overwhelming, as it
can be today.[20] Alexander wanted to cross the Hyphasis, to keep on fighting,
even to reach the Ganges, but not his troops. As Curtius remarked, they "saw
things differently: while his thoughts encompassed worldwide empire and his

[18] Bosworth 1996, pp. 6–8; Dahmen 2007, pp. 6–9, 109–110; Bhandare 2007; and especially
Holt 2003. Ten of these medallions exist.
[19] Arrian 6.5.21–24, with Seibert 1969, pp. 23–25.
[20] Worthington 2014, pp. 283–288.

programme was still set in its initial stages, the men were exhausted by the hardships of the campaign and wished only to enjoy what profits from it lay closest to hand."[21]

So they mutinied.[22] Where Ptolemy's sympathies lay is not known. Coenus voiced the feelings of the men, and although Alexander tried to shame them into following him, they refused to budge. On the third day, he had no choice but to abandon his plans to push deeper into India and turn back. Before he did, he built twelve stone altars dedicated to the Olympian gods, each 80 feet high, to mark the eastern boundary of his empire. Shortly after, Coenus, who had defied Alexander at the river, was found dead, struck down by some mysterious illness. Coincidence? No ancient writer accuses Alexander of having anything to do with Coenus' death, but, as we have seen, once anyone crossed Alexander, redemption was out of the question.

Setbacks and Revolt

Alexander still wanted to sail the Southern (Indian) Ocean, so the army moved back to the Hydaspes, where Craterus had been building a large fleet. In November, amid great fanfare, the fleet set sail, but at the confluence of the Indus and Acesines rivers bad weather wrecked and damaged many of the ships. Rather than waste time while the ships were repaired, Alexander raided the territory of the Malli (Malavas) peoples, which lay on both sides of the Hydraotes, in the lower Punjab. They had not sent him tokens of surrender or had any diplomatic contact with him, so he decided these were good enough grounds to see them as his enemies. He divided his army into several separate divisions, each under an individual commander, who would attack different parts of the area. Ptolemy was instructed to remain at the base camp for three days and then follow them, again to mop up any survivors.

In only one week, all of the Mallian towns west of the Hydraotes were taken and their inhabitants slaughtered in this "conquest through terror."[23] The remaining natives fled for refuge to a citadel in a city also named Malli. The city fell quickly, but the citadel held fast.[24] Alexander's men were not giving their all in trying to take the citadel—probably they had had enough of sieges—so to exhort them he ran up a scaling ladder to the battlements. His example did the

---

[21] Curtius 9.2.11, trans. Heckel and Yardley 2003, p. 260. Army discontent: Briant 2010, pp. 63–66.

[22] Austin, no. 12, pp. 25–26 (= Arrian 5.28–29.1), with Worthington 2014, pp. 251–253.

[23] Bosworth 1996, p. 144.

[24] Worthington 2014, pp. 253–256.

trick, but unfortunately they all rushed up the scaling ladders, which broke beneath their weight. Alexander, along with Peucestas, Leonnatus, and Abreas, were now sitting ducks at the top of the wall.

Led by Alexander, they jumped into the midst of the enemy, prepared to fight to the death. Abreas quickly fell to an enemy arrow, and another arrow penetrated Alexander's chest and came out of his neck. It must have punctured a lung, for in his *History* Ptolemy tells us that "air was breathed out from the wound together with the blood."[25] Peucestas' managed to shield Alexander until the troops outside, terrified that Alexander might be dead, broke into the citadel to save them. They massacred everyone inside it in retaliation for Alexander's dreadful wound. His doctor saved his life in the nick of time, but it took him several weeks to recover.[26]

The siege of Malli presented Ptolemy with an excellent opportunity to add himself to the action in his *History*, yet for some reason he says nothing about any role he played in it. Arrian speaks of the belief that Ptolemy was with Alexander in the citadel and that it was him, not Peucestas, who held a shield over the king when he fell, yet Arrian then goes on to discuss the inconsistencies in our sources: "There are some who have recorded that Ptolemy, son of Lagus, in company with Peucestas, mounted the ladder with Alexander, that Ptolemy held his shield over him when he lay wounded, and that he was called Soter ["Savior"] on that account. And yet Ptolemy himself has recorded that he was not even present at this engagement, but was fighting battles against other barbarians at the head of another army."[27] The question has been rightly asked (even though it cannot be answered): Who were these "barbarians" that Ptolemy was fighting, and why did Arrian and our other writers not mention his mission?[28] Perhaps Ptolemy was at Malli after all, and his silence may again be to mask the fact that as one of the royal bodyguards he had not protected his king properly—he seems to have done the same in his treatment of Cleitus' murder in 328.

Alexander's brush with death at Malli sharply highlighted a critical failing on his part – if Alexander had died, who would have succeeded him as king? He still had no heir. Even more worrying for the soldiers was who would have taken over from him to lead them back home. The differing personalities of the various commanders and the distrust they felt for each other meant that

[25] Ptolemy, *FGrH* 138 F 25 = Arrian 6.10.1.
[26] Curtius 9.5.21 and Pausanias 1.6.2 claim that Ptolemy saved Alexander's life, but that is false, and Ptolemy says nothing about this deed in his *History* (Arrian 6.11.8).
[27] Arrian 6.11.8 (from Ptolemy, *FGrH* 138 F 26a).
[28] Welles 1963, pp. 114–115; see too Roisman 1984, p. 382; Bosworth 1988, pp. 79–83. On Ptolemy's *History*, see Appendix 1.

no single one of them would have been acceptable to the others, as the aftermath of Alexander's death proved. Hephaestion and Craterus had even come to blows at one point in the campaign, and to keep them apart Alexander had placed them on opposite banks of the Indus as he sailed down it. By giving each of his senior staff various duties and commands as a means of "checks and balances" to prevent any trouble from them, Alexander may well have fostered their dislike of each other, which became even more evident during the Wars of the Successors.[29]

Further campaigning followed, marked by increasing brutality, a trend that we first started to track in Bactria. In a campaign against a prince named Oxycanus and a certain Sambus, west of the Indus, 80,000 Indians were slaughtered. Not even India's most holy of men, the Brahmans, were spared. The Brahmans were a mixture of philosophers, soldiers, and counselors to kings, a combination Alexander and his men never had encountered before.[30] During the Malli campaign the invaders attacked the town of Harmatelia, populated by Brahmans, and killed all of them.[31] This massacre proved to be a dreadful error, as the Brahmans now began to incite their countrymen to revolt against Alexander.

During the attack on Harmatelia, many of the invaders, Ptolemy included, suffered wounds from the Brahmans' arrows that were dipped in snake venom.[32] They began to die, and Alexander was said to have kept watch over Ptolemy in his tent, dreaming that a snake appeared to him with a plant in its mouth. The plant was the antidote, which Alexander quickly found; he rubbed it on Ptolemy and saved his life as well as the lives of other wounded men.[33] The story about the dream is clearly fiction, not least because Ptolemy in his *History* does not relate it, and we should be very surprised if he missed the chance to speak of Alexander saving his life.[34]

In the summer of 325, Alexander arrived at Patala (perhaps Hyderabad in southern Pakistan), and from there he sailed down the Indus into the Indian Ocean, which he claimed as the southern boundary of his empire. Ptolemy accompanied him, as he commanded one of the triremes.[35] This would be the last

---

[29] See Heckel 2002.

[30] On the Brahmans and their role in Indian society, see Worthington 2014, pp. 257–258.

[31] Eggermont 1975, pp. 114–125, accepts that Alexander besieged Harmatelia but places the town in Baluchistan, i.e. Gedrosia (cf. Strabo 15.2.7), which Alexander marched through after he had left India (see below).

[32] Diodorus 17.103.3–8; Curtius 9.8.21–28; Justin 12.10.3. Arrian says nothing about the episode.

[33] The plant is a type of oleander (*Nerium odorum Sol.*): Ellis 1994, p. 13, citing sources.

[34] Although Welles 1963, p. 115, believes that either Ptolemy ignored the episode because it was too "trivial or romantic" or that Ptolemy did write of it and Arrian ignored it.

[35] Arrian, *Indica* 18.5.

time Alexander enjoyed any success in India. Even as he returned to Patala, the Brahmans, in tandem with various princes, spearheaded a revolt against the invaders. Alexander had opened up India (as well as Bactria) to the West, and the Seleucid kings built on what he had achieved, but for now the revolt was an ignominious end to Alexander's campaign in India—in fact, Bactria and Sogdiana likewise rebelled against Macedonian rule as he marched westward toward Babylon.

Westward Bound

Instead of leaving India by the same route as he had entered the country, Alexander took about 30,000 men, together with a baggage train of their Asian spouses, families, and belongings, and marched along the desolate Gedrosian coastline (Makran, in Baluchistan), and then through the Gedrosian Desert into Carmania. His motive was personal: he wanted to do better than legendary rulers such as Semiramis, Queen of Assyria, and Cyrus the Great, who had lost almost all of their men to the terrible desert conditions. In doing so, Alexander committed arguably the biggest military blunder of his entire reign.[36]

Alexander set off via present-day Karachi and the Las Bela plain, over the Kirthar Range, and into the Gedrosian Desert. Ptolemy must have been with him on this terrible march, from early October to early December of 325, of over 450 miles across the Dashtiari Plain to the north of the Bampur River and eventually to Pura (perhaps modern Iranshahr), the capital of Gedrosia.[37] The contemporary writer Aristobulus painted a vivid picture of what everyone endured.[38] Many of the men succumbed to the intense heat by day, simply falling down and dying where they lay. As Arrian soberly remarked, this march was worse than all the fighting of the previous decade.[39] Flash flooding was also a major problem: one night the army had encamped in a dry river bed, but a sudden torrential downpour turned it into a raging river, which swept away the entire baggage train, including the men's families. It is small wonder that when the men did reach Pura they ate and drank without pause, and then embarked on a wild, week-long drinking binge as they crossed westward through Carmania. Alexander dressed as Dionysus and danced atop a special chariot, evoking among other things his association with this god and his belief in

[36] Worthington 2014, pp. 261–263.
[37] Ptolemy: Ellis 1994, p. 13.
[38] Aristobulus, *BNJ* 139 F 49a = Arrian 6.24.
[39] Arrian 6.24.1.

his own divinity.[40] The king went on to boast that he had outdone Cyrus and Semiramis, but at what cost?

Alexander marched from Carmania via Pasargadae (where he visited the tomb of Cyrus the Great) to Persepolis, where Ptolemy makes another appearance. In India, Alexander had persuaded one of the Brahmans, Calanus by name, to accompany him on his campaign. Calanus had fallen ill in Pasargadae and by the time he reached Persepolis he knew his end was near. In keeping with his religious beliefs, he elected to die by self-immolation, and asked Alexander to arrange a funeral pyre for him. Alexander thought highly of Calanus, and tasked Ptolemy with building the pyre.[41] When it was ready Calanus climbed to the top, while trumpets sounded out and the men cheered him, and then sat unmoving while the pyre was lit and the flames burned him to death. Alexander honored Calanus' death with games and festivities, including a drinking contest, so excessive that thirty-five men died during it and six not long after.[42]

From Persepolis, Alexander marched to Susa, arriving in late February or March of 324. There he held a mass marriage, in which he and over ninety of his senior staff married Persian noblewomen.[43] Many of the bridegrooms would have left wives back home in Macedonia, but these wives were not a problem because the Macedonians were polygamists. Alexander married Stateira, the eldest daughter of Darius III, and Parysatis, the youngest daughter of Artaxerxes III. Ptolemy married Artacama, daughter of Artabazus.[44] He also received a gold crown (as did the other bodyguards) as a wedding gift.[45] We know next to nothing about Artacama, and Ptolemy may even have divorced her after Alexander died.

The mass marriage is a puzzling affair at first sight. It has been considered part of an idealistic policy on Alexander's part, together with his integration of foreigners into the army and administration; the *prosyknesis* attempt; his marriage to Roxane; and his prayer for harmony among people a few months later at Opis (see below), to try to unite the races in a brotherhood of mankind. But Alexander was no idealist; he was a pragmatist, pure and simple. No Greek women came from the mainland to marry Persian noblemen, as we might

[40] Alexander's divinity: Worthington 2014, pp. 265–269. Ptolemy does not record this drunken march in his *History* (Arrian 6.28.2), perhaps because it cast an unsavory light on the king.

[41] Arrian 7.3.2.

[42] Chares, *FGrH* 125 F 19a = Athenaeus 10.437a-b. See too Plutarch, *Alexander* 70.1.

[43] Austin, no. 14, pp. 27–29 (= Arrian 7.4.4-5), with Worthington 2014, pp. 275–277.

[44] Arrian 7.4.6; Plutarch, *Eumenes* 1.3, wrongly gives her name as Apame (this was the name of Seleucus' wife: Plutarch, *Demetrius* 31.3). On Ptolemy's marriages, see Chapter 7.

[45] Arrian 7.5.6.

expect if he had truly wanted a unity of mankind from these Susa marriages. They were intended to pollute the Persian bloodline, to ensure that there would never be another Iranian who might claim to be Great King and oppose Alexander, and to produce the next generation of commanders and administrators, who with mixed Irano-Macedonian blood would not be seen as foreign conquerors. Likewise, foreigners in the army boosted manpower reserves and provided specialist military skills, like mounted archers and javelin men, and natives in the administration provided a liaison role between the people and Alexander.

From Susa the army marched to Opis, reaching there in the summer of 324. By now Alexander was planning to invade Arabia, so it was abundantly clear to the men that he had no intention of returning to Greece. After he announced that he was giving honorable discharges and money to all the veterans and wounded soldiers to return home, the troops' simmering discontent boiled over unexpectedly: they mutinied again.[46] The mutiny is surprising, as it made sense to discharge those who might be unfit for the Arabian expedition, but it appears that the catalyst was the recent arrival of 30,000 youths from Lydia, Lycia, Syria, Egypt, and the northeast satrapies, whom Alexander had ordered to be trained in Macedonian warfare as he passed through those areas. Alexander intended these new arrivals to replace his own men, and even referred to them as a counterbalance (*antitagma*) to the Macedonian phalanx.[47] The discharge announcement was therefore taken as a lack of confidence in his own soldiers.

Alexander immediately executed thirteen of the most vocal protesters, but to no avail. He delivered a long harangue to his men that praised his father's exploits almost as much as his own.[48] Again, to no avail. For three days his troops held out on him, until finally he began to replace senior Macedonian personnel with Persians, as well as transferring Macedonian titles for his Foot Companions and Companion Cavalry onto Persian troops. This proved too much, and his men capitulated. Alexander forgave them, and that night held a banquet of reconciliation, during which he prayed for harmony among everyone. His prayer has sometimes been given an idealistic motive, that he was praying for harmony among the races as part of his wish to create a brotherhood of mankind, but again, it was pragmatic: Alexander did not want any disharmony among the ranks during his Arabian campaign.

Alexander appointed his general Craterus to take the 10,000 discharged infantrymen and 1,500 cavalrymen veterans from Opis back to their homes

---

[46] Austin, no. 15, pp. 29–32 (= Arrian 7.8–9, 11), with Worthington 2014, pp. 277–280.

[47] Diodorus 17.108.3.

[48] Arrian 7.9.6–7.10.7.

in Greece. More than that, it appears that Craterus was to assume the 73-year-old Antipater's duties as guardian of Greece and, in turn, Antipater was to bring 10,000 reinforcements to Alexander at Babylon.[49] Antipater suspected Alexander's motives, however, and for his own protection he sent his son Cassander and no troops in his place—which could of course have placed his son at considerable risk. Cassander arrived in Babylon shortly before the king's death in 323 and renewed his friendship with Ptolemy, whom he had not seen in a decade.

The King Is Dead

None of Alexander's boyhood friends was closer to him than Hephaestion, with whom he likely had a homoerotic relationship.[50] In the fall of 324, when the army had moved from Opis to Ecbatana, Hephaestion died. He had fallen ill after a drinking party and developed a fever, for which his doctor put him on a strict diet. He was recovering when he threw caution to the wind and consumed a whole chicken and half a gallon of chilled wine in one sitting. Death came the same day. Alexander was grief-stricken, among other things holding games in Hephaestion's memory and cutting his own hair (reminiscent of how Achilles reacted when Patroclus was killed); crucifying the unfortunate doctor; ordering the entire empire to observe a 3-day mourning period; and—resented especially by the Persians—quenching the sacred fires for this period, something reserved only on the death of a Great King. Perdiccas was to take Hephaestion's body to Babylon for a ceremonial burial in a ziggurat over 200 feet high, costing 10,000 talents.[51]

The extent of Alexander's grief shows us his increasing feeling of isolation. During the winter of 324/323 he waged a 40-day campaign against the Cossaeans of the Zagros mountain range that bordered on Media (in modern Luristan), southwest of Ecbatana. This was the last campaign he ever undertook, and he did so, Plutarch claimed, to take his mind off Hephaestion's passing.[52] The Cossaeans controlled important communications routes and levied a toll on travelers between Ecbatana and Babylon. He starved the various tribes into surrender, and may have decided to abolish their right to charge passage. Ptolemy took part in this campaign, and seems to have contributed

[49] Arrian 7.12.4.

[50] Alexander's relationship with Hephaestion: Ogden 2011, pp. 155–167.

[51] When he moved to Egypt, one of Ptolemy's first actions was to cancel a planned shrine there, a sign of the enmity felt by Alexander's senior personnel toward Hephaestion.

[52] Plutarch, *Alexander* 72.3–4; cf. Arrian, *Indica* 40.6–8.

greatly to its success, although the account of it we have in Arrian (presumably from Ptolemy's *History*) does not go into much detail.[53]

Of importance in the story of Ptolemy is the odd anecdote that at this time Alexander appointed him his *hedeatros*, or taster.[54] It is very unlikely, however, that Alexander would risk the life of one of his royal bodyguards, whom he had personally picked, merely to taste his food and drink.[55]

Alexander's reliance on Ptolemy in the Cossaean campaign may well be because his other generals were occupied with other tasks, such as Craterus leading the veterans back to Greece and Perdiccas taking Hephaestion's body to Babylon. Yet Alexander could easily have given the latter task to Ptolemy; that he did not, but relied on him so heavily in the campaign, is a sign that Ptolemy was finally coming into his own. But one person whose power began to rise spectacularly after Hephaestion's death was Perdiccas, who was also a royal bodyguard. Alexander came to see him as his right-hand man, and likely promoted him to Hephaestion's former position of second-in-command, or *chiliarch*.[56] Perdiccas' authority was something that he exploited in the aftermath of the king's death, as we shall see in the next chapter.

From Ecbatana, Alexander marched to Babylon. He had by now abandoned any pretense of returning to Greece, and intended Babylon to be his launching point to invade Arabia. After that, he might even have been contemplating an attack on Carthage as part of a wider operation in the western Mediterranean. But fate was against him. Before he could invade Arabia, Alexander the Great died, in the late afternoon of June 11, 323, a few weeks shy of his thirty-third birthday.[57] He had collapsed after another night of drinking, lapsed into a semi-comatose state, and a week later was dead.[58] Although poison has been suspected, it is more likely that he died of natural causes, brought on by his punishing lifestyle, numerous wounds (including the near fatal one at Malli), and excessive drinking.

Alexander did not leave stability in his realm when he died, as Philip had done, nor did he leave an undisputed heir; he was a great general, but not so great as a king, and his legacy paled against that of his father.[59] Indeed, what

---

[53] Arrian 7.15.1–3, with Seibert 1969, pp. 25–26.

[54] Chares, *FGrH* 125 F1 = Athenaeus 4.171b.

[55] Heckel 1992, p. 226 n. 54; though see Collins 2013, who argues the office was more important and involved other duties.

[56] Collins 2001; Meeus 2009a.

[57] Depuydt 1997.

[58] Death: Worthington 2014, pp. 293–296. See too Doherty 2004, although his thesis that Ptolemy was responsible for the murder and deliberately styled his later account of the reign to exonerate himself is surely incorrect. Source problems surrounding Alexander's death: Bosworth 1971 and 1988, pp. 157–184.

[59] Worthington 2014, pp. 302–309; see too Squillace 2015.

the Macedonians of the mainland thought of Alexander and their empire in 323, thanks to the way he had forsaken his own kingdom for his personal reputation, and his pretensions to personal divinity, was probably very different from what they thought of Philip and their growing influence at the end of his reign in 336.[60] Alexander's legacy included the warfare and chaos that gave birth to a new era and a new world, the Hellenistic (Map 3). It was also one in which Ptolemy, as we shall see, played an instrumental role in shaping.

[60] I argue this in Worthington 2014, pp. 105–109 (Philip) and pp. 300–302 (Alexander), the central thesis being that Philip was the greater king for Macedonia than Alexander.

5

Ptolemy and the Rise of the Successors

We cannot construct as coherent and extensive a picture of all the events of the first few decades after Alexander's death as we can for earlier periods in Greek history, given that many of our ancient sources are fragmentary or treat episodes sparingly. Diodorus in particular furnishes us with the most information on the Wars of the Successors until 301, when his interest in them wanes. We are reasonably well informed of Ptolemy's movements until the final few years of his life, although we have to resort to conjecture at times. On the ancient sources, see Appendix 2.

After Alexander's Death

When he was growing weaker, Alexander had given his signet ring (the seal of authority) to Perdiccas, now his second-in-command, to make sure that the business of imperial administration continued uninterrupted.[1] It was Perdiccas who ordered that all fires be ritually put out the night Alexander died as a mark of respect. The other senior officers accepted Perdiccas as Alexander's stand-in, at least while the king was alive, but it was a different matter after he died. It is an overstatement that "breath had hardly left Alexander's body before the ambitious [Perdiccas] himself dreamt of the succession."[2] But Perdiccas was ambitious, and saw his position as merely a stepping stone to ruling all of Alexander's empire.[3]

---

[1] For example, Curtius 10.5.4; Justin 12.15.12; Nepos, *Eumenes* 2.1. Perdiccas: Heckel 1992, pp. 134–163.

[2] Elgood 1938, p. 2.

[3] For example, Curtius 10.5.4; Justin 12.15.12; Nepos, *Eumenes* 2.1.

As Alexander's health declined, his generals gathered by his bedside to ask him to whom he intended to leave his empire. According to Ptolemy, Alexander answered "to the best man."[4] As a royal bodyguard, Ptolemy would have been present to hear Alexander's response, but why did Alexander simply not name someone? In fact, why ask the question in the first place? It did not occur to anyone, regardless of rank, that someone who was not of the Argead dynasty would succeed Alexander as king. Roxane was still pregnant, and clearly if she bore a son he would succeed his father. If she gave birth to a daughter, there was always Alexander's half-brother Arrhidaeus, the son of Philip and his third wife, Philinna of Thessaly. Arrhidaeus, born in 357, was apparently mentally incompetent, and had been passed over as heir by his father in favor of his younger son, Alexander.[5] But even so, Arrhidaeus could still continue the Argead line, and, as has been rightly said, "what Alexander had conquered belonged to Macedonia, and Macedonia belonged to the Argead dynasty."[6] Too much has been made of the question and Alexander's apparent response; if it were asked of the dying Alexander, his generals were probably not asking who was going to succeed him as king, but simply who would be in charge of affairs until Roxane gave birth.

Still, a decision had to be made about governing the empire. Normally when a Macedonian king died, his son would succeed him if he were of age, or a regent would be appointed if the heir was a minor.[7] Macedonia had been in crisis before. The last time was in 359, when its king (Perdiccas III) had been killed in battle against an invading Illyrian tribe, and the heir (Amyntas) was only a boy. The kingdom was about to be invaded on two fronts by two different tribes, and at the same time two pretenders vied for the throne. Then, Amyntas was set aside and his uncle, Philip, was proclaimed king (Chapter 1).[8]

But Babylon in 323 was a world removed, geographically and chronologically, from the Macedonia of 359. Alexander's child was still unborn; the generals were in unchartered waters. The royal court was with the king in Babylon, not back in Pella, and instead of powerful barons in service to the king at the capital, there were powerful generals with substantial armies scattered

---

[4] Diodorus 18.1.4; Arrian 7.26.3 (= Ptolemy, FGrH 138 F 30); Curtius 10.5.5; Justin 12.15.8 ("the most deserving"). "To the best" is *to aristo* in Greek; possibly Alexander had meant to say "to Craterus," who was not present at Babylon at the time, and Plutarch, *Eumenes* 6.1–2, speaks of the Macedonians wanting him to succeed Alexander. On the last words, see Antela-Bernárdez 2011; on Craterus, see n. 53 below.

[5] Diodorus 18.2.2; Plutarch, *Alexander* 77.5, with Greenwalt 1985; Carney 2001; Worthington 2008, p. 175.

[6] Ellis 1994, p. 24; see also Schur 1934.

[7] Hatzopoulos 1986.

[8] Worthington 2008, pp. 20–22.

throughout Asia—not to mention Antipater on the mainland, and Craterus in Cilicia with the 10,000 troops discharged at Opis in 324. Alexander as king expected his orders to be obeyed by everyone in both the western and eastern halves of his empire, but that was because he was the rightful king. With no one to control his senior officers, it was only a matter of time before their animosities rose to the fore.[9] Indeed, Alexander's last words "had given the signal for war amongst his friends, or thrown amongst them the apple of Discord."[10] It was indeed a constitutional crisis.[11]

Eager for personal power, the Successors had no qualms in dividing up Alexander's disparate empire, or in making or breaking alliances with each other over the years as suited their purposes. In doing so, they plunged the Greek world into a battleground for forty years, which among other things saw the end of the 300-year-old Argead dynasty and the emergence of Ptolemy on the center stage of history.[12]

King Who?

It is often thought that events moved quickly after Alexander died, but no ancient writer says so.[13] It would have taken time for Perdiccas to finalize arrangements for Alexander's body and to deal with other pressing matters, not least reassuring the restless army that all would be well—we are told that the men "felt abandoned so far beyond the Euphrates, surrounded by enemies, who were far from happy with the new rule [of Macedonia]," and that they warned of civil war because there was no heir to the throne.[14] This meant that each commander would be after his own power, and so cause yet more bloodshed after all the deaths in Asia.

---

[9] Heckel 2009.

[10] Justin 12.15.11; cf. 13.1.8–15.

[11] Bosworth 2002, pp. 29–34.

[12] On the Wars of the Successors, see Schur 1934; Cloché 1959; Will 1984a and 1984b; Bengtson 1987; Hammond and Walbank 1988, pp. 117–244; Green 1990, pp. 5–134; Heckel 2002; Bosworth 2002 and 2007; Braund 2003; Adams 2007 and 2010; Bennett and Roberts 2008 and 2009; Romm 2011 (only to 316); Roisman 2012; Waterfield 2012; Anson 2014a; and the essays in Hauben and Meeus (2014). On the economic effects of the wars (including Alexander's invasion) on the empire, see Rostovtzeff 1941, vol. 1, pp. 126–187.

[13] Yet the prevailing opinion is that everyone acted with breakneck speed; for example, Waterfield 2012, p. 19: "the whole business reeks of haste," and Romm 2011, p. 37: "it is certain that on June 12," but there is no evidence for their views, especially for Romm's certainty of the day after Alexander's death.

[14] Curtius 10.5.12–13.

Perdiccas would have enjoyed controlling affairs for as long as he could, so some days may have elapsed before he called a meeting of the senior staff at Babylon to decide what to do.[15] The principal players here, as they concern us in Ptolemy's life, were Perdiccas; Antigonus Monophthalmus ("one-eyed," who, after Issus in 333, had been given the satrapy of Phrygia in west central Asia Minor, and who had at his disposal a huge army);[16] Ptolemy himself;[17] Seleucus;[18] Leonnatus (another royal bodyguard);[19] Lysimachus (also a bodyguard);[20] Cassander (Antipater's son who had arrived at court in 324); Antipater (guardian of Macedonia and Greece);[21] and Craterus (who was then in Cilicia, on his way back to Macedonia with the veterans Alexander had discharged at Opis in 324).[22] There is no indication that anyone presumed that Antipater, Craterus, or Antigonus would make the journey to Babylon, in which case everyone, the army included, was expected to abide by the decisions made there. Likewise, no one could have suspected that Antigonus in Phrygia would strive the most to resurrect Alexander's old empire, and so would dramatically impact events of the next two decades.[23]

Perdiccas took command of the proceedings by virtue of his position. Antipater actually ought to have brought everyone together since Alexander had made him his deputy when he first left for Asia in 334, but Antipater was thousands of miles away in Greece, and Perdiccas for obvious reasons was not going to request his presence in Babylon. Our ancient writers (all later) do not provide us with a complete picture of the discussions, and what they do say is often confused and contradictory, not least when it comes to Ptolemy's role at Babylon.[24] Diodorus, who gives us the most information on the entire period

---

[15] Background and settlement at Babylon: Bouché-Leclercq 1903, pp. 6–10; Rosen 1967 and 1968; Wirth 1967; Seibert 1969, pp. 27–38; Errington 1970; Martin 1983 (1987); Billows 1990, pp. 52–58; Bosworth 1993 and 2002; Ellis 1994, pp. 24–27; Meuss 2008; Waterfield 2011, pp. 19–29; cf. Romm 2011, pp. 37–55; Anson, 2014a, pp. 14–28.

[16] Heckel 1992, pp. 50–56.

[17] One of the seven *somatophylakes*, who were Leonnatus, Lysimachus, Aristonous, Perdiccas, Ptolemy, Pithon, Peucestas (Arr. 6.28.4): see Heckel 1992, s.vv.

[18] Heckel 1992, pp. 253–257.

[19] Heckel 1992, pp. 91–106.

[20] Heckel 1992, pp. 267–275.

[21] Heckel 1992, pp. 38–49.

[22] Heckel 1992, pp. 107–133.

[23] In detail: Billows 1990 and Champion 2014.

[24] Austin, no. 22, pp. 41–43 (= Arrian, *FGrH* 156 F1, 1–8; Diodorus 18.3.2–5); Arrian, *FGrH* 156 F.1, 1–8; Curtius 10.6–10.8 (the most details on events at Babylon); Justin 13.2.1–4.25; on the source problems, especially relating to chronology, see Roisman 2012, pp. 61–71, properly preferring Curtius' version of events; *contra* Bosworth 2002, pp. 29–44, and see too Lane Fox 2014, pp. 168–170.

of the Successors, at least until the battle of Ipsus in 301, omits entirely the issue of Roxane's baby, and makes it it sound like Arrhidaeus was always the preferred choice when it came to choosing the next king. Fortunately for our purposes, we do not need to discuss the ins and outs of the sources' veracity, and the following account of events, following Curtius' narrative, is the most plausible.

Only the senior personnel met in the royal palace at Babylon, attended also by the royal bodyguards (Ptolemy included), to decide what to do. Arrhidaeus was also in Babylon, but Perdiccas had not invited him to the meeting. Perdiccas cunningly had brought into the room Alexander's throne, royal robe, diadem, and weaponry, and he placed the king's signet ring on the throne, as if pretending to give it back, telling everyone that they had to elect a leader until Roxane gave birth and the boy (significantly) came of age.[25] He was clearly expecting the men present to demand he reclaim the signet ring, and, as we shall see, may have prepped someone to put him forward as regent of the baby king. Curiously, everyone in Babylon seems to have expected Roxane to give birth to a boy; no one seems to have wondered what would happen if she had a daughter.

Then Perdiccas' plan came unstuck. Suddenly the anxious troops who had been waiting outside the palace burst inside, wanting to make their own demands and to hear what was being discussed.[26] Their presence ended the smaller, closed shop meeting, for now the rank and file could show their approval (or not) of any plan.[27] Roxane's baby (if male) was obviously the main contender for the kingship. But then Nearchus, Alexander's admiral, suggested Heracles, Alexander's illegitimate son from his *de facto* relationship with Barsine, daughter of Artabazus.[28] Barsine and Heracles were living in Pergamum when Alexander died. Heracles had been born in 327, so he was only a few years old at this time.[29] That this suggestion came from Nearchus is interesting. Acting on Alexander's orders as he left India, Nearchus in 324 had sailed the one thousand miles of the Makran coastline in an epic voyage,[30] and had been given as a wife in the mass marriage at Susa in 324 a daughter of Barsine. Thus his favoring of Heracles (his brother-in-law) was an obvious attempt to gain influence. His plan

---

[25] Curtius 10.6.4–9; Justin 13.2.5.

[26] Errington 1970, pp. 50–51; Meeus 2008, p. 44.

[27] Roisman 2012, p. 63.

[28] Curtius 10.6.10–12. Justin 13.2.6–8 has Meleager putting Heracles and Arrhidaeus forward, but Justin has probably confused Meleager with Nearchus. On Heracles, see Tarn 1921, Brunt 1975.

[29] Heracles was either 17 (Diodorus 20.20.1) or 15 (Justin 15.2.3) in 310.

[30] Voyage: Worthington 2014, pp. 269–270.

backfired, however, because Heracles was a bastard, and would never have been accepted as a ruler in place of a legitimate Argead. Even Ptolemy, who at Susa had married Artacama, sister of Barsine, was astute enough not to support Heracles' candidacy. The troops clashed their spears on their shields to show how much they were against Nearchus' proposal, although he refused to withdraw it.

Then Ptolemy spoke.[31] According to Justin, Ptolemy was against Arrhidaeus becoming king because of his disability and the belief that his mother had been a whore before marrying Philip II. However, in Curtius' account Ptolemy delivered a scornful speech against Heracles and Roxane's baby, given that the mother's Bactrian birth would make Alexander's heir only half Macedonian, and "whose very name Europe will be ashamed to hear."[32] Whatever the motives of the ancient writers in presenting Ptolemy as they did, it is unlikely that he would be so vehemently opposed to Arrhidaeus, whose father was Philip. But his adverse feeling about Roxane's child does betray how the Macedonians looked down on anyone not of their own blood.

Ptolemy followed up his vocal attack with a radical proposal: to form an advisory body to administer the empire, with all of its members having equal status[33]—"those who used to advise [Alexander] should meet as a body whenever there is a need to decide anything, and what the majority decides shall be approved, and obeyed by the generals and other troop commanders."[34] "Better, he said, to choose from those who stood close to their king in personal qualities, who were the governors of provinces, who were entrusted with military campaigns—rather than be subjected to the domination of unworthy men while the king had but nominal power."[35] Ptolemy's proposal meant that in place of the Argead single kingdom, there would be a series of united, yet distinct, satrap-states. He was clearly angling for a place on that advisory body, based on his authority as a bodyguard, which would see him propelled overnight from bodyguard to satrap, and so on a par with his more influential comrades who had been generals or satraps.[36] Perdiccas and

[31] Curtius 10.6.12–15; Justin 13.2.11–12; cf. Pausanias 1.6.2. Diodorus says nothing about Ptolemy in the lead-up to the settlement; see further Bosworth 2002, pp. 40–43, Mooren 1983, especially pp. 233–240.

[32] Cf. Meleager's similar critique of Roxane: Justin 13.2.9–10.

[33] Mooren 1983, for the argument that Ptolemy's proposal showed he believed that the Macedonian empire could survive without a king.

[34] Curtius 10.6.15.

[35] Justin 13.2.11–12.

[36] Schur 1934, p. 132; Rosen 1979, p. 465; Seibert 1969, pp. 32–33; Errrington 1970, pp. 74–75; Mooren 1983, p. 233; Meuss 2008, pp. 48–50, and 2014, pp. 270–271. Mehl 1986, p. 25, is too extreme in that Ptolemy wanted to bring an end to the empire.

the others must have seen through Ptolemy's crafty plan, and although some agreed with it, ultimately it was rejected. Nevertheless, Ptolemy had made his mark, and when a settlement was reached a week later, his boldness paid off: he was made satrap of Egypt, although there were strings attached, as we shall see.

After Ptolemy's speech, one of the other bodyguards, Aristonous, spoke in favor of Perdiccas being Alexander's "best man," and that he should also take back the signet ring. Aristonous was clearly Perdiccas' man, especially as Curtius speaks of Perdiccas pretending to waver, thinking that the more he appeared modest, the more he would be encouraged to take the the ring and assume the regency until Roxane's boy came of age.[37] Aristonous may have spoken as he did when he saw that more of those present favored Ptolemy's proposal than that of Perdiccas; certainly Ptolemy in his *History* ignored him completely, perhaps because his speech helped to foil Ptolemy's plan.[38] Then the battalion commander Meleager undid any support that Aristonous might have generated for Perdiccas by lambasting the latter in an impassioned speech, warning of his ambition, and even going so far as to say that if Alexander had anointed Perdiccas his successor "that should be the only one of his orders that you should disobey."[39]

An unknown person, clearly representing the troops, then put forward Arrhidaeus to be proclaimed king as Philip III.[40] They had deliberately selected Philip as the name to emphasize continuity in the Argead line, and were not prepared to wait until Roxane gave birth, probably a reaction to her bloodline.[41] Perhaps sensing their proposal would be disregarded, the troops began to turn violent, even threatening to kill the others for holding the discussion without Arrhidaeus present. At that point, Meleager brought Arrhidaeus into the meeting, where he was hailed king. Perdiccas and some of the others fled and hid in different parts of the palace in fear of their lives, and for the best part of a week there was considerable turmoil as the various battalions of the infantry faced off against the cavalry, who owed allegiance to different generals.[42]

---

[37] Curtius 10.6.16–19.

[38] Errington 1969, pp. 235–236.

[39] Curtius 10.6.22; his speech: Curtius 10.6.20–24.

[40] Curtius 10.7.1–2. Justin 13.2.8 has Meleager proposing Arrhidaeus.

[41] Errington 1978, pp. 114–115. Cf. Arrian, *FGrH* 156 F 1, 1: "Arrhidaeus was proclaimed king, and his name was changed to Philip."

[42] Diodorus 18.2.2-4; Arrian, *FGrH* 156 F 1, 2; Curtius 10.7.11-9.11; Justin 13.3.5-10. On the rift between the different factions and the role of the infantry and cavalry, see Roisman 2012, pp. 71–81.

Eventually a compromise was reached: Philip III would be sole king until Roxane gave birth. If she had a son, then he would be made a joint ruler with Philip III; Perdiccas would be the *chiliarch*, answering directly to the monarch, and Meleager would be promoted to Perdiccas' second-in-command.[43] Perdiccas' position meant that he would be the most powerful man in the Macedonian Empire, but he was far from happy, as was Ptolemy, for Meleager had not featured in his proposal. Nevertheless, Perdiccas had no choice but to agree to Meleager's terms: although the cavalry supported Perdiccas, the infantry did not, and numbers spoke. Eventually, all sides swore to this compromise before Alexander's corpse.[44]

A week had gone by, during which time Alexander's body had been embalmed, a break from the Macedonian tradition of burning a body on a pyre. Since Perdiccas had determined that Alexander was to be buried at Aegae in Macedonia, it was essential to preserve his corpse for its long journey there. There is a belief that Alexander wanted to be buried at Siwah, home of the Oracle of Zeus Ammon, which Alexander had visited in 331 to find out if he was a god.[45] If so, then Perdiccas' decision to bury the body at Aegae could be seen as a claim to regnal authority since it was the responsibility of a successor to bury his predecessor. Possibly also Perdiccas saw Ptolemy as a threat to him, given his proposal about a ruling committee, and wanted to deny Ptolemy the political advantage he would gain from burying Alexander in Egypt. Not that it mattered: within two years Ptolemy had kidnapped the corpse and buried it in Egypt (Chapter 6).

Despite the agreement, Perdiccas never intended to allow Meleager to wield the influence he had suddenly gained. Cunningly ordering a review of troops to mark the acclamation of Philip III as king, Perdiccas dramatically accused Meleager and 300 of his men of treachery, and had them trampled to death by war elephants.[46] We should note that this was on his orders, not those of Philip III, who was already being disregarded.[47] Meleager was spared, but only for show: he was soon executed, apparently while claiming sanctuary in a temple.[48]

---

[43] Cf. Arrian, *FGrH* 156 F 1, 1; Justin 13.4.1-4. Meleager: Heckel 1992, pp. 165–170.

[44] Justin 13.4.4.

[45] Diodorus 18.3.5, 28.3; Curtius 10.5.4; Justin 12.15.7, 13.4.6; see further Badian 1967, pp. 185–189; Seibert 1969, pp. 110–113; Billows 1990, pp. 58–67; Erskine 2002, p. 171; Meuss 2008, pp. 66–68.

[46] Diodorus 18.4.7; Arrian, *FGrH* 156 F 1, 4; Curtius 10.9.11–19; cf. Justin 13.4.7–8.

[47] Cf. Curtius 10.9.19: "Philip did not stop or order [the executions], and it was obvious he would not admit to doing anything himself unless the result was a justifiable one."

[48] Diodorus 18.4.7 (after the divison of the empire); Arrian, *FGrH* 156 F 1, 4 and Curtius 10.9.20–21 (before the division), with Errington 1970, p. 57; Meees 2008, pp. 58–59.

The Babylon Settlement

With Meleager dead, Perdiccas quickly called another meeting of the senior personnel to lock in a settlement with similar terms as he had intended earlier.[49] Pausanias claims that Ptolemy was primarily responsible for the division of the empire, but Perdiccas was clearly in charge.[50] Perdiccas was made regent of Philip III and, if Roxane had a son, of the baby king as well. We do not know how heavily pregnant Roxane was; the sources say she was either five or eight months pregnant when Alexander died, so clearly the wait would not be too long.[51] Perdiccas' position, as Curtius suggests in Aristonous' speech, meant that he was one step closer to realizing his ambition.[52] Then Perdiccas proceeded with the rest of his arrangements. His object was to isolate and occupy the attention of his fellow generals and direct competitors—"isolate" by sending them to the various regions of the far-flung empire, and "occupy" them with controlling their areas, leaving him free to act as he wished. Perhaps taken aback at how quickly and ruthlessly Perdiccas had brought down Meleager, the others had little choice but to agree to his arrangement. Ptolemy, while no ally of Perdiccas, seems content to have played second fiddle to him for the moment.

Antipater and Craterus were made joint generals of Greece and Macedonia, which effectively gave them control of the western part of the empire, although Antipater was always the senior of the two men. Their joint command was a stroke of genius on Perdiccas' part because in 324 Alexander may have intended Craterus to succeed Antipater in Greece.[53] Perdiccas was thus counting on Antipater and Craterus to be at loggerheads with each other, allowing him to operate as he wished. However, any anticipated dissension did not happen: they joined forces in successfully putting down the Greek revolt, and then turned on Perdiccas (see below).

Antigonus was still in his fortress capital at Calaenae.[54] He was made satrap of Greater Phrygia, Lycia, and Pamphylia, which meant that he would be preoccupied with affairs in the lion's share of western Anatolia. Antigonus was

---

[49] Arrian, *FGrH* 156 F 1, 5–8; Dexippus, *BNJ* 100 F 8; Diodorus 18.3.1–4; Curtius 10.10.1–4; Justin 13.4.5, 9–25, with Anson 2014a, p. 22.

[50] Pausanias 1.6.2.

[51] Five months: Curtius 10.6.9; eight: Justin 13.2.5; cf. Errington 1970, p. 58, for her giving birth in September.

[52] Curtius 10.6.16–19; see too Wirth 1967, Bosworth 1993.

[53] Ashton 1991, pp. 125–131, for the view that Craterus stood the most to gain from Alexander's death: he was "the right man, in the wrong place, at the wrong time" (p. 131).

[54] Antigonus under Alexander: Anson 1988; Billows 1990, pp. 36–48; Champion 2014, pp. 12–18.

something of an unknown entity because he had been living in one place as satrap for much of Alexander's Asian campaign, but presumably the others felt no anxiety about reappointing him to his satrapy.

Ptolemy received Egypt, the adjoining portion of Arabia, and Libya. But Perdiccas added the stipulation that the current satrap of Egypt, Cleomenes, remain in the country, ostensibly to assist him.[55] On the one hand, it made sense for Ptolemy to have help because he had no understanding of administration, and no real experience of leading more than the occasional troop of men. More likely, though, is that given Ptolemy's opposition to Perdiccas in the first meeting at Babylon, Perdiccas wanted to keep tabs on him, and so Cleomenes would be Perdiccas' spy.[56]

Lysimachus received Thrace, which took him from Asia to the European side of the Hellespont. The military problems he faced in the north against the Odrysian Thracians led by Seuthes III effectively sidelined him for several years (as Perdiccas doubtless intended).[57] But then Lysimachus emerged as one of the most influential of the Successors, and toward the end of his life he was even king of Macedonia (Figure 5.1).[58]

Leonnatus was appointed satrap of Hellespontine Phrygia, which promised him considerable wealth. Eumenes, the only successor who was a Greek (from Cardia in Thrace), and had been Alexander's principal secretary and a cavalry commander, received the rebellious Cappadocia and Paphlagonia in Asia Minor, with the orders to expel the local Iranian ruler there, Ariarathes. Antigonus and Leonnatus were ordered to assist him. Eumenes would prove to be a formidable opponent over the next several years.[59]

Finally, Seleucus was made commander of the Companion Cavalry, an interesting post, given that he had as much claim to territory as any of the others. He may, however, have preferred to stay on the sidelines, suspecting

[55] Arrian, *FGrH* 156 F1, 5; Justin 13.4.11; Pausanias 1.6.3 (he was Perdiccas' man).

[56] On Cleomenes, see Vogt 1971; Seibert 1979 and 1969, pp. 39–51; Le Rider 1997; Caroli 2007, pp. 37–43; Burstein 2008a; Baynham 2015.

[57] Lund 1994, pp. 20–33, 53–54; Shipley 2000, pp. 47–51; cf. Archibald 1998, pp. 304–316. Lund 1994, pp. 20 and 54, argues that he was not actually a satrap but was acting as a general under Antipater, but this seems unlikely: Delev 2000, p. 384. Justin 15.3.15 claims that Lysimachus received Thrace because of his courage, and as an example tells of the time Alexander, as punishment, shut him into a room with a lion, but Lysimachus killed the beast by ripping out its tongue (15.3.7–9).

[58] Lysimachus: Austin, no. 45, pp. 83–86 (= Pausanias 1.9.5–10). In detail: Landucci Gattinoni 1992 and Lund 1994.

[59] Plutarch, *Eumenes*; Nepos, *Eumenes*, with Westlake 1969; Briant 1972 and 1973; Schäfer 2002; Bosworth 2002, pp. 98–168; Anson 2004 and 2014, pp. 47–115; Romm 2011; Roisman 2012, pp. 119–136, 145–152, 158–236; Champion 2014, pp. 37–68. The Successors later turned on Eumenes not simply because he was Greek but because of his unmilitary status: Anson 2014.

Figure 5.1 Portrait of Lysimachus. © Vanni Archive / Art Resource, New York

that the Babylon settlement would be ephemeral, given the personalities involved. He was right; it was not long before trouble broke out, wrecking the pact. Seleucus' careful strategy paid off: he became ruler of Babylonia, and founded a dynasty, the Seleucid, that ruled one of the most extensive territories of the Hellenistic world and was second only to the Ptolemaic in longevity (Figure 5.2).[60]

Thus came about this "bad-tempered compromise."[61] These men were not kings but satraps, subservient to Philip III, though he hardly held the power or generated the respect that Alexander had. However, Perdiccas was in a unique position to control the empire from Babylon. He may also have commanded the largest number of Alexander's veterans—the core fighting power of the

[60] Austin, no. 46, pp. 86–47 (= Appian, *Syrian Wars* 52–55, 57–58, 62–63); Seleucids: Bevan 1902; Bouché-Leclerq 1914; Bikerman 1938; Rostovtzeff 1941, vol. 1, pp. 422–551; Mehl 1986; Grainger 1999 and 2014; see too Tarn and Griffith 1952, pp. 126–163; Grant 1982, pp. 48–64; Walbank 1993, pp. 123–140; Shipley 2000, pp. 271–325; Bosworth 2002, pp. 210–245; Austin 2003; Errington 2008, pp. 36–39, 111–142.

[61] Errington 2008, p. 15.

Figure 5.2 Portrait of Seleucus. © The Metropolitan Musuem of Art, Purchase,
H. Dunscombe Colt Gift, 1974, www.metmuseum.org.

Macedonian army—than any other of his comrades apart from Craterus.[62]
The events of the next few years show that these men never took the Babylon
settlement seriously. The constant jockeying for power, given their personalities and ambitions, meant that their alliances would always be self-serving
and short-lived. No one was ever content with what he possessed, and no one
could ever settle down. In part this stemmed from the phenomenal influence
that Alexander's conquests had had on them, which fed their imperial aspirations.[63] But also no one could trust anyone else—even in 323 it was observed
of Perdiccas that "everyone was suspicious of him and he of them."[64] And
Plutarch adds that Antigonus "was not swayed by Perdiccas' edicts, and was already ambitious and scornful of all his comrades."[65] It is no surprise that their

[62] Roisman 2012, p. 87, and on the veterans with Craterus, including their role in the Lamian
War (on which, see below), see pp. 110–118.
[63] Strootman 2014a.
[64] Arrian, *FGrH* 156 F 1, 5.
[65] Plutarch, *Eumenes* 3.3.

opinions of each other all too often dictated their policies with disastrous and bloody consequences.[66]

Some time later Roxane gave birth to a boy, whom she named Alexander after her husband. Thus the dual monarchy of Philip III and Alexander IV became a reality, with Perdiccas their regent.[67] At no time was Roxane considered as regent, even though she was Alexander's widow and mother of a king. Royal wives and widows, like Olympias or Philip III's wife Eurydice, often played a political and military role in history, but not Roxane, who would be callously put to death with her son in 310 (Chapter 7). The reason that she was so marginalized presumably stems from her Bactrian ancestry and the intent of the Successors to legitimize their power by controlling the kingship.[68]

The events of the next two decades can be divided into two periods. The first, 323–320, was dominated by Perdiccas' personal ambition, which proved his downfall.[69] The second, 320–301, witnessed the ascendancy of Antigonus Monophthalmus, whose imperial dreams likewise brought about his demise. Antigonus, who had been treated peripherally by Perdiccas in the settlement at Babylon, may have been unhappy at being forced to assist Eumenes.[70] If so, he would soon show he was not someone to be trifled with, and of all the Successors, it was he and later Seleucus who came closest to ruling the entire Macedonian Empire.

Egypt and Ptolemy's Ambition

Ptolemy's choice of Egypt was not capricious. Like the man himself, it was pragmatic and shrewd. The Greeks already knew a great deal about Pharaonic Egypt from Homer, Herodotus (who devoted an entire book of his history of the Persian Wars to Egyptian affairs), Greek tragedy (Euripides' *Helen* of 412, for example, had much to do with Egypt), and even (later) the various contemporary accounts of Alexander's campaigns, for example by Hecataeus of Abdera.[71] Greeks had also enjoyed trading contacts with the country for some

---

[66] On the origins of the Successors' distrust of each other and the influence Alexander played in it, see Heckel 2002.

[67] The notion that Philip was sole ruler until the time of his death (317) and only then did Alexander become king, or even that Alexander was a subordinate king to Philip, is exploded by Habicht 2006a. It was a joint kingship on equal terms from the outset.

[68] Schäfer 2014.

[69] Rathmann 2005.

[70] Billows 1990, pp. 56–58.

[71] These authors had a very Greek perception of Egypt, described as an "Egyptian mirage": Lloyd 2010b; see too Morrison 2010, pp. 756–758.

centuries, ever since Pharaoh Amasis II of the 26th Dynasty established the city of Naucratis as a trading colony in the sixth century.[72] In fact, in a poem perhaps commissioned by King Amyntas of Macedonia in the fifth century, the lyric poet Bacchylides had spoken of Egypt's great wealth and its grain, a much-coveted crop by the Greeks.[73] Egypt and what it offered therefore were well known.

But there were other reasons for why Ptolemy was attracted to Egypt, which presumably he had noted during his time there with Alexander. For one thing, the country was small (23,000 square kilometers), and it was easily defensible, thanks to the harsh deserts of Libya to the west, Arabia to the east, and the marshes of the Nile delta—Isocrates' description of the Nile as Egypt's "immortal wall" was well taken (Map 4).[74] As we shall see, Ptolemy's choice of satrapy paid off for him on several crucial occasions.

Egypt also had good mineral resources and was fertile thanks to the Nile Valley. It had a population of about seven million (most of which lived in small towns and villages), a functioning administrative system with a mixture of Egyptian and Macedonian elements thanks to Alexander, a well-established trading and commercial network with Greece and the East, and it was wealthy. Ptolemy would also have been well aware of the stimulus that the new city of Alexandria would offer trade, even to the extent of eclipsing Naucratis. Further, Cleomenes had built up a considerable financial reserve of 8,000 talents.[75] On top of that were the 4,000 troops and thirty triremes that Alexander had left in Egypt to help maintain control.[76]

More important, though, Egypt was geographically removed from the areas that would be contentious between so many of the Successors: Asia and Greece/Macedonia. Choosing Egypt allowed Ptolemy to remain on the sidelines while building up finances, manpower, and security until the time was right to increase his personal power. He knew that Perdiccas would hardly embrace living out his days in Babylon, and probably suspected that Antigonus would not be content to remain in his satrapy or help Eumenes pacify Cappadocia. Ptolemy therefore was content to bide his time, and when the time came, he struck decisively.

One of the biggest, perhaps *the* biggest, questions concerning Ptolemy is whether he had ambitions to turn Egypt into an imperial power and vie for

[72] Caroli 2007, pp. 110–123.

[73] Discussed by Lianou 2014, pp. 379–380.

[74] Isocrates 11, *Busiris* 4.

[75] Pseudo-Aristotle, *Oeconomicus* 1352a–1353b. It is worth nothing that Strabo 1.8 claims that Ptolemy went after Egypt because of his greed.

[76] Arrian 3.5.3–5; Curtius 4.8.4.

the Macedonian throne. If not, was he a mere "onlooker," who occasionally profited from his rivals' conflicts, but was content to rule only Egypt?[77] Or, as is also sometimes believed, did he choose Egypt for "separatist" reasons—in other words, he intended to secede from the rest of the empire and set up his own autonomous state well away from everyone else?[78] The general opinion leans toward the defensive policy, most often with repercussions for Egyptian security, for which he is usually blamed.[79]

Nothing, though, is further from the truth: Ptolemy was as much an imperialist as his comrades. Even our ancient writers treat him no differently from the other Successors in their personal ambitions and greed for greater slices of Alexander's old empire.[80] In fact, Ptolemy moves so quickly and decisively, militarily and diplomatically, over the next few years that it is hard to imagine we are dealing with the same man who was only a name to us during so much of Alexander's Asian campaign.

We can start to chart Ptolemy's rise to power when he went from bodyguard to satrap of Egypt in a matter of days thanks to the Babylon settlement. Much has been written on this settlement, but one question that has not been asked, as far as I know, is why Ptolemy spoke at this decisive meeting. Scholars seem unconcerned that a member of the royal bodyguard, albeit an elite and important position, but wielding nothing like the power of a general or satrap, would stand up to Perdiccas, who was then the most powerful official in the Macedonian Empire. That Ptolemy's proposal was voted down does not alter the fact that he wanted his voice to be heard. He clearly had something in the back of his mind as early as this conference, and over the years he prudently and skillfully set out to build up his power.[81] He likely requested Egypt himself, and if so, his boldness paid off handsomely; other bodyguards received nothing or, like Lysimachus and Leonnatus, were sent to far-flung places in political and military turmoil.

Ptolemy did not elect to stay in the background; the reason that he put forward his startling proposal for a ruling council was that he was ready for a real command.[82] Despite being one of Alexander's boyhood friends, he had seen others promoted to influential posts, and had lived in the shadow of

---

[77] Shipley 2000, pp. 201–202.

[78] Bouché-Leclercq 1903, p. 9; Rosen 1979, p. 465; Hölbl 2001, p. 12.

[79] This is the critical stance of Seibert 1969 (for example pp. 84–90, for general comments on his foreign policy); note the reaction of Hauben 1977a.

[80] Meeus 2014, pp. 265–268, quoting and analyzing the sources, especially Diodorus 20.37.4, who says that they all courted Cleopatra, Alexander's sister, as a means of gaining the entire empire; see also Lane Fox 2014. On Ptolemy and Cleopatra, see pp. 152–153.

[81] Will 1984a, pp. 27 and 36.

[82] Meeus 2014, pp. 270–271.

Alexander's commanders throughout his campaign. The few times Alexander had tapped him for military operations he had performed his duties well, but they were relatively minor operations, and that was not enough. Alexander's death and the future of the Macedonian empire afforded Ptolemy the opportunity to leave the shadows.

Ptolemy, then, was anxious for power from the outset, and that did not change throughout his time as ruler of Egypt.[83] And like all the Successors, he had an active foreign policy well beyond his borders that began as soon as he got to Egypt, as we shall see. There is no question that (over the years) control of Cyrenaica to his west, of Coele-Syria ("hollow Syria," from the depression of the Jordan Valley), Palestine, and Syria to his northeast, of Cyprus, of the Eastern Mediterranean, and the islands of the Aegean, as well as a close alliance with Rhodes, were all essential for his security, but they were also part of a shrewd economic and military policy. They provided him with many of the natural resources he could not get in Egypt, such as timber for his fleet, and contributed to his manpower reserves and revenues.[84] Eventually, though, in 308 Ptolemy would set his sights on Greece and Macedonia, intending to be Alexander's successor, a bid that collapsed on him.

Ptolemy actively engaged with the other Successors as and when needed, and he involved himself in overseas ventures for security and self-aggrandizement. He cleverly chose a country away from the major hotspots, which offered him a high degree of safety from invasion, until he was ready to extend his part of the empire. Even transferring the capital of Egypt from Memphis to Alexandria, given that city's location on the Mediterranean and its connection to Alexander, and his reliance on his fleet, showed that he was casting his eyes beyond his own satrapy.[85]

His time in Egypt, as we shall see, charts the progression of his ambition, from a desire to enjoy ruling power to the need to be viewed as an equal and then a better by the other Successors. His extension of Egypt's possessions and thus his own standing in the Hellenistic world; his proclamation of kingship; his bid on what all the Successors saw as the ultimate prize, Macedonia and Greece; and his crafting of a dynasty to ensure that the Ptolemies remained in control of Egypt for almost three centuries, stand as a testament to his aspirations and success.[86]

---

[83] Though Seibert 1969, p. 88, and Huss 2001, pp. 185 and 192, for example, believe that Ptolemy's ambition changed over the years, and he became less imperialistic, but not so.

[84] Rostovtzeff 1941, vol. 1, pp. 332–351, and 1954, pp. 126–130; Bagnall, 1976, pp. 224–229; Lianou 2014; cf. Caroli 2007, pp. 70–71 and 99–104.

[85] Pollard 2010, pp. 449–450; Strootman 2014a, pp. 314–315; see too Hauben 2014, Meeus 2014.

[86] Cf. the comment of Turner 1984, p. 122: "the first fifty years of Ptolemaic rule in Egypt can be characterized only through the actions of [Ptolemy]." Ptolemy I's rule: Bouché-Leclercq 1903,

The Gathering War Clouds

On the Greek mainland, Alexander's death was at first disbelieved—if it were true, the whole world would smell his corpse, quipped the Athenian orator Demades.[87] But once the news was confirmed, the Athenians led a revolt against Macedonian rule, which threatened the western half of the empire. The Greeks called this revolt the Hellenic War but, following Diodorus, it is more commonly called the Lamian War after the town of Lamia in Thessaly, where Antipater was almost captured or killed.[88] When the revolt broke out, Antipater moved quickly to suppress it, but a Greek army under the Athenian general Leosthenes defeated him at Thermopylae and blockaded him in Lamia for the winter of 323–322. Antipater's reversal was in no small part due to his lack of Macedonian soldiers, the result of Alexander's many demands for troops from 334 to 331, which had depleted his manpower reserves.[89]

Fortunately, in the spring of 322 Antipater received help from Leonnatus, who joined him from Phrygia with 20,000 infantry and 1,500 cavalry, including battle-hardened veterans from Alexander's army.[90] Leonnatus was able to rescue Antipater from Lamia but was killed in the fighting; nevertheless, Antipater made his way safely back to Macedonia. Then, in June 322, the Macedonian admiral Cleitus rendezvoused with Antipater's fleet and defeated the Greek fleet twice, the first time off Abydus (in the Hellespont) and the second off the island of Amorgus in the Aegean. Cleitus' victories finally allowed Craterus, who had been shut up in Cilicia because of the Greeks' control of the seas, to take the 10,000 troops he had led from Opis to Antipater.[91] Their arrival was a game-changer.

In August (322), Antipater's army of 48,000 troops met and defeated a Greek force of 28,000 in battle at Crannon in central Thessaly.[92] The Lamian War ended, and Macedonian control of Greece was reimposed. But it was a

pp. 1–140; Bevan 1927, pp. 18–55; Elgood 1938, pp. 1–40; Seibert 1969; Turner 1984, pp. 119–133; Ellis 1994; Hölbl 2001, pp. 12–34; Caroli 2007; Lloyd 2010a; Lane Fox 2014.

[87] Plutarch, *Phocion* 22.3.

[88] Lamian War: Diodorus 18.9–13, 15–18.6; Arrian, *FGrH* 156 F 1, 9, with Hammond and Walbank 1988, pp. 107–117; Schmitt 1992; Habicht 1997, pp. 36–42; Bennett and Roberts 2009, pp. 27–40; Worthington 2013, pp. 330–333; Anson 2014a, pp. 33–41.

[89] Bosworth 1986 and especially 2002, pp. 64–97; *contra* Hammond 1989b, pp. 56–68, Billows 1995, pp. 183–206, Badian 1994, pp. 261–268.

[90] Diodorus 18.15.1–4, with Roisman 2012, pp. 111–112.

[91] Diodorus 18.16.4–5. Waterfield 2011, p. 39, suggests that all three men came together because of dissatisfaction over their treatment by Perdiccas in the Babylon settlement, but this seems unlikely—it had not diluted Antipater's power in Greece, for example.

[92] Diodorus 18.17.1–8.

different kind of rule; the League of Corinth, which Philip had established and Alexander continued, and which had supposedly allowed the Greeks the freedom to make their own decisions, was abolished, and in its place Antipater installed garrisons in key towns, to rule with an iron fist. Athens, the ringleader, was dealt with the harshest: a garrison was set up in the Piraeus, Athenian democracy was abolished, and a wealth qualification for citizenship was imposed, gutting the number of citizens.[93] Anti-Macedonian politicians were condemned—the most vocal, since Philip's day, was the famous orator Demosthenes, who fled the city and committed suicide on Calauria (modern Poros).[94]

Craterus now married one of Antipater's daughters, Phila, which bound the two men closer together. However, Antipater was clearly the more powerful partner, not least because he "helped [Craterus] to prepare for his return to Asia," also as a means of getting him out of the way.[95] But both of them soon faced trouble from Perdiccas, who by now had set his eyes on Antigonus' satrapy. The latter was actually forced to flee to Macedonia that winter, where he persuaded Antipater and Craterus to form a coalition against Perdiccas.[96] Their action was an informal declaration of war, and Perdiccas responded by framing plans to march against them and win control of Macedonia and Greece for himself. To thwart his plan, Antipater, Craterus, and Antigonus decided to invade Asia Minor and bring Perdiccas to battle. The invasion never took place because Ptolemy, as we shall see, decided to enter the fray, forcing Perdiccas to invade Egypt instead.

[93] Diodorus 18.18.3–6; Plutarch, *Demosthenes* 28–30, *Phocion* 29 and 33; Pseudo-Plutarch, *Moralia* 846e–847b, 847d, 849a–d, with Worthington 2013, pp. 334–335.

[94] Demosthenes' last days: Worthington 2013, pp. 326–337.

[95] Diodorus 18.18.7.

[96] Diodorus 18.23.3–4, 25.3–6; Justin 13.6.8–13.

6

Securing Egypt

When Ptolemy left Babylon for Egypt is unknown.[1] There was little love lost between him and Perdiccas, so Ptolemy probably stayed in Babylon at least while Roxane was pregnant to ensure that Perdiccas did nothing to jeopardize the recent settlement. We are told that Eumenes did not leave immediately for Cappadocia, but continued dealing with the army; given how suspicious the Successors were of each other, Ptolemy might well have wanted to make sure no one would overstep his bounds.[2] Besides, thanks to Cleomenes, Egypt was not rife with any of the turmoil affecting other parts of the empire, so Ptolemy had no need to worry about instability in the country or of the need to be there as soon as possible. One ancient writer claims that Ptolemy ruled Egypt for 40 years, seventeen as satrap and twenty-three as king, which means that he did not go to Egypt until 322.[3] There are grounds for believing this if we consider when Ptolemy had Cleomenes put to death (see below).

What troops did Ptolemy take with him to Egypt? He had been a royal bodyguard, so he did not command any large contingents like the other officers, and in the chaotic days of the Babylon settlement he would hardly have attracted die-hard soldiers to him. He must therefore have hired some mercenaries. Since he knew that Cleomenes had collected 8,000 talents for Egypt's treasury, Ptolemy may have promised his mercenaries additional remuneration on the understanding that he could pay them only when he was actually in Egypt and had access to the treasury.[4] It is no surprise

---

[1] Bevan 1927, p. 18, claims that Ptolemy arrived in Egypt five months after Alexander died, but cites no sources for this, nor is there evidence that "the new satraps at once took off for their fiefs": Green 1990, p. 9; cf. Bouché-Leclercq 1903, pp. 10–11 (arriving November 323).

[2] Plutarch, *Eumenes* 3.1.

[3] Porphyry, *BNJ* 260 F 2. On the year Ptolemy became king, see pp. 160–162.

[4] Diodorus 18.14.1. No moves were made against him, even though Alexander's so-called Dissolution Decree of 324, which forbade satraps to have their own armies, was still in effect: Diodorus 17.106.3, with Worthington 2014, p. 264.

that Ptolemy made manpower his foremost priority when he came to control Egypt—by the time he fought the battle of Gaza in 312, he had actual Macedonian troops, probably because by then he had proved himself an equal to the former generals.[5]

Ptolemy and Cleomenes

Ptolemy had to be careful about Cleomenes, who had with him 4,000 Macedonians troops based in Egypt and may also have been Perdiccas' mole, reporting all of Ptolemy's movements.[6] Cleomenes would hardly have welcomed the Babylon settlement, which demoted him from satrap to assistant, and meant he would have to contend with a superior who was actually living in Egypt. It was obvious from the moment that he arrived that Ptolemy had little time for Cleomenes—in fact, at some point after he arrived in Memphis he executed Cleomenes.[7]

Exactly when Cleomenes was put to death is not known. One ancient writer claims that it was before Ptolemy seized Alexander's corpse, when it was en route to Macedonia in the late summer or fall of 321 (see below). If true, it is hard to accept that Ptolemy put up with Cleomenes in person for almost two years if he went to Egypt soon after the Babylon settlement, especially if he suspected that Cleomenes was spying on him. More likely is that Ptolemy went to Egypt in 322, well after the settlement, and tolerated Cleomenes because of his experience with Egyptian administration. When relations between Ptolemy and Perdiccas were deteriorating, Ptolemy, already suspicious of his subordinate's loyalty, had him executed.

Presumably the rapid downfall of Cleomenes made Ptolemy popular with the Egyptians since the former satrap was extortionate. Ptolemy would have been well aware that he was an unknown entity to the Egyptians, his power not set in stone, and he must have expected tension between himself and the native peoples, as well as with the other Successors. He had seen how the Egyptians had turned their backs on the Persian satrap Mazaces when Alexander arrived in Egypt in 332 because of their hatred of Persian rule, and he had no desire to be another Mazaces should one of his opponents try to snatch Egypt from him. Since we are told that he "took over Egypt without difficulty and was treating

---

[5] Numbers: Diodorus 18.14.1, 21.7, 28.5, 33.3–4; Gaza: Diodorus 19.80.4; see Bosworth 2002, p. 82, that Ptolemy had no veterans.

[6] Cf. Pausanias 1.6.3, with Seibert 1969, pp. 39–51; Ellis 1994, p. 27.

[7] Pausanias 1.6.3, with Seibert 1969, p. 112.

the inhabitants with kindness,"[8] we can see his careful attitude from the outset to win over his subjects while he worked to build up a support base.[9]

Removing Cleomenes to garner support also explains Ptolemy's diplomatic moves to placate the priests, a powerful element in Egyptian society, especially as it was said that Cleomenes had taken some of their temple treasuries from them.[10] He gave his assurance that he, like Alexander, would do nothing against the native religions, and even observed the mourning period for one of the sacred Apis bulls that had died as he arrived in Egypt, generously giving the large sum of 50 talents to help defray the burial costs. In return, the priests tolerated Ptolemy's rule, and approved his elevation to Pharaoh two decades later. We will discuss Ptolemy's relations with his subjects, including his administrative and religious policy, in Chapter 11.

There was nothing that Perdiccas could do to save Cleomenes, as Ptolemy doubtless suspected. If Diodorus is right that Ptolemy "well knew that Perdiccas would attempt to wrest from him the satrapy of Egypt," then his removal of Cleomenes can only be seen as ruthlessly pragmatic, one of Ptolemy's traits as ruler.[11] Most likely, he now gave the Macedonian troops in Egypt the one-twelfth of their annual pay that Cleomenes had kept for himself, presumably promising them that they would not be underpaid again to ensure their loyalty to him. Ptolemy had thus moved quickly and decisively to make it plain to all and sundry that he had no need of assistants and was his own man— "Egypt was Ptolemy's estate."[12] In all the measures he took, even when he first arrived there, we see Ptolemy laying the foundations for Egypt's security and its expansion in the world.[13]

Ptolemy's First Campaign

Ptolemy first lived in Egypt's traditional capital Memphis to give the impression of a continuity of rule to the people, but he intended to govern Egypt eventually from Alexandria, which Alexander had founded in 331. Construction of the city had been ongoing since that year, but it was Ptolemy who was instrumental in its completion and added greatly to it beyond what

---

[8] Diodorus 18.14.1.
[9] Cf. Justin 13.6.18–19 on winning over the Egyptians.
[10] Pseudo-Aristotle, *Oeconomicus* 1352a–b.
[11] Quote: Diodorus 18.14.2.
[12] Tarn and Griffith 1952, p. 207.
[13] Meeus 2014, pp. 271–272.

Alexander had likely envisaged (see Chapter 8). Alexandria was also going to be the base for his fleet, but its site presented a problem to his security. Natural frontiers protected his western, eastern, and southern borders, but Alexandria was on the coast to his north, so it was vulnerable to attack from the Mediterranean.

To help protect Alexandria and the northern coastline, Ptolemy made strategic alliances with several of the nine kings of neighboring Cyprus, who had been allies of Alexander. To one of them, Eunostus of Soli, he married Eirene, his daughter by Thais, the same woman who was believed to have encouraged Alexander to burn down the palace at Persepolis.[14] Cyprus' location and its natural resources (metals, timber, and grain), which were critical for Egypt and its economy, explain Ptolemy's move; in fact, all the Ptolemies followed his lead, which is why the island was the longest held of all that dynasty's possessions.[15]

Ptolemy's diplomatic intervention in Cyprus was soon followed by a military campaign to his west in independent Cyrenaica (northeast Libya). Some time ago, in the Greek colony of Cyrene (near Shahhat in eastern Libya), founded in 630 by settlers from Thera (Santorini), a civil war had broken out between oligarchs and democrats.[16] In 324, during this strife, some exiled democrats from Cyrene gained help from a Spartan mercenary commander named Thibron, who had just killed Alexander's disgraced imperial treasurer Harpalus on Crete.[17] Thibron absorbed Harpalus' 7,000 mercenaries into his own army and took them to Cyrene. Instead of supporting the exiled democrats' cause, Thibron wrested power for himself, and besieged the city. He forced terms on the Cyrenaeans, including further military forces for his army and a payment of 500 silver talents, and allowed his men to plunder the surrounding areas. With no relief in sight, the desperate oligarchs appealed to Ptolemy for help. Recognizing the opportunity that had suddenly come his way, Ptolemy lost no time. In probably late summer 322, he ordered his general Ophellas (from Olynthus) to take a fleet and land army to Cyrene.[18] Ophellas defeated Thibron and his

[14] Marriage: Athenaeus 13.576e; on the alliance, see Rosen 1968, pp. 197–198; Seibert 1969, pp. 113–114; Caroli 2007, pp. 83–85.

[15] Bagnall 1976, pp. 38–79; see too Mitford 1953.

[16] *Parian Marble*, *BNJ* 239 B 10–11; Diodorus 18.14.1, 19–21; Arrian, *FGrH* 156 F 9, 16–18, with Seibert 1983, pp. 101–104, and 1969, pp. 91–95; Huss 2001, pp. 98–103; Caroli 2007, pp. 71–73. On Cyrenaica during Ptolemy's reign, see Bartson 1982.

[17] Worthington 2014, pp. 290–291.

[18] Diodorus 18.21.7–9, with Seibert 1969, pp. 91–95. *Parian Marble*, *BNJ* 239 B 10, places the capture in 322/321.

men, later hanging Thibron in Cyrene. Afterward, Ophellas handed over the whole of Cyrenaica to Ptolemy.[19]

Ptolemy imposed a moderate oligarchy on the Cyrenaeans, supported by garrisons in their cities, with himself as their general and the sole authority in selecting their officials.[20] He also started to strike his own coinage in Cyrene, further evidence that he controlled the region.[21] To be on the safe side, though, he kept Ophellas and a large contingent of troops there.[22] Just like today, foreign campaigns are costly, and the maintenance of troops in Cyrenaica, as well as his other incursions well beyond his borders, explains his bureaucratic innovations to generate revenue (see Chapter 11). Cyrene now remained in Ptolemaic hands until 96 (when Ptolemy Apion left it in his will to the Romans, who promptly freed the cities), even though it was often a problem area for them.[23]

Ptolemy's action in Cyrenaica can only have added to Perdiccas' suspicion of him, and Perdiccas may even have been aggrieved that he had not been consulted about the campaign in the first place. But Ptolemy knew, as with his execution of Cleomenes, that there was nothing Perdiccas could do; if the latter protested, then Ptolemy could simply say he was protecting Egypt's borders, which, after all, was one of his tasks as satrap.

Stealing Alexander

We can understand Ptolemy's need to shore up his western defenses, hence his eagerness to control Cyrenaica, to prevent anyone threatening him. But his preoccupation with Cyrene may also have had something to do with Alexander. Cyrene was the stopping-off point on the African coastline for overseas visitors to the Oracle of Zeus Ammon at Siwah. It lay on the road to Paraetonium, about 350 miles to the east, from where began the route southward through the desert to Siwah.[24] Indeed, Cyrene's position in relation to Siwah explains the growth of the town in the first place. The cult of Zeus Ammon was well known to the Greeks, and Alexander (accompanied by Ptolemy) had made a special visit to the oracle when he was in Egypt.

---

[19] Arrian, *FGrH* 156 F 9, 19; Diodorus 18.21.9; Justin 13.6.20.
[20] *SEG* 9.1.1–46.
[21] Bagnall 1976, pp. 183–185.
[22] Diodorus 20.40.1; Hölbl 2001, p. 15.
[23] Will 1960, pp. 269–290; Bagnall 1976, pp. 25–37; Bartson 1982.
[24] Bevan 1927, p. 9.

There is a tradition that Alexander wanted to be buried in Siwah.[25] By taking over Cyrene, Ptolemy would control not only the caravan route to the most important oracle in this part of the world but also the only way to Alexander's tomb. Perdiccas, however, was intent on burying Alexander at Aegae, which was his way of laying claim to the throne of Macedonia, as the next king was responsible for burying his predecessor. Perdiccas' recent marriage to Antipater's daughter Nicaea and his attempt to win the hand of Cleopatra, one of Philip II's daughters and Alexander the Great's only living sister, also show his ambition.[26] Given that relations were crumbling rapidly between Ptolemy and Perdiccas, and that Ptolemy stood to lose the opportunity to bury Alexander in Egypt, Ptolemy decided to abandon any semblance of collegiality with Perdiccas. He went to Damascus (in Syria), and there, as the funeral cortege rumbled its way from Babylon to Macedonia, he stole Alexander's corpse from its elaborately carved hearse.[27] Probably this was in the late summer or early fall of 321.[28] Arrhidaeus (not the king), who commanded the cortege's guard, put up no fight, which might suggest he had made some previous arrangement with Ptolemy.[29] Although Perdiccas sent a force under Pithon and Attalus to the rescue, it arrived too late.[30] Ptolemy returned to Egypt with the body, but rather than bury it in Siwah, he took it with him to Memphis; later he would move it to Alexandria.[31]

Ptolemy's kidnapping of Alexander's body is one of the most audacious events of this period. It is going too far to say that he seized the corpse in a "brazen bid" to wrest power from Perdiccas.[32] But given the ramifications that Ptolemy would have known his action would have, the hijacking is very much an overt declaration of his ambition. His message was clear: he was no longer

[25] Diodorus 18.3.5, 28.3; Curtius 10.5.4; Justin 12.15.7, 13.4.6, with Seibert 1969, pp. 110–113; Erskine 2002, p. 171; Meeus 2008, pp. 66–68.

[26] Diodorus 18.23.1, 3; Justin 13.6.4–6.

[27] Diodorus 18.28.2–3; Arrian, FGrH 156 F 9, 25; Pausanias 1.6.3, with Bouché-Leclercq 1903, pp. 19–20; Erskine 2002, pp. 167–171. On the hearse (with a drawing of it), see p. 130.

[28] Diodorus 18.28.2; Strabo 17.1.8; perhaps even winter as the cortege had set off from Babylon after the searing heart of the summer was dying down: Anson 1986, pp. 212–217.

[29] Pact: Bevan 1927, p. 19. Justin 13.4.6 says that Philip III Arrhidaeus intended to accompany it, but this is not so.

[30] Arrian, FGrH 156 F 9, 25 (cf. F 10, 1), says that Arrhidaeus successfully took the body from Perdiccas so he could give it to Ptolemy.

[31] Memphis: Parian Marble, BNJ 239 B 11; Diodorus 18.28.3; Curtius 10.10.20; Pausanias 1.6.3; Strabo 17.1.8. Alexandria: Chapter 8. Bosworth 2000, p. 219, accepts that Alexander was to have been buried at Siwah, as outlined in Alexander's alleged will, and that Ptolemy acted on the king's wishes by kidnapping the corpse to foil Perdiccas' plan of burying it in Greece. Even though Ptolemy buried Alexander in Alexandria, that was still in Egypt, and so according to Alexander's wish. The will was a fiction, invented by Ptolemy as a propaganda tool against his rivals, as Bosworth 2000 properly argues; see further, pp. 153–154.

[32] Romm 2011, p. 152.

a bodyguard, but an equal. Perdiccas had Alexander's signet ring, but Ptolemy now had Alexander's body, which helped to legitimize his control of Egypt by binding himself closer to the Argeads.[33] We will revisit Ptolemy's seizure of Alexander and how it benefited himself and his new capital in Chapter 8.

Ptolemy's diplomatic relations with Perdiccas, already on rocky ground after the execution of Cleomenes, were now irrevocably broken. Perdiccas, as Ptolemy would have suspected, saw Ptolemy's action as an attack on himself as regent, as well as a major blow to his attempt to claim the Macedonian throne. At first he tried to have Ptolemy condemned by his army for treason, but he was acquitted. Probably the vote went Ptolemy's way because he was more popular than Perdiccas and the army Assembly was doing all it could to avert a civil war.[34] Therefore, Perdiccas prepared to invade Egypt to "take down Ptolemy, install a satrap of his own in Egypt in place of Ptolemy, and get the body back."[35] This conflict between the two of them may have been brewing for some time, with Perdiccas merely using Alexander's body to justify his attack and so mask his personal agenda in order to keep the support of his men.[36]

Putting aside his plan to attack the coalition of Antipater, Craterus, and Antigonus Monophthalmus as part of his bid to take over Macedonia (p. 88), Perdiccas marched to Egypt; thus began the First War of the Successors.[37] All in all, there would be four of these wars between now and 301, which resulted in the deaths of thousands of troops and civilians in the affected areas. In actuality, there was really only the one unbroken war, as has been noted, divided into these phases that grew out of the conclusions of the previous events.[38]

Perdiccas Invades Egypt

Perdiccas marched toward Egypt with a large army including war elephants, animals that the Macedonians had first encountered in India, and which became a staple of Hellenistic armies. He also had Philip III, Alexander IV, and Roxane in tow since technically, as regent, he was invading Egypt in the kings' names.

In the meantime, there was a surprising turn of events in Cappadocia. Antipater and Craterus had earlier invaded Asia Minor, intent on preventing

[33] Lianou 2010, pp. 127–128; Meeus 2008, pp. 67–68, and 2014, pp. 273–277.

[34] Hammond and Walbank 1988, pp. 121–122 with n. 5 (p. 121).

[35] Arrian, *FGrH* 156 F 10, 1; Diodorus 18.29.1; Pausanias 1.6.3, with Bouché-Leclercq 1903, pp. 22–25; Seibert 1969, pp. 117–121; Caroli 2007, pp. 47–46.

[36] Roisman 2012, pp. 93–95.

[37] Diodorus 18.25.6, 33–37. See further, Hauben 1977b; cf. Waterfield 2011, pp. 57–60; sources and discussion on the war between Ptolemy and Perdiccas: Seibert 1969, pp. 96–108.

[38] Waterfield 2011, p. 57.

Perdiccas from attacking them in Macedonia. Antipater took up a position in Cilicia, while Craterus' mission was to defeat Perdiccas' ally Eumenes, who had been doing a sterling job in his territories, especially as the expected help from Antigonus and Leonnatus had never arrived (the former had not wanted anything to do with Cappadocia, and the latter had died in Greece in 323 during the Lamian War). Afterward, Antipater and Craterus were to rendezvous and march south against Perdiccas, neatly trapping him between themselves and Ptolemy. However, Eumenes defeated and killed Craterus in battle.[39] News of this shocking result does not seem to have reached Perdiccas or Ptolemy before the former closed in on Egypt in May or June of 320.[40]

Perdiccas' invasion of Egypt was a disaster.[41] At Pelusium his soldiers began to desert him, perhaps because Ptolemy had spies or at least sympathizers among the enemy troops since he routinely resorted to bribery or offered higher pay to mercenaries to weaken an opponent's forces.[42] But "what harmed Perdiccas more than the strength of his enemy was the loathing he incurred by his arrogance; this won the hatred even of his allies."[43] Even though he was a battle-hardened soldier from his experiences with Alexander, he could never instill in his men the same sort of devotion they had shown their king.

From Pelusium, Perdiccas marched by night about 130 miles to the Fort of Camels, not far from Memphis, and a good crossing point on the Nile.[44] There he made ready to cross the river and attack the capital. Unfortunately for him, the Fort of Camels was garrisoned. Ptolemy, who may have heard from the deserters of Perdiccas' plan to take the fort, moved quickly to increase the garrison's manpower, bringing the reinforcements himself. When Perdiccas attacked the fort at dawn, Ptolemy was clearly visible on the ramparts—"with utter contempt of the danger, striking and disabling those who were coming up the ladders, he sent them rolling down, in their armor, into the river," and he even speared one of their elephants. Ptolemy's Homeric fighting style, reminiscent of the way he had fought in India (pp. 54–55), bravery, and his emulation of Alexander's leadership skills in always leading from the front, paid off:

[39] For example, Diodorus 18.30.5–60; Arrian, *FGrH* 156 F 9, 26–27; Plutarch, *Eumenes* 7; Nepos, *Eumenes* 4.1–4. Discussion: Bennett and Roberts 2009, pp. 41–54; Roisman 2012, pp. 127–134; Anson 2014a, pp. 63–68.

[40] Diodorus 18.37.1 and Plutarch, *Eumenes* 8.2, state that word reached the Perdiccan camp two days after Perdiccas invaded Egypt; *contra* Diodorus 18.33.1 (before Perdiccas invaded).

[41] Diodorus 18.33–37; Arrian, *FGrH* 156 F 9, 28; Pausanias 1.6.3; Justin 13.8.1–2, 10, with Seibert 1969, pp. 114–128; Romm 2011, pp. 163–167; Roisman 2012, pp. 93–107, and 2014; Anson 2014a, pp. 68–70.

[42] Diodorus 18.33.1–3, with Errington 1970, p. 65; Ellis 1994, p. 37.

[43] Justin 13.8.2.

[44] Diodorus 18.33.6–34.5. The following quote at Diodorus 18.34.2.

his men rallied around him, and forced back Perdiccas' troops, who may well have been battling fatigue after their night march. Perdiccas had no choice but to abandon the siege.

Perdiccas then decided on a surprise forced march to capture Memphis while Ptolemy was still at the fort. His idea was a good one, and his quick strategic thinking to capitalize on an enemy's circumstances illustrates why Alexander had chosen him as his second-in-command. Again, he pushed his men hard after their forced march the night before and setback at the fort, and again fate was against him, this time in the guise of the Nile. He decided to cross in stages to an island in the river's eastern branch opposite Memphis. The first batch of troops made the crossing successfully, despite facing strong currents and water that was chest high. In an effort to help the rest of his men, Perdiccas deployed some elephants upstream from the island on the left and cavalry downstream on the right to make smoother conditions—and catch any of his men that were swept away, as Macedonian soldiers were generally not good swimmers.[45] Unfortunately, the animals moved so much to keep their balance that they added to the swell of the water, and many men in the next contingent drowned as they were in full armor.

Given the setback at the Nile, and perhaps also worried that Ptolemy and his men might suddenly catch up to his troops in their disarray, Perdiccas decided to move his location and called the men on the island back to him. They had noticed that their comrades' heavy armor had contributed to their drowning, so they shed their own armor before they began to swim back. Still, many of them drowned or were swept away and were eaten by "the animals in the river"—crocodiles and perhaps even hippopotami.[46] Over 2,000 of Perdiccas' men had died in the course of one to two days, and enough was enough: that night, after much mourning and criticism, two of his commanders, Pithon and Seleucus, stabbed Perdiccas to death in his tent.[47]

Ptolemy was quick to capitalize on Perdiccas' demise to win over his soldiers. He had already cremated the enemy dead and sent their ashes back to their families, a solemn task that fell to a commander.[48] His action was not necessarily meant to win over Perdiccas' men, for by nature Ptolemy seemed to

[45] Roisman 2012, p. 101 n. 41, with references.

[46] Diodorus 18.35.5; Polyaenus 4.19.

[47] Diodorus 18.36.5; Pausanias 1.6.3; cf. Justin 13.8.10, with, Seibert 1969, pp. 122–126. Tent: Diodorus 18.36.5. Arrian, *FGrH* 156 F 9, 28, says that he was killed in battle by his companion cavalry, which is untrue. Strabo 17.1.8 claims that soldiers impaled him with their sarissas, but this cannot be right because a tent could not accommodate the length of these weapons (at least 14 feet). Nepos, *Eumenes* 5.1, has Seleucus and Antigenes killing Perdiccas by the Nile, which is also suspect.

[48] Diodorus 18.36.1.

have been a kind and caring person, traits that appealed to people. Then the day
after he rode into the Perdiccan camp, taking presents for the kings to show his
loyalty, and to counter any criticisms that he was a traitor because Perdiccas had
invaded Egypt in their name.[49] It was a clever move, and it worked: Philip III
accepted Ptolemy's allegiance to both kings. As a further sign of his loyalty,
Ptolemy seems to have been behind the building of a sanctuary to Philip in the
temple of Karnak, which bears the king's name in hieroglyphics (one of a very
few instances of his name in Egypt); it is an interesting example of the priests'
willingness to recognize Philip as their king.[50]

With the two kings on his side, Ptolemy addressed Perdiccas' troops. He
promised them food and a place in his own army if they surrendered to him,
or a safe passage out of Egypt. This was obviously a pragmatic move, as his
own army was not large, and he would have been on the lookout to increase
his numbers wherever and whenever he could. We also wonder whether his
experiences with Alexander had taught him the need to win over any enemy.
He had been present when Alexander had treacherously killed Indian mercenaries at Massaga after promising to spare them, which had stiffened local
resistance to him (p. 56). Ptolemy was always careful to appeal to enemy
troops.

Perdiccas' men apparently pleaded with Ptolemy to take on their former
commander's position, including regency of the two kings.[51] But Ptolemy
said no, and instead put forward Pithon and Arrhidaeus (the man in charge
of Alexander's funeral cortege) as regents.[52] Ptolemy's refusal of the powerful regency has been taken as another sign that he wanted nothing to
do with the empire and planned to separate Egypt from it, but that is too
much of a stretch.[53] Indeed, whether Ptolemy was even offered the regency
is debatable, and the whole episode may have been invention on the part
of the biased Diodorus to show Ptolemy's "selflessness, moderation, and
friendship."[54]

But perhaps we are not dealing with invention after all. One matter
that we would most expect to be discussed when Ptolemy met with the

[49] Diodorus 18.36.6–7; Arrian, *FGrH* 156 F 9, 29. Errington 1978, p. 118: Ptolemy may not
have gone in person but sent an embassy, especially as he was worried about his western border
with Cyrene (on which see below).

[50] Schäfer 2014, pp. 442–447.

[51] Diodorus 18.36.6–7, with Seibert 1969, pp. 126–128; Errington 1970, p. 60; Bosworth
2002, 14–15; Anson, 2014a, p. 70.

[52] Arrian, *FGrH* 156 F 9, 30, with Errington 1970, p. 66, and 1978, p. 121, for the view that this
election was Ptolemy's idea.

[53] Will 1966, p. 37; Errington 1970, p. 71; Ellis 1994, p. 39; *contra* Meeus 2014, pp. 277–278.

[54] Roisman 2012, pp. 106–107.

kings would be Alexander's corpse, but there is no mention of this ex-change in our sources. Did Philip III really not care if Ptolemy returned his half-brother for burial in Aegae, especially as it was the duty of the next king to bury his predecessor? The silence is significant and indicative of Ptolemy's Machiavellian work behind the scenes. To begin with, Pithon and Arrhidaeus were odd choices as regents. If Ptolemy had been in con-tact with Arrhidaeus from the time he hijacked Alexander's hearse, and, as is likely, had spies in Perdiccas' camp, he may well have made some tacit agreement with Arrhidaeus when Perdiccas first entered Egypt. Perdiccas was a very capable soldier, and Ptolemy could not predict how successful his invasion would be. It is even possible that he was behind Perdiccas' murder, since one of the assassins was Pithon, a former bodyguard and someone Ptolemy would have known well.[55]

What we may have is a scenario that only someone with Ptolemy's cunning could bring about. He condoned Perdiccas' assassination, with the expecta-tion that he would be offered the regency, which he would refuse in favor of Pithon and Arrhidaeus. What did he stand to gain? The answer is, simply, to be left alone in Egypt—and to keep Alexander's body for the influence it gave him. He knew that another general settlement was needed, given the recent events and deaths, and in any case he had urgent matters to attend to in Cyrene (see below). If Philip III had demanded the return of Alexander's body, he was disregarded.

The final decision made in the camp at this time was to outlaw Eumenes and at least fifty other Perdiccan supporters, condemning them all to death *in absentia*.[56] This resolution had to have been influenced by the news of Eumenes' killing of Craterus, and it marked the start of a formal purge of Perdiccan loyalists. The two kings and Roxane then left for Macedonia, leav-ing Alexander's body with Ptolemy. Since the Babylon settlement was clearly in shreds, in the early fall of 320 the remaining Successors, with the excep-tion of Ptolemy, met at Triparadeisus in upper Syria (a lavish game park, to judge by the "triple game reserve" name, possibly Baalbek) to thrash out a new agreement.[57]

---

[55] Errington 1970, pp. 65–66 (cf. Anson 2014a, p. 69); arguments against Ptolemy involved in the assassination: Roisman 2012, pp. 103–104.

[56] Diodorus 18.37.1, 59.4; Arrian, *FGrH* 156 F 9, 30; Justin 13.8.10, 14.1.1; cf. Plutarch, *Eumenes* 8.1–3, Errington 1970, p. 67.

[57] Diodorus 18.39; Arrian, *FGrH* 156 F 9, 34–38 (= Austin, no. 24, pp. 45–46); Polyaenus 4.6.4. Narrative: Bouché-Leclercq 1903, pp. 25–28; Caroli 2007, pp. 46–47; Romm 2011, pp. 173–177; Waterfield 2011, pp. 66–68. Discussion: Errington 1970; Billows 1990, pp. 64–71; Green 1990, pp. 12–17; Anson 2003; Roisman 2012, pp. 136–144; Landucci Gattinoni 2014.

The Triparadeisus Settlement

The chronology of the following decade is much disputed, and two different chronological schemes have been advanced for it, "low" and "high"; I follow the so-called low chronology, which dates events one year later than high chronology, hence the Triparadeisus settlement in 320 (low), not 321 (high).[58]

Antipater, now well into his eighties, arrived at Triparadeisus from Cilicia, expecting to chair the proceedings because of his seniority. But things did not go smoothly thanks to the fiery Eurydice, wife of Philip III. Angry that she was being overlooked as the guardian of the two kings, even though she was queen, she whipped the army into a fury, perhaps over pay that had been due to them for some time.[59] In response, Pithon and Arrhidaeus surrendered the regency to Antipater, who with some difficulty was able to restore order to the proceedings and negotiate a settlement.[60] Possibly he was successful not so much from any diplomatic prowess on his part but because he promised the men their money.

Antipater was named guardian (*epimeletes*) of Macedonia and Greece and of the two kings. Ptolemy was reconfirmed as satrap of Egypt and ruler of Libya—as Diodorus states, "it was impossible to displace him, since he seemed to be holding Egypt by virtue of his own prowess as if it were a prize of war."[61] Ptolemy was also allowed to campaign in "the lands beyond," referring to the west of Libya.[62] Thus he could do what he wanted in the west, but not the east, where there was resistance to his expansion in places like Palestine and Phoenicia. His gains come as no surprise, as after the defeat of Perdiccas his position could hardly be challenged, except by a major invasion, which no one at that time felt like trying. Even more a sign of Ptolemy's power is Diodorus' mention of Egypt as a prize of war, which has affinities with Alexander's invasion of Asia in 334—after he crossed the Hellespont, and before he disembarked from his ship, he threw a spear into the foreign soil, claiming all Asia as his "spear-won territory."[63] The phrase signified territory that belonged to the king by right of conquest.[64] Ptolemy was therefore adopting the same attitude

---

[58] Low chronology: Errington 1970, pp. 75–77, and 1977; Anson 1986, 2003, and 2014a, pp. 58–59; Billows 1990, pp. 64–80; Roisman 2012, pp. 136–144. For the higher chronology, see Bosworth 1992 and 1993; cf. Wheatley 1995. Dating issues generally: Seibert 1969, pp. 70–81, and for a compromise between the two chronologies, see Boiy 2007.

[59] Diodorus 18.39.1–4; Arrian, *FGrH* 156 F 9, 31–33, with Errington 1970, p. 67.

[60] Diodorus 18.39.4–7; Arrian, *FGrH* 156 9.31–33; Polyaenus 4.6.4. On the episode, see Roisman 2012, pp. 136–12, 157–158, and 2015, p. 79.

[61] Diodorus 18.39.5, 43.1.

[62] Arrian, *FGrH* 156 F 9, 34.

[63] Diodorus 17.17.2.

[64] Schmitthenner 1968, pp. 31–46.

toward Egypt, and in fact by 311 all the Successors had come to see their lands in the same light.

Pithon received Media and other eastern areas as a reward for dispatching Perdiccas. Arrhidaeus was given Hellespontine Phrygia, together with 1,000 troops. Nicanor, a son of Antipater, replaced Eumenes, who was officially an outlaw, in Cappadocia. And Seleucus now came out of the shadow of his former commander Perdiccas; he was given Babylonia, and so finally became a satrap.

Antigonus gained the most, with responsibilities akin to those of Craterus before his death.[65] He was confirmed satrap of Phrygia and took over Perdiccas' army in Asia, thereby becoming general of Asia; Antipater's son Cassander became his second in command. Moreover, as part of the moves against the Perdiccans, Antigonus was given a mandate to hunt down Eumenes, who still had a considerable army with him. With Antipater's blessing, Craterus' widow Phila (Antipater's daughter) married Antigonus' son Demetrius. Why Antipater allowed Antigonus to wield so much power is not known, though he was still as much an enigma as he had been at Babylon two years previously. Antipater certainly did not see him as his successor.[66] Most probably, Antipater believed he was the only man who could reasonably defeat Eumenes and his supporters in Asia, and in that respect he was right.[67] Thus the settlement made Antipater the most powerful man in the West, and Antigonus that in the East.

When Antipater had finalized the arrangements, he returned to Macedonia with the two kings. It was not long before Antigonus revealed his true colors, executing Pithon for treason, conducting a minor purge of other officials, and later systematically looting, to the tune of 25,000 talents, the great palace treasuries at Ecbatana, Persepolis, and Susa to pay his men and to finance future campaigns.[68] He had a formidable army in Asia under his command of 60,000 infantry, 10,000 cavalry, and 30 war elephants, and was ably assisted by his son, Demetrius Poliorcetes ("the Besieger"), one of the period's more colorful characters, as we shall see (Figure 6.1).[69]

Antigonus' actions ought to have surprised no one, as Polybius, when discussing the aims of Philip V of Macedonia (r. 221–179), claimed that all the Antigonids wanted universal dominion.[70] For five years father and son

[65] Champion 2014, p. 25.

[66] Cf. Billows 1990, pp. 69–70.

[67] It has sometimes been assumed that Antigonus did not have these wide-sweeping powers, especially the command of a large army, until he had wiped out the Perdiccans, but there was no time limit on his powers: Billows 1990, pp. 70–71; Champion 2014, pp. 199–200 n. 17.

[68] Diodorus 19.46.6, 48.7–8.

[69] Cf. Diodorus 19.81, and especially Plutarch, *Demetrius* (Plutarch pairs him with Mark Antony), with Manni 1951.

[70] Polybius 5.102.1.

Figure 6.1 Portrait of Demetrius Poliorcetes. © The Metropolitan Musuem of Art, Gift of C. Ruxton Love Jr., 1967, www.metmuseum.org.

ignored Egypt, which allowed Ptolemy valuable time to introduce administrative and bureaucratic measures and to try to create some harmony between the native peoples and the Greeks and Macedonians living in the country (see Chapter 11). After the Triparadeisus settlement, Ptolemy had married Antipater's daughter Eurydice, a union that must have had Antipater's blessing. She was his third wife, and she was in Macedonia when she was betrothed to him. This marriage is an excellent example of the complex inter-dynastic political marriages (often polygamous) of the Successors (and their descendants) to ensure that they, the Macedonians, remained the ruling elite of the Hellenistic world.[71] By the time Eurydice arrived in Memphis for the marriage, it would have been late 320; accompanying her was her niece, Berenice, whom Ptolemy would marry in 317.

Ptolemy might have been disappointed at what he had received at Triparadeisus, given that he had faced Perdiccas alone, but his marital tie

[71] Cf. Waterfield 2011, p. 41. On polygamy for political purposes, see Greenwalt 1989.

to Antipater cunningly aligned himself with the man he at least considered the most influential of the remaining Successors. In this he was wrong, as Antigonus' actions over the next two decades proved.

Extending Egypt

Ptolemy was suspicious of Antigonus, so after the Triparadeisus settlement he resolved to shore up the eastern defenses of Egypt. Over the winter of 320–319 he sent troops under his general (and one of his friends) Nicanor into Coele-Syria and Phoenicia, and annexed the region to Egypt (Map 4).[72] Apparently he had first tried to bribe the satrap of Syria, Laomedon (a Greek from Amphipolis, who, like Ptolemy, had been one of Alexander's boyhood friends, and had been exiled for his part in the Pixodarus affair of 337), to hand Syria over to him. When Laomedon refused, Ptolemy sent Nicanor to capture him. Probably during this brief campaign Ptolemy's army seized Jerusalem—on the Sabbath, so the Jews, as he knew, would not put up resistance on this holy day. Ptolemy encouraged a goodly number of Jews to move to Alexandria, and its Jewish quarter was eventually second in population to only Jerusalem itself.[73]

In acting as he did, Ptolemy did not merely increase his kingdom's security but its possessions: Coele-Syria and Phoenicia provided him with a buffer zone between himself and his nearest possible rival, gave him control of the Phoenician ports and fleet, and allowed him access to raw materials that Egypt did not have.[74] In fact, the Ptolemies as a whole were always careful to control these areas, until they lost Syria to the Seleucids in the second century.[75] Moreover, control of Syria gave Ptolemy a launching point should he ever need to attack Cyprus or move into the eastern Mediterranean. It cannot be overlooked that Ptolemy's systematic annexation of key strategic regions was not just to protect Egypt; his campaign now was another example of his growing ambition.

For the moment, Ptolemy was left alone. Probably now he was forced to intervene in Cyrene, where discontent was growing against Ophellas and his supporters. Ptolemy drew up the so-called constitution of Cyrene, a document

---

[72] Diodorus 18.43 (cf. 73.2, where Diodorus calls Ptolemy's action unjustified); Appian, *Syrian Wars* 52; Pausanias 1.6.4; cf. *Parian Marble, BNJ* 239 B12. On this campaign, see Bouché-Leclercq 1903, pp. 32–34, Seibert 1969, pp. 129–130, and Wheatley 1995, arguing in favor of the high chronology, putting Ptolemy's invasion in summer 320.

[73] For example, Josephus, *Jewish Antiquities* 12.7, 8–9; cf. Caroli 2007, pp. 89–91.

[74] Cf. Ellis 1994, p. 41; Huss 2001 pp. 122–123; Vandorpe 2010, p. 169.

[75] Abel 1935, pp. 567–575; Bagnall 1976, pp. 11–24.

Figure 6.2 Portrait of Cassander. Public domain.

that sheds light on the relationship between the king, cities, and land, which gave the oligarchs local power while he gave himself supreme authority, backed by a garrison.[76] Cyrene therefore ceased to be a free city, and Ptolemy's western border was again secure.

In the summer of 319 came a thunderbolt from the west, introducing a period of chaos: Antipater had died.[77] His son Cassander, then about forty years old, prepared to take up his father's guardianship of the two kings and control of the West (Figure 6.2). It was not to be. Shortly before his death, Antipater had decided that job should go to one of Alexander's infantry officers and Craterus' former second-in-command, Polyperchon, then in his midsixties, and had tapped Cassander to be his second-in-command.[78] Possibly

[76] *SEG* 9 1, lines 1–46 = Austin, no. 264, pp. 443–445 (dating the constitution to Ptolemy's first inervention in Cyrene, see above), with *SEG* 18.726; trans. Harding 1985, no. 126, pp. 159–161; see too Larsen 1929; Bagnall 1976, pp. 28–29; Fraser 1972, vol. 1, pp. 48–49, 95, 98–99, 786–788; Seibert 1983, pp. 102–104; Laronde 1987; Caroli 2007, pp. 6–83.

[77] Austin, no. 25, pp. 47–48 (= Diodorus 18.48.4–50).

[78] Diodorus 18.48.4–5. Polyperchon: Heckel 1992, pp. 188–204.

Antipater was avoiding the notion that he was trying to set up an Antipatrid dynasty, something that might have upset Macedonian barons.[79] More likely is that Polyperchon was a better choice because of his experience and reputation than Cassander, for after Antipater and Craterus marched into Asia to attack Perdiccas, Polyperchon was left in charge of Greece, and the Macedonians regarded him highly.[80] Another explanation that we ought not disregard is that Antipater simply disliked his son. After all, he had had no qualms in sending Cassander by himself to Alexander in 324, even though the king had asked specifically for Antipater to come with troops, and Cassander might well have suffered for his father's disobedience.

Cassander was incensed. Diodorus gives two versions of his response. The first is that he immediately began to seek support from among his friends to wrest control from Polyperchon, while at the same time sending envoys in secret to Ptolemy as well as the other "commanders" (presumably Lysimachus and Antigonus) asking for their military support.[81] The second is that after marshaling his friends, he went to Antigonus in Asia, seeking his assistance, and telling him that he had already received a positive response from Ptolemy.[82] Antigonus gave him 4,000 troops and 35 warships, ostensibly because of his relationship with Antipater, but in reality he wanted to distract Polyperchon and seize Macedonia and Greece himself.

Why Ptolemy supported Cassander as he did is not known. It has been suggested that he was now implementing—in a sense—his proposal in Babylon that there should be a ruling council, and that Cassander may have held a similar view.[83] On the other hand, the two were friends, and as Cassander's brother-in-law, Ptolemy may simply have wanted to continue the alliance forged with Antipater at Triparadeisus. However, we can see in his eager response to Cassander a similar motive to that of Antigonus—in other words, his own serious interest in Greece, something that manifested itself in 308.

The upshot of all this was that yet another settlement of the Successors was shattered. Antipater's decision to give power to Polyperchon set in motion the course of events of the next years. Polyperchon was never really taken seriously—he had never held a high command under Alexander, and so could not hold his own with the others. His invitation to Olympias to return to Macedonia from Epirus and help look after Alexander IV and his pleas to

---

[79] Errington 2008, pp. 21–22.

[80] Diodorus 18.48.4.

[81] Diodorus 18.49.1–3. Lysimachus' allying with him suggests he may have been setting his sights beyond Thrace, even to include Macedonia, but against this see Lund 1994, pp. 55–57.

[82] Diodorus 18.54.2–4.

[83] Anson 2014a, p. 84.

Eumenes for military support were likewise viewed with resentment.[84] Eyes now turned to the prized kingship of Macedonia, plunging the kingdom into dynastic chaos with no fewer than six rulers (including Cassander) until 276, when Antigonus II Gonatas finally brought stability and established the Antigonid dynasty.[85]

[84] Diodorus 18.49.4, 57.3–4; Justin 14.5.

[85] Macedonia and Greece in this and the Hellenistic eras: Hammond and Walbank 1988, pp. 95 and passim; Walbank 1993, pp. 79–99; Shipley 2000, pp. 116–152; Errington 2008, pp. 21–32, 45–56, 79–82.

7

Taking on the Enemy

All of the Successors had put a portrait of Alexander on their coinage to exploit their relationship to him, but in 319 Ptolemy went further with a new iconography on the obverse of his coins: Alexander's head, wearing an elephant scalp and the horns of Zeus Ammon; on the reverse was Zeus sitting on a throne, holding an eagle and thunderbolt with the legend "of Alexander" (Figure 7.1).[1] The elephant scalp associated Alexander with India, especially his victory at the battle of the Hydaspes River in 326 and his later commemorative medallions, one of which featured him (probably) on horseback attacking an elephant (p. 60). Also, Indian elephants were a feature on the Alexander sarcophagus.

Why would Ptolemy introduce this change, and why the visual association to India specifically? We do not know. Perhaps, as has been pointed out, he wanted to highlight his rise to prominence in the Indian part of Alexander's campaign, which is why he devoted much of his *History* to his exploits in India.[2] But would people really associate Ptolemy's new iconography with his own military rise, rather than, in keeping with the original purpose of the medallions, Alexander's invasion of India?

Ptolemy was responsible for a wide-ranging monetization policy that included a lighter standard of coinage, which we will consider as part of his administrative and economic reforms in Chapter 11. It is likely that the new coin under discussion here was simply a new image of Alexander, which was for propaganda and economic reasons. After all, his next major innovation came eight years later in 311, when he added his own name to the coin legend on some of his silver types to make "Ptolemy's Alexander (coin)."[3] A short while later, he

---

[1] Stewart 1993, pp. 229–243; on Ptolemy's coinage, see too Emmons 1954, Lorber 2005. All of the Successors exploited Alexande's image on their coins and artwork: Stewart 1993, pp. 229–323; Meeus, 2009b.

[2] Meeus 2014, pp. 279–283, citing further studies.

[3] *Alexandreion Ptolemaiou*; date: Lorber 2005, pp. 63–64.

Figure 7.1 Coin portrait of Alexander wearing elephant scalp. © The Trustees of the British Museum.

reverted to Alexander's name alone. The eight-year gap from 319 is significant, as indeed is his swiftness in removing his own name, presumably because of an adverse reaction he had caused. In both instances (319 and 311) he was simply emphasizing his association with Alexander and the Argead house to give his rule legitimacy. He maintained that association even after he took the royal title in 306, for silver drachmas with the portrait and name of Alexander on them continued in official circulation.

Cassander and the Greek Mainland

Antigonus had decided he was not answerable to the kings or their guardians anymore, but was set on building up his own power.[4] To this end, he decided to increase his holdings in Asia Minor; he took Ephesus, capturing ships and

---

[4] Diodorus 18.49.1–2.

700 talents of bullion meant for Polyperchon in Macedonia. His support of Cassander was already a major concern for Polyperchon, and when Cassander made his move into Greece from Asia, Polyperchon knew that the combination of the two men was a serious threat to him. Thus began the Second War of the Successors (319–316), in which Ptolemy took little part.[5]

The convoluted events, especially on the mainland, of the following few years involving the main protagonists—Cassander, Polyperchon, Antigonus, and Eumenes—do not concern us much here.[6] As Polyperchon's support declined drastically in Greece because of Cassander's inroads, helped by the substantial troops he had received from Antigonus, Polyperchon issued a proclamation offering the Greeks their freedom. This garnered little support, and if anything was viewed suspiciously.[7] Over the next years, many of the Successors, Ptolemy included, would issue their own such proclamations, all of which were merely to win favor.[8] When the most important city on the mainland, Athens, sided with Cassander in 317, Polyperchon's fate as far as control of Greece went was sealed.[9] He withdrew to the Peloponnese, where he continued his intrigues against Cassander. To ensure Athenian passivity, Cassander installed a Macedonian garrison and governor in Athens, the Aristotelian philosopher Demetrius of Phalerum (the nearest coastal town to Athens).[10]

Demetrius, although not yet 40 years old, was a graduate of Aristotle's Lyceum and one of the period's foremost intellectuals. For the next decade he ruled Athens absolutely in Cassander's name, introducing a series of laws to restrict Athenian extravagance, while he himself enjoyed lavish banquets and numerous courtesans. Nevertheless, Athens enjoyed a period of peace, and intellectual life flourished in the city. This was the period when Theophrastus of Eresus (Aristotle's successor as head of the Lyceum) wrote diverse works on botany and biology, not to mention his *Characters*, satirical character sketches of thirty different types of unpleasant people.[11] The genre of New Comedy

[5] Diodorus 18.55–57, with Seibert 1969, pp. 129–137, 159–163; Billows 1990, pp. 82–109; Caroli 2007, pp. 47–50. Huss 2001, pp. 131–132, suggests that Ptolemy cared little for his allies, hence his low profile.

[6] See Bouché-Leclercq 1903, pp. 34–39; Green 1990, pp. 18–20; Waterfield 2011, pp. 75–83.

[7] Diodorus 18.56, with Hammond and Walbank 1988, pp. 133–134; Dmitriev 2011, pp. 113–114, 116–119.

[8] Dmitriev 2011, pp. 112–134.

[9] For example, Diodorus 18.64, 68, 74–75, with Hammond and Walbank 1988, pp. 134–137.

[10] Demetrius of Phalerum's regime: Ferguson 1911, pp. 38–94; Mossé 1973, pp. 102–108 (described as a "philosophical tyranny"); Green 1990, pp. 36–51; Tracy 1995, pp. 36–51; Habicht 1997, pp. 53–66; O'Sullivan 2009.

[11] Theophrastus: for example, Green 1990, pp. 68–71; Habicht 1997, pp. 121–123.

became a fixture in cultural life, of which the greatest writer was Demetrius' student Menander. New Comedy had romantic and escapist plots, and its plays were set in rural areas, unlike the sharp political Old Comedy of the fifth and early fourth centuries. There was a reason for this change: Demetrius' rule was a stark reminder for the Athenians of their military and political impotence; the plays of New Comedy made them forget for a while the reality of Macedonian control.[12]

In the meantime, Cassander set his eyes on Macedonia. For some time, Polyperchon had been intriguing with Olympias, Alexander's mother, to bring her back to Macedonia and rally the people to his cause. However, another force to be reckoned with was Philip III's wife Eurydice, who had no desire to see Olympias regain influence at court, especially as she would be championing her grandson (Alexander IV) over Eurydice's husband. Therefore, as Olympias approached Macedonia with troops from Epirus, Philip and Eurydice led their own army against her. Eurydice had been trained (unusually for a woman) as a fighter, and she appeared in full armor to exhort her army.[13] However, loyalty to Alexander's mother trumped any feelings for his half-brother, and the troops of Philip and Eurydice mutinied on them.[14] Olympias, a "passionate and embittered woman,"[15] exploited their demise by walling Philip and Eurydice up in a tiny space, where they were fed only through a small opening. Eventually, taking advantage of Cassander's absence from Macedonia, Olympias ordered Philip to be stabbed to death, and sadistically sent Eurydice a sword, a noose, and some hemlock, telling her to choose the manner of her death—defiantly, Eurydice hanged herself with her girdle.[16]

Olympias had put an Argead king to death to pave the way for Alexander IV's rule as sole king. Regicide was a heinous crime, but then she went even further. Since Cassander at the time was besieging Tegea, attempting to win over cities in the Peloponnese taken earlier by Polyperchon, Olympias felt secure enough to kill Cassander's brother Nicanor and 100 other Macedonian nobles she personally hated and who had sided with Cassander and Eurydice.[17] Her actions earned her the disgust of the Macedonians. Cassander knew he needed to return to Macedonia before Polyperchon and Olympias became too

[12] Menander, drama, and politics: Grant 1982, pp. 159–162; Green 1990, pp. 65–68, 71–79; Habicht 1997, pp. 98–105.

[13] Athenaeus 13.560f.

[14] Diodorus 19.11.2; Justin 14.5.9–10.

[15] Hammond and Walbank 1988, p. 140; though note Diodorus 19.51.6 that she "had attained to the highest dignity of the women of the day."

[16] Diodorus 19.11.4–7.

[17] Diodorus 19.11.8–9; Justin 14.6.1–2.

powerful for him to overcome, so he broke off the siege of Tegea and headed home.[18]

At the head of an army, Cassander seized Macedonia. Olympias fled to Pydna, taking with her Alexander IV, Roxane, and various supporters. Cassander besieged Pydna, and as the winter dragged on, many of the defenders died of famine, forcing the non-Greek defenders to eat their corpses to survive. Eventually, the city capitulated and Olympias was captured.[19] Rather than risk putting her on trial and turning her into a martyr, Cassander had her executed (possibly by stoning) as a traitor for murdering Philip and Eurydice as well as Philip's II's seventh wife Cleopatra and her baby daughter in 336.[20] Her corpse was supposedly to be left unburied.[21]

Cassander had avenged the murder of a Macedonian king, which endeared him to the people. He assumed guardianship of the young Alexander IV, and that summer, as he "began to embrace in his hopes the Macedonian kingdom," he married Thessalonice, a half-sister of Alexander the Great (the daughter of Philip II and his Thessalian wife Nicesipolis).[22] The benefit of this political marriage, which tied him to the Argead house, was not lost on Ptolemy when he set his eyes on Greece in 308. Cassander was now Alexander IV's uncle, but he had no intention of letting either the king or his mother have influence at court—he had them taken under guard to Amphipolis and put under house arrest there, devoid of the trappings of royalty.[23] He next arranged an elaborate burial for Philip III and Eurydice at Aegae to further emphasize his ruling power.[24] Ostensibly as part of an urbanization policy, he also founded two cities, Cassandreia (named after himself), on Pallene in the Chalcidice, and Thessalonica (named after his wife) at the head of the Thermaic Gulf.[25] In addition, and with monetary support from wealthy individuals and states, in 316 he refounded Thebes, which Alexander had destroyed in 335.[26] Naming

---

[18] Diodorus 19.35.1; Justin 14.5.8, 6.2. *Parian Marble, BNJ* 239 B 14, dates his return to the summer of 316.

[19] Diodorus 19.35.4–36, 49–50; Justin 14.6.5. Cannibalism by the "non-Greeks": Diodorus 19.49.4.

[20] Diodorus 19.51; Justin 14.6.6–12; Pausanias 9.7.2 (stoning); cf. 1.11.4, with Hammond and Walbank 1988, pp. 136–144; Anson 2014a, pp. 115–116. Chronology: Errington 1977; see too Anson 2014a, pp. 116–121.

[21] Justin 14.6.6–12.

[22] Diodorus 19.52.1; Justin 14.6.13. The quotation from Diodorus 19.52.1.

[23] Diodorus 19.52.4; Justin 14.6.13.

[24] Diodorus 19.52.5.

[25] Diodorus 19.52.2, with Errington 2008, pp. 27–28. He may even have added the entire Chalcidice to his possessions when he founded Cassandreia: Billows 1995, pp. 134–135.

[26] Diodorus 19.53.2, 54.1, 63.4; Pausanias 9.7.1. Donations and other help by individuals: Diodorus 19.54.2; Pausanias 9.7.1; *IG* VII 2419; *SIG* 337; trans. Harding 1985, no. 131, pp. 164–165.

Cassandreia after himself rather than after Alexander IV clearly showed how Cassander viewed himself, as did the refounding of Thebes, which helped him maintain control of Greece.[27] He was here to stay.

Ptolemy was well aware of Cassander's rising arc, although he did not commit himself fully to this new successor war, probably because it was not worth the risk for so little personal gain. Egypt was enjoying peace and prosperity, and he now ruled a substantially larger territory than he had in 323, stretching to Libya in the west and Syria in the east. He also effectively controlled Cyprus because of his alliances with several of its kings, and had cunningly negotiated a series of accords with several Aegean islands to strengthen his hold of the seas. But Ptolemy would not remain on the periphery of world events much longer.

Ptolemy's Marriages

Although the date is not known for certain, Ptolemy married his fourth and most influential wife Berenice (later Berenice I—the name was popular among the Ptolemaic family) most likely in 317.[28] Ptolemy married four times, and had children who we know of by three of his wives.[29] He probably did not divorce a wife to marry another, as we are told that he was polygamous; his wives would therefore have lived together at court.[30] Whether they all got along with each other is another thing; there was tension between Philip II's various wives, who lived together in the palace at Pella, although this was probably due more to the presence of the meddlesome Olympias.[31]

Ptolemy's first wife was Thais, the Athenian courtesan who was said to have persuaded Alexander to set fire to the palace at Persepolis in 330. Ptolemy may have met her earlier than this episode, as she complained of the many hardships wandering through Asia, which suggests that she was one of the many courtesans who accompanied the army on its campaign.[32] Only one ancient writer tells us that Ptolemy was actually married to Thais.[33] However, it is

[27] Hammond and Walbank 1988, p. 145 n. 3; Landucci Gattinoni 2010. Pausanias 9.7.2 claims that Cassander restored Thebes because of his hatred of Alexander and everything to do with the Argead family.

[28] Ellis 1994, p. 42; Caroli 2007, pp. 105–108; van Oppen de Ruiter 2011.

[29] Marriages: Ogden 1999, pp. 68–73, and especially Caroli 2007, pp. 104–108.

[30] Plutarch, *Comparison of Demetrius and Antony* 4.1, with, for example, Bouché-Leclercq, 1903, pp. 94–95; Ellis 1994, pp. 42, 45. Pausanias 1.6.8 speaks of Ptolemy inheriting from his father (if he were Philip) a passion for women by his marriages, which might indicate polygamy. On polygamy, see Greenwalt 1989.

[31] Carney 2000, pp. 23–27, 29–31.

[32] Plutarch, *Alexander* 38.3, with Ellis 1994, p. 8.

[33] Athenaeus 13.576e.

likely they were married, given that he named one of their sons Lagus after his grandfather. First-born sons were normally named after their grandfathers, and it would be hard to imagine Ptolemy giving his first son the name Lagus if he was a bastard. We remember that Alexander's first son was illegitimate, and he was not named Philip, after his grandfather, but Heracles.

With Thais, Ptolemy had two sons and a daughter.[34] He never seems to have expected either of their sons to succeed him, and they played no part in the succession on his death. One son, Lagus, was an Olympic competitor in 308, and the other, Leontiscus, was taken prisoner on Cyprus by Antigonus' son Demetrius in 306, but released without ransom. As for the daughter Eirene, Ptolemy married her off to Eunostus, king of Soli in Cyprus, soon after he moved to Egypt.

Ptolemy took a second wife, or rather had one forced upon him by Alexander, in 324 as part of the mass marriage at Susa. Artacama of Persia is unknown to us, and there is no record that she and Ptolemy had children.[35] Certainly none materialized on his death claiming the Egyptian throne. Exactly what her status was is unknown, but she was not in the same aristocratic league as the wives of Alexander's closer commanders and friends. Ptolemy may even have divorced her, given the circumstances of the marriage, for it seems that all but one of the men who had had to marry foreign wives at Susa divorced their wives after the Babylon settlement.[36] The only exception we know about was Seleucus, who stayed married to Apama, Spitamenes of Bactria's daughter.[37]

Ptolemy's third wife was Eurydice, the daughter of Antipater, whom he married in probably 320. With Eurydice he had two sons for sure, Ptolemy Ceraunus ("thunderbolt") and Meleager, and possibly a third, Argaeus, as well as two daughters, Lysandra and Ptolemais. Ceraunus and Meleager became Macedonian kings for a very short time in the late 280s to 279. Lysandra married Lysimachus of Thrace's son Agathocles in 300, and Ptolemais married Demetrius Poliorcetes in 287. (On Argaeus, see below.)

Ptolemy's fourth and most influential wife was Berenice, who had moved to Memphis in about 320 (Figure 7.2). Berenice had been married previously to a fairly obscure Macedonian, of lowly origin, named Philip, who presumably had died by the time she went to Egypt.[38] She and Philip had three children, a son, Magas, and two daughters, Antigone and Theoxene.[39] In 316 or

---

[34] Athenaeus 13.576e.

[35] Name: Arrian 7.4.6; but Plutarch, *Eumenes* 1.3, wrongly calls her Apama.

[36] Bevan 1927, p. 51; Ellis 1994, p. 15; Hölbl 2001, p. 14.

[37] Cf. Plutarch, *Demetrius* 31.3.

[38] Pausanias 1.7.1.

[39] Scholiast to Theocritus 17.61.

Figure 7.2   Ptolemy and his wife Berenice. © The Trustees of the British Museum / Art Resource, New York

315 Berenice's marriage to Ptolemy produced a daughter Arsinoe, and in the winter of 309 she gave birth to a son, Ptolemy, on Cos.[40] There was also another daughter, Philotera, whose birth year is unknown. Of these children, Magas became Ptolemy's governor of Cyrene in 300, Antigone married Pyrrhus of Epirus in 296, and Ptolemy succeeded his father as ruler of Egypt from 285. Their daughter Arsinoe (II) inherited her mother's ambitious genes, for she married her brother Ptolemy when he was ruling Egypt, thereby beginning the Ptolemaic tradition of brother-sister marriage.[41] That marriage earned Ptolemy II the epithet Philadelphus ("lover of his sister") and ridicule from a well-known obscene poet named Sotades, whose line "You're pushing your cock into an unholy hole" had him drowned in a lead coffin on Ptolemy's orders.[42]

[40] For the date: *Parian Marble, BNJ* 239 B no. 19.
[41] On the marriage practice, see Criscuolo 1994; Ager, 2005; Buraselis 2008; and the comments of Koenen 1983, pp. 157–161.
[42] Athenaeus 14.621a.

Ancient writers claimed that of all his wives, Ptolemy thought the most of Berenice, and that their marriage was a love match.[43] She likely became his mistress not long after arriving at his court with Eurydice.[44] She quickly became a force with which to be reckoned—when Pyrrhus of Epirus was sent as a hostage to Egypt in 298, he found her to be the most influential of all the wives, and paid special attention to her because of it.[45] Just as Olympias was always ambitious for her son Alexander, so was Berenice for her son Ptolemy, and she may have persuaded her husband to make him Egypt's next king, rather than his eldest boy Ptolemy Ceraunus.[46] We will take up the succession when dealing with Ptolemy I's final years in Chapter 12.

Of incidental interest is that none of Ptolemy's daughters was given what became the most famous of female names associated with Egypt—Cleopatra. That name was introduced much later—the first Cleopatra was in fact a member of the Seleucid ruling house, the daughter of Antiochus III, who married her cousin Ptolemy V Epiphanes (r. 204–181) in 195, when he was 13 years old. The name evidently caught on.

The parentage of Ptolemy's and Eurydice's son Argaeus is controversial because Pausanias, a Greek author writing in the second century AD, claims that Ptolemy II had his brother Argaeus executed for treason (together with an unnamed brother who is said to have been Eurydice's son).[47] If this is true, then Eurydice could not have been Argaeus' mother, but Berenice, since she unquestionably gave birth to Ptolemy (II) on Cos. One way of explaining the controversy is that Pausanias did not mean Ptolemy's full brother (by the same mother) but his half-brother. However, Pausanias in the same passage refers to Magas as Ptolemy II's half-brother, so he was clearly aware of the difference between full- and half-brother status. Pausanias, who was not a historian, may have simply made a mistake about Argaeus' status, and hence his mother.[48] There is no need to go to the lengths of a recent study arguing that Argaeus was not Ptolemy's son by any of his wives, but an illegitimate son of Alexander the Great and Thais, whom Ptolemy willingly adopted when Alexander was done with Thais and gave her, pregnant (with Argaeus), to Ptolemy.[49]

---

[43] Theocritus 17.38-40; cf. Plutarch, *Pyrrhus* 4.4, on her influence on Ptolemy.

[44] There is a belief based on a corrupt source that Eurydice was actually Ptolemy's sister, which, if true, meant that he began the Ptolemaic practice of brother-sister marriage, not his son, but this belief is erroneous: Ogden 1999, p. 70.

[45] Plutarch, *Pyrrhus* 4.4.

[46] Pausanias 1.6.8; cf. Appian, *Syrian Wars* 62.

[47] Pausanias 1.7.1.

[48] Cf. (that he was Eurydice's son) Bouché-Leclercq 1903, p. 26 n. 4; Bevan 1927, p. 53; Ogden 1999, pp. 68, 75; Hazzard 1987, p. 149.

[49] van Oppen de Ruiter 2013, citing sources and bibliography.

On the Offensive

With Cassander calling the shots in Macedonia and Greece, Antigonus swallowed up more of Asia. In the process, he hunted down and captured the tough and resilient Eumenes after a campaign stretching for several years, which saw both parties suffer reversals, in 316.[50] Ptolemy had also waged his own campaign against Eumenes when the latter had begun to recruit substantial numbers of mercenaries in areas such as Coele-Syria, Phoenicia, and Cyprus, which came under Ptolemy's sphere of influence. In 318 Ptolemy embarked with a fleet to Zephyrium (near Cyinda), in Asia Minor, from where he attempted to win over as many of Eumenes' men as he could while castigating the commanders at Cyinda for supporting him.[51] He was completely unsuccessful, not so much, perhaps, because of the men's personal loyalty to Eumenes, but because the two kings, in tandem with Polyperchon and Olympias, had ordered them to obey only Eumenes.[52] Ptolemy therefore abandoned his missions and returned home.

But by 316 the threat from Eumenes was over. Antigonus imprisoned his worthy adversary for several days, and was apparently reluctant to kill him, until the matter was taken out of his hands and some guards strangled Eumenes to death; Antigonus sent his ashes to his widow and children in Cappadocia.[53] Antigonus now had an enormous army, ruled a vast area of Asia, and had access to the huge treasuries at the palace centers of Susa, Ecbatana, and Persepolis. Despite his advanced age, his aim was to resurrect the empire Alexander had ruled, and that meant taking over Greece and Macedonia for himself. Meeting his goal was something the others could not allow.

Apart from his attempt to weaken Eumenes' troop numbers, Ptolemy had remained on the sidelines while the preceding events took place, but in 315 he was brought sharply into the growing conflict. Late that summer Antigonus traveled to Babylon, where he had a violent dispute with Seleucus, apparently over how the latter was conducting his financial affairs, which ended with Seleucus fleeing to Ptolemy.[54] Antigonus' disagreement, however, may have had more to do with resenting Seleucus' popularity and his control of

---

[50] Diodorus 18.58–63, 19.12–34, 37–44; Nepos, *Eumenes* 7–10; Plutarch, *Eumenes* 9–18; Justin 14.1–5, with Seibert 1983, pp. 110–114; Billows 1990, pp. 83–104; Bosworth 2002, pp. 141–158; Waterfield 2011, pp. 93–102; Roisman 2012, pp. 212–236; Champion 2014, pp. 37–68.

[51] On this brief campaign, see for example Roisman 2012, pp. 186–187.

[52] Diodorus 18.61.1–2.

[53] Murder: Plutarch, *Eumenes* 19.1; Nepos, *Eumenes* 12.4; cf. Didorus 19.44.2 (Antigonus "had him put to death"); ashes: Didorus 19.44.2; Plutarch, *Eumenes* 19.1; Nepos, *Eumenes* 13.4.

[54] Diodorus 19.55.2–5; Pausanias 1.6.4, with Billows 1990, pp. 106–107.

Alexander's last capital, Babylon. Seleucus fled through Mesopotamia and Syria to Ptolemy, not so much because, in Diodorus' words, "word had spread abroad of Ptolemy's kindness and of his cordiality and friendliness toward those who fled to him," but more because Ptolemy was really his only option for refuge.[55] It was uncertain whether Cassander could maintain his position in Greece should Antigonus attack him, and Lysimachus still had his hands full pacifying Thrace.

Ptolemy was in a quandary. If he turned his back on Seleucus, he risked making an enemy of him forever; on the other hand, if he supported him, he would incur the wrath of Antigonus. In the end he chose the latter, perhaps because he knew that relations were rocky between him and Antigonus anyway, and so he needed all the allies he could get. And so he welcomed Seleucus as a former comrade and friend.

Seleucus warned Ptolemy that Antigonus and his formidable army intended to take over the entire empire and be another Alexander.[56] As sensational as Seleucus' claim was, it could not be overlooked that Antigonus controlled all of Alexander's eastern empire, and that the other satraps in the area were either his supporters or lived in fear of him—as had been his plan since Antipater's death in 319.[57] He may even have cajoled his own Macedonian troops to confer the regency on him, perhaps at Tyre.[58] Ptolemy decided on a proactive approach to restore Seleucus to Babylon, and in this was followed by Lysimachus and Cassander, whom Seleucus also persuaded to join his cause.[59]

In later 315, a deputation from Ptolemy, Lysimachus, and Cassander met with Antigonus in upper Syria, and ordered him to allow Seleucus to return to Babylon.[60] In a further attempt to reduce Antigonus' territory, they demanded that Ptolemy be given control of all Syria, Lysimachus Hellespontine Phrygia (which would mean his kingdom would straddle both sides of the Hellespont), and Cassander Cappadocia and Lycia, and that Antigonus should give them a share in the spoils from his defeat of Eumenes – otherwise, it was war.[61] Not surprisingly, Antigonus, who stood to lose most of his eastern possessions under their terms, laughed off the ultimatum; no diplomatic negotiations for him. While Seleucus had certainly been treated badly, Ptolemy, Lysimachus,

---

[55] Diodorus 19.55.5.
[56] Diodorus 19.56.
[57] Champion 2014, p. 73.
[58] Simpson 1957, pp. 371–373.
[59] Diodorus 19.56.3; Pausanias 1.6.4.
[60] Diodorus 19.57.1 (cf. 85.3); cf. Justin 15.1.2; Bouché-Leclercq 1903, pp. 45–49.
[61] Diodorus 19.57.1, with Billows 1990, p. 109.

and Cassander had no grounds for their demands. Thus began the Third War of the Successors (315–311).[62]

Antigonus marched south into Phoenicia, sending his envoy Agesilaus to make alliances with the Cypriot kings who were not allied to Ptolemy, while he tried to persuade the Rhodians to build a fleet for him. These moves were clearly intended to put pressure on Ptolemy, who knew Egypt's vulnerability to attack from the direction of these islands and Palestine. Agesilaus, however, scored success only with some minor Cypriot kings, not the powerful ones, like Nicocreon, who remained loyal to Ptolemy. Again we see that Ptolemy's earlier, careful diplomatic policy toward Cyprus paid off for him.[63]

In 314 Antigonus hit back at the coalition of Ptolemy, Cassander, and Lysimachus when he denounced Cassander for murdering Olympias, imprisoning Roxane and Alexander IV in Amphipolis, and forcing Thessalonice to marry him.[64] He sent Polyperchon, who was still in the Peloponnese, 1,000 talents to shore up support against Cassander,[65] and then dramatically issued an edict promising the Greeks of the mainland and Asia their freedom and autonomy, without foreign garrisons in their cities.[66] His motive was purely pragmatic: to undermine Cassander's military power and secure allies at this time.[67] However, his decree also impacted the other Successors because it prevented them from garrisoning any Greek city throughout the entire empire—of course, none of them took any notice of it.

In a bid to outdo Antigonus and act against Cassander, Ptolemy issued a similar proclamation to the Greeks, claiming that he was just as concerned as Antigonus with their freedom.[68] His proclamation adroitly set himself up as

---

[62] Diodorus 19.57.2–62; see too Seibert 1969, pp. 138–151; Will 1984a, pp. 46–52; Hammond and Walbank 1988, pp. 150–162; Billows 1990, pp. 109–134; Caroli 2007, pp. 50–56; Champion 2014, pp. 69–97; Anson 2014a, pp. 129–149; on chronology: Wheatley 1998; Anson 2006; Meeus 2012.

[63] Caroli 2007, pp. 85–86. Seibert 1969, pp. 143–144, sees Agesilaus' minor diplomatic successes as evidence of Ptolemy's failed Cyprus policy (it did not speak of "eine erfolgreiche, aktive Zypernpolitik"), but against this, see Hauben 1977a, p. 265.

[64] Diodorus 19.61.1–2; Justin 15.1.3.

[65] Diodorus 19.57.5, with Billows 1990, pp. 369–370; see further, Simpson 1957.

[66] Austin, no. 29, pp. 54–56 (= Diodorus 19.61–62.2). On what was meant by "freedom" as it affected the Greeks and Antigonus' dealings with the Greeks, see Heuss 1938, pp. 146–152; Simpson 1959; Dixon 2007; Dmitriev 2011, pp. 115–129; see too Seibert 1983, pp. 179–183; cf. Green 1990, pp. 23–25 and Billows 1990, pp. 194–197, and pp. 189–236 on Antigonus' relations with the Greeks (not just of the mainland but also Asia Minor and islands) during his life.

[67] Cf. Manni 1951, pp. 111–114, and in detail Heuss 1938; Seibert 1983, pp. 179–183; Simpson 1959; cf. Billows 1990, p. 114; Anson 2014a, pp. 133–134. For a detailed treatment of the events of the next three years (involving the other Successors), see for example Waterfield 2011, pp. 109–120; ·Anson 2014a, pp. 129–149.

[68] Diodorus 19.62.1–2, with Heuss 1938, pp. 150–151; Kolbe 1916; Seibert 1969, pp. 180–183; Hauben 1977c, p. 322; Grabowski 2008, p. 35; Dmitriev 2011, pp. 115–120; see too Lehmann 1988a.

a liberator regardless of whether Antigonus, Polyperchon, or Cassander triumphed over the other.[69] Of course Ptolemy, like Antigonus, did not care a jot about the best interests of the Greeks, and it was not lost on them that he had installed garrisons in Cyrene and in many of the surrounding towns.[70] But Ptolemy's move shows his ambition: he was competing with Antigonus to be a hero in the eyes of the Greeks, and he may even have been laying the groundwork for his bid on Greece in 308 (see Chapter 9).[71]

By 312 Polyperchon had managed to win over a number of key towns in the Peloponnese from Cassander, who was also under pressure on his borders. This would have been a good time for Antigonus to halt his campaign in Syria, where he had recently won over Palestine and Phoenicia from Ptolemy, and invade Macedonia. However, Ptolemy was becoming more of a threat to him every day. His navy was far more powerful than that of Antigonus, and its commander, Polyclitus, had earlier defeated Antigonus' fleet, thereby thwarting Antigonid involvement in Cyprus and getting ships from Rhodes.[72] In fact Seleucus (who had been serving as an admiral under Ptolemy) and 100 Ptolemaic triremes had joined with Ptolemy's brother, Menelaus, to win over all of Cyprus for Ptolemy.[73] Ptolemy had followed up that success with some swift campaigning that was worthy of Alexander. After putting down a revolt of Cyrene in 313, Ptolemy personally led an army to Cyprus to kill or take prisoner four kings who had recently thrown in their lot with Antigonus, and made his longtime friend and ally Nicocreon, the king of Salamis, general (*strategos*) over all Cyprus.[74] Prudently, though, he kept Menelaus as a general on the island and to keep tabs on Nicocreon.[75] Afterward, Ptolemy besieged two cities in northern Syria, sailed to Cilicia, where he captured Malus and sold its inhabitants into slavery, and then returned to Egypt.[76]

Ptolemy's growing influence led Antigonus to declare war on him, despite currently besieging Tyre.[77] He ordered Demetrius, his son, into Syria to take on Ptolemy.[78] But Ptolemy had long since gone. In spite of Antigonus' unexpected

---

[69] Simpson 1959, p. 390.

[70] Their cynical exploitation of freedom for their own advantage: Diodorus 19.62.2.

[71] Strootman 2014a, pp. 317–318; Meeus 2014, pp. 286–287.

[72] For example, Diodorus 19.58.5–6: how Seleucus used Ptolemy's naval superiority at the siege of Tyre. On the Ptolemaic navy, see for example Pollard 2010, pp. 449–450.

[73] Diodorus 19.62.3–5; 100 triremes: Diodorus 19.58.5.

[74] Cyrene: Diodorus 19.79.1–3; Cyprus: Diodorus 19.79.4–7.

[75] Bagnall 1976, pp. 39–42 and Hauben 1987a, p. 224, on Nicocreon and Menelaus.

[76] Diodorus 19.79.6–7, 80.3.

[77] Diodorus 19.61.5; siege: Billows 1990, pp. 111–112, 117.

[78] Diodorus 19.69.1, 80.1–2.

difficulties in besieging Tyre, which with Ptolemaic support held out against him for 15 months, he ordered Demetrius to invade Egypt.[79] At the old Philistine city of Gaza, Demetrius found Ptolemy (supported by Seleucus) and his army waiting to engage him.[80] Antigonus' generals Nearchus and Pithon, who accompanied Demetrius, advised him to wait, but Demetrius wanted only to attack, and exhorted his men to do so.[81] Although he was still only in his early twenties, he had fought with his father against Eumenes, and now he had his first independent command. Understandably, he wanted to prove himself. Just south of Gaza, the two sides met on a wide plain to do battle; it was late fall of 312.[82]

The Battle of Gaza

Ptolemy's army comprised 18,000 infantry and 4,000 cavalry, most of which were Macedonians, Greeks, and mercenaries, as well as a "mass" (*plethos*) of Egyptians.[83] Some of these Egyptians served as soldiers, while others helped to carry equipment and missiles. Presumably the Egyptians (who must all have been infantrymen) would not have been trained in Macedonian fighting tactics, so Ptolemy was expecting his own men to carry the day, as his reliance on the cavalry, none of which was Egyptian, proves. But the fact that he called upon Egyptians to fight for him—the first time we are aware that he used the natives in his army—shows he was not taking Demetrius lightly. Nor should he, for the invading army consisted of 12,500 infantry, 4,500 cavalry, and 43 war elephants. As yet Ptolemy had no elephants in his army, which is a surprise; although he did not have access to elephants from India, he could have made use of African ones.

The battle was going to be a hard-fought one.[84] Like Alexander at the Hydaspes River battle in 326, Ptolemy realized his greatest danger was from his opponent's elephants and cavalry, so he dug spikes into the ground and set up chains across his line to impede the elephants' progress. Further, also echoing Alexander at the Hydaspes, he prepared his archers and javelin-throwers to wound the animals and dislodge the mahouts so that in disarray and pain

[79] The chronology of the next few years is controversial: see Seibert 1969, pp. 164–175, and especially Hauben 1973 and Wheatley 1998.

[80] Diodorus 19.80.3–5.

[81] Diodorus 19.81.

[82] Diodorus 19.84.6 for the plain. Dating: Anson 2014a, pp. 159–160. Plutarch, *Demetrius* 5.2: Demetrius was twenty-two years old; Diodorus 19.81.4–5 refers to him as a youth.

[83] Diodorus 19.80.4.

[84] Battle: Diodorus 19.82–84.5; Plutarch, *Demetrius* 5; Appian, *Syrian Wars* 54; Pausanias 1.6.5; Justin 15.1.5–9, with Bouché-Leclercq 1903, pp. 73–75; Seibert 1969, pp. 164–175; Kertész 1974; Devine 1984 and 1989b; Bennett and Roberts 2010, pp. 89–100; Champion 2014, pp. 91–97.

the giant animals would stampede back onto their own line. That Demetrius or Antigonus did not anticipate this form of counterattack was a failing on their part: although neither of them had been present at the Hydaspes to see Alexander's gruesome tactic in action, Demetrius did have veteran generals like Nearchus with him who had been at the battle, and would have reported Alexander's tactics.

Demetrius commanded his left wing, comprising 4,400 infantry (including his 200-man personal bodyguard) and 30 elephants. On his right flank he deployed 1,500 cavalry; the remaining infantrymen and thirteen elephants were stationed in the center. Demetrius planned his strategy around the cavalry on his left flank routing the enemy line, and deploying the cavalry on his right flank as Ptolemy's line crumbled. Ptolemy made some minor adjustments when he saw Demetrius' line; he personally commanded his right wing, supported by Seleucus, and 3,000 cavalry. He kept only 1,000 cavalry on his left wing because he needed to reinforce his right wing against the larger number facing it.[85] Thanks to his experience of fighting with Alexander and observing this brilliant general in action, Ptolemy knew that the mass of cavalry at the greatest tactical points would help him carry the day.

Demetrius unleashed his powerful left flank, as expected, against Ptolemy's right, but Ptolemy's cavalry did not buckle as Demetrius had hoped, and actually began to push the enemy cavalry back, while at the same time the invader's elephants were rendered impotent by the spikes and a barrage of missiles aimed at them and their drivers. With no one to control them, the elephants stampeded back or were captured. The failure of the elephant charge disheartened Demetrius' men, and the battle turned into bitter hand-to-hand fighting, in which Ptolemy's men always had the advantage. In panic, Demetrius' cavalry retreated, closely followed by the infantry, hoping to escape to safety at Gaza. However, Ptolemy bore down on them so quickly that Demetrius had to flee further north, through Phoenicia, Cilicia, and eventually into northern Syria. Despite the intensity of the fighting, Demetrius lost only 500 troops (which must have included cavalry).[86] Ptolemy and Seleucus allowed Demetrius to recover the dead and returned various prisoners to him unransomed.[87] Still, Ptolemy had captured 8,000 enemy troops and their elephants, which was a blow to Antigonus in Asia. He scattered his new men on allotments of land (*kleroi*) throughout Egypt, which they farmed until called up for active duty.

---

[85] Makeup of lines and strategy: Devine 1989b, pp. 31–34.

[86] On preferring Diodorus 19.84.3, which gives the number slain as 500, in contrast to Plutarch, *Demetrius* 5.2, who gives 5,000: Seibert 1969, pp. 164–175; Devine 1984.

[87] Diodorus 19.85.3; Justin 15.1.8–9 (adding that Ptolemy released Demetrius' friends and gave them gifts).

Gaza was Ptolemy's first major battle, and he had proved he was a fierce adversary in the field and more than a competent general of an army. After his victory, he captured Gaza and marched into Phoenicia and Syria, where Sidon surrendered to him immediately, although Tyre defied him.[88] Later, the commander of Tyre's garrison, Andronicus, fell into his hands. Rather than punishing him, Ptolemy pardoned him for his earlier defiance, and welcomed him to his court, a benevolent act that, claims Diodorus, showed he was "exceptionally gentle and forgiving and inclined toward deeds of kindness. It was this very thing that most increased his power and made many men desire to share his friendship."[89] Diodorus' effusive evaluation of Ptolemy betrays the fact that Ptolemy was as ruthless and cunning as any of the Successors. At the same time, we should remember that Alexander the Great had been careful to treat many of his enemies with respect, again for pragmatic reasons, and Ptolemy had witnessed his actions firsthand.

When Ptolemy heard that Demetrius had moved into Upper Syria from Cilicia, he sent his general and friend Cilles after him.[90] Cilles was not up to the task; Demetrius defeated him, capturing him and 7,000 of his troops without a fight. Perhaps as a quid pro quo for Ptolemy's treatment of his commanders after Gaza, Demetrius sent Cilles unharmed back to Ptolemy. When Antigonus heard the news of the battle of Gaza, he reportedly said that Ptolemy had merely defeated "a crowd of beardless youths and would now have to fight real men."[91] He then marched to join his son, intent on taking on Ptolemy. Rather than risk facing a vengeful Antigonus and his army so far from home, Ptolemy, on the opinion of his advisers, decided the time had come to return to Egypt.[92] He pulled out of Syria, and on his way home his men destroyed several important towns, including Akka, Joppa, and Gaza, perhaps to thwart Antigonus.[93] If so, his plan did not work, for Antigonus was able to take over all of Syria and Phoenicia.

The Satrap Stele—and Nubia?

Ptolemy's successful incursion in Syria was recorded on the so-called satrap stele (Figure 7.3), which was set up in November 311 by the priests of Buto

---

[88] Diodorus 19.84.8, 85.4–86.2.

[89] Diodorus 19.86.2–3.

[90] Diodorus 19.93.1–2; Plutarch, *Demetrius* 6.1–3; Pausanias 1.6.5.

[91] Plutarch, *Demetrius* 6.1. Diodorus 19.93.4 claims that Antigonus rejoiced at the news, given that Demetrius was so young, and that his victory over Cilles showed he was worthy to be a king.

[92] Diodorus 19.93.4–7; Pausanias 1.6.5.

[93] Bosworth 2002, p. 242.

Figure 7.3 The satrap stele, granite "satrap stela" of Ptolemy I, probably originally from Buto, Egypt, 311 BC, Cairo CG 22182 Public domain image from Ahmed Bey Kamal, *Stèles, ptolémaiques et romaines* (Cairo: Institut français d'archéologie orientale, 1904–1905), pl. 56. Photograph by Aidan Dodson.

(at Pe and Tep) and commemorated his restoration of their lands—and revenues—in the northwest Delta, east of Alexandria, which had been taken away by the Persians: "I, Ptolemy, the satrap, restore to Horus, the avenger of his father, the lord of Pe and to Buto, the lady of Pe and Tep, the territory of Patanut, from this day forth and for ever, with all its villages, all its town, all its inhabitants, all its fields, all its waters, all its oxen, all its birds, all its herds, and all things produced in it, as it was aforetime, together with what has been added since by the gift, made by the king, the lord of both lands, Khabbash, the ever living."[94]

The stele was discovered in 1871 in Cairo, and today is in the Egyptian Museum there. Written in hieroglyphics, the monument is a unique Egyptian literary source for at least one of Ptolemy's military campaigns, and therefore for his reign. It also shows us that the priests were quick to see in his generous action a didactic and propagandistic advantage. In representing him as a good ruler on the stele, they hoped this would influence him and future Ptolemies to rule a peaceful, united Egypt. Further, even though only those able to read hieroglyphics would understand its message, the priests would still garner prestige for themselves and their temple throughout Egypt as news of the stele was spread by word of mouth.[95]

Ptolemy's benevolence to these priests was supposedly out of gratitude for the gods' granting him his recent military successes and safe return. But there was more to it than that. Ptolemy must have been concerned about reprisals from Antigonus, and Alexandria and the northwest Delta were especially vulnerable to invasion.[96] That was why he had made alliances with Cypriot kings shortly after moving into Egypt. Therefore his grant to the priests of this area was really nothing to do with benevolence, but all to do with the strategy of having them—and the gods—on his side in the event of attack. He thus exploited religion for military considerations, as we shall see when we discuss his religious policy (Chapter 11).

The satrap stele is important for two other reasons. First, it tells us that by the time it was set up in 311, Ptolemy had moved to Alexandria as his capital.[97] Exactly when he did so is not known, but 314 is a possibility because in that year Antigonus expelled all of Ptolemy's garrisons in Syria so as to give him an easy march into Egypt.[98] Ptolemy presumably expected Antigonus not to

[94] Translation: Bevan 1927, p. 31. On the stele, see Seibert 1983, pp. 224–225; Caroli 2007, pp. 91–94; Lane Fox 2014, pp. 194–195; and especially Sethe 1916, pp. 11–122 no. 9; Goedicke 1985; and Burstein 2014 and 2015. Full translation in Bevan 1927, pp. 28–32 and Ritner 2003, pp. 392–397.

[95] Schäfer 2014, pp. 447–452, calling the stele a kind of manual on how to rule.

[96] On which, see Robinson and Wilson 2010.

[97] Diodorus 18.26.3, 28.2–4; Strabo 17.1.8; Aelian, *Varia Historia* 12.64, with Fraser 1972, vol. 1, pp. 7, 15–16 n. 79, and vol. 2, p. 12; Swinnen 1973, pp. 116, 120; Lorton 1987; Stewart 1993, pp. 221–223, 369–375; Erskine 2002, pp. 170–171. Gambetti 2009, p. 26, dates the move to 314.

[98] I am grateful to Prof. Sandra Gambetti for her thoughts on the chronology here.

make the same mistake as Perdiccas had in trying to cross the Nile to attack him in Memphis, but to invade from Pelusium to his west. If that were to happen, Ptolemy needed to be in a better position than Memphis to protect Egypt, and so he moved to Alexandria for strategic purposes.

The satrap stele also records a second campaign undertaken by Ptolemy I "to the territory of Irem" as retaliation for what its people had done to Egypt, and how he returned to Egypt with "their people, both male and female, and their gods." It has been vigorously argued that this campaign was to Nubia, on Egypt's southern border, which Ptolemy undertook in 312 or early 311, because of a Kushite incursion on that border.[99] There is no question that Ptolemy II campaigned in Nubia in the 270s, where he established a colony on the Red Sea, and that his successors were active in Nubia.[100] But did Ptolemy II take an army into Nubia in response to a recent Kushite invasion of Egypt, as is commonly thought, or was he following in the footsteps of his father?

The state of the evidence will not allow a precise answer, but in any case, other evidence makes Ptolemy II the first to go there.[101] Nor does the name "Irem" on the stele shed light on the matter; it is a Nubian toponym, but given the different vocalizations of hieroglyphs, the word might also refer to people in another area, such as Arabs or Jews in Palestine, or even Arabs in the Sinai Peninsula.[102] It has also been suggested that Ptolemy waged the campaign to increase his manpower reserves, given that he allowed these people to keep their own slaves (referring to the men and women of the inscription) and religion, something he would not have allowed had they been mere prisoners of war.[103]

Given Ptolemy's concern with Antigonid reprisals after his Syrian expedition, as may be seen in why he restored the lands to the priests, it seems unlikely that he would march to his southern border and, while being so far away, allow Antigonus relatively easy access to Alexandria should he choose to invade Egypt.

The End of the Argeads

In late 312 or possibly even the spring of 311, Ptolemy gave Seleucus 1,000 troops (800 infantry and 200 cavalry) to help him return to Babylon.[104] Seleucus expelled the Antigonid garrison there, and by May 311 had reasserted control

---

[99] Burstein 2008b, 2014, and 2015.
[100] Theocritus, *Idyll* 17, lines 86–87, and see too Burstein 2008b.
[101] Diodorus 13.7.5, quoting Agatharchides, *BNJ* 86 F 19.
[102] Burstein 2015, pp. 122–123, for details.
[103] Goedicke 1985, pp. 34–35.
[104] Diodorus 19.86.5, 90–92; Appian, *Syrian Wars* 54; Justin 15.4.11. Seleucus' campaign: Billows 1990, pp. 136–138; van der Spek 2014.

of his former lands. That the people welcomed his return may have been because Antigonus had shown little consideration for them.[105] Now feeling secure,
Seleucus boldly declared himself General of Asia, and the long Seleucid dynasty
is dated from that year (311–65).[106] Understandably, Seleucus' daredevil declaration upset not only Antigonus (probably as Seleucus had intended), since he
had been General of Asia, but also Ptolemy, Cassander, and Lysimachus.

The aftermath of the battle of Gaza was that all sides were exhausted and suspicious of each other. It was time for another round of peace negotiations, which
were held in an unknown location in the fall of 311; all the major protagonists, with
the exception of Polyperchon and Seleucus, were present.[107] There, Antigonus,
Cassander, Ptolemy, and Lysimachus divided up much of Antigonus' territory
among themselves, thus bringing to an end the Third War of the Successors. It
is interesting to see how the others were beginning to take Lysimachus more
seriously, who in 313 had successfully campaigned in the Pontic region and had
defeated an Antigonid army there.[108] He had "merely bided his time somewhat
longer" than the others, and it was paying off handsomely for him.[109]

Cassander was to control Europe and to be guardian of Alexander IV;
Lysimachus was reconfirmed (again) in Thrace, but he had to give up
Hellespontine Phrygia; Ptolemy retained Egypt (by now including Cyprus
and Libya), and some territory in Arabia, but he had to renounce Phoenicia
and Palestine; and Antigonus remained as General of Asia (taking over
Hellespontine Phrygia), albeit without all the territories he had conquered
since 319. It is wrong to refer to this agreement as a peace settlement, not least
because none of the parties viewed it seriously, but as a breathing space in
their hostilities.[110] Ptolemy and Antigonus did make peace with each other,
but their relations remained strained over Ptolemy's retention of Cyprus
(which Antigonus saw as part of his Asia) and Syria, where Antigonus had
based troops, and which Ptolemy wanted all for himself.[111] Moreover, neither
Polyperchon (who was still in Greece) nor Seleucus were members of it—in
fact, Seleucus and Antigonus never made peace with each other, thus continuing their war that had begun in 315.[112]

[105] Anson 2014a, pp. 147–148, citing bibliography.

[106] But see Bevan 1902, p. 52, for 312. Seleucids: see the works cited in Chapter 5 n. 60.

[107] Austin, no. 30, pp. 56–57 (= Diodorus 19.105.1–4), with Simpson 1954; Seibert 1983, pp.
123–127. See too Austin, no. 31, pp. 57–59, and Harding 1985, no. 132, pp. 165–167 (Antigonus'
letter to Scepsis about the peace).

[108] Lund 1994, pp. 40–43; Anson 2014a, pp. 141–142.

[109] Strootman 2014a, pp. 315–316.

[110] Rosen 1968, pp. 205–207 (the end of the empire); Huss 2001, p. 168; Meeus 2014, p. 289.

[111] Errington 2008, p. 40.

[112] Simpson 1954, pp. 30–31; Mehl 1986, p. 137; Champion 2014, pp. 98–103.

Built into the settlement was also the proclamation of Greek freedom put forward by Antigonus and Ptolemy at the start of the war, to which all members swore. The freedom of the Greek cities was cynically exploited by the Successors, for anyone impeding Greek autonomy in any way would be at the mercy of others—it was, as has been noted, a "permanent *casus belli*, a convenient pretext to inflict war on less fortunate or propaganda-minded opponents."[113] As we shall see in the next chapter, Ptolemy exploited it the following year to declare war on Antigonus.

Antigonus still had at his disposal a large army, abundant supplies, and vast hoards of bullion, despite the loss of some of his territories. However, he was clearly not content to allow Seleucus to retain Babylon, for shortly after the settlement he began a series of attacks to oust him again (the so-called Babylonian War), but eventually in 309 he gave up, and the two men came to an agreement.[114] Likewise, by 310 Ptolemy was accusing Antigonus of unlawful attempts on cities in Cilicia, and calling on Lysimachus and Cassander to join with him against Antigonus, perhaps evidence that Ptolemy had been crafting his own plans even as he swore to uphold the settlement.[115]

What the Successors agreed to in 311 was to remain in force until the thirteen-year-old Alexander IV came of age.[116] However, a single Argead king ruling all territories and served by his satraps, as in the days of Alexander, was an impossibility now. As has been adroitly said: the Successors "read the treaty clause 'when Alexander comes of age' as 'if Alexander should come of age.'"[117] And in doing so, Alexander's death warrant was signed. In the spring of 310, Cassander conveniently forgot Olympias' act of regicide five years earlier, and had Alexander IV and Roxane poisoned by their jailer.[118] Alexander (at least) was buried in Aegae. That none of the other Successors tore strips off Cassander showed their tacit approval and relief—and the hypocrisy of politics, for Antigonus had earlier denounced Cassander for imprisoning Alexander and Roxane. Indeed, if Diodorus is to be trusted, "Cassander, Lysimachus, and Ptolemy, and Antigonus as well, were relieved of their anticipated danger from the king [that is, of his being released and ruling in his own right]; for henceforth, there being no longer anyone to inherit the realm, each of those who had rule over nations or cities entertained hopes of royal power and held the territory that had been placed under his

---

[113] Hauben 2014, p. 237; see too Dmitriev 2011, pp. 120–122.

[114] Watefield 2011, pp. 125–127.

[115] Diodorus 20.19.3–4, with Seibert 1969, pp. 176–183.

[116] Diodorus 19.105.1. Hölbl 2001, p. 19, suggests that he was approaching fourteen, and so would soon join the ranks of the royal pages, but this is unlikely as he was already king.

[117] Waterfield 2011, p. 129.

[118] Diodorus 19.105.2; see too Justin 15.2.5; Pausanias 9.7.2, with Hammond and Walbank 1988, pp. 164–167.

authority as if it were a kingdom won by the spear."[119] Again we see the justification of their right to rule based on military conquest.[120]

The same lack of reaction is true a year later when Heracles, the illegitimate son of Alexander, who had been suggested as a potential king at the Babylon conference in 323, was killed. Polyperchon had brought Heracles to Greece, hoping to use him to oust Cassander, but the latter made a deal with the now elderly Polyperchon, giving him lands in Macedonia and making him governor of the Peloponnese. In return, the contemptible Polyperchon ordered Heracles and his mother Barsine to be strangled to death.[121]

With Alexander's IV's death, the Argead dynasty ended, and so formally did the single Macedonian Empire, which had reached its zenith in the reigns of Philip II and Alexander. Significantly, and perhaps surprisingly, the remaining Successors—now no longer satraps—did not immediately proclaim themselves kings (basileis)—and in Babylonia and Egypt the regnal years of Alexander IV continued for several more years.[122] The Successors would wait another four years, until 306, before taking on the title of king. Perhaps they did so because it took time for them to get used to not serving an Argead king for the first time in their lives, and this was because of their own doing. Perhaps, even, no one actually dared to assume that title for fear the others would use the move against the person, until Antigonus, given his pretensions to empire, decided the time had come. The Successors were now absolute rulers based not on legitimacy but on their military power, and they were imperialists, always working to extend their possessions and maintain that military mastery.[123]

[119] Diodorus 19.105.3–4.
[120] Schmitthenner 1968; Caroli 2007, pp. 171–175.
[121] Diodorus 20.28.1–2; Justin 15.2.3 (before killing Alexander IV and Roxane); Pausanias 9.7.2 (poisoned). On the decision to kill Alexander and Heracles, and the order of these deeds: Hammond and Walbank 1988, pp. 165–168.
[122] Skeat 1954, p. 9.
[123] Billows 1990, pp. 241–248; Chaniotis 2005, pp. 57–68.

8

Alexander's Corpse

Ptolemy's hijacking of Alexander's corpse in 321 and its subsequent burial in Egypt were meant to give him an edge in the Wars of the Successors, and by extension promote Egypt's place in the world. So too was his completion of much of Alexandria and his founding of the famous Library and Museum there. In doing so, he set Egypt apart from any of the other Successor kingdoms throughout the Hellenistic and well into the Roman eras. But it was the pull of Alexander's name that endured the most. Three centuries after his death, in 30, Octavian, the future emperor Augustus, arrived in Alexandria, and was asked if he wanted to see the tombs of the Ptolemies, which lay next to that of Alexander. "I wish to see a king, not corpses," he supposedly replied.[1]

Stealing Alexander

Alexander's funeral cortege had finally set off on its long journey from Babylon to Aegae in probably September 321. It had been held up for so long because it had taken two years to build the elaborate hearse, a "small Ionic temple on wheels,"[2] carrying the king's body (Figure 8.1). The contemporary writer Hieronymus of Cardia described this hearse in detail, his account preserved by Diodorus.[3] It was 18 feet wide and 12 feet long, bedecked with jeweled columns, bells, and garlands, boasted the first-ever shock absorbers, and was pulled by 64 mules. Alexander's gold sarcophagus, draped in his purple robe, his weapons around it, was in its interior, hidden from view by a gold net, its

---

[1] Suetonius, *Augustus* 18.1; cf. Dio 51.16.5.

[2] Stewart 1993, p. 216.

[3] Diodorus 18.26–27; it is hardly a surprise that it was famous for its splendor, and attracted crowds of spectators along its route (Diodorus 18.28.1–2). See Stewart 1993, pp. 216–220, including a more detailed description of its ornateness; Erskine 2002, pp. 167–171; Seibert 1969, pp. 96–102, 110–112.

Figure 8.1 Alexander's hearse. © Drawing by Candace H. Smith

entrance to the chamber guarded by two gold lions. Greek, Macedonian, and
Asian artistry abounded on the vehicle. Over each side hung a spectacular
picture. One was of Alexander seated in a chariot flanked by Macedonian
Companions on one side and a Persian guard on the other. Another featured
war elephants carrying Indian soldiers with Macedonian infantry behind
them. A third depicted cavalry squadrons, and the final one was of a war fleet.
All the paintings were propaganda, signifying the power of the Macedonians
over their enemies (past, present, and even future), and also sending out a
warning message to potential rebels along the route to Greece.

At some point between late summer and winter of 321, Ptolemy took control of Alexander's funeral cortege at Damascus.[4] Evidently, Arrhidaeus (the
man in charge of the cortege) was taken by surprise, or he may even have made
some earlier pact with Ptolemy, for he offered him no resistance. Ptolemy

[4] Diodorus 18.28.2–3; Strabo 17.1.8; cf. Pausanias 1.6.3, with Erskine 2002, pp. 163–167. The
kidnapping was perhaps in winter as the cortege most likely set off from Babylon only after the
searing summer heat was dying down: Anson 1986, pp. 212–-217. On Ptolemy perhaps honoring
Alexander's wish to be buried in Egypt, see pp. 94–95.

returned with the body to Memphis, celebrating its arrival with games.[5] We never hear of the ornate hearse again.

There is a bizarre anecdote in a writer of the third century AD that Ptolemy swapped Alexander's corpse on the hearse for a dummy, which he dressed in the deceased king's clothes. When Perdiccas caught up to the cortege, Ptolemy fled back to Egypt, but Perdiccas did not pursue him because he believed he had saved Alexander's body. When he discovered he had been duped, it was too late to chase Ptolemy.[6] None of our other sources even hints of Ptolemy acting in this way, and it is safe to reject this story as a curiosity.

Ptolemy buried Alexander's body in Memphis, but his tomb was only a temporary one since Ptolemy intended to make Alexandria his capital. Certainly, "a few years later,"[7] he had Alexander's body transported to Alexandria, which must have been by 311 when the satrap stele tells us that he was living there (pp. 124–125). There is a tradition that his son Ptolemy II ordered his brother Argaeus to transfer Alexander's corpse from Memphis to Alexandria, but this is highly unlikely, and the accounts of our other ancient writers, that Ptolemy I moved it, are to be preferred.[8] Even more unlikely is that this Argaeus was an illegitimate son of Alexander the Great and Thais, whom Ptolemy raised, which explains why he, as Alexander's bastard son and Ptolemy's stepson, was entrusted with moving the body.[9]

It is surely the case that Ptolemy I took the body to Alexandria.[10] His action also fulfilled a prophecy that "the land that received the corpse would remain forever blessed and unravaged."[11] It paid off to listen to these prophecies. Alexander's undoing of the Gordian knot in 333 must have been psychologically demoralizing for the Persians, given the prophecy that whoever undid that knot was destined to rule Asia.[12] Ptolemy would have witnessed that. Now, Alexander's body gave him a source of authority for the Macedonian veterans, not to mention immense propaganda value, and showed his intention

---

[5] Thompson 1988, p. 4.

[6] Aelian, *Varia Historia* 12.64.

[7] Curtius 10.10.20; cf. Diodorus 18.28.3–4.

[8] Tradition: Pausanias 1.7.1; other accounts: Diodorus 18.28.3, 4; Curtius 10.10.20; Strabo 17.1.8. Greenwalt 1988 argued in favor of the Pausanias passage, but is demolished by Habicht 2006a, pp. 153–154. Pausanias does make mistakes on Ptolemaic matters; for example, see p. 203 (Ptolemy abdicates in favor of Ptolemy II).

[9] van Oppen de Ruiter 2013. Ptolemy's children: pp. 112–115.

[10] Bouché-Leclercq 1903, p. 142 n. 2; Fraser 1972, vol. 1, pp. 15–16, and vol. 2, pp. 31–33.

[11] Aelian, *Varia Historia* 12.64, with Fraser 1972, vol. 1, p. 16.

[12] For the myth's impact on the historical and legendary Alexander, see Ogden 2011, pp. 65–67, 76–77. See too Fredricksmeyer 1961.

to establish his own power and that of Egypt in the Hellenistic world.[13] We cannot overlook the implications of his careful burial of the body, which was the traditional task of a successor. As we have seen, his seizure of the royal corpse destroyed any semblance of relations with Perdiccas, who likewise claimed the body for the political advantages it gave him. In an attempt to retrieve it, he invaded Egypt, with disastrous consequences (see Chapter 6).

Ptolemy interred the body in a purpose-built mausoleum, which was called both *soma* (body) and *sema* (tomb), in Alexandria.[14] This would have been in the Brucheum district of the city (see below). We are told that Ptolemy IV Philopator (221–204) built a *sema*, and interred in it his mother and the previous three Ptolemaic kings alongside Alexander, and that it was part of the palace complex.[15] From then on, the *sema* became the burial place of all Ptolemaic rulers. Most likely, then, is that Ptolemy I built a tomb for Alexander, which was abandoned or demolished when Ptolemy IV built his new one to house his family and Alexander.[16] The mausoleum was part of the royal palace structure, as we know from the account of Strabo, who was living in Alexandria in the 20s BC and described the city in his day: "Also part of the royal palaces is the so-called *Soma*, which was an enclosure containing the tombs of the kings and that of Alexander."[17] The message of the multiple burial complex was clear: "living or dead, the Ptolemies were inseparable from Alexander."[18]

Ptolemy I had introduced a cult to Alexander in Memphis, although how the priests reacted to this, given that the city was Egypt's religious center, is not known.[19] After the move to Alexandria, Ptolemy had Alexander deified, and so worshipped there.[20] This is not surprising, as Alexander had founded the city, and traditionally the founder of a city (*ktistes*) was so revered. An eponymous priesthood was also set up (one priest was Ptolemy's brother Menelaus), as were statues of Alexander in various parts of the city. Ptolemy's actions were less for piety and more for politics, of course: the *sema*, statues, and cult of Alexander would constantly remind people of Ptolemy's connection to Alexander and

---

[13] Cf. Meeus 2008, pp. 67–68, and 2014, pp. 273–277. I disagree with his view (2014, pp. 276–277) that taking the body was less likely to appeal to Ptolemy's soldiers, since the troops had mutinied at the Hyphasis River in 326 and at Opis in 324, wanting to go home, and therefore they would not have been enthused at staying in Egypt. Meeus does not take into account that the army by 323 was very different in composition, and many of its troops were from the east: see Bosworth 1980b.

[14] Fraser 1972, vol. 1, pp. 15–17, 225–226; Stewart 1993, chap. 8.

[15] Ptolemy IV: Zenobius 3.94; location: Strabo 17.1.8, with Łukaszewicz 2014, pp. 198–200.

[16] Fraser 1972, vol. 1, p. 16; Stewart 1993, p. 224 n. 97.

[17] Strabo 17.1.8.

[18] Erskine 2002, p. 165.

[19] Taylor 1927. On this and the following, see Seibert 1983, pp. 226–227; Fraser 1972, vol. 1, pp. 215–226; Stewart 1993, pp. 243–245.

[20] Fraser 1972, vol. 1, pp. 215–219.

thus the Argeads. They gave his rule a "special aura of authority,"[21] and as a result, the *sema* attracted visitors throughout history and enabled Alexandria to become a focal point in the Hellenistic world.

Alexander's body, then, was of profound importance to Ptolemy, but subsequent Ptolemaic rulers and even the Alexandrines themselves held it in equal esteem.[22] Further, Ptolemy's actions attracted people to move to Egypt as civilians and soldiers, which was a boost to the Egyptian economy and armed forces as well as his own personal prestige. Diodorus neatly summed up this aspect: "Entombing [Alexander] and honoring him with heroic sacrifices and magnificent games, [Ptolemy] won fair recompense, not only from men but also from the gods. For because of his graciousness and nobility men eagerly came from all sides to Alexandria, and gladly enrolled in his army."[23]

Alexandria

Now Egypt's second largest city with a population of about 4.5 million people, Alexandria was founded officially on April 7, 331, by Alexander the Great.[24] It was the capital of Hellenistic, Roman, and Byzantine Egypt for a thousand years until AD 641, when the Muslims conquered Egypt, and founded what became the new capital of Cairo. The power of Alexandria in the Hellenistic period is reflected by the fact that by the mid-second century the city was referred to as Alexandria *by* (not "in") Egypt.[25] The very country in which it was located seemed to rank second place to its capital city; it was as if Alexandria were an independent polis along the Greek model, rather than the country's capital. In fact, it was both: since Alexandria was created from scratch by Alexander, it was always going to be a Greek city, and in essence it remained one, despite its diverse population and reputation as a cultural melting pot.[26]

After Alexander had moved into Egypt and received the country's surrender from its Persian satrap Mazaces, he had set off from Memphis to visit the Oracle of Zeus Ammon at the oasis of Siwah. He broke the journey at coastal Lake Mareotis, about a dozen miles west of the Canopic mouth of the Nile, where a

---

[21] Hammond and Walbank 1988, p. 123, citing Diodorus 18.28.4–5. Statues: Stewart 1993, pp. 243–252; cult: Fraser 1972, vol. 1, pp. 215–226.

[22] Erskine 2002, pp. 163–167.

[23] Diodorus 18.28.4.

[24] Fraser 1972, vol. 1, pp. 3–6; Bagnall 1979, pp. 46–49.

[25] Bell 1946.

[26] Bouché-Leclercq 1903, pp. 121–140; Bevan 1927, pp. 91–104; Tarn and Griffith 1952, pp. 183–186; Fraser 1972; Bernand 1995; Grimm 1998; Pollard and Reid 2009; Hinge and Krasilnikoff 2009; cf. Bowman 1986, pp. 203–233; Caroli 2007, pp. 258–304.

narrow isthmus connected the lake to the Mediterranean.[27] Almost a mile offshore lay a narrow, three-mile-long island, named Pharos, which was mentioned
in Homer.[28] When Alexander came to the area and saw its strategic location for
trade and commerce, he recounted the lines of Homer and decided to found a city,
which he would connect to the Nile by a canal, and build a mole out to Pharos to
create a harbor on each side of the mole.[29] This was in similar fashion to the way he
had linked Tyre to the mainland with a mole during his siege of that city.

Alexander may have intended his new foundation to be only a trading one
with the entire Mediterranean basin. In this respect he may have wanted to
build an equivalent of Tyre, given the latter's commercial supremacy.[30] At the
same time, he recognized the area's strategic location for defensive purposes.
In other words, the famed Alexandria of the Hellenistic period may not have
been anything like the young conqueror had envisaged, but was due more
to Ptolemy's vision, his need to increase revenues, and his exploitation of
Alexander's name.[31] In the process, Memphis, the traditional capital of Egypt
since the Old Kingdom (2686–2125 BC), was eclipsed, which was to be expected as its position so far south was hardly suited for a commercial and economic capital, as Alexandria was intended to be.

The sources dispute when Alexander actually planned the city. Arrian
and Plutarch, drawing on Ptolemy, claim that he drew up plans when he first
stopped at the site en route to Siwah, while Diodorus, Curtius, and Justin,
based on Aristobulus, put this on the return journey.[32] There is also a tradition
that Alexander himself came up with the actual layout of the city:[33]

> [Alexander] ordered his architects to trace the circuit of the city to
> be founded. But as they had no clay to do so, he happened to see a
> threshing-floor with wheat on it and ordered them to place the grains
> around and use them instead of clay in marking he circuit. They did so.
> The following night fowls came and picked up the grain. This seemed

[27] Diodorus 17.52.1 says the site was home to the small fishing town of Rhacotis when
Alexander came across it.

[28] Homer, Odyssey 4.354–355: "There is then an island in the midst of the stormy sea, in front
of Egypt; Pharos they call it."

[29] Austin, no. 7, pp. 17–18 (= Arrian 3.1.5–2.2, Plutarch, Alexander 26.3–10).

[30] Bevan 1927, p. 4.

[31] Howe 2014.

[32] Diodorus 17.49.2–52.7; Arrian 3.3.1–4.5; Curtius 4.7.5–4.8.2; Justin 11.11.13; Plutarch,
Alexander 26.6, with Fraser 1972, vol. 1, pp. 3–6. Welles 1962 argues that Alexander went to
Siwah to ask the oracle about where he should found a new city, but this is wrong: Ellis 1994,
pp. 85–86 (n. 24); Hölbl 2001, p. 10. On the sources for the founding, see Howe 2014, pp. 74–77.

[33] Anonymous History of Alexander, FGrH 151 F 11, trans. Robinson 1953, ad loc.

to be a sign: some said it portended ill (the city to be founded would
be captured); Alexander however said it was a good omen (though it
was made clear that many would be fed by that city) and at once built
a large city there, which he called Alexandria, after his own name.

Diodorus even says that he designed the streets to take advantage of the Etesian
winds and so keep the city cool.[34] If Alexander had done any such planning,
he may have focused only on the area of the harbors, with his eye to trade and
defense, rather than on the actual streets and neighborhoods of the city.

   As designer and to oversee construction, Alexander appointed the leading
architect of the day, Deinocrates of Rhodes.[35] Whether the king wanted his
new foundation to have all the trappings of a Greek city—including an agora,
a gymnasium (a training facility and a place for social and intellectual gather-
ings), an odeum for music, a theater, and sanctuaries for Greek gods—is unknown, but all these date from Ptolemaic times. They may well have had their
origins in Ptolemy's desire to exploit Alexander's association with Alexandria
as part of his bid to rival the other Successors and to promote Greek civilization in Egypt, just as Alexander had brought Greek civilization to Asia.[36]
Against this background, we can understand why Ptolemy wanted to move the
country's capital to there and to bury Alexander in it—and to make it a great
intellectual center with the Museum and the Library (see below).

   How much of Alexandria was built in the decade or so from its foundation
date to when Ptolemy moved to Egypt is not known. Since Cleomenes, the
satrap of Egypt, had been instructed to make sure construction proceeded at
a goodly pace when Alexander left Egypt, a great deal of the city may have
been built. The mole connecting Pharos to the mainland must been con-
structed since it was intended to protect the twin harbors that it created, the
westerly (man-made) one for commerce (Eunostus, "happy returns"), and the
easterly (natural) one for war. The mole was called the *heptastadion* because
it was seven stades (about seven-eighths of a mile) long; over the centuries,
silt built up around the mole, so that what used to be the island is now part of
the mainland (similar to what used to be the island city of Tyre). Also built
were the major roads, waterways underneath them, and several buildings
at least. Cleomenes may even have built a mint in the fledgling city, which
Ptolemy would have taken over when he moved there.[37] Unfortunately, little

[34] Diodorus 17.52.2.
[35] Mansuelli 1983.
[36] Howe 2014. Alexander and Greek civilization: Austin, no. 19, pp. 35–37 (= Plutarch, *Moralia* 328c–329d).
[37] Fraser 1972, vol. 1, p. 7.

of Ptolemy's Alexandria remains—as does, in fact, little of the city throughout the Ptolemaic era, as most of the archaeological evidence is from the Roman period.[38]

Ptolemy clearly added to the city, and perhaps the detailed description by the first-century geographer Strabo helps us to deduce its ground plan in Ptolemy's time (Figure 8.2).[39] Alexandria was laid out in a rectangle four miles long from east to west and three-quarters of a mile from north to south. It had two major roads, one running north-south (from the sea to Lake Mareotis) and the other running east-west (the Canopic, from the Canopus Gate in the east to another gate in the west), which thus cut the city into quarters.[40] Each of these roads was one hundred feet wide (an unprecedented width compared to the narrow streets of mainland Greek cities), and both roads would pre-sumably have been completed by the time Ptolemy moved to Egypt, together with the structures that lined them, such as houses, shops, and colonnades. So too would have been the various public buildings, such as law courts, theater, and the gymnasium, which were grouped into a square where the two roads crossed in the center of the city.[41] The city was very much a multicultural one, even in Ptolemy's day, with the different ethnic races in the city living in three separate districts, all speaking their own languages: the native Egyptians in the Rhakotis, the Greeks and Macedonians in the Brucheum, and the Jews (speaking Hebrew or Aramaic) in their own area. At the same time, these quarters effectively segregated the different populations and emphasized the superiority of the Macedonians and Greeks, who lived in the more exclusive Brucheum district, home to the royal palace, Museum, and Library.

What had not been built when Ptolemy first moved into Egypt was the great temple to Sarapis, the new god he introduced to help unite his Greek and Egyptian peoples (Chapter 11), the *sema* to house Alexander's body, the Museum, Library, and lighthouse on Pharos, a cemetery (outside the city walls), and the protective walls.[42] He did not proceed with a temple to Hephaestion, Alexander's boyhood friend, assuming Arrian is correct that Alexander ordered Cleomenes to build one there in honor of his deceased com-panion.[43] Since no ancient writer suggests that Alexander ever intended to take

---

[38] Łukaszewicz 2014.

[39] Strabo 17.1.6-10 (= Austin, no. 232, pp. 388–392 abr.), with Fraser 1972, vol. 1, pp. 7–37 (through to late Ptolemaic times).

[40] Fraser 1972, vol. 1, pp. 7–37.

[41] The civic structure of the city—its constitution—is not fully known: Fraser 1972, vol. 1, pp. 93–131.

[42] Diodorus 17.5.2–3 and Arrian 3.1.5 say that Alexander planned city walls, and Tactitus, *Histories* 4.83.1, that it was Ptolemy who built them.

[43] Arrian 7.23.6–8.

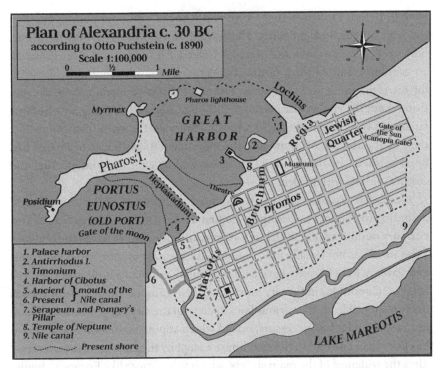

Figure 8.2 City plan of Alexandria. William Shepherd, *Historical Atlas* (New York: Henry Holt, 1911), pp. 34–35. Courtesy of the University of Texas Libraries, The University of Texas at Austin. Perry-Castañeda Library Map Collection. Used under the Creative Commons License.

up residence in Alexandria, it is safe to assume that a palace that would have befitted him was never built. Perhaps one of the reasons why Ptolemy stayed in Memphis so long was that he was waiting for the palace in Alexandria, which faced north over the harbor toward the Mediterranean, to be built for him.

Alexandria was one of three Greek cities in Egypt, the others being Naucratis and Ptolemais.[44] Naucratis had been founded for trading purposes in the sixth century. Ptolemais in Upper Egypt (to the south, on the site of an ancient village named Psoï) was founded by Ptolemy and named after himself; it was the farthest south he ever traveled, and clearly was meant to spread Ptolemaic control along the entire Nile Valley.[45] It became his capital of Upper Egypt, and with its own constitution and elected officials it too was a Greek polis.

Alexandria dominated everywhere, though. Naucratis' pull as a commercial center declined as that of Alexandria grew, and Ptolemais always lived in the capital city's shadow. But Alexandria's sway extended outside Egypt

[44] Bevan 1927, pp. 90–91, 104–108; Rowlandson 2003, p. 254; Caroli 2007, pp. 304–308.
[45] Thompson 2003, p. 106.

as well. Before Ptolemy's time, Tyre and Rhodes had monopolized trade in the Aegean, but their influence diminished as Alexandria, thanks to its harbors, grew in importance and prestige. Indeed, Alexandria was more than just an economic and cultural center; thanks to Ptolemy, it became a blueprint for town planning and the public and administrative organization of cities throughout the Hellenistic period.[46] Although Alexandria really only became famous in the Hellenistic world after Ptolemy's death, when institutions like the Library and the Museum and the monumental lighthouse of Pharos had been finished, the origins of its greatness and its enormous intellectual and cultural pull lie with Ptolemy.[47]

Alexandria was also the largest and most civilized city in the known world according to Diodorus, writing in the first century BC, who states that its free citizenry numbered 300,000. If this is true, and allowing for wives and children (who were free but usually not counted with men as part of a free population) and slaves, we could easily have a total population of half a million at the city's height.[48] Conditions in the city must have been cramped, though. Ptolemy was likely responsible for the various laws to do with the city's organization that we hear about under his successors, one of which stipulated that no house was to be closer than one foot to the next house except by the consent of the owners.[49] Thus the wideness of the main streets, which sound more like European boulevards, was in sharp contrast to the cramped housing conditions and side streets.

One thing that Alexandria lacked was security. Unlike Memphis to the south, Alexandria (and Egypt) was vulnerable to attack from the Mediterranean. Nevertheless, Ptolemy did not give a second thought to making it his capital; his reasoning was entirely political—to give him an edge in the Wars of the Successors. First, the city had an intimate connection with Alexander the Great, which Ptolemy further capitalized on by burying the conqueror and instituting a cult to him there. Although many of the Successors did name or rename cites after Alexander, none had the pull of Alexandria.

Second, a new capital symbolized a new rule. Ptolemy was with Alexander in 330 when the ceremonial palace at Persepolis burned to the ground. That destruction was meant to symbolize "out with the old and in with the new": the era of the Great Kings of Persia was gone; in its place was Macedonian rule.

[46] Caroli 2007, pp. 278–280. On the importance of cities and changes in their structure in the Hellenistic world, see Billows 2003 and Graham, Shipley, and Hansen 2006.

[47] Bouché-Leclercq 1903, pp. 121–140; Bevan 1927, pp. 91–104; Hazzard 2000, pp. 36–46; Łukaszewicz 2014, pp. 201–205.

[48] Population: Fraser 1972, vol. 1, pp. 38–92.

[49] For a translated part of Alexandrian city laws of the mid-third century, see Bagnall and Derow 1981, no. 104.

Likewise, moving Egypt's capital from Memphis to Alexandria proclaimed a new era and a new ruling dynasty. That was why he went to such lengths in his *History* to associate the founding with Alexander, even going so far as to say that the conqueror himself laid out the ground plan, which allowed Ptolemy—literally—to build on it.[50]

Third, Alexandria was a Greek city, something Ptolemy consciously encouraged as a means of appealing to his Greek and Macedonian subjects. It became, then, part of his policy of administering and controlling Egypt.[51] Finally, perhaps differing from Alexander's original intention, Ptolemy wanted Alexandria to be a great intellectual center, greater than any city any of his rivals might found or enhance. Throughout the Classical period, Athens had been the intellectual and cultural center of the Greek world; Ptolemy wanted his Alexandria to be the scholarly heart of the entire Mediterranean world.

We tend to think of the Library and the Museum as the scholarly hub of Alexandria, with their groundbreaking literary and especially scientific accomplishments. But there was also an influential Alexandrian school of art, excelling in wall painting and mosaics (as had artists in these media back home in Macedonia). The Alexandrian artists borrowed from Egyptian models to form an artistic "duality," and in turn they influenced Roman artists.[52]

The Museum and the Library

Ptolemy's other famous additions to Alexandria were the Museum (*Mouseion*, literally the sanctuary of the Muses), the Library, and the lighthouse at Pharos. Exactly when he began work on them is unknown, but they were all unfinished on his death, and were completed in the reign of Ptolemy II.[53] The Museum and the Library, set in spacious gardens and walled off from the general population, were located close to the royal palace area and the tomb of Alexander in the northern Brucheum district, the area in which the Macedonians and Greeks lived.[54] Whether the Museum and the Library were separate buildings or were joined together in one is unknown, but each was a distinct entity with its own scholars and officials; together they functioned as a center of learning

---

[50] Arrian 3.1.5, with Howe 2014, pp. 77–78.

[51] Caroli 2007, pp. 258–304, especially pp. 264–273. On administration, see Chapter 11.

[52] Whitehouse 2010, especially pp. 1017–1020 on mosaics.

[53] Bevan 1927, pp. 124–127; Fraser 1972, vol. 1, pp. 321–322, 469, 475; Pfeiffer 1968, pp. 95–102.

[54] Strabo 17.1.8; on them, see Fraser 1972, vol. 1, pp. 305–335.

and teaching for a community of scholars that produced some of the finest literary and scientific work of antiquity.

The Museum, as its literal name suggests, was a shrine to the Muses, who were said to inspire man's creative and intellectual thoughts. It was not a museum in the modern sense of the word, but was in essence a religious institution, devoted to mathematics and science.[55] Strabo gives us a good description of the building in his time, and it might not have changed greatly from Ptolemy's design: it had a covered walkway, meeting rooms, lecture rooms, gardens, and a dining room for those who lived and worked there.[56] Interestingly, Strabo does not mention the Library, which might indicate that it was part of the same building, and people generally referred to both institutions as the Museum. The Library was not just a repository of works, which were written on papyrus scrolls housed on open shelves (ancient stacks), with labels to identify them, and were catalogued; it was also a center for studying literature and (to use the modern term) literary criticism.

In setting up the Museum and the Library, Ptolemy was ably helped by Demetrius of Phalerum, Cassander's puppet ruler of Athens from 317 to 307 (pp. 109–110).[57] After Demetrius (Antigonus' son) expelled him from Athens, Demetrius of Phalerum ended up in Alexandria in 297, where he befriended Ptolemy. The latter had unsuccessfully tried to lure Theophrastus, Aristotle's successor as head of the Lyceum in Athens, to Alexandria, and so settled for his student, Demetrius. He gave Demetrius a great deal of money to start collecting books for the Library and appointed him overseer of the intellectual life of the Museum. His bid for Theophrastus and the trust he placed in Demetrius indicate that Ptolemy was attracted to Aristotle's school in Athens, with its focus on learning and inquiry. In fact, the Lyceum was its own Mouseion, as it had a shrine to the Muses and a library.[58] It is perhaps too much of a coincidence that Ptolemy wanted the same in Egypt—actually not the same, but better. Perhaps Ptolemy's preoccupation with Aristotelian philosophy and teaching is a sign that Aristotle had tutored him along with the young Alexander. If so, it was an experience Ptolemy never forgot, and he made arrangements for his son and heir to be tutored by one of the Aristotelian school, Strato of Lampsacus.

Why did Ptolemy want these centers of learning? Several reasons come to the fore, all interlinked. On one level, he was following in the tradition of

[55] Fraser 1972, vol. 1, pp. 312–319.
[56] Strabo 17.1.8. See, for example, Parsons 1952; Canfora 1990; MacLeod 2000; Caroli 2007, pp. 284–291; Pollard and Reid 2009; Berti and Costa 2010; cf. Ellis 1994, pp. 54–57, Green 1990, pp. 84–91.
[57] Fraser 1972, vol. 1, pp. 312–335; Caroli 2007, pp. 284–286.
[58] Green 1990, p. 85; Erskine 1995, pp. 39–40.

Macedonian kings, who patronized intellectuals and attempted to give their courts a literary or artistic bent. King Archelaus, for example, managed to lure Euripides to his court, Perdiccas III patronized Plato's Academy in Athens, and Philip II enjoyed contacts with leading Athenian orators and philosophers such as Isocrates and Speusippus, and had hired Aristotle to tutor Alexander. Ptolemy, although first and foremost a soldier, was interested in writing— his history of Alexander's exploits was a major, albeit misguided, source for Arrian's later account of Alexander's reign (Appendix 1). Nevertheless, it too played a role in stimulating Alexandria's intellectual life.

A significant difference between the intellectual tradition of these kings and Ptolemy's initiative was patronage: with the exception of Euclid (see below), Ptolemy was not inviting prominent intellectuals to his court as a sort of "artist in residence" scheme; he was sponsoring scholarly activity in existing intellectual institutions.[59] In other words, he wanted great minds to be attracted to what the Museum and the Library offered as research centers. Of course it did not hurt that those who worked there were paid handsome salaries (which were not taxed) and enjoyed free board and lodgings. But Ptolemy had introduced a subtle twist, and here we can see the ancestor of the modern think tank or research center, with people free to pursue their own research, receiving pay, room and board, and gathering to eat together and for other social activities.

By exploiting the link with Aristotle, Ptolemy may well have been further associating himself with Alexander to legitimize his position in Egypt. Moreover, the institutions gave the Greek inhabitants of Egypt a connection to their own heritage in an alien country, which had its own history and culture.[60]

Of course there was always politics at work—the mainstay of the Hellenistic period—not to mention later competition with rival libraries (see below).[61] Ptolemy intended his Museum and Library to counterbalance Egyptian and Greek literary and scientific knowledge, and even art; it was to be a center of learning and teaching that would associate it uniquely with the Ptolemies. He wanted to boast the greatest repository of works from as many cultures as possible that had been translated into Greek for his world. Furthermore, he wanted those who worked there to publish their writings, from local history to poetry to mathematics to science, as significant additions to existing scholarship. No other Successor in his lifetime could match him in these regards, thus showing that the Museum and the Library were as much political institutions as they were intellectual ones.

---

[59] Erskine 1995, p. 40.
[60] Erskine 1995, pp. 41–43; cf. Peremans 1976; Caroli 2007, pp. 284–304.
[61] Erskine 1995, pp. 38–48.

To ensure the Museum's protection and to stimulate research work, there was a special priest of the Muses, appointed by Ptolemy himself.[62] The chief librarian and Museum director were usually the most eminent scholars, and often the appointment went hand in hand with tutoring the royal children. Those who worked in the Museum covered all fields of scientific knowledge, including mathematics, physics, astronomy, and medicine, whose work had a lasting impact even today.[63] One of these men, Euclid, Ptolemy personally patronized—the only case of individual sponsorship, as opposed to the ongoing institutional patronage as noted earlier. Euclid wrote the *Elements of Geometry* in thirteen books at Alexandria. The story goes that Ptolemy found the work too difficult and asked if there was an easier way to master it, to which Euclid replied that there was no royal road to geometry.[64] This was a reference to the famous Royal Road of the Persian Empire, which linked Sardis to faraway Susa and was meant to facilitate quicker and easier travel.

Other great names in the life of the Museum included Heron (who invented a steam engine); Aristarchus of Samos (an astronomer, whose work on the planetary system influenced Archimedes' view that the planets orbit the sun); Herophilus (the father of anatomy, who dissected corpses and greatly added to knowledge of the brain, eye, liver, and sex organs); and Eratosthenes of Cyrene (the father of geography, and the first person to identify prime numbers and to calculate the earth's circumference). Archimedes himself spent some time in Alexandria before going to Syracuse, from where he remained in contact with Alexandrian scholars.

The first chief librarian was, surprisingly, not Demetrius of Phalerum, but Zenodotus of Ephesus (a grammarian and Homeric scholar), who was appointed in 284, toward the end of Ptolemy's life. Demetrius continued writing philosophical and literary works at the Library, including his treatise *On Fortune*, which argued that Fortune had bestowed on the Macedonians all the wealth of Persia, but warned them that the same Fortune could just as easily take it away at any time. Other literary giants included Strato of Lampsacus (a philosopher and tutor to the future Ptolemy II); Apollonius of Rhodes (who wrote the *Argonautica*, succeeded Zenodotus as chief librarian, and tutored the future Ptolemy III); Aristophanes of Byzantium (a Homeric scholar and grammarian; also a chief librarian); and Callimachus of Cyrene (who under Ptolemy II first catalogued the contents of the Library, known as the *Pinakes* or "*Tables*," in 120 volumes).

[62] Strabo 17.1.8.
[63] Alexandrian science: Fraser 1972, vol. 1, pp. 336–446.
[64] Proclus, *Commentary on Euclid Book 1*, 68.

Men such as these were responsible for introducing the basic tenets of literary criticism that guide us today. Among other things, they studied the Homeric poems to try to determine whether there was only one Homer or whether his poems were fashioned by multiple poets, and they came up with a more definitive text.[65] Their commentaries on the poems and analyses of their language and other textual problems paved the way for Homeric scholars in the Renaissance and beyond. The emphasis on Homer, who held a special place in Greek life and education, supports the view noted earlier that the Museum and the Library provided a cultural link for the Greeks living in Egypt to their heritage.

All foreign works had to be translated into Greek before they were included in the Library's collection, and there is even a tradition that Ptolemy II began the translation of the Old Testament (Hebrew Bible) into Greek (which became known as the Septuagint). This translation practice has a downside, highlighting the cultural gap between Greek and non-Greek. In fact, in early Ptolemaic Egypt, scholars and intellectuals were attracted to Alexandria more often than not from within the Ptolemaic sphere of influence, especially Cyrene, Cos, and Samos. No Egyptian scholars are found at the Library until closer toward the middle of the third century, even though Ptolemy kept company with them. They included the historian and priest Manetho, whose *Aegyptiaca* (*History of Egypt*) is of fundamental importance for the reigns of the Pharaohs.[66] Yet Greek literature in Alexandria, indeed in Egypt, throughout the entire Ptolemaic period incorporated Egyptian traditions, and by fusing both cultures together, rather than highlighting divisions, appealed to Greeks as well as Greek-speaking Egyptians (like Manetho).[67]

Ptolemy laid the foundations of the Library's future greatness, but it was under Ptolemy II that it became the biggest repository of works in the known world—the ancestor of the British Library and Library of Congress. Ptolemy II had an army of scribes, who were responsible for borrowing books and copying them from around the world. They used a reed pen and an ink made from vegetable gum, soot, and water, and meticulously copied texts onto papyrus scrolls, the papyrus being a plant found all over the Nile delta. They wrote on the papyrus leaf in vertical columns, and more leaves were added (using the natural gum of the papyrus to attach them) depending on the length of the text. When finished, the entire papyrus copy was rolled up on a stick. To

---

[65] See Bouché-Leclercq 1903, pp. 121–140; Barker 1954; Pfeiffer 1968, pp. 87–233; Fraser 1972, vol. 1, pp. 447–479; Turner 1984, pp. 171–174; Caroli 2007, pp. 292–298; Morrison 2010; Rihll 2010.

[66] Peremans 1976; Caroli 2007, pp. 168–170.

[67] Morrison 2010, pp. 758–778.

read the text, the scroll was held in the left hand, and unrolled with the right. Ptolemy III was manic in his collection of works: it was said that any and every book found on ships that docked in Alexandria was confiscated, copied (the originals were marked "from the ships"), and only the copies returned to the owners.[68] At its height, the Library was said to have held several hundred thousand papyrus scrolls, which is a staggering number when one thinks that all of them were written by hand.

When Julius Caesar went to Egypt in 48, he was said to have deliberately set fire to the Library, destroying thousands of papyrus rolls. Whether he was guilty of one of the greatest acts of vandalism in world history or whether the Library caught fire by some other means is unknown. But because of that fire, we have only a fraction of the many Greeks works that were copied.

What one has, others want. Important libraries were later founded at Antioch by the Seleucid kings after Ptolemy's death and, more famously, at Pergamum by Attalus I (241–197) and his son Eumenes II (197–169).[69] A fierce rivalry developed between the libraries at Alexandria and Pergamum, which led to Egypt banning the export of papyrus in an effort to stop the Pergamene scholars from copying texts. Instead, the latter simply switched to sheepskin. Still, no other library could match that of Alexandria in reputation or longevity.

The Pharos Lighthouse

According to one ancient source, when Pyrrhus returned to Epirus in 297, Ptolemy began construction of a huge white limestone or marble lighthouse on the eastern end of the island of Pharos after it had been joined to the mainland by the mole (*heptastadion*).[70] Since the water was shallow and strewn with rocks close to the entrance to the eastern harbor, a lighthouse made perfect sense to help steer ships safely into harbor. At the same time, the structure could have had a military function as a signal or warning tower.[71] The lighthouse cost the enormous sum of 800 talents. It was the first of its kind and was quickly copied, so again we can credit Ptolemy with an innovation that has come down to us today. At over 400 feet tall, the lighthouse was enormous; in fact, only the Great Pyramid at Giza (480 feet) eclipsed it in height at that time. Built in three, tapering sections, a statue of Zeus the Savior sat atop the

---

[68] Fraser 1972, vol. 1, p. 325.

[69] Pfeiffer 1968, pp. 234–251; Hansen 1971, pp. 390–433.

[70] *Suda*, s.v. Pharos. See further, Fraser 1972, vol. 1, pp. 17–20, with p. 21 on the *heptastadion*; Rihll 2010, pp. 412–413; Łukaszewicz 2014, pp. 201–204.

[71] Łukaszewicz 2014, pp. 203–204.

Figure 8.3 The Pharos lighthouse. © Album / Art Resource, New York.

structure (Figure 8.3).[72] The light from its top (situated just below the statue) came from a furnace at night and from a mirror reflecting the sun's rays by day, and it could be seen almost forty miles away.[73]

The lighthouse thus gave Alexandria a tremendous "wow factor" as people sailed into the harbor, and it is no surprise that it was one of the seven wonders of the ancient world.[74] It stood for almost an entire millennium until an earthquake in AD 1323 destroyed it.

There is a tradition that a man named Sostratus from Cnidus was responsible for its construction, which included its costs.[75] Certainly the dedication on the lighthouse names him: "Sostratus the Cnidian, friend of the sovereigns, dedicated this, for the sake of the safety of those who sail the seas." Sostratus was probably Ptolemy II's ambassador at Delos in the 270s, in which case he was not the lighthouse's architect (whose identity is unknown), but a wealthy

[72] The identification of the god is controversial: Fraser 1972, vol. 1, pp. 18–19.
[73] Josephus, *Jewish War* 4.10.5, says 300 stadia, so about 37 miles.
[74] Clayton 1988.
[75] Strabo 17.1.6.

courtier who took up the plan of Ptolemy I, and as a gift to the city brought it to completion in Ptolemy II's reign.[76]

Overall, Alexandria's splendor was unparalleled; its buildings became famous, and no other Hellenistic city could match it as an intellectual center. It was thus the ultimate symbol of Ptolemaic grandeur and wealth.

[76] Meeus 2015.

9

From Satrap to King

The settlement of 311 was doomed to fail, not least because Antigonus' continued moves fostered suspicion on the part of the Successors toward him and each other.[1] However, the wrecking ball came the following year, when Ptolemy embarked on a series of campaigns to include control of Macedonia and Greece. Ptolemy was always suspicious of Antigonus, and had even reached out to Cassander and Lysimachus to join him in limiting Antigonus' power before it was too late.[2] In 310 he decided to move against Antigonid bases in Cilicia and Cyprus, followed by a personal campaign in southern Asia Minor. Then the opportunity presented itself for him to intervene actively in Greek affairs when quarrels erupted between Antigonus' two sons, Demetrius and Philip, and his nephew, Polemaeus, who was in charge of the Antigonid forces in Greece, and who had suddenly allied with Cassander. By 308 we find Ptolemy in Greece itself, and making his own bid for the throne of Macedonia. His campaigns in these years had nothing to do with shoring up Egypt's defenses, nor were they merely to outdo his old rival: they were openly imperialistic.[3]

Ptolemy the Imperialist

In 310 Ptolemy charged Antigonus with illegally garrisoning cities, thus breaking the "freedom clause" of the 311 settlement, and prepared for war against him.[4] He sent his general Leonides into Cilicia to conquer the cities

[1] Cf. Diodorus 20.19.3, with Huss 2001, p. 166.

[2] Diodorus 20.19.4, with Seibert 1969, pp. 176–183.

[3] On the campaign and his ambition, see Seibert 1969, pp. 186–189; Bosworth 2000; Huss 2001, pp. 166–180; Grabowski 2008; Waterfield 2011, pp. 131–132; Hauben 2014, who describes these years as "the least transparent and the most intriguing" (p. 235); Lane Fox 2014, pp. 180–190; Meeus 2014.

[4] Diodorus 20.19.3–4, with Seibert 1969, pp. 184–185; Caroli 2007, pp. 57–58; Dmitriev 2011, p. 128.

that Antigonus controlled there. Ptolemy was probably spurred to act as he did because Antigonus at the time was busy with Seleucus in the east, which kept both of them out of Egyptian affairs. Demetrius, however, was able to overcome Leonides' troops, who retreated (or were recalled) from the area; nevertheless, Ptolemy had made his presence known in the eastern Mediterranean. He had more success on Cyprus, where he had appointed his brother Menelaus as king of Salamis (succeeding Nicocreon, who had died in 311).[5] Ptolemy was concerned that Nicocles, king of Paphos, had made an alliance with Antigonus, who might use the island against him, given its strategic location. Menelaus and his troops had supported two of Ptolemy's friends, Argaeus and Callicrates, who forced Nicocles to commit suicide for intriguing with Antigonus.[6] Paphos was the wealthiest of Cyprus's cities, and its influence extended over most of the western half of the island. Thus Ptolemy ended up controlling virtually all of Cyprus, in the process netting abundant timber supplies for his fleet.[7]

In the summer of 309, Ptolemy himself marched into Lycia, in southwest Asia Minor.[8] He won over Phaselis and Xanthus (in which Antigonus had installed a garrison), and then sailed to Caria, where he captured Caunus (also home to an Antigonid garrison), Myndus (on the coast of Asia Minor opposite the island of Cos), and perhaps also Iasus, before moving to Cos, located on the "border" of the eastern Mediterranean and the Aegean Sea.[9] He set up camp on the island for the winter of 309, during which time his pregnant wife Berenice, who had accompanied him on his campaign, gave birth to his son Ptolemy (the future Ptolemy II).[10] But Ptolemy was not content merely to play the role of new father that winter. He summoned Polemaeus, commander of Antigonus' troops in Greece, to him. Polemaeus had recently sent troops to the satrap of Hellespontine Phrygia, Phoenix, which the latter was using to garrison several Greek cities.[11] Ptolemy seems to have wanted to use Polemaeus against Antigonus in some way, but after an argument he had

---

[5] Nicocreon of Salamis should not be confused with Nicocles of Paphos, as sometimes happens: Bagnall 1976, pp. 39–42; Gesche 1974; on Nicocreon and Menelaus, see too Hauben 1987a, p. 224.

[6] Diodorus 20.21, with Bagnall 1976, pp. 39–40; Daszewski 1987.

[7] Cf. *Parian Marble, BNJ* 239 B17. Only Soloi was autonomous, which was ruled anyway by Ptolemy's son-in-law Eunestus: Hauben 1987a, pp. 217–222; cf. Caroli 2007, pp. 86–87.

[8] Diodorus 20.27, with Bouché-Leclercq 1903, p. 61; Caroli 2007, pp. 58–59.

[9] Cos and Myndus: Diodorus 20.37.1–3, with Wörrle 1977, p. 54. Iasus: Bagnall 1976, pp. 89–91; Garlan 1975; Giovannini 2004; Dmitriev 2011, pp. 125–126; Hauben 2014, p. 246.

[10] *Parian Marble, BNJ* 239 B 19; Theocritus 17.58–76. Born November 12: Grzybek 1990, p. 182.

[11] Diodorus 20.19.2; on the events mentioned here, see Anson 2014a, pp. 151–152.

Polemaeus put to death. He recruited Polemaeus' solders into his own army, further increasing his manpower reserves.[12] Although Ptolemy's attempt to take Halicarnassus (opposite from Cos) met with no success, thanks to the intervention of Demetrius,[13] he likely entered into diplomatic contacts with the nearby Rhodians, and may even have drafted the document that he soon declared was Alexander's will, which he gave them for safekeeping (see below).[14]

Ptolemy's successes must have taken everyone by surprise. In addition to the distraction his operations caused the Antigonids, all of the places he took gave him strategic ports for his fleet, skilled seamen, and additional revenues, especially from the important cities of Xanthus and Caunus.[15] Moreover, the extension of his influence in Cos and its area expanded his trade and communication routes to Greece. It would not have been lost on the other Successors that after his involvement the previous year in the eastern Mediterranean, Ptolemy was switching his attention to the Aegean—and, in keeping with Macedonian military tradition, commanding his troops in person. Given the areas that Ptolemy now controlled, the next logical step was Greece itself. Ptolemy must have intended this move from the outset of the campaign, since he had remained for the winter on Cos, a convenient stopping-off point on the way to Greece. Thus, Ptolemy's moves in these years are significant for showing the low opinion he held of the likes of Demetrius and Cassander in Greece, as well as his own imperial aspirations.

In the early spring of 308, Ptolemy sailed from Myndus to Greece.[16] En route he liberated Andros, strategically close to Attica, in the Cyclades, from a garrison of Antigonus' men.[17] At this time he may have won over the island of Delos from Athens.[18] These islands were part of a League of the Islanders, or Cycladic League, allied to Antigonus since 314. Eventually, by 286, Ptolemy would control all the islands of this league, but that was evidently not his

---

[12] Diodorus 20.27.3, with Seibert 1969, pp. 177–178.

[13] Plutarch, *Demetrius* 7.3, with Seibert 1969, p. 186.

[14] Hauben 1977c, pp. 336–337; Bosworth 2000, p. 217. Ptolemy and Rhodes in general: Seibert 1969, pp. 225–230.

[15] Giovannini 2004, pp. 69–87. It is likely that Ptolemy subdued other places that Diodorus does not mention in his abbreviated account: Seibert 1969, pp. 185–186; Hauben 2014, p. 246.

[16] Diodorus 20.37.1. Background: Bouché-Leclercq 1903, pp. 62–66; Will 1984a, pp. 55–56; Caroli 2007, pp. 59–60. Date: Huss 2001, p. 177.

[17] Diodorus 20.37.1. Huss 2001, p. 177, on the garrison; Kolbe 1916, p. 531, argues that the garrison belonged to Cassander.

[18] Hauben 2014, pp. 251–252, insists that the first stop was Delos for propaganda reasons, given the religious importance of the island (the earlier home of Apollo) if Ptolemy was already making it clear he intended to liberate the Greeks, and suggests (p. 249) that Ptolemy made his liberation campaign known from Cos during the winter, whereas it is universally accepted that he did so only when he landed in Greece.

present intention, perhaps because he wanted to get to Greece as quickly as possible. From Delos it was plain sailing to Corinth in the Peloponnese. There was no resistance to him. He made Corinth his base, took over Sicyon, installing garrisons in both cities, and proclaimed his intention to liberate the Greek cities and award them their freedom.[19]

Ptolemy most likely intended to resurrect and head the League of Corinth, which Philip II had created in 337.[20] Antipater had abolished the league in 322, but Greece had suffered greatly in the Wars of the Successors, so Ptolemy was likely expecting that the Greeks would welcome the chance to live in a similar period of peace (and prosperity) as they had in the days of the league.[21] Ptolemy also made himself president of the Isthmian Games at Corinth, part of the Olympic Games cycle, at which his son Lagus (by Thais) competed in the chariot race.[22] Ptolemy intended his presidency to increase his support among the Greeks, and here was following Cassander's precedent, who had earlier presided over the Nemean Games.

Since 311, Ptolemy had been slowly but steadily extending his power in Asia Minor, Lycia, and Caria, the Aegean, and the Peloponnese. His moves betray a ruler not content with ruling only Egypt. True, he had worked solidly and successfully to protect Egypt's borders and build up buffer states between himself and the nearest Successors who might pose a threat to him. But even from the time he had first moved to Egypt, he had established himself as a force with which to be reckoned, as his annexation of Cyrenaica and especially his hijacking of Alexander's corpse proved. But in involving himself in Greek affairs now, did he intend to rule Macedonia and Greece, or, as has been suggested, did he merely want to be taken more seriously by the other Successors and seen as their bona fide equal?[23] Surely not. By 308 Ptolemy had ruled Egypt for fifteen years, had thwarted two invasions of his country, and had more than proved he was as good as, if not better than, his rivals. Although he was well entrenched in Egypt, and living in luxury in Alexandria, the lure of the jewel in the Successors' crown—kingship of Macedonia—was too much even for him.

Ruling Macedonia and Greece really did have this pull. When the Successors began to call themselves kings in 306 (see below), only Cassander was actually king of the Macedonians. That rankled with the others, who all

[19] Diodorus 20.37.1–2; Polyaenus 8.58.
[20] Kolbe 1916; Seibert 1969, pp. 182, 187, and 1983, pp. 183–185; Horat Zuffa 1971–1972; Will 1984a, p. 55; Billows 1990, pp. 144–145; Huss 2001, pp. 177–178; Dixon 2007, pp. 173–175; Dmitriev 2011, pp. 130 and 139–141.
[21] Prosperity: Worthington 1994; Shipley 2000, pp. 130–133, and 2005.
[22] Diodorus 20.37.1, and especially *Suda*, s.v. Demetrios. Huss 2001, p. 176, for the date; Ellis 1994, p. 47, for Lagus.
[23] Errington 2008, p. 42.

constantly proclaimed a connection to Alexander. Among other things, they issued coins with Alexander's image on them and later their own, but still with some imitation of him.[24] They put out stories to do with the great king, such as Seleucus' claim that Alexander had visited him in a dream and told him he would be great.[25] Some commissioned artworks, such as Craterus' statue in 322 at Delphi depicting how he saved Alexander's life during a hunt, and Cassander's painting of Alexander and Darius in battle (possibly the precursor to the famous Alexander Mosaic).[26] Ptolemy had eclipsed all of them with what he did to Alexandria, Alexander's city, as well as interring Alexander's body in a specially built tomb there, and establishing a cult to him. Yet only Cassander could call himself king of the Macedonians, as on a bronze statue base at Dium, the Macedonian religious center.[27] The others might well be kings of their own territories, but Macedonia gave Cassander the edge; under him, the kingdom entered a new phase.[28] Ptolemy's desire to bring back the League of Corinth from the days of Philip and Alexander shows that he wanted to be king of Macedonia.[29]

Spreading Rumors: Ptolemy, Son of Philip, and Alexander's Will

We have already discussed whether Lagus or Philip II was Ptolemy's father (pp. 9–10). I believe Ptolemy's incursion into Greece gives us a context for his putting out the rumor that he was Philip's illegitimate son, and further, that he was guided by Cassander's earlier actions to bind himself closer to the Argead family.

It has been suggested that Ptolemy claimed Philip as his father in 306, when he became king of Egypt, since he or his detractors had no need to do so earlier, for example at the time of the Babylon settlement (323).[30] But Ptolemy surely felt no need to legitimize his position in any way in 306, for he had just become king. Like the other Successors, he regarded his territory as spear won;

[24] Stewart 1993, pp. 229–323, and 2003; Dahmen 2007; Meeus 2009b. See too Lianou 2010.

[25] Diodorus 19.90.4.

[26] Plutarch, *Alexander* 40.5, with Waterfield 2011, p. 50. Mosaic: Worthington 2014, pp. 170–171.

[27] Green 1990, p. 31 n. 58.

[28] Errington 1978.

[29] See further the analysis of the sources on Ptolemy and the league by Seibert 1969, pp. 180–182 and 187–188. Hauben 2014, pp. 235–261, is right to argue that Ptolemy was intent on extending his influence in the Greek mainland, but stops short of considering that Ptolemy sought the Macedonian crown.

[30] Ellis 1994, p. 3; Ogden 1999, p. 67.

his right to rule was, like Alexander's rule of Asia, based on military power, not legitimacy. If anything, Ptolemy ought to have made the claim about his alleged parentage in 323, given that he was in a weaker position than so many of the others at Babylon, but he did not. We need to find another date and a better context for his assertion about Philip.

Three dates emerge: (1) 314, when Ptolemy issued his "freedom of the Greeks" to disadvantage Antigonus (p. 118); (2) 309–308, when Ptolemy intended to invade Greece; and (3) 295, when he went to Athens' assistance (p. 177). The first and third ventures fizzled out quickly, but the second is the likelier occasion because of his marriage proposal to Cleopatra, Alexander's sister—in fact, Alexander's *only* full sister (her mother was Olympias)—before he set sail for Greece.

Cleopatra at the time was living in Sardis under a governor who reported directly to Antigonus.[31] Perdiccas, Cassander, Antigonus, and Lysimachus, to name but four, had previously vied for her hand, but she had accepted Ptolemy's proposal. Since he had probably not seen her since their childhood days in Macedonia, he was hardly wanting to marry her for love, nor could she have been enamored of him. No, Ptolemy wanted to marry Cleopatra to tie himself to the Argead family, the same motive that had driven all the other Successors in wanting to take her as wife.[32] Why, then, did Cleopatra choose to marry Ptolemy? The other men, as Diodorus tells us, had made it clear they were simply using her to help gain power, and Ptolemy was no different here. Besides, Cleopatra may have wanted to stake her own claim to the throne, so marrying any of the others would have helped her realize that ambition.[33] Possibly Cleopatra simply disliked her other suitors, and felt she had more in common with Ptolemy. But a better explanation is that one of the provisions of her brother Alexander's will, which Ptolemy now circulated (see below), was that she should marry Ptolemy. This document is spurious, as we shall see, but she did not know that. Since it fell to a Macedonian king to arrange the marriages of family members, she thus had no choice but to follow the stipulation of the will and marry Ptolemy. This was a brilliantly cunning move on his part.

Ptolemy's intended marriage to Cleopatra has affinities with Cassander's marriage to Thessalonice, a half-sister of Alexander (and the half-sister of

---

[31] Diodorus 20.37.3; Seibert 1969, pp. 180–182, 184–189; Hammond and Walbank 1988, p. 169; Billows 1990, pp. 144–145; note the caution of Ellis 1994, p. 46.

[32] Diodorus 20.37.4; see too Diodorus 18.23.3 (Perdiccas "was bent upon marrying Cleopatra, believing that he could use her to persuade the Macedonians to help him gain the supreme power"), and Justin 13.6.4–6 ("to bolster his strength with royal dignity, Perdicas turned his thoughts to marriage with Cleopatra").

[33] Meeus 2009c.

Cleopatra), in 317. In fact, Cassander's marriage might have influenced Ptolemy to exploit Cleopatra as he did. When Cassander marched on Macedonia in 317, he became guardian of Alexander IV; however, his marriage into the ruling family made him Alexander IV's uncle, and was the stepping stone to personal rule.[34] Ptolemy had seen how the marriage had elevated Cassander. Now he needed to counteract Cassander's power in Greece, and I suggest that he took a leaf out of Cassander's book by marrying an Argead. If so, his intention, like Cassander's marrying Thessalonice, was to bid for the Macedonian throne.[35] But marriage alone might not have been enough for the people—after all, Cassander had already been guardian of the rightful king before he married his Argead wife. Therefore, Ptolemy invented a familial connection with the Argeads through Philip II. That he was able to use his own name added weight to his claim, for Philip had had a stepfather named Ptolemy, who ruled Macedonia from 368 to 365.[36]

Into this scenario we may also bring one of the curiosities of the early Hellenistic period, Alexander's will, supposedly read out by Perdiccas to the army in Babylon.[37] The will is quoted in the version of Alexander's death found in the *Alexander Romance*, a fantastic, later account of Alexander's life. The will had a number of detailed provisions in it concerning Alexander's heir by Roxane and the future of his empire, including that Ptolemy was to become satrap of Egypt and marry Cleopatra, and it was said to have been entrusted to the Rhodians for safekeeping.

The will is a fictitious document; it was believed that Perdiccas in 321 or Polyperchon in 317 was its author to bolster their claims to power; however, it has been persuasively argued that Ptolemy composed the will after 311, most likely in 309, to give him an edge over Cassander and Antigonus.[38] The clue to this date is the claim that the will was deposited on Rhodes. We have seen that the proximity of the island to Egypt made it valuable to Ptolemy, and he was well aware that its powerful fleet was a threat to him if the Rhodians allied

---

[34] Simpson 1957, pp. 371–372, and Huss 2001, p. 139, argue that the marriage shows that Cassander had given up on ruling the empire, but it is hard to see how this follows.

[35] Elgood 1938, p. 31, suggests that Ptolemy went to Greece to recruit men for his army, but he had no need to do so by now.

[36] It might even be now that to further his association with the Argead monarchy Ptolemy also circulated the story that the founder of the Ptolemaic family was the god Dionysus, for a fragment of Satyrus gives a genealogy of the early Ptolemies, citing Ptolemy's mother (Lagus' wife) Arsinoe as a descendant of Dionysus: Satyrus, *BNJ* 631 F 1, with Gambetti's commentary *ad* F 1.

[37] Diodorus 18.4.1–6.

[38] Bosworth 2000, pp. 207–241, also reviewing other arguments, and critiquing the various provisions of the will, and Lane Fox 2014, pp. 185–187. On Ptolemy apparently kidnapping Alexander's body to prevent it from going to Greece, since the will claimed he wanted to be buried in Egypt, see p. 94.

with his opponents. That was why he was always careful to court the Rhodians diplomatically and not use use military force against them; entrusting them with Alexander's will showed the esteem he had for them.[39]

Descent from Philip II thus gave Ptolemy more of a claim to the Macedonian throne than Cassander had, even if that supposed descent was not legitimate. In Babylon in 323, Alexander's illegitimate son Heracles had been cast aside from any consideration for the throne because of his status, but since then the Successors had done anything and everything to expand their influence. In his clashes with Antigonus and Cassander, Ptolemy decided that convincing the Macedonians he was a bastard son of Philip was better than no connection to that king and family. Another asset in his efforts was possessing Alexander's will, with its unashamed denigration of all his opponents, the arrangement for him to marry Cleopatra, and thus the message that he deserved the kingship.

Ptolemy's bid to win Greece and especially Macedonia was a serious one, especially for Antigonus—so serious that as Cleopatra left Sardis to join Ptolemy, Antigonus had her put to death.[40] With her demise, Ptolemy's grand plan swiftly collapsed. But the preceding scenario offers a plausible context for when and why Ptolemy claimed he was a bastard son of Philip, to which we can connect the oddity of Alexander's will, and thus see Ptolemy for what he really was: an imperialist who went to any lengths to achieve his goals.

Ptolemy's Return

Since Ptolemy's plan to wrest Macedonia and Greece from Cassander relied so heavily on marrying Cleopatra and her physical presence with him, he probably had not heard of her death before he sailed from Myndus to Greece. The collapse of that marital tie brought about the end of his Greek campaign. He also failed to win any positive support from the Greeks themselves, despite his proclamation of freedom, and even his self-proclaimed presidency of the Isthmian Games had little effect on the Peloponnesians, who did not supply him with expected food and money. It is not surprising that the Greeks were dubious of how friendly a person who appealed to liberty yet set up garrisons could be. Once the news about Cleopatra reached him, he knew his grand plan would not succeed. Therefore, he made his peace with Cassander and returned home.[41] However, he was still able to maintain control

[39] Bosworth 2000, pp. 217–218, 236–238.
[40] Diodorus 20.37.5–6, with Seibert 1969, pp. 184–189.
[41] Diodorus 20.37.2 (much telescoping of events); Hauben 2014, pp. 255–256, notes that the reason for Ptolemy's departure is not known, but that his ambitious undertaking did not "collapse like a house of cards."

of the strategic and economically powerful cities of Sicyon and Corinth.[42] This might even suggest not a total withdrawal on his part. but rather a calculated retreat until a better day.[43] As we shall see, we find him again involving himself in Greek affairs in 288.

In any case, it was prudent for Ptolemy to return to Egypt. Antigonus, then on his way home from the east, could have seized the opportunity of Ptolemy's absence to launch an attack on the country.[44] Aside from hypotheticals, Ptolemy's western border had been compromised. Ophellas, the governor of Cyrenaica, was persuaded by the tyrant of Syracuse, Agathocles, to attack Carthage, and marched there with over 10,000 mercenaries from the mainland.[45] Although he was invaluable as a governor, Ptolemy would hardly have overlooked Ophellas' audacious action. His bid came to nothing anyway because Agathocles assassinated him as soon as he arrived (in 308).[46] However, Cyrenaica seems to have been in revolt for the next several years until 300. Ptolemy must have realized that he could not leave Egypt for any length of time if he wanted to maintain stability of rule.

Ptolemy's plan in 308 had failed, but nevertheless he had added to Egypt's naval dominance in the Aegean and eastern Mediterranean and laid the foundations of the thalassocracy that his first two successors also strove to maintain. Although aspects of the first three Ptolemies' foreign policy was defensive, as has been well argued,[47] we cannot deny that Ptolemy had the same imperialistic ambition as his former comrades, and that he had made Egypt an imperial power. The campaign of 310–308 was part of a careful and long-term plan, not mere "uncharacteristic aggression."[48] He had patiently waited in the wings during Alexander's invasion of Asia for a slice of power, and when he got it, he was prepared to wait equally patiently before making his move, believing he was worthy to be Alexander's successor.[49] At the same time, he was not out to resurrect Alexander's empire, but to add to his own territory and prestige.

[42] Diodorus 20.37.1–2, 102.2.

[43] Cf. Huss 2001, p. 178.

[44] Wheatley 2002, pp. 45–46.

[45] Diodorus 20.40–42; Justin 22.7.4–5 (Ophellas' motive was to control all of Africa), with Will 1964; Laronde 1971; Mørkholm 1980; Seibert 1983, pp. 133–136; Huss 2001, pp. 179–180; Caroli 2007, pp. 75–76.

[46] Diodorus 20.42.3-5; Justin 22.7.5-6.

[47] Will 1966, pp. 153–208; cf. Walbank 1993, pp. 100–103.

[48] Ellis 1994, p. 46.

[49] Cf. Seibert 1969, p. 187. Hauben 2014, pp. 257–261, concludes that Ptolemy had a grand plan for Greece that went beyond a more defensive imperialism, but sees Ptolemy's move as opportunistic. I disagree, as Ptolemy had been carefully building up his lines of communication and defenses with his moves into Asia Minor as early as 310, in an effort to keep Antigonus at bay while he made a bid for the throne.

The days of a single empire under one king, as Ptolemy had seen at Babylon in 323, were indeed long gone.

Athens: A New Era

In the meantime, Antigonus was again turning his attention to Greece. In the early summer of 307, he sent his son Demetrius to Greece with 250 war-ships and 5,000 talents to liberate the cities there from Cassander, begin-ning with Athens.[50] He gambled that his action would endear him to the rest of the Greeks where Ptolemy had failed. Thus began the Fourth War of the Successors (307–301).[51]

Leaving the bulk of his fleet at Cape Sunium, on the southern tip of the peninsula of Attica, Demetrius took two dozen ships with him to Athens. The story goes that the garrison commander in the Piraeus (the port of Athens) mistook him for Ptolemy sailing to Corinth, and did not give the order to set up chains across the Piraeus to protect it from attack. His oversight allowed Demetrius to sail into the port, and claim the city.[52] He overcame Cassander's garrison, and expelled Demetrius of Phalerum, who fled first to Thebes, and then to Ptolemy in Alexandria.[53] He befriended Ptolemy, and continued writ-ing philosophical and literary works, as well as overseeing the organization of the Museum and the Library (Chapter 8).

Demetrius grandly declared the Athenians free from Cassander's rule, gave them various gifts, including 150,000 bushels of grain, timber for their fleet, and money, and allowed them to re-establish their democracy, which had been on hiatus for a decade.[54] The Athenians were hardly free, though, and had simply swapped one master for another. Nor were they able to restore the widespread radical democracy of the Classical period. In fact, most of the de-crees now shepherded through the Assembly (the decision-making body of the democracy) by politicians such as Habron (son of the fourth-century states-man Lycurgus), Demochares (a nephew of Demosthenes, the great orator and politician of the same era), and Stratocles (a politician who came to promi-nence during Antipater's control) honored Demetrius and his supporters,

[50] Diodorus 20.45.1

[51] Caroli 2007, pp. 60–66; Waterfield 2011, pp. 134–154; Anson 2014a, pp. 153–157; Champion 2014, pp. 109–114.

[52] Plutarch, *Demetrius* 8.3–5, with Diodorus 20.45.2–4.

[53] Diodorus 20.45.4.

[54] Diodorus 20.45.5, 46.1; Plutarch, *Demetrius* 10, with Habicht 1997, pp. 66–68; Dmitriev 2011, pp. 130–131. See also Oliver 2007.

and continued in this way throughout the Antigonid occupation of the city (307–301).[55]

Of course the restoration of even this limited democracy was an illusion, for Demetrius treated Athens as his personal property. Nevertheless, a grateful Athenian populace went so far as to grant divine honors to Demetrius and his father as savior gods—for bringing about the end of Demetrius of Phalerum's oppressive regime and some return to democracy. The people gave them their own cult, annual procession, and statues in the Agora; further, in 306 they even called the two men kings, and added two new Athenian tribes, Antigonis and Demetrias, to the existing ten in which all Athenians were enrolled.[56]

At that point, Antigonus recalled his son and gave him orders to wrest Cyprus from Ptolemy and win over Rhodes and the eastern Mediterranean as a precursor to invading Egypt.[57] Why Antigonus did not himself launch an offensive against Cyprus, and so let Demetrius remain in Athens, is simple: he was getting old, and was increasingly turning to his young son to conduct his military operations. In Antigonus' case, the spirit of conquering everyone was willing, but the flesh was weak.

Ptolemy Dashed

The strategic location of Rhodes and Cyprus, as we have said, made control of both of them desirable. Cyprus was also rich in grain, copper, and especially timber, which Ptolemy needed for his fleet, and he and the other Ptolemies always worked to maintain some sort of influence over the island.[58] Likewise, Rhodes was an important commercial center for Egyptian grain, and a transit point for all goods shipped to Egypt throughout the Hellenistic period.[59] The large number of Rhodian amphorae found in Alexandria testifies to the commercial contacts between the two places, and the Rhodians probably furnished Ptolemy with warships and let him use their island as a port for his fleet.[60] Both islands had been allies of Alexander and had close ties to Ptolemy, but

[55] Diodorus 20.46.2–3, with Habicht 1997, pp. 71–74. Plutarch's abhorrence of Stratocles is evident in his description of him at *Demetrius* 11 as "a disgusting man" and "living a debauched life," and that he was contemptuous of the people.

[56] Austin, no. 36, pp. 65–67 (= Plutarch, *Demetrius* 10); Diodorus 20.46.1–2; Plutarch, *Demetrius* 10.3, 12.1; Appian, *Syrian Wars* 54, with Ferguson 1911, pp. 95–123; Mossé 1973, pp. 108–114; Habicht 1997, pp. 68–69; Errington 2008, pp. 47–48.

[57] Diodorus 20.46.5; Plutarch, *Demetrius* 15.1.

[58] Bagnall 1976, pp. 38–79; cf. Mitford 1953.

[59] Rostovtzeff 1941, vol. 1, pp. 169–173, and especially Berthold 1984.

[60] Hauben 1977c, pp. 322–330. Ptolemy and Rhodes in general: Seibert 1969, pp. 225–230.

then again, the Rhodians had made alliances with practically every Successor at some point.[61] Cyprus especially had been a bone of contention between Ptolemy and Antigonus for years, so if Demetrius were to take both islands he would strike a blow at Egypt's economy and security, as well as assuring Antigonid control of the eastern Mediterranean.

In the spring of 306, Demetrius set out to Cyprus with 15,000 infantry, 400 cavalry, and at least 163 warships. En route he tried to win over the Rhodians, but they refused his diplomatic advances, preferring to maintain their amity (and trading prerogatives) with Ptolemy.[62] Both Antigonus and Demetrius viewed the Rhodian reaction as a *causus belli*, and decided to deal with the island later.[63] Demetrius sailed on to Cyprus, landing near Salamis with his infantry and cavalry. Close to that city he did battle with Menelaus, Ptolemy's brother, who had 12,000 infantry and 800 cavalry, and defeated him.[64] Menelaus escaped into Salamis and managed to send urgent word to his brother Ptolemy before Demetrius laid siege to the city. His enormous siege engines, taller than the ramparts of the city, included the fearsome, multi-storied armored *helepolis*, designed by Epimachus of Athens; at over 100 feet high, with a 40-foot base, it could launch missiles weighing over 175 pounds a staggering 650 feet (Figure 9.1).[65]

Ptolemy sailed at once to relieve his brother with at least 140 warships and 200 transport vessels carrying 10,000 troops.[66] Landing at Paphos, he received reinforcements from some of the Cypriot cities and made plans to join up with Menelaus' own fleet of sixty warships.[67] But Demetrius moved quickly to barricade Menelaus in the harbor of Salamis, and then as Ptolemy arrived (probably unaware of Menelaus' fate), Demetrius attacked him.[68] Both fleets included huge quadriremes and quinquiremes, so their enormity of size, numbers, and the other armaments must have made the entire scene breathtaking in scale. The epic naval battle, characterized by daredevil prow on prow ramming of the warships and Demetrius' use of catapults mounted on ships (reminiscent of Alexander's use of siege towers and battering rams on boats at Tyre), provided

[61] Hauben 1997c; Berthold 1984, pp. 38–58.

[62] Diodorus 20.82.1; cf. 81.4 (importance of revenues from trading with Egypt).

[63] Billows 1990, p. 202.

[64] Diodorus 20.47.3, 7; Plutarch, *Demetrius* 15.2; Pausanias 1.6.6.

[65] Diodorus 20.48.2–3, 91.2–8, with Marsden 1971, pp. 84–85; Bennett and Roberts 2009, pp. 124–128.

[66] Diodorus 20.49.1–2.

[67] Diodorus 20.49.3–5; Plutarch, *Demetrius* 16.1; Polyaenus 4.7.7.

[68] Battle: Diodorus 20.50–52; Plutarch, *Demetrius* 16; Justin 15.2.6–9; Pausanias 1.6.6; Polyaenus 4.7.7; Appian, *Syrian Wars* 54, with Bouché-Leclercq 1903, pp. 68–70; Seibert 1969, pp. 190–206; Bennett and Roberts 2009, pp. 146–153; Champion 2014, pp. 115–120. See too Hauben 1976.

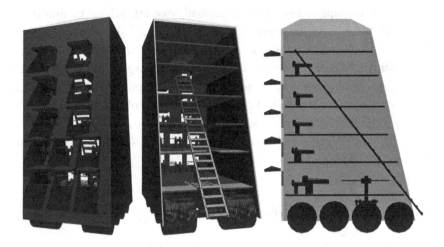

Figure 9.1 The *helepolis* Drawn by Evan Mason. Used under the Creative Commons License.

"an excellent case study for how best to attack or defend a coastal city with the aid of a fleet," and became a "textbook example" for the next century.[69] Demetrius' left wing successfully drove back Ptolemy's right wing, enabling Demetrius to maneuver into the space and attack Ptolemy's center, which also was pushed back (precisely what Ptolemy had intended to do to his opponent's line). Ptolemy had no choice, given Demetrius' relentless assault, but to retreat to Citium in utter defeat.[70]

Ptolemy's losses are not properly known, but at least forty warships and one hundred supply ships were captured and eighty damaged, with 8,000 men taken as prisoners of war, to Demetrius' twenty ships damaged.[71] Menelaus' only option now was to surrender Cyprus to Demetrius, and Ptolemy to return to Egypt with his tail between his legs, although "not at all humbled in spirit by the defeat."[72] Thus Demetrius had his revenge for his defeat six years earlier at Gaza, and the Antigonids now became the dominant naval power. Among the captives at Salamis were Menelaus and Leontiscus (Ptolemy's son by Thais), whom Demetrius allowed to leave unharmed and without a ransom.[73] Another captive was the courtesan (*hetaira*) Lamia, who had accompanied Ptolemy

[69] Murray 2012, p. 105, with pp. 105–111 on the battle, and especially Seibert 1969, pp. 190–206.

[70] Seibert 1969, pp. 202–203, is overly critical of Ptolemy, accusing him of panic in his abandonment of Cyprus, but Ptoleny had no option but to leave; cf. Hauben 1977a, p. 266.

[71] Diodorus 20.52.6; Plutarch, *Demetrius* 16.2, with Seibert 1969, pp. 200–202.

[72] Diodorus 20.53 (the quote at 53.3).

[73] Justin 15.2.7.

to Cyprus, perhaps as his mistress, but had been left behind by him there. Although older than Demetrius and "past her prime," she seduced him and became one of his numerous mistresses in Athens for many years.[74]

Ptolemy would not regain his ascendancy in the Aegean until 294. He still had Egypt and Cyrene, and some cities in the Peloponnese, but these were far from the possessions he had painstakingly accumulated over the past sixteen years.[75] Worse was to come later that year when, as we shall see in the next chapter, Antigonus and Demetrius decided to invade Egypt to topple him from power once and for all.

Ptolemy Becomes King

Soon after news of his son's crushing victory at Salamis in 306 reached him, Antigonus, at the grand old age of 79, began to wear a diadem and took the title of king, the first of the Successors to do so.[76] He then sent a diadem to his son in Cyprus and allowed him to be called king as well. Lysimachus, Seleucus, Cassander, and Ptolemy quickly proclaimed themselves kings so that they would not be considered inferior, as satraps, to Antigonus and Demetrius as kings.[77]

Antigonus' move formally ended the mirage of satrapal status. Although Justin claims the Successors had refused the title of king "as long as sons of the king [Alexander the Great] had been able to survive . . . such was the respect they felt for Alexander that, even when they enjoyed the royal power, they were content to forego the title 'king' as long as Alexander had a legitimate heir," Alexander IV, the "legitimate heir," had been put to death four years previously.[78] That it took that long for the Successors to call themselves kings of their territories was perhaps because they had brought down the dynasty to which they had sworn allegiance and had lived under all their lives. The world of 306 was very different from that of 310, and appearance could now give way to the reality of kingship. Suddenly this new world went from no king to

---

[74] Plutarch, *Demetrius* 16.3, 27.

[75] Wörrle 1977, pp. 52–54, downplays the loss, but it was in fact a major blow for Ptolemy.

[76] Diodorus 20.53.2; Justin 15.2.10; Plutarch, *Demetrius* 18.1; Appian, *Syrian Wars* 54, with Bouché-Leclercq 1903, pp. 70–71; Gruen 1985, pp. 254–257; Billows 1990, pp. 156–157 (cf. pp. 158–160 on the nature of Antigonus' kingship).

[77] Austin, no. 36, pp. 65–67 (= Plutarch, *Demetrius* 18); Diodorus 20.53.3–4; Justin 15.2.11–12, 15; Appian, *Syrian Wars* 54; cf. Billows 1990, pp. 155–160; Lund 1994, pp. 156–158. See also Gruen 1985, pp. 253–271; Strootman 2014a, pp. 317–320. Attitude (drawing on Plutarch, *Moralia* 823c): Cohen 1974.

[78] Justin 15.2.13–14 for the quote.

a multitude of them. Ptolemy's army apparently acclaimed him king.[79] Exactly when this occurred is unknown, and scholars are split into two camps over a date in 306 or 304.[80] The ancient sources seem to suggest that Ptolemy (and the others) became kings in the same year as Antigonus so as to match his authority.[81] Since Ptolemy was an ambitious ruler, we would not expect him to have been content in a subordinate position once the others were calling themselves kings. In fact, Ptolemy even backdated his kingship to include his years as satrap after Alexander's death in 323.[82]

But would Ptolemy have assumed the kingship in 306, when Demetrius had so recently and decisively defeated him off Salamis? This question has given rise to the belief that Ptolemy became king only in 304, after Demetrius' lengthy siege of Rhodes had ended, during which Ptolemy had given the defenders valuable assistance and had also warded off an Antigonid invasion of Egypt (see next chapter).[83] Thus he was again enjoying the sorts of victories that people would expect of a king. Moreover, the year 305/304 fits in with the chronology of Egyptian documents, which dated his kingship to that year, as the Egyptian year ran from November 7 to November 6, and the siege of Rhodes was over by the spring of 304. He may have become king on the first day of the Egyptian New Year in 305 (November 7), but did not celebrate his accession until the anniversary of Alexander's death, which fell in the following year; this in turn became the anniversary of his accession.[84]

However, no ancient writer states that any of the Successors who declared themselves king needed an actual victory to shore up their claim, merely

[79] Justin 15.2.11; Appian, *Syrian Wars* 54. Plutarch, *Demetrius* 18.1, says he was acclaimed king by the "the followers of Ptolemy in Egypt"—presumably not the Egyptians but a slip for "Macedonians." Diodorus 20.53.3 simply says he assumed the diadem and signed himself king.

[80] Bosworth 2000, pp. 228–238, argues that Ptolemy had been using the title since 309, at least informally, but this seems very early, and in any case we would expect Antigonus and the others to have followed his lead then.

[81] *Parian Marble*, BNJ 239 F B 23, though the chronology of this document is frequently erroneous; on this passage, see the commentary of Sickinger, BNJ, *ad loc.* A papyrus fragment, possibly from a Rhodian historian, also claims that Ptolemy became king around the time of Demetrius' invasion of Egypt, which followed the capture of Cyprus, in fall 306: Lehmann 1988b, pp. 2–7. Porphyry, BNJ 260 F 2, says that Ptolemy ruled Egypt for forty years, seventeen as satrap and twenty-three as king. That would put Ptolemy moving into Egypt in 322/321 (as I suggested on p. 89), and becoming king in 305. In demotic documents, the native scribes dated his reign from 305: Samuel 1962, pp. 11–24.

[82] Skeat 1954, pp. 2–4, 38; Samuel 1962, pp. 11–24; Seibert 1983, pp. 139–140; Grzybek 1990, pp. 90, 96–97; but note Jones 1997.

[83] Gruen 1985, pp. 257–258; cf. Thompson 2003, p. 105.

[84] Bouché-Leclercq 1903, pp. 70–72; Samuel 1962, pp. 4–11; Grzybek 1990, pp. 95–97.

that they did so out of rivalry with each other.[85] Also, for what it is worth, Plutarch notes that Ptolemy's "followers" called him king so as not to give the semblance of being depressed by their recent rout at Cyprus.[86] Too much has been made of this defeat for dating Ptolemy's kingship; even though it was catastrophic for his naval ascendancy, his overall military prowess at the time was still formidable, and Egypt was hardly a backwater on the periphery of the Hellenistic world. Given his personal aspirations and relations with his rivals, it simply was not in Ptolemy's character to have delayed calling himself king, defeated or not. In fact, as we shall see in the next chapter, not long after his loss at Salamis, Ptolemy blocked Antigonus and Demetrius with a massive army of nearly 90,000 troops and 250 ships from invading Egypt.His victory in sending this enormous Antigonid force packing must surely have redeemed him for the disaster at Cyprus, as Pausanias notes.[87] It likely spurred his victorious army to declare Ptolemy a king, and further, may have caused the people of Egypt to bestow on him the surname *soter* or "savior" (see next chapter), both of which put him on a par with the recently vanquished Antigonids.

The Egyptian records that date Ptolemy's kingship to 305 may have done so because the priests did not come to call him king until after they had crowned him Pharaoh in that same year.[88] Taking that title was a significant departure from Alexander, who had merely adopted all the rights and powers associated with it.[89] While the year of Ptolemy's kingship is important, absolute certainty is impossible, though on balance 306 is the most likely. And in keeping with the way he exploited Alexander's name, Ptolemy waited for the anniversary of his death to celebrate his own accession. Soon he began to mint coins with his own portrait on them and the inscription "King Ptolemy."[90]

Ptolemy's elevation to king shows that he was far from a spent force, and was already bouncing back, even in the same year as his terrible loss at Cyprus. If anything, he emerged from each conflict better positioned to interact with the other Successors than before. Patience to achieve his goals was his virtue, and in this respect he must surely be regarded as the most calculating, farsighted, and successful of the Successors.

[85] Diodorus 20.53.4; cf. Meeus 2014, pp. 294–301, summarizing bibliography and arguments in detailed notes.
[86] Plutarch, *Demetrius* 18.1.
[87] Pausanias 1.6.6.
[88] Lehmann 1988b, pp. 8–9; cf. Hölbl 2001, pp. 20–21; Caroli 2007, pp. 129–131 (chronology).
[89] Burstein 1991; Caroli 2007, pp. 123–129.
[90] Meeus 2014, pp. 300–301, citing bibliography.

The Emergence of Hellenistic Kingship

We have moved from officers under Alexander, to satraps, and now to kings—kingship being one of the defining characteristics of the Hellenistic period.[91] Kingship changed the face of political power in the Hellenistic world forever. Hellenistic rulers like Ptolemy relied on civil administrators, their so-called friends (*philoi*), when it came to seeking advice.[92] As Alexander's Successors established their own kingdoms, they created personal armies owing loyalty only to them in place of the one army commanded by a single Macedonian king. Ptolemy, like all the new kings, did not rule constitutionally but by right of conquest, which comes as no surprise, as they were all military men.[93] In doing so, they—like Alexander—were faced with all manner of new challenges to rule a multicultural subject population.

One way of maintaining rule and promoting harmony and loyalty in their domains was by worship, and eventually an actual ruler cult. The kings received cult names—in our period, *soter* ("savior") for Antigonus and Demetrius in 307, and for Ptolemy in 306 (see next chapter). They were thus revered not for who they were but for what they had done for a particular people.[94] At first, the kings did not allow their own people to worship them, but a change came with their successors. In Egypt, Ptolemy II deified his father on his death in 283 and instituted a cult to him as a savior god. He followed these actions with a cult to himself and his sister-wife Arsinoe II as *Theoi Adelphoi* (brother/sister gods) in 272 while they were alive.[95] In doing so, he promoted the trend of ruler cult in the Hellenistic world.[96] Like kingship, ruler cult was one of the characteristics of the Hellenistic period and influenced Roman imperial rule, with Ptolemy and his peers playing a role in its origins.[97]

[91] Tarn and Griffith 1952, pp. 79–125; Mooren 1983; Walbank 1984a; Samuel 1989, pp. 21–28; Hammond 1993a and 2000; Shipley 2000, pp. 59–107; Bosworth 2002, pp. 246–278; Ma 2003; Caroli 2007, pp. 170–187; Errington 2008, pp. 63–76.

[92] Samuel 1993.

[93] Billows 1995, pp. 20–24, and passim; see too Strootman 2014a.

[94] Tarn and Griffith 1952, pp. 53–54.

[95] See Hölbl 2001, pp. 101–104, for excellent comments on Arsinoe II's divine status.

[96] Koenen 1983; Samuel 1989, pp. 67–81; Caroli 2007, pp. 188–193; Pfeiffer 2008; Carney 2013, pp. 97–100; *contra* Hölbl 2001, pp. 92–94, that it was Ptolemy who deified the dynasty.

[97] Habicht 1970; Seibert 1983, pp. 186–188; Walbank 1984a, pp. 87–100, and 1993, pp. 210–218; Shipley 2000, pp. 156–163; Hölbl 2001, pp. 90–98; Chaniotis 2003; Waterfield 2011, pp. 203–206; Erskine 2014. More specifically on Ptolemy I and II: Samuel 1989, pp. 67–81; Caroli 2007, pp. 188–193; Pfeiffer 2008; Vandorpe 2010, pp. 163–164.

10

First among Equals

Taking advantage of Ptolemy's defeat at Cyprus, Antigonus and Demetrius invaded Egypt.[1] At the head of a huge army—80,000 infantry, 8,000 cavalry, and 83 war elephants—Antigonus set off from Antigoneia (northern Syria) to Egypt, while Demetrius with an equally substantial fleet of 150 warships and 100 transport vessels sailed to join him at Gaza. They were to rendezvous there in late October, eight days before the setting of the Pleiades (early November), which signaled the end of the sailing season in the eastern Mediterranean and the onset of the winter storms.[2]

Antigonus arrived at Gaza, where he was advised to delay his campaign because of the Pleiades.[3] He refused, and ordered his men into Egypt. However, a major storm with high north winds wreaked havoc with Demetrius' fleet at Raphia; many vessels were sunk or damaged, and the remainder of them were unable to anchor in port but had to remain off the coast past Gaza because of dangerous shoals close to land.[4] Even though Antigonus arrived in that area, he was unable to unite with his fleet, which impacted the invasion severely.

In the meantime, Ptolemy had set up his camp at Pelusium, and had already installed garrisons at key points along the route Antigonus' army would take. He had also slyly sent word to the enemy mercenaries that he would offer them more money than Antigonus—as much as one talent for commanders of troops—if they defected to him.[5] As Ptolemy's garrisons continued to harass the enemy troops on their march to Pelusium, and as more of the invaders became bogged down in the Nile delta, a number of the enemy

---

[1] Diodorus 20.73–76, with Seibert 1969, pp. 207–224; Hauben 1975/76; Billows 1990, pp. 162–164; Champion 2014, pp. 124–129.

[2] Date: Anson 2014a, p. 165, citing bibliography.

[3] Diodorus 20.73.3.

[4] Diodorus 20.74; Plutarch, *Demetrius* 19.1–2; Pausanias 1.6.6.

[5] Diodorus 20.75.1.

deserted to Ptolemy. A frustrated Antigonus had no choice but to withdraw; as he returned to Syria the high winds further laid waste his fleet, enabling Ptolemy to capture a number of the enemy vessels. Back in Alexandria, Ptolemy hosted lavish entertainment, made a thank-offering to the gods, and wrote to Cassander, Seleucus, and Lysimachus about his triumph and the number of men who had defected to him.[6]

Demetrius is usually condemned for the utter failure of his invasion, but Antigonus must share in the blame, for he had refused to wait until spring when weather conditions improved.[7] Ptolemy has also been criticized for not chasing down Demetrius as he sailed away in disarray.[8] But Ptolemy would not have had a straightforward mopping-up operation, given the weather, and there was always the danger that Antigonus would try to engage Ptolemy if he believed his son in danger. Despite "his huge size and weight making it harder even than his old age for him to undertake campaigns," Antigonus was still a formidable adversary.[9] It was therefore better to let Demetrius go, even if that meant more conflict—which soon came.

As we discussed in the last chapter, Ptolemy's enthusiastic army, riding on its success against the Antigonid invasion, proclaimed him king. This may also be the time when his people conferred on him his famous surname *soter* ("savior"). However, the more common belief is that he received it from the Rhodians in 304 for helping them resist Demetrius' siege of their city. It seems preferable, therefore, to deal with the surname issue after discussing that siege.

The Siege of Rhodes

Demetrius had not forgotten his diplomatic rebuff at the hands of the Rhodians in 306 before he besieged and took Cyprus that same year. In the summer of 305, he ordered the Rhodians to surrender 100 hostages and open all their harbors to him. When they refused, he laid siege to their island.[10] Ptolemy had

---

[6] Diodorus 20.76.7.

[7] Billows 1990, p. 164; Wheatley 2014, blaming Antigonus for the miscalculation of invading Egypt and being outmatched by Ptolemy; *contra* Champion 2014, p. 128.

[8] Seibert 1969, pp. 219–224, on reasons why Antigonus withdrew; on p. 222 he argues that Ptolemy's lethargy is another example of his defensive foreign policy, but aganst this see Hauben 1977a, p. 266.

[9] Plutarch, *Demetrius* 19.3.

[10] Austin, no. 39, pp. 69–70 (= Diodorus 20.81, 20.100.1–4); Diodorus 20.81–88, 91–100.3; Plutarch, *Demetrius* 20.5–22; Pausanias 1.6.6; Polyaenus 4.6.16, with Hauben 1977c, pp. 328–339 (but note the criticisms of Billows 1990, pp. 165–166 n. 5); Seibert 1983, pp. 142–145, and

no choice but to support Rhodes, not from any feelings of loyalty because its people had earlier sided with him against the Antigonids, but because of the great threat to Egypt if it fell into Demetrius' hands. Ptolemy was still recovering from his naval loss off Cyprus, so he could send only large amounts of provisions and probably 1,500 troops to help the defenders.[11] Cassander and Lysimachus likewise sent aid, both fearing that a successful Demetrius would move against them next.[12]

Demetrius had 40,000 troops, 200 warships, and over 170 transport vessels carrying siege towers to be deployed on land as well as mounted on ships. His siege equipment included the gigantic and terrifying *helepolis* (see Figure 9.1). Despite Demetrius' great numbers and the severe pounding that his siege engines inflicted on the walls of Rhodes, the defenders resisted with relentless determination. As the siege dragged on into 304, Demetrius, eager to get involved in Greece again with his father, decided to cut his losses. He may also have been worried because Ptolemy was already rebuilding his fleet. Therefore, he came to terms with the Rhodians; he recognized their autonomy and did not install a garrison in the city. They agreed to be his allies, hand over the hostages, and support the Antigonids in their campaigns—significantly though "except in a war against Ptolemy."[13]

The siege had lasted for one year, and it became famous for two reasons. First, even though he had failed, Demetrius was nicknamed Poliorcetes ("Sacker of Cities") because of the massive size and formidable power of his siege equipment.[14] Second, as a thank-offering to the gods, the Rhodians built a colossal, 105-foot-tall bronze statue of their patron deity, the sun god Helios, which they stood next to their harbor. It cost the whopping sum of 300 talents, which they paid for by selling some of Demetrius' abandoned siege equipment. This statue, which took 12 years to build and is known more famously as the Colossus of Rhodes, was one of the seven wonders of the ancient world.[15] It was destroyed in an earthquake half a century later, and lay in ruins until it was melted down after an Arab invasion in AD 653.

1969, pp. 225–230; Berthold 1984, pp. 66–80; Ellis 1994, pp. 48–49; Pimouguet-Pédarros 2001; Bennett and Roberts 2009, pp. 121–132; Murray 2012, pp. 111–117; Champion 2014, pp. 130–142. Chronology: Anson 2014a, pp. 184–185.
   [11] Diodorus 20.88.9, 94.3, 96.1, 98.1, 99.2, 100.3.
   [12] Diodorus 20.96.3, 100.2.
   [13] Plutarch, *Demetrius* 22.4.
   [14] Diodorus 20.92.2, 103.3.
   [15] Higgins 1988.

Ptolemy the Savior

The grateful Rhodians erected statues of Cassander and Lysimachus in their city, but since Ptolemy had sent them the most help, they inquired of the Oracle of Zeus Ammon at Siwah if they could honor him as a god, and when their request was granted, they built a shrine to him (the Ptolemaeum) in their city with his own cult.[16] Further, when describing the statues of the various Ptolemaic kings that stood in front of the Odeum (music hall) in Athens in his day, Pausanias tells us that each king was also given his own surname (*epiklesis*), and that the Rhodians had bestowed the surname *soter* ("savior") on Ptolemy.[17]

It is, however, not certain that Ptolemy was called *soter* at this time, and thus Pausanias, writing four hundred years after the events in question, was mistaken.[18] For one thing, Pausanias gets several facts about the Ptolemies wrong, such as Ptolemy II bringing Alexander's body to Alexandria or Ptolemy I abdicating in favor of Ptolemy II.[19] Since Diodorus, our principal source for this period, says nothing about the surname when discussing the Rhodian honors, and Rhodian priestly inscriptions from Ptolemy's lifetime down to the first century never refer to him as *soter*, Pausanias might indeed have erred. In fact, elsewhere in his work he includes the tradition that Alexander named Ptolemy *soter* for saving his life in the siege of the Oxydracae, when, in fact, Ptolemy was not even there, and says so in his *History*![20]

We should not try to second guess Diodorus' silence on the matter—after all, in his account of the Babylon settlement, for example, the most significant event in the immediate aftermath of Alexander's death, he says nothing about Roxane's baby being considered as Alexander's successor. Diodorus might therefore have omitted facts about Ptolemy for his own reasons. The lack of the epithet in the Rhodian priestly inscriptions is surprising, but perhaps *soter* has nothing to do with a cult title or divine honors, but simply means "savior" in a

---

[16] Diodorus 20.100.3–4.

[17] Pausanias 1.8.6. This was likely also his cult name: Hauben 1977c, p. 339; on the bestowal of the surname, see too Seibert 1969, pp. 229–230; Berthold 1984, pp. 74–76, 78; Ellis 1994, pp. 49–50; Huss 2001, pp. 189–190; Caroli 2007, pp. 194–194; Muccioli 2012, pp. 81–94.

[18] Hazzard 1993, Worthington 2016 (from the civilian population of Egypt); *contra*, for example, Huss 2001, pp. 238–239; Hauben 2010.

[19] p. 131 and p. 203, respectively.

[20] Pausanias 1.6.2. Not present: Ptolemy, *FGrH* 138 F 26b; Curtius 9.5.21. Cleitarchus, *BNJ* 137 F 24, has Ptolemy present, but it may come from an even later source, perhaps Timagenes; cf. the commentary of Prandi, *BNJ* 137 F 24, citing bibliography. Arrian 6.11.8 (from Ptolemy, *FGrH* 138 F 26a) mentions that the rescue took place at the siege of Malli, yet Ptolemy was also not there; cf. Hazzard 1993, p. 53, and 2000, pp. 14–15, 150, 151.

secular sense; if so, we would not expect the word to appear in these religious documents.[21]

It has been suggested that Ptolemy II first called his father *soter*, perhaps in 263, since a silver tetradrachm coin has the portrait of Ptolemy on the obverse and the inscription *Ptolemaiou Soteros* on the reverse.[22] However, an inscription of the mid-280s records that the League of the Cycladic Islands bestowed divine honors on Ptolemy, calling him "savior."[23] Since he liberated this league from Demetrius' control in probably either the 290s or 280s (see below), he clearly received the surname in his lifetime.

We cannot definitively know who first called Ptolemy a savior, and the consensus is still in favor of the Rhodians.[24] But if not the Rhodians, who else? The obvious candidates are his own people, given that Ptolemy had saved them from invasion three times. We can rule out the first time, in 320, when Perdiccas invaded Egypt, as the Egyptians had lived under Ptolemy for two years at best; for all they knew, Perdiccas might have been a better ruler than him. This leaves two other contexts: when Ptolemy defended Egypt from Demetrius' threat in 312, after defeating him at Gaza, and when he rescued the country more recently from the major Antigonid invasion.

This third occasion (in 306) has the edge. Even if bad weather had disabled Demetrius' fleet, Ptolemy had still held off Antigonus' huge land army, and so saved Egypt. His success more than likely led his army to declare him king, and the civilian population followed this lead by naming him *soter*, following the precedent of the Athenians, who called Antigonus and Demetrius savior gods for liberating them from Cassander in 307. That there was no cult attached to Ptolemy in Egypt was in line with his refusal to be associated with divine honors, having witnessed firsthand the reaction to Alexander's pretensions to personal divinity.[25] Although there was a cult to Ptolemy on Rhodes after 304 (and in the Cyclades after 286), these places were not Egypt. Like Alexander, Ptolemy adopted the rights and responsibilities of the Pharaohs, which for the Egyptians, but not the Greeks and Macedonians, included divinity, but he did so only to promote his public image in Egypt, as we will see in Chapter 11. Thus his Greek and Macedonian subjects in Egypt could call him a savior, without the surname being connected to a cult.[26]

---

[21] Johnson 2000.

[22] Hazzard 2000, pp. 3–24. By 261, other coins with the same legend on them were issued at Tyre, Sidon, Ptolemais, and Joppa, and soon after Ptolemy II began calling himself the son of Ptolemy *Soter* in literary documents.

[23] Hauben 2010, pp. 108–118; the inscription is the decree of Nicuria (restored).

[24] Hauben, 2010, pp. 105–108.

[25] Alexander's Divinity: Worthington 2014, pp. 265–269.

[26] The same is true of Antiochus I, the son of Seleucus I, who saved his kingdom by defeating the Gauls in 275, for which he was named *soter*.

The Battle of Ipsus and the Death of Antigonus

After his failure at Rhodes in 304, Demetrius returned to Greece, intent on freeing the Greeks from Cassander's and Polyperchon's influence.[27] There, Athens was embroiled in a war with Cassander, who in 304 was besieging the city.[28] The Athenians successfully appealed for help to Demetrius, who, with 330 ships and several thousand troops, expelled Cassander from Attica and drove him north through Boeotia as far as Thermopylae, in the process winning over these areas to their cause.[29] The grateful Athenians allowed Demetrius to live in the rear chamber of the Parthenon, where his debauched lifestyle with several courtesans and young men shocked the people and, they believed, insulted the goddess Athena.[30] They were incensed when he demanded a surprise tax of 250 talents, a colossal sum, which they scrambled to put together with great difficulty—only to see him give it to Lamia and his other courtesans to buy soap.[31] Even worse was his decision to be initiated into the Mysteries, one of the holiest of Greek religious sects, forcing the Athenians to collapse the standard initiation period of one year into one month in order to pander to his wishes.[32]

In this period Demetrius gradually reduced Cassander's influence in Greece, and in 302 he liberated Sicyon and Corinth from their Ptolemaic garrisons, and changed the name of Sicyon to Demetrias after himself.[33] At Corinth, Demetrius announced to embassies from the Greek cities his father's intention of reconstituting the League of Corinth with himself and Antigonus as its leaders.[34] Their intention, however, was not to use the league as the means for Macedonia to rule Greece, as in the days of Philip and Alexander, but as a Greek alliance against Cassander and as a springboard for invading Macedonia.[35] Accordingly, Demetrius was elected commander of the Greek

[27] Diodorus 20.100.6, 102.1.
[28] Habicht 1997, pp. 74–77.
[29] Plutarch, *Demetrius* 23.1–2.
[30] Plutarch, *Demetrius* 23.3–24, 25.9; cf. Athenaeus 6.253a, with Habicht 1997, pp. 67–81; see Ogden 1999, pp. 173–177, on his courtesans (and wives).
[31] Plutarch, *Demetrius* 27.1.
[32] Diodorus 20.110.1; Plutarch, *Demetrius* 26.
[33] Diodorus 20.102–103; Plutarch, *Demetrius* 25.1–2.
[34] Diodorus 20.102.1, Plutarch, *Demetrius* 25.3. Translation of an inscription from Epidaurus recording this: Austin, no. 42, pp. 76–78, and Harding 1985, no. 138, pp. 172–174. Background: Heuss 1938, pp. 189–192; Ferguson 1948; Seibert 1983, pp. 179–183; Hammond and Walbank 1988, pp. 176–178; Billows 1990, pp. 228–232 (the league was meant to create a "United States of Greece"); Dixon 2007, pp. 176–177.
[35] Simpson 1959, p. 397; Green 1990, p. 34.

forces (as had Philip and Alexander before him). Cassander did not intend to fight, however, and offered terms of surrender to the octogenarian Antigonus as the senior Antigonid, who at once instructed his son to refuse them: he wanted Cassander out of Greece and Macedonia for good.[36]

A defiant Cassander renewed his alliance with Ptolemy, Lysimachus, and Seleucus, who decided to take the fight to Antigonus in Asia rather than see him win control of Macedonia and then attack them.[37] Their plan would not only prevent the aged Antigonus from invading Macedonia but also force him to recall Demetrius, and so save Cassander. In the summer of 302, Cassander turned to deal with Demetrius in Greece, while Lysimachus invaded Asia Minor to rendezvous with Ptolemy and Seleucus, who brought with him 20,000 infantry, 12,000 cavalry, and 100 scythed chariots.[38] Ptolemy did not join them but merely sent troops.[39] In an exemplary display of looking after his own interests, he took advantage of Antigonus' situation to invade Syria and Phoenicia, capturing Antigonid garrison posts including Byblos and possibly Damascus, and so occupied Coele-Syria a third time.[40] During his siege of Sidon, Ptolemy apparently received a report that Antigonus had defeated Lysimachus and Seleucus in battle, forcing him to make a truce with the Sidonians and return to Egypt. The news was false though.

Sure enough, Antigonus recalled Demetrius, leaving him no choice but to come to terms with Cassander (who had stayed in Greece).[41] In the spring of 301, the two sides met in battle at Ipsus, a small town in central Phrygia. The battle was a crucial one, for if Antigonus won he stood poised to conquer the kingdoms of all his opponents and fashion an empire on a par with that of Alexander.[42] We know little about this important battle because of the paucity of the ancient sources. The coalition force was under the overall command of Lysimachus, which showed how important he had become in the last few years.[43] He was personally in charge of the infantry, while Seleucus' son and successor, Antiochus (by the Persian Apame), directed the cavalry. Under them were 64,000 infantry,

[36] Diodorus 20.106.1–2.

[37] Diodorus 20.106.2–5, 21.1.4; Justin 15.2.16–17; cf. Plutarch, *Demetrius* 28.1–2, with Seibert 1969, pp. 231–240.

[38] Diodorus 20.107.1–2.

[39] Diodorus 21.1.5.

[40] Diodorus 20.113.1–2; Pausanias 1.6.8; Seibert 1969, pp. 231–233.

[41] Diodorus 20.111.1–2; cf. Plutarch, *Demetrius* 28.1–2, with Billows 1990, pp. 176–185, for details; see too Seibert 1983, pp. 154–155.

[42] Battle: Diodorus 21.1.2–4; Plutarch, *Demetrius* 28.3–29; Polyaenus 4.7.4 and 12.1, with Billows 1990, pp. 181–184; Bennett and Roberts 2009, pp. 101–113; Champion 2014, pp. 158–161.

[43] Lund 1994, pp. 70–77.

10,500 cavalry, 400 war elephants, and 120 scythed chariots.[44] Plutarch claims that the opposing Antigonid army consisted of 70,000 infantry, 10,000 cavalry, and 75 war elephants.[45] Fighting with Antigonus and Demetrius was Pyrrhus, the young king of Epirus.[46]

Both sides deployed their lines with the heavier phalanx in the center, lighter infantry on each side of it, and cavalry reinforcing each flank. Demetrius was on the right wing and Antigonus was stationed in the center, behind the infantry. Exactly where Seleucus or Lysimachus was positioned on their lines is unknown; Antiochus was on the left wing, so his father may have been with him or even in charge of the elephant corps, which was ranged in front of the infantry.

Demetrius took his troops around the enemy elephants to attack and rout Antiochus. He was gaining the upper hand over Antiochus, but as he pursued the retreating cavalry he found he had gone too far and was effectively isolated from his own men. His horses were also fearful of the sight and smell of the elephants, and his own right flank was exposed. Enter Seleucus, who boldly rode up and down Demetrius' wing encouraging his men to desert to him. A substantial number of cavalry did so, while more fled. Although Antigonus tried to exhort his men, desperate for Demetrius to return, it was not to be. Surrounded by the coalition infantry, Antigonus fell victim to a "cloud of javelins."[47] His very size may well have been a hindrance on the battlefield.

Demetrius managed to escape to Ephesus with 5,000 infantry and 4,000 cavalry.[48] Alexander had treated his enemies, such as Darius III or the Indian raj Porus, with the respect that befitted their positions; so too did Lysimachus and Seleucus, who buried Antigonus with all the pomp and trappings of royalty.

Thus ended the Fourth War of the Successors, and with it came the end of Antigonus Monophthalmus, a victim of his own ambition, who had risen "from private station to high power and became the mightiest king of his day, [who] was not content with gifts of Fortune, but undertook to bring unjustly into his own hands the kingdom of all the others."[49] Antigonus had shaped the history of the Hellenistic world for the past two decades; in that respect, Ipsus really was the end of an era.[50] But it was far from being the end of the

---

[44] So Plutarch, *Demetrius* 28.3; Diodorus actually states 480 elephants, but this is probably his error; cf. Mehl 1986, pp. 201–202.

[45] Plutarch, *Demetrius* 28.3.

[46] Plutarch, *Pyrrhus* 4.3.

[47] Plutarch, *Demetrius* 29.5; cf. Diodorus 21.1.4; Pausanias 1.6.7.

[48] Plutarch, *Demetrius* 30.1. Diodorus 21.1.4 says he sailed to Salamis in Cyprus. Neither source mentions Pyrrhus, who must also have escaped.

[49] Diodorus 21.1.1.

[50] Cf. Seibert 1969, p. 235; Ellis 1994, p. 51; Huss 2001, p. 190.

Antigonids. Demetrius still possessed Cyprus, some bases in Greece and Asia Minor, Sidon, Tyre, the League of the Cycladic Islands (including the strategic Euboea, off Attica's eastern coastline), and the largest fleet in the Mediterranean.[51] By the mid-290s we will discover that he was ready to avenge his father's defeat at Ipsus, and conquer Greece, and his son would go onto found the Antigonid dynasty, which lasted until the Roman era.

For the moment, a fragile period of calm existed between the only three of Alexander's original Successors still alive: Ptolemy, Lysimachus, and Seleucus.

Ptolemy's Position after Ipsus

The Successors now carved up the Antigonid territory "as if it had been a huge carcass," each man taking his portion.[52] Lysimachus received all of Asia Minor to the Taurus mountain range, a substantial increase to his kingdom; Cassander was reconfirmed ruler of Macedonia and Greece, so nothing new for him; likewise for Ptolemy, who had retrieved all of Syria and Palestine himself. That these two men were not given more is probably because they had not risked their lives in the battle. The big winner was Seleucus, who took over the remainder of Antigonus' holdings, thereby vastly increasing his own territory to as far east as Afghanistan. Although he wisely stayed out of India, he did make an alliance with its new king, Chandragupta, the founder of the Mauryan Empire, whose own position owed much to Alexander's example.[53] Seleucus thus laid the foundation for what would be the most geographically extensive of the Hellenistic kingdoms, and second only to the Ptolemaic in longevity.[54]

Ptolemy's earlier support of Seleucus' return to Babylon in 312 seems to have been disregarded as the two men now got into an intense squabble over Phoenicia. Seleucus demanded control of the area because Ptolemy did not deserve any reward for not fighting at Ipsus.[55] Ptolemy countered with the fact that he was still a member of the coalition, and had been promised Phoenicia.[56] Seleucus' behavior was less to do with Ptolemy's absence from the battle, and more with who would control the two principal cities of Tyre and Sidon (currently held by Demetrius).[57] The area was also a strategic military buffer zone

---

[51] Merker 1970, p. 142.

[52] Plutarch, *Demetrius* 30.1.

[53] Alliance: Appian, *Syrian Wars* 53; Alexander and Chandragupta: Worthington 2014, p. 261.

[54] On the Seleucids, see the works cited in Chapter 5 n. 60.

[55] Diodorus 21.1.5, with Seibert 1983, pp. 156–158.

[56] Polybius 5.67, with Mehl 1986, pp. 207–212.

[57] Anson 2014a, p. 174.

between the two kings, and each one would profit from its grain crop, oil, and wine, and its access to the so-called spice route, which began in Saudi Arabia and ended in Coele-Syria.

Eventually Seleucus relented, but their clash was a sign of deteriorating relations, all the more so when Seleucus stated that "for friendship's sake he would not for the present interfere, but would consider later how best to deal with friends who chose to encroach."[58] The issue of who owned Ptolemaic Syria, officially known as the province of "Syria and Phoenicia," the second largest foreign possession of the Ptolemies next to Cyrenaica, remained a major bone of contention between the two dynasties.[59]

In probably 300 the revolt of Cyrenaica ended, which had broken out in 308 when its governor, Ophellas, had been betrayed and executed by Agathocles of Syracuse (p. 155). Cyrenaica had severed its ties with Ptolemy, but he could not allow it to be independent because of its value on his western border. He appointed his stepson Magas as governor.[60] Apart from a brief attempt at independence in 258–246, Cyrenaica remained a key Ptolemaic possession for more than two centuries, until 96.

Ptolemy took Seleucus' ominous warning, quoted earlier, to heart, because in the same year, or possibly even the very early 290s, he arranged two political marriages to shore up his relations with the increasingly influential Lysimachus.[61] The number of inter-dynastic marriages in these years is not an anomaly, as political marriages were a feature of the Hellenistic period. Ptolemy's daughter Arsinoe (by Berenice) married the elderly Lysimachus, and another daughter, Lysandra (by Eurydice), was betrothed to Lysimachus' son Agathocles.[62] Lysimachus was glad of the alliance because of the strength of the Egyptian navy, which Ptolemy had been rebuilding since his defeat at Cyprus in 306. Lysimachus expected to use this fleet against several towns in Asia Minor loyal to Demetrius.

Seleucus, with no navy of his own and feeling vulnerable, cast his eyes around for a new ally. In 298 he settled on, of all people, Demetrius, a classic example of "the enemy of my enemy is my friend." In reality he had no other choice, but Demetrius welcomed his advance as it gave him the opportunity to start rebuilding his own influence. To cement their accord, Seleucus married

---

[58] Diodorus 21.1.5.

[59] On the relationship between their dynasties, and indeed all Hellenistic dynasties, see Davies 2002.

[60] Pausanias 1.6.8; Seibert 1983, pp. 133–136; Bagnall 1976, pp. 25–26.

[61] Bouché-Leclercq 1903, pp. 85–86; Lund 1994, pp. 88–90; Caroli 2007, pp. 66–67. Ipsus in fact shaped the marriage alliances of the next several years: Cohen 1974.

[62] Plutarch, Demetrius 31.3; Pausanias 1.9.6, 1.10.3; Carney 2013, pp. 31–48.

Demetrius' daughter (by Phila) Strationice.[63] A bizarre postscript to this marriage is that Seleucus' son, Antiochus, fell in love with Strationice; when Seleucus found out in 293, he made his son king of upper Syria—and gave him Strationice as his wife.[64]

From these diplomatic alliances, a new grouping of protagonists was emerging: Ptolemy and Lysimachus versus Seleucus and Demetrius. Cassander played no role in any side, probably because he was occupied entirely with Greece, whereas the others were concerned with Asia Minor and the eastern Mediterranean. But then Seleucus unexpectedly tried to make amends with Ptolemy and reconcile him to Demetrius by arranging that Demetrius marry Ptolemais, Ptolemy's daughter by Eurydice.[65] Why Seleucus acted in this way is unknown: he may have wanted to rebuild his bridges after the tussle over Phoenicia, or even gather as many allies as he could in case Lysimachus should turn against him.[66] Ptolemy accepted Seleucus' compact because after Ipsus he was more concerned with events in Egypt and avoiding conflict with the other kings. Yet, at the same time, he was very careful of Demetrius, prudently demanding hostages to ensure that he kept his side of the bargain.[67]

Although Demetrius had had little say in these diplomatic marriages, and was clearly playing second fiddle to Seleucus and Ptolemy, his power was slowly but steadily on the rise. He had taken over Cilicia, and in 296 moved to Cyprus, just before Lysimachus took Cilicia for himself.[68] The loss of Cilicia did not concern him, for he was now focused on Greece. At the same time, he could not afford to upset Ptolemy or Seleucus. Therefore, he played the age-old game of keeping friends close, and enemies closer. After the defeat at Ipsus, his ally Pyrrhus had lost the throne of Epirus and fled into exile; Demetrius now sent him as a hostage to Ptolemy to show his good intentions toward the Egyptian king while keeping in Seleucus' good books.[69] But then, in 295, Demetrius' ambition became an open book when he sailed to take over Greece and Macedonia, prompting Ptolemy to intervene one more time on the mainland.

[63] Plutarch, *Demetrius* 31.3–4.

[64] Plutarch, *Demetrius* 38; Appian, *Syrian Wars* 59–61.

[65] Plutarch, *Demetrius* 32.3. Waterfield 2011, pp. 177–178, suggests that Ptolemy was actually behind this marriage to offset any move that Seleucus might make in lower Syria.

[66] Anson 2014a, p. 176.

[67] Seibert 1969, pp. 30–31.

[68] Plutarch, *Demetrius* 32.4–5, with Waterfield 2011, pp. 178–179. On Demetrius in the following period, cf. Will 1984b.

[69] Plutarch, *Pyrrhus* 4.3.

Ptolemy's Further Involvement in Greece

In May 297, Cassander died of tuberculosis at Pella.[70] Philip IV, his eldest son, succeeded him, but he succumbed to tuberculosis only four months later.[71] His death was followed by the joint kingship of Cassander's two other sons, Antipater I and Alexander V, with their mother Thessalonice as regent.[72] Although she favored Alexander over Antipater, she insisted on a joint rule; most likely Alexander controlled Macedonia west of the Axius River and Antipater east of it. Thus Macedonia all but returned to its separatist days before Philip II, whose union of Upper (western) and Lower (eastern) Macedonia in 358 had paved the way for his country's prosperity and power.

Ptolemy had stayed clear of the conflicts in Greece and Asia for some time, but now his personal ambition was again whetted because of Cassander's death and Pyrrhus' presence in Egypt. Ptolemy saw in the young Pyrrhus a means to reassert himself into Greek affairs by restoring him to the throne of Epirus. He married him to Antigone, Berenice's daughter by her previous husband Philip, and in 297 sent him with troops to Epirus.[73] Pyrrhus remained a close ally of Ptolemy, always "eager to do him every favor he could and to deny him nothing."[74] Under Pyrrhus' rule, Epirus was propelled to prominence in the Greek world. Pyrrhus himself was one of the period's great military leaders, even invading Italy and defeating the Romans at Heraclea in 280 and Asculum in 279. His victories there nonetheless devastated his troop numbers, and gave rise to the term "Pyrrhic victory."[75]

Another person exploiting the disunity in Macedonia was Demetrius, who in 295 decided the time was ripe for his bid on the Macedonian throne. After Ipsus, the Athenians had turned their backs on him, despite their leading politician Stratocles urging them to stay loyal to him. He had set off from Ephesus to Athens, but at Delos an Athenian delegation caught up with him; it told him that no king was welcome in their city, and that his wife Deidameia (Pyrrhus' sister, whom he married in 302) had been expelled to Megara.[76] Demetrius

[70] Pausanias 9.7.2 ("dropsy"); Justin 16.1.1. Date: Hammond and Walbank 1988, p. 208 n. 3.
[71] Plutarch, *Demetrius* 36.1; Pausanias 9.7.2; Justin 16.1.1.
[72] Plutarch, *Demetrius* 36.1. Her status as guardian or regent is controversial, but see Hammond and Walbank 1988, p. 210 n. 3, for her having this role; *contra* Errington 1978, p. 126 n. 124.
[73] Marriage: Plutarch, *Pyrrhus* 4.4; Pausanias 1.11.5; military support: Plutarch, *Pyrrhus* 5.1; Pausanias 1.6.7, 11.5.
[74] Plutarch, *Pyrrhus* 6.3.
[75] Plutarch, *Pyrrhus*; cf. Austin, no. 47, pp. 90–92 (= Plutarch, *Pyrrhus* 8.1–7, 14); Lévêque 1957; Garoufalias 1979; Champion 2012.
[76] Plutarch, *Demetrius* 30.2–3.

took the news with icy calmness, requesting that the Athenians return some ships belonging to him that were still in the Piraeus, which they did.[77] The Athenians also opened relations with Lysimachus.[78] All of their actions were naïve, and proved to be costly errors for them.

After some initial campaigning in the Peloponnese (where he was shot in the jaw by a catapult bolt during the siege of Messene), Demetrius took his revenge on the Athenians, and besieged their city.[79] The people were already hard-pressed due to a grain shortage, which made them pay 300 drachmas for a measure of grain when the regular price was only five; so bad did the situation become that the Athenians' military leader Lachares (an ally of Cassander, who had seized power in 300), negotiated gifts of grain from Lysimachus in 299 and 298.[80] Demetrius' siege caused a famine in the city, the horror of which is captured by Plutarch's anecdote of a father and son fighting tooth and nail over a dead mouse.[81] Ptolemy sent 150 ships to the Athenians, although his fleet prudently remained off the island of Aegina when it saw Demetrius' huge flotilla of 300 ships bearing down on it, which may well have tarnished Ptolemy's reputation somewhat.[82]

In April 294, a split among the Athenians occurred, and a faction hostile to Lachares persuaded the people to surrender to Demetrius; in fear of his life, Lachares fled to Thebes. Thus Demetrius again won control of Athens. The people knew they would suffer his wrath for their earlier treatment of him and his wife, but he generously gave them 100,000 bushels of grain to alleviate their suffering. At the same time, he installed garrisons in the city (on the Hill of the Muses, across from the Acropolis) and in the Piraeus, and set up (perhaps not immediately, as decrees show the democratic Assembly was at work a little longer) an oligarchy of his own men.[83]

Mastery of Athens gave Demetrius mastery of Greece, and after a brief campaign against Sparta he turned to Macedonia in the fall of 294. There, in a bizarre turn of events, Antipater I had put his mother Thessalonice to death

---

[77] Plutarch, *Demetrius* 36.1–2.

[78] Hammond and Walbank 1988, p. 204.

[79] Wound: Plutarch, *Demetrius* 33.2. Demetrius and Athens: Plutarch, *Demetrius* 33.3–34, with Dreyer 2000.

[80] Austin, no. 54, pp. 106–107 (*IG* v.2. 344). Lachares: Habicht 1997, pp. 82–83; see too Seibert 1983, pp. 163–165.

[81] Plutarch, *Demetrius* 34.2. Athens in this period: Hammond and Walbank 1988, pp. 206–207, 211–218; Green, 1990, pp. 123–125; Habicht 1997, pp. 81–87. Grain shortage: Marasco 1984.

[82] Plutarch, *Demetrius* 33.4.

[83] Plutarch, *Demetrius* 34.3–5. Background (including chronology): Ferguson 1911, pp. 132–138; Hammond and Walbank 1988, pp. 211–212; Green 1990, pp. 124–125; Habicht 1997, pp. 86–87; Anson 2014a, p. 186.

and expelled his brother Alexander V so he could rule the kingdom himself.[84] Alexander was not prepared to let Antipater get away with this and solicited help from Demetrius (then in the Peloponnese) and Pyrrhus. Demetrius left his son Antigonus Gonatas ("knock-kneed") in charge at Athens, and headed north. However, he moved slowly, unlike Pyrrhus, who was geographically closer in any case. Pyrrhus drove out Antipater, but as his price for helping Alexander he took over the parts of southwest Macedonia that bordered his own kingdom.

Demetrius was still marching north while all these events were going on. At Dium, in the foothills of Olympus, he received a message from Alexander that he was not needed after all. That was Alexander's fatal mistake.[85] Pretending that nothing was wrong, Demetrius invited the insolent young man to a banquet, and had him murdered for plotting against him, or so he said. Demetrius then proclaimed himself King of Macedonia, and the people had little choice but to accept him.[86] In many respects, given the length of his marriage to Phila (Cassander's sister), his own and his father's general loyalty to the Argeads, and his tenacity, Demetrius was well suited for the kingship.[87]

Seeing the writing on the wall, Antipater I now abandoned Macedonia and fled to Lysimachus. There was no help for him there because while leading troops against the Getae of northern Thrace, Lysimachus was defeated by their king and was imprisoned for the best part of the year in their capital, Helis.[88] At the time of Lysimachus' misfortune, Demetrius had just finished a successful campaign in Thessaly, and was then attacking Boeotia, where he seized a number of towns, including Thebes, which he garrisoned. He left Boeotia to march immediately on Thrace, hoping to add it to his domain, but returned to Macedonia when news reached him that the wily Lysimachus had escaped.[89]

Ptolemy's Final Campaigns

Despite the lackluster effort of his fleet off Athens, Ptolemy was quick to seize more of Demetrius' possessions while he was busy in Macedonia. In 294 Ptolemy finally recaptured Cyprus, lost to him twelve years previously in 306.[90]

---

[84] Plutarch, *Demetrius* 36.1; Diodorus 21.7; Pasusanias 9.7.3; Justin 16.1.1–4. On this and the following events: Hammond and Walbank 1988, pp. 212–218.

[85] Plutarch, *Demetrius* 36; Justin 16.1.8–9; cf. Diodorus 21.7.1.

[86] Plutarch, *Demetrius* 37; Justin 16.1.10–17, with Habicht 1997, p. 21.

[87] Demetrius as king: Hammond and Walbank 1988, pp. 219–229; Waterfield 2011, pp. 186–190, 193–196.

[88] Diodorus 21.12; Pausanias 1.9.6, with Lund 1994, pp. 43–49.

[89] Plutarch, *Demetrius* 39.3; cf. Diodorus 21.14.1–2.

[90] Plutarch, *Demetrius* 35.3–4.

He besieged Salamis on the island and faced Demetrius' wife Phila, who conducted the island's overall defense, and bravely rallied the defenders until the city was overcome. She was captured, along with her children, but remembering Demetrius' noble action of returning his son Leontiscus to him, Ptolemy sent her to her husband with presents.[91] It would be over two centuries before Cyprus, in 58, was again lost to the Ptolemies, thanks to the Romans.

Most probably at this time Ptolemy took over Demetrius' Aegean possessions, including the League of the Cycladic Islands, originally founded by Antigonus, perhaps in 314.[92] Ptolemy's action gave Egypt control of the entire Cyclades and the Aegean sea routes for the next half century until 245.[93] A *nesiarchos* ("commander of the islands") was appointed.[94] In gratitude, the league established a cult to Ptolemy as a savior.[95] He also seized Sidon, Tyre (expelling Demetrius' garrisons in both places), and all of Lycia, and brought these areas under Ptolemaic control—by the end of 288 we find two *oikonomoi* (financial administrators) there.[96] Philocles, the king of Sidon, whom Ptolemy allowed to rule presumably as his vassal, became one of his top generals and helped to ensure Ptolemaic dominance of the Aegean and Asia Minor until the early years of Ptolemy II's reign.[97] Also at this time, Ptolemy may have seized Pamphylia, for a *pamphyliarch* (governor) is attested by the end of 278, during Ptolemy II's reign.[98] Since Ptolemy II continued his father's administrative policies, it is plausible that Ptolemy I had established this office, and hence took over Pamphylia. Ptolemy's empire was now considerable, for which he deserves credit.

For the next year or two there was an uneasy calm between the kings, who for the most part remained in their kingdoms.[99] Seleucus could not have been happy with Ptolemy's new possessions, especially as he had set his sights on them after Ipsus, but nevertheless he did nothing. Then, in 291, Demetrius soured his relations with Pyrrhus when he married one of Pyrrhus' wives, Lanassa, who willingly left her husband to be with him. Pyrrhus had earlier made an unsuccessful foray into Thessaly, which had been a buffer zone between Macedonia and central Greece since the days of Philip II, to undo Demetrius' influence there.[100] In 290, after holding his own Olympic festival in

---

[91] Plutarch, *Demetrius* 38.1.
[92] Diodorus 19.62.9.
[93] Merker 1970; Seibert 1983, pp. 117–120; see too Bagnall 1976, pp. 136–141.
[94] Austin, no. 218, pp. 359–361 (decree recording the appointment).
[95] Hauben 2010, pp. 108–118.
[96] Wörrle 1977.
[97] Seibert 1970; Hauben 1987b.
[98] Bagnall 1976, pp. 111–113; Mehl 1986, p. 273.
[99] Background and subsequent events: Anson 2014a, pp. 179–184.
[100] Plutarch, *Demetrius* 40.1–3.

Athens because he could not attend the Pythian Games at Delphi, Demetrius invaded Epirus, but achieved little.[101]

For a while now, Demetrius' opulent lifestyle had been the source of grave dissatisfaction among the Macedonians, who cherished austerity, even of their kings. Demetrius had so many different clothes, including purple robes embroidered with gold, ostentatious hats, and gold-embossed shoes, that "there was something theatrical about him."[102] The Macedonians were also fuming over the contempt in which he held them, refusing to read their petitions and not granting them audiences, and they were hardly enamored with his grand plan of invading Asia, with an enormous army—"which no man had possessed since Alexander"—of 98,000 infantry, 12,000 cavalry, and 500 warships (including some "super warships" of fifteen and sixteen banks of oars), funded by the Macedonian treasury.[103]

At all costs, Demetrius had to be stopped from invading Asia. Ptolemy, Lysimachus, Seleucus, and Pyrrhus (despite his earlier truce with Demetrius) banded together for the sole purpose of ending his rule. This Fifth War of the Successors, breaking out in the summer of 288, was over almost as soon as it began.[104] Ptolemy sailed to Greece to win over cities loyal to Demetrius.[105] At the same time, Pyrrhus invaded Macedonia from the west and Lysimachus from the east. Demetrius, who was in Greece, immediately marched north, leaving Gonatas to protect his interests in Greece.

This time luck was not with Demetrius. Many of his men deserted to Lysimachus and Pyrrhus, so he fled in disguise (wearing a black cloak instead of his usual royal robe) to Cassandreia, leaving behind his wife Phila—unable to deal with her husband's misfortune, she committed suicide by taking poison.[106] From Cassandreia, Demetrius rejoined Gonatas in Corinth, intent on regaining his influence in Greece. Lysimachus and Pyrrhus divided up control of Macedonia between each other, and to ensure that they had no opposition to the throne, Lysimachus had his son-in-law, the former joint king Antipater I, put to death.[107] Demetrius embarked on a lightning and successful

---

[101] Games: Plutarch, *Demetrius* 40.4; Demetrius and Epirus: Plutarch, *Demetrius* 41.1–2. Demetrius and Pyrrhus later reconciled: Plutarch, *Demetrius* 43.1.

[102] Plutarch, *Demetrius* 41.4–5; cf. 44.6.

[103] Contempt: Plutarch, *Demetrius* 42; size of his force: Plutarch, *Demetrius* 43.2–3; quote: Plutarch, *Demetrius* 44.1. On the following events, see Hammond and Walbank 1988, pp. 238–248.

[104] Plutarch, *Demetrius* 44, *Pyrrhus* 10–12; Justin 16.2.1–3, with Hölbl 2001, p. 24.

[105] Plutarch, *Demetrius* 44. 2.

[106] Plutarch, *Demetrius* 45.1.

[107] Hammond and Walbank 1988, pp. 229–238; Lund 1994, pp. 98–100; Anson 2014a, pp. 180–181.

campaign in the Peloponnese, but his aim to retake Greece was foiled by the Athenians. When in 287 Demetrius marched on their city (which had revolted from him), the people urgently appealed to Pyrrhus and Ptolemy.[108] The latter sent grain, money, and 1,000 mercenaries under Callias of Sphettus (an exile from Athens then serving in Ptolemy's army), who were based on Andros, and kept his fleet on stand-by.[109] With their help, the Athenians defied Demetrius, who abandoned his siege—and Greece. Gonatas was to hold his remaining possessions in Greece, while Demetrius crossed to Asia Minor, intent on undoing Lysimachus' influence there.[110]

Demetrius fared poorly though. After some initial successes, including the capture of Sardis, he was systematically beaten back by Lysimachus' son Agathocles, losing 8,000 men. In despair he wrote for help to Seleucus, who insisted on his surrender, and then imprisoned him.[111] Although Lysimachus offered Seleucus 2,000 talents to execute him, the latter refused.[112] Three years later, in 282, Demetrius drank himself to death, at age fifty-four. Seleucus had his ashes put into a golden urn bedecked with purple and with his diadem, which he returned to his son Antigonus in Greece, who buried his father at Demetrias (on the Gulf of Pagasae).[113]

Ptolemy's control of Cyprus, the League of the Cycladic Islands, and his naval base on Andros meant that he dominated the entire Aegean and eastern Mediterranean.[114] However, after Demetrius' failure at Athens, Ptolemy had withdrawn from the coalition; he had not personally taken part in any fighting on the mainland, probably because he was about eighty by then, and perhaps in deteriorating health. As far as we know, this was his last campaign. We hear nothing more about him until 285, when he made his younger son joint ruler, and his death in 283 (Chapter 12).

The End of the Successors

When Demetrius fell into Seleucus' hands in 285, Lysimachus decided that the time was ripe for him to seize all of Macedonia. His invasion was a complete

---

[108] Plutarch, *Demetrius* 46.1–2.

[109] Plutarch, *Pyrrhus* 11.2. See further the decree in honor of Callias (*SEG* 28.60 = Austin, no. 44, pp. 80–83); Shear 1978; Osborne 1979; Habicht 1997, pp. 95–97. Ptolemy's aid: Callias decree, lines 11–42 (Shear 1978, pp. 2–3), with Habicht 1997, pp. 127–129.

[110] Plutarch, *Demetrius* 46.2–5.

[111] Plutarch, *Demetrius* 47–51.

[112] Diodorus 21.20; Plutarch, *Demetrius* 51.3, with Lund 1994, p. 104.

[113] Death: Plutarch, *Demetrius* 52.1–3; Burial: Plutarch, *Demetrius* 53.

[114] Hammond and Walbank 1988, pp. 228, 232; Green 1990, pp. 128–129.

success; Pyrrhus was forced back to Epirus, and so Lysimachus became sole king of Macedonia.[115] Like Ptolemy and Seleucus, Lysimachus had come a long way since the settlement at Babylon in 323. After Ptolemy had died in 283, only Lysimachus and Seleucus of the original Successors were still alive; Seleucus by then was 75 years old, and Lysimachus 72. Neither man would last much longer.

Arsinoe (II) and her half-brother Ptolemy Ceraunus had long since set their sights on taking Thrace as a stepping stone to ruling Greece and Macedonia. Arsinoe now schemed to have Lysimachus suspect his eldest son (and heir) Agathocles of treason, and the unfortunate and innocent Agathocles was executed. Lysimachus followed this action with a purge of his friends, who fled for safety to Seleucus.[116] They included Ptolemy Ceraunus and his sister Lysandra (Agathocles' widow). Seleucus interpreted the flight as a sign of his rival's weakness, and Lysandra and her brother very probably fed his belief. Therefore, in the winter of 282, Seleucus invaded Asia Minor, and Lysimachus assembled am army to meet the invader. In 281 they fought each other at the battle of Corupedion, where Seleucus defeated and killed Lysimachus.[117] Seleucus then added Thrace and Macedonia to his kingdom—now it was his turn to rule an empire second only to Alexander's in size.

That summer (281) Seleucus crossed to take possession of Macedonia— the first time he had been back to his homeland since 334, when he invaded Asia with Alexander. Unfortunately for him, another man also had his eyes set on the Macedonian throne—Ptolemy Ceraunus. This Ptolemy treacherously murdered Seleucus and proclaimed himself king. His rule was a short one to say the least. In 279 a major Gallic invasion of Greece took place, with the Gauls penetrating as far as Delphi and Asia Minor. Ptolemy Ceraunus was killed in battle against them in 279, his head impaled on top of an enemy spear in triumph. For two more years the Gauls ran amok, but in 276 Gonatas defeated them in battle at Lysimacheia (Thrace), and took the Macedonian throne as Antigonus II Gonatas (r. 276–239). He founded the actual Antigonid dynasty, which lasted until the Romans made Macedonia and Greece a province of the Roman Empire in 168.[118]

With the assassination of Seleucus in 281, the Wars of the Successors finally ended after 40 years of bloodshed, intrigue, murder, and turmoil, out of which

---

[115] Plutarch, *Pyrrhus* 12; Justin 16.3.2, with Lund 1994, pp. 105–106.

[116] Lund 1994, pp. 185–198.

[117] Seibert 1983, pp. 165–167; Lund 1994, pp. 199–206.

[118] Gonatas: Tarn 1913; Gabbart 1997; cf. Hammond and Walbank 1988, pp. 251–258; Waterfield 2011, pp. 197–212. Conquest by Rome: Errington 1971; Gruen 1984; Eckstein 2006; Waterfield 2014; cf. Green 1990, pp. 414–432.

arose the great Hellenistic dynasties: the Ptolemies in Egypt; the Seleucids in Syria, Mesopotamia, and Iran; and the Antigonids in Macedonia and Greece. All of their rulers traced their lineage back to Alexander's senior staff, and thus their empires back to Alexander the Great himself. In this respect, they were all worthy of succeeding him—some, like Ptolemy, more than others.

11

Ptolemy and Egypt

Although Egypt's population during Ptolemy's reign is not properly known, at the end of the Ptolemaic period it was about seven million, including Greeks, Macedonians, Thracians, Illyrians, those from the Asian areas of Alexander's conquests, Jews, and of course Egyptians.[1] The vast majority lived in small towns and villages in the three main areas of the country: Upper and Middle Egypt, and the Fayum, an area that Ptolemy greatly expanded for both farming and settlement. The capital Memphis was on the Nile, not far south of the delta, and had a population in the tens of thousands.[2] Although Ptolemy switched the capital to Alexandria by 311, Memphis continued to be a religious and ceremonial center. The other Successors were clearly a threat to Ptolemy's control of Egypt, but he also faced the problem of how to govern his multicultural country effectively. Unlike the Pharaohs, he had no legitimate right to rule, so he embarked on a complex policy that was ultimately anchored in religion and an understanding of other cultures to secure his acceptance.

Our ancient sources tell us next to nothing about how Ptolemy ruled Egypt, or what his people really thought of him, in contrast to the Ptolemaic rulers who followed him. Yet by considering some aspects of all Ptolemaic rule, we can get glimpses into what Ptolemy did, and why, as well as Alexander's influence on him. Accordingly, this chapter is divided into Ptolemy's three main areas of governance—relations with the people, administration and economy, and religion—although all three overlap.

But here a word of warning: I do not deal with many socioeconomic and cultural topics, for example family life, differences between rural and urban areas, social order, and law, because once again our information is post–Ptolemy I, and applying it to Ptolemy is too hypothetical. However, many of the citations in the notes refer (often unavoidably) to the entire Ptolemaic period.[3]

---

[1] Number: Diodorus 1.31.6–8, with Manning 2003, pp. 47–49; Fischer-Bovet 2011; cf. Bevan 1927, pp. 114–118.

[2] Thompson 1988, pp. 32–35.

[3] The most comprehensive treatment of all aspects of Ptolemaic (and Pharaonic) Egypt is Lloyd 2010c; see also the extensive chapters in Walbank, Astin, Frederiksen, and Ogilvie 1984c.

Relations with the People

To begin with, what was the nature of Ptolemy's rule?[4] A Macedonian king had the final say in all domestic and foreign policy—*l'état, c'est moi* existed long before Louis XIV. For advice the king could turn to his closest companions (*hetairoi*), who often formed an advisory council, especially when on campaign. Although the kings need not heed their advice, Ptolemy, like the other Successors, turned to friends and companions for guidance on state matters. As a result, we see a change in the nomenclature of advisers, with friends (*philoi*) eclipsing *hetairoi*. Even though not elected to any actual office, the *philoi* became powerful in their own right because rulers relied on them.[5] In the case of Egypt, these *philoi* (and later *archisomatophylakes*, or "Gentlemen of the Bodyguard") were Macedonians and Greeks, not natives, at least during Ptolemy's time.[6] Antigonus Monophthalmus appeared to have had a *synedrion* (council) composed of his *philoi*, and Ptolemy will have had something similar.[7] Such was Ptolemy's "court," although at the end of the day everyone knew that he was an autocrat—in other words, a typical Macedonian king.

Ptolemy's greatest challenges were to bridge the divide between the Egyptians and the other population groups—Greeks, Macedonians, Asiatics, Thracians, and Jews—living under him, and to have everyone accept him as ruler.[8] This presented more of a dilemma when it came to the Egyptians. After all, the Macedonians were living in Egypt as conquerors, and no one likes to be conquered. Ptolemy was helped by the Egyptians' custom of obeying a leader: in Pharaonic times the people had followed the will of the priests and the Pharaohs. This rigid system enabled Alexander to rule Egypt; he was not a Pharaoh, but he strove to ensure that the age-old ideal of *maat* ("right order") prevailed in Egypt, something that was expected of a Pharaoh. So too did all the Ptolemies. Although Ptolemy transferred the capital to Alexandria from Memphis (where the Pharaohs were associated with Ptah, father of the gods), and his kingship followed the Macedonian model, he was still responsive to

---

[4] See further, Manning 2010, pp. 30–34, 73–116, for example.

[5] Billows 1990, pp. 246–250; Habicht 2006b; Mooren 2010.

[6] Strootman 2014b, pp. 126–131, on the ethnicity of the *philoi*, especially after Ptolemy II.

[7] Diodorus 18.50.5, 19.46.4, 48.1, 57.1.

[8] On the people and society see, for example, Bevan 1927, pp. 79–90, 109–114; Rostovtzeff 1941, vol. 1, pp. 316–332; Tarn and Griffith 1952, pp. 197–207; Bowman 1986, pp. 122–125; Samuel 1989, pp. 35–48; Thompson 2001, pp. 301–322; Bingen 2007, especially pp. 104–133, 240–255; Manning 2010, pp. 141–152 and passim; Cruz-Uribe 2010, pp. 492–497; Strootman 2014b, pp. 111–135.

Egyptian customs, religion, and laws.[9] He deliberately continued the close association Alexander had forged with Amun Re to show he was chosen by the god and a beloved son, both phrases that were part of his official throne name, and which signified divine support of his rule. Reliefs on a temple in Oxyrhynchus (some 200 miles south of Alexandria) show him offering *maat* for Egypt's prosperity, so he clearly took his Pharaonic duties seriously.[10]

In this way the Egyptians saw Ptolemy as king and Pharaoh, and the priests of Buto even called him "great ruler of Egypt" on the satrap stele. His Greek and Macedonian subjects also accepted him as, in turn, he measured up to their expectations of a ruler. The "dual nature" of Ptolemy's rule is exemplified by his secular portrait, wearing a diadem, on his coins and his depiction as Pharaoh on temples (see Figures 1.1 and 1.2). These representations also highlight another factor of Ptolemaic Egypt: that under these rulers the country was neither Egyptian nor Greek, but a hybrid in all aspects of its life and society.[11] Ptolemy was not merely King of Egypt, but King and Pharaoh. In taking on the title of Pharaoh, the Ptolemies were not just establishing their political legitimacy over Egypt, but bringing about a new type of rule and ruler. Ptolemy, like Alexander when he began calling himself King of Asia, was faced with new challenges each day and had no precedent to fall back on; what Ptolemy cleverly did was to exercise power not over society, but through it.[12]

Like Alexander in the eastern half of his empire, Ptolemy faced a myriad of different customs.[13] A Macedonian king had never ruled Persia before, so Alexander had to adapt quickly. He called himself King of Asia, a term that best described his new kingship, and wore a combination of Macedonian and Persian clothing, despite the animosity this caused among his men.[14] While the revolts of Afghanistan and India proved that the people did not accept him as their king, what he did, or rather tried to do, and the successes and failures he faced, were a remarkable learning experience for all the Successors when it came to dealing with their diverse subject populations.

Alexander had allowed the Egyptians to practice their own religion when he first took over the country, even sacrificing to the native god Apis (who was in the form of a bull), and Ptolemy would have seen the effect this had on the people. Even in Persia, Alexander had allowed freedom of religion and

[9] Samuel 1993; on royal ideology and religious policy, see especially Koenen 1993; cf. Hölbl 2001, pp. 77–90.

[10] Hölbl 2001, p. 86, citing bibliography.

[11] Manning 2010, p. 3.

[12] Manning 2010.

[13] Worthington 2010, and 2014, pp. 196–201, 214–216, 239–241.

[14] Curtius 6.6.1–10; Plutarch, *Alexander* 45.1–4. On the title and its implications, see Fredricksmeyer 2000.

social customs, but it was a different story in Bactria and India. For example, he banned the Bactrian practice of dogs eating elderly and sick people alive, and in India he committed atrocities against the revered Brahman philosophers. On the one hand, the Bactrian ritual was as abhorrent to the Greeks as it is to us, but nonetheless, Alexander's unilateral move interfered with local customs, and was seen as that. He made no attempt to understand why the Bactrians had this practice, and in India he either failed to grasp, or simply did not care about, the deep role that the Brahmans played in Indian politics, religion, and society.

Ptolemy had no desire to face the same sorts of issues that had plagued Alexander. He doubtless won popularity with the native peoples when he executed the extortionate Cleomenes, and he was careful to allow the Egyptians to abide by their own laws, have their own courts, and keep their religious beliefs and social customs.[15] He also had little choice but to maintain good relations with the Egyptian elite (his association with the priest and historian Manetho is one such example) because, like Alexander, he needed the upper echelon of society to accept his rule, and thereby help to "sell" it to the other social strata of society. In this respect he allowed many of the native elite to continue in his administration, a practical move anyway because they knew the native language and customs.

While he paid due respect to the powerful and venerated Egyptian priests, his reasons, though, were always pragmatic. For example, in 311, his restoration of the lands to the priests of Buto that the Persians had seized from them was less for piety and more to do with gaining their goodwill should he face an Antigonid invasion from that area (see p. 124). The grateful priests did set up the satrap stele in his honor, which no doubt helped to legitimize his rule in the eyes of the natives, but it surely would not have been lost on the people that when Ptolemy founded Ptolemais (sometimes called Ptolemais Hermiou) in the Thebaid in or soon after 312, he did so to spread Ptolemaic influence southward to counteract Thebes as the capital of Upper Egypt.[16] Nor did the Egyptians have much say in the cult of Sarapis, which Ptolemy introduced, as a means of binding native and non-native together (see below).

Ptolemy deliberately encouraged foreigners, especially Macedonians and Greeks, to move to Egypt. He did so not only to boost the size of his army but also because these immigrants had the experience of living in a monetary economy, and Ptolemy was intent on introducing such an economy to replace Egypt's reliance on bartering (see below).[17] Greeks quickly comprised the

---

[15] On law and order, see Manning 2010, pp. 165–201; Mélèze Modrzejewski 2014; and futher discussion in this chapter.

[16] On Ptolemais, see, for example, Bevan 1927, pp. 104–108; Mueller 2006, especially pp. 166–168.

[17] Rostovtzeff 1941, vol. 1, pp. 263–264.

largest immigration group, living side by side with the native inhabitants in both rural and urban areas.[18] Indeed, Greeks remained the largest group of settlers throughout the Hellenistic period.[19] As a result, Greek became more widely spoken throughout the country, and more than that, Ptolemy made it the official language of his administration. There was probably no overnight change; however, the steady creep of the Greek language also had an impact on Egyptian literacy, as the native language became less used in official circles.[20]

Although there was never a royal edict forcing anyone to learn, write, and speak Greek, non-Greek speakers found it difficult to impossible to take part in the bureaucracy, and so felt marginalized. Egypt was never a bilingual country, but by the later third century some of the Egyptians were bilingual—not so much out of desire but necessity so they could take part in the bureaucracy.[21] Significantly, no Greek or Macedonian was expected to read and speak Egyptian—of all the Ptolemaic rulers, only the polyglot Cleopatra VII did so.[22]

Ptolemy was also eager for Jews to move to Egypt. A large number of them were already living in Elephantine in southern Egypt, but they began to move to the country in greater numbers after the battle of Gaza in 312. They played an important role in society under all the Ptolemies and into the Roman period.[23] Many were farmers or artisans, but a goodly number were employed in the administration as tax-gatherers and even law enforcement, for which they too had to speak and write Greek.

Ptolemy's counselors were never Egyptians, and, since the language of Ptolemaic administration was Greek, natives had to learn this language if they wanted to take part in the bureaucracy, which could not have been easy.[24] Alternatively, they might adopt a Greek name, such as Menches, a village scribe at the tail end of the second century, who changed his name to Asclepiades.[25] His job was to provide reports on various farming activities in his village, including rents, to his superiors.

Natives may also have been largely marginalized in Ptolemy's army and navy. Egyptian troops played a significant role in the battle of Raphia, fought

---

[18] Rowlandson 2003; Bingen 2007, pp. 104–113 and 240–255.

[19] A focused treatment of documented Greeks in Egypt, which is also a survey on Greeks generally in the country, is Lewis 1986; cf. Rowlandson 2003.

[20] See, for example, Thompson 1992; cf. Cruz-Uribe 2010, pp. 492–493.

[21] Hölbl 2001, p. 25, and especially Peremans 1983. For a letter from the third century by an Egyptian who was bilingual, see Bagnall and Derow 1981, no. 113, p. 193.

[22] Plutarch, *Antony*, 27.4.

[23] Bevan 1927, pp. 111–114, and especially Kasher 1985.

[24] Cf. Falivene 1991.

[25] Austin, no. 260, pp. 437–438, with Lewis 1986, pp. 104–123.

between Ptolemy IV and the Seleucid king Antiochus III in 217, and are found more prominently in Ptolemaic armies after this date. Before then, we hear of Egyptians fighting only in 312, when at the battle of Gaza they supported Ptolemy against an Antigonid army. It has been suggested that Ptolemy, or his immediate successors, did not use natives in their armies until after Gaza because of the linguistic differences between them and Greek soldiers.[26] That is possible, but then again, natives were used as light armed infantry, so the different languages do not seem to have been a major problem.[27] Perhaps, then, the Ptolemies felt no need to train locals as front-row fighters until much later, given that they had a ready supply of trained Greeks, Macedonians, and mercenaries, who had settled permanently in the country thanks to Ptolemy.

Ptolemy evidently enjoyed the loyalty of his men, and his generosity and generalship skills clearly attracted soldiers to serve under him. The troops of Perdiccas and Antigonus did desert them on occasion, for example, and it is even more instructive that after Ptolemy's loss to Demetrius at Cyprus in 306, many of his men refused to serve in the victor's army, despite how much he was going to pay them, but tried to return to Egypt.[28]

But the divide between the native and non-native population was never fully bridged. The impetus Ptolemy gave to Alexandria, especially with its Museum and Library, was intended to endear his rule to Greeks and Egyptians, for bustling Alexandria was a Greek city; it was a hub of civilization, and it helped to promote Egypt as a cultural center in the Mediterranean world (see Chapter 8). Yet there was a clear preference given to non-Egyptian scholars, which would not change for the best part of a century. Further, Ptolemy may have been responsible for establishing ethnic quarters for Egyptians, Greeks, and Jews in Alexandria. Although the city was a melting pot of different cultures, peoples, and languages, these different quarters highlighted the social divisions of its inhabitants.[29]

It is no surprise that, as time continued, problems developed between the foreign and native populations in all aspects of public and private life, presumably largely brought on by the preponderance of Macedonians and Greeks in the administration and in the decision-making process at court.[30] Also

[26] Peremans 1978 and 1983, pp. 273–277; Hammond 1996; cf. Pollard 2010, pp. 447–449.

[27] Rodriguez 2004; Fischer-Bovert 2013 and 2016; see too Lloyd 2002, pp. 120–122, on Egyptians in early Ptolemaic armies based on hieroglyphic evidence; cf. Lewis 1986, pp. 20–26; Clarysse 1985.

[28] Diodorus 20.47.4.

[29] See further, Fraser 1972, vol. 1, pp. 38–92; Peremans 1976.

[30] Mooren 2010: on pp. 126–127, Mooren refers to the forty members of the *philoi* and *archisomatophylakes* from the entire Ptolemaic period, of which only two were Egyptian. See too Peremans 1976, 1980/81.

unpopular were other practices to which the Ptolemies had to resort, including the forced billeting of officials and troops in villages and towns. This was something that happened frequently in the Greek world as contingents of troops could be spread far and wide to meet any situation. Because space was limited in Egypt thanks to the annual flooding of the Nile, townships probably had to put up large numbers of men, and discontent at the costs that the local people had to shoulder and abuses on the part of soldiers grew. A letter of Ptolemy II from the middle of the third century speaks of his awareness of "increased violence as [the soldiers] are not receiving lodgings from the *oikonomoi* [officials] but break into the houses themselves, expel the inhabitants and settle there by force," and he goes on to order that the men stop doing this, and that when they are billeted with families they must leave the homes in good shape.[31] We do not know whether these abuses occurred in Ptolemy I's time, but they may well have, given his dependence on the army and deployment of troops throughout Egypt.[32]

The picture we have been painting seems to be of a country that was losing its national identity, and becoming more "Greek" with every passing year. But that is not so. For one thing, Egyptian culture and customs impacted those who lived in Egypt. For example, Greeks in their own literature wrote about Egypt and Egyptians, and early Ptolemaic portraiture was heavily affected by Egyptian styles.[33] Trappings of Egyptian religious beliefs found their way into Greek religion, the worship of Sarapis being the most obvious, and the Greeks also took up the cult of Isis (Osiris' sister). Greeks in rural areas especially adopted Egyptian irrigation practices, and the nuts and bolts of the Pharaonic bureaucratic system shaped the Ptolemaic. Further, a study of hieroglyphic evidence from the early Ptolemaic period (down to Ptolemy IV) suggests that the upper echelons of Egyptian society, from which came priests and generals, for example, still exercised influence in the various areas in which they lived, and that experienced Egyptian generals served in the Ptolemaic army.[34] While Egypt in the Hellenistic period was never as uniquely Egyptian as in Pharaonic times, its native people still worshipped their own gods, practiced their own social customs, and spoke their own language; in short, Egypt was

---

[31] Austin, no. 249, p. 422; cf. no. 250, pp. 422–423, on Ptolemy II's other decrees to safeguard internal security. See too Bagnall and Derow 1981, nos. 114–115, pp. 193–195, for two individual complaints about abusive treatment.

[32] Army: Bouché-Leclercq 1907, pp. 1–69; Bevan 1927, pp. 165–177; Lewis 1986, pp. 20–26 (pp. 21–24 on billeting); Pollard 2010, pp. 447–451; and especially Fischer-Bovet 2014.

[33] Morrison 2010, pp. 758–778; Ashton 2010, pp. 971–977. See also Figure 1.3.

[34] Lloyd 2002, pp. 117–136.

"a society of two faces, Greek and Egyptian, resulting in an ongoing symbiosis of both cultures."[35]

Despite the differences between his foreign and native populations, Ptolemy was accepted as a ruler, for we hear of no discontent against him. Perhaps he did deliberately cultivate a gracious and generous image to win him popularity and to help legitimize his rule, for our sources stress these aspects of his nature. Diodorus speaks of his "treating the natives with kindness," and Justin of how he "won the support of the Egyptians by his exceptional restraint, and he had put the neighboring monarchs in his debt by his benefactions and indulgent behavior towards them."[36] These traits were certainly different from Alexander, who toward the end of his reign was paranoid and apparently instilled fear in everyone at court. Nor did Ptolemy harbor pretensions to personal divinity as had Alexander, causing him to lose touch with his army and people.[37] If so, Ptolemy was again learning from Alexander's successes and failures. In reality, the gap between foreign and native elements of the population could never have been bridged. However, by not losing contact with the rank and file of his army and his own people, and by championing the religious and social customs of all his subjects, Ptolemy was able to rule as successfully as he did.

Administration and Economy

Nearly all of what we know about Ptolemaic administration and the economy comes from the time of Ptolemy II (r. 283–246) and his successors.[38] Ptolemy II in particular introduced many new taxes and laws, in the process creating "the most elaborate and far-reaching bureaucracy the world had ever known."[39] However, he must have added to a bureaucracy that had its origins with his father. The same is also true of Ptolemaic economic policy, in which Ptolemy I played a far greater role than has often been assumed.[40]

[35] Vandorpe 2010, pp. 171–179; the quote is on p. 178.

[36] Diodorus 18.14.1; Justin 13.6.19.

[37] Worthington 2014, pp. 265–269.

[38] Bouché-Leclercq 1906, pp. 123–402; Bevan 1927, pp. 132–188; Préaux 1939; Rostovtzeff 1941, vol. 1, pp. 261–415 (only six pages on Ptolemy I!) and 1954; Tarn and Griffith 1952, pp. 186–197; Bagnall 1976, pp. 3–10 and passim; Turner 1984; Bowman 1986, pp. 56–64; Lewis 1986, pp. 104–123; Samuel 1989, pp. 51–65 (all post–Ptolemy I); Hölbl 2001, pp. 58–63; Bingen 2007, pp. 157–205; Caroli 2007, pp. 213–256; Manning 2010, pp. 117–164 and passim (almost all post–Ptolemy I); Rowlandson 2010, pp. 238–243; Waterfield 2011, pp. 155–170 (comparing Ptolemaic administration to Seleucid).

[39] Grant 1982, p. 40; Manning 2010; cf. Rowlandson 2010, pp. 243–245.

[40] Lianou 2014.

When Ptolemy first occupied Egypt, he took over Alexander's existing system of administration. In this structure, Egyptians had played a role in the administration of their country, and Cleomenes had been tasked with collecting all taxes; later, in 325, Alexander made Cleomenes satrap. Since Pharaonic times, Egypt had been divided into forty nomes (*nomoi*) or areas, with an equal number in both Upper and Lower Egypt; each one was subdivided into places (*toparchoi*) and villages (*komai*). Each nome was presided over by a governor who was both judge and tax collector. The governors were under the control of the *dioiketes*, the king's chief civil servant, and were subservient only to the king himself. In continuing with these divisions and officers (often natives), as well as using a flood of officials in the nomes who performed minor duties (for example, collecting local taxes, registering estates and lands, overseeing farming property, even acting as a police force), Ptolemy can be seen to be fusing together Macedonian and Egyptian practices, and in doing so was using Alexander as his model.[41]

Once Alexander had toppled the Persian Empire, he was faced with the thorny problem of how to rule it.[42] In the late fifth century, the Persian king Darius had divided the empire into twenty satrapies because of its huge size. Each satrapy was under the control of a satrap, who was virtually autonomous—all he had to do was ensure that taxes were paid to the Great King and muster troops when needed. Alexander adopted this practice, but necessarily had to adapt it. For example, after 330 he allowed native aristocrats to be satraps, but he took away their military and financial powers and placed these in the hands of Macedonians.

Alexander's action was purely pragmatic: he needed men who had the same social and religious customs and spoke the same language and local dialects as the ordinary people. He also anticipated that by using natives as satraps they would show loyalty to him and so help to reconcile the people to Macedonian rule, even if they were now no more than titular figureheads. He also introduced the post of imperial treasurer to streamline taxation collection and management. Also as part of his administration, Alexander founded various cities, which also acted as military outposts and stimulated trade and communication.[43]

[41] Austin, no. 262, pp. 440–442; Ellis 1994, pp. 44–45; Falivene 1991, pp. 203–227; Caroli 2007, especially pp. 110–167, 193–256; Lloyd 2010a. On nomes and their officials: Bevan 1927, pp. 139–144, 157–165; Tarn and Griffith 1952, pp. 196–197; Caroli 2007, pp. 251–253.

[42] Alexander's administration: Worthington 2014, pp. 196–201.

[43] Plutarch, *Moralia* 328e, claims over 70 cities, but see Fraser 1996 for Alexander's founding only nine, including Alexandria.

Egypt was far smaller than the Persian Empire, but Ptolemy still had the issue of dealing with a diverse subject population and maintaining his rule, as we have noted earlier. However, he saw first hand how Alexander had addressed the problem of administration, and he learned from it. Thus it made sense to have an official who acted as intermediary between the various officials in rural Egypt and the court in Alexandria, hence the *dioiketes* took on the guise of imperial treasurer. Ptolemy also replaced the previous Egyptian governors of the nomes with Greeks and Macedonians, although by necessity he had to use many locals in lower and middle posts in the nomes. He probably set up a *strategos* or general in each nome, who was in charge of military affairs, responsible only to him. In time, the *strategos* came to wield more powers, which may even have included judicial, for it appears that there were Greek courts in the various towns of each nome, which surely existed in Ptolemy's time.[44] Ptolemy's action again followed Alexander's practice of appointing his own men to high-level positions. Even his founding of Ptolemais and his expansion of Alexandria have an affinity with Alexander's policy of founding cities.

After Ptolemy had done away with Cleomenes, all taxes now flowed to him. Yet despite the country's wealth and resources, it did not have enough fighting manpower for his army or timber for his fleet and copper for his coinage. Therefore, he embarked on an ambitious economic plan, which aligned with his foreign policy, to make himself and his country wealthier and to help pay the enormous costs of his army.[45] In doing so, all his policies more than laid the groundwork for Ptolemy II's later economic reforms: they made Egypt part of the Greek world, no longer a country that was previously seen as merely part of Asia.[46]

Ptolemy, like his sucessors, encouraged trade and agriculture throughout Egypt.[47] Among other things, his stimulus to agriculture included irrigation and land reclamation projects, all designed to increase the amount of cultivable land and hence crops. Equally important was turning Alexandria into a major commercial center and port. This was one of his main reasons, perhaps his major reason, for making the city his capital, as Memphis was situated far away from the major trade networks of the Mediterranean and the Aegean. Ptolemy's construction of the *heptastadion* (mole) to create Alexandria's two ports, as well as the lighthouse at Pharos, was as much a part of his economic policy as a means of lending grandeur to the city. The move to Alexandria

[44] Law: Bouché-Leclercq 1907, pp. 196–275; Bevan 1927, pp. 157–165; Rowlandson 2010, pp. 243–244; Mélèze Modrzejewski 2014.

[45] Lianou 2014.

[46] Lloyd 2010a, pp. 83–105.

[47] Rostovtzeff 1941, vol. 1, pp. 274–296; Lianou 2014, pp. 385–391.

would therefore have dramatically increased commercial activities and hence revenues. Also benefiting the state coffers were Ptolemy's various overseas possessions, especially Cyrenaica, Coele-Syria, Cyprus, Asia Minor, and the islands of the Aegean. His activities in these areas were not just for defensive and imperialistic reasons, for they provided him with the natural resources that were unavailable to him in Egypt, in particular timber for his fleet.

The people were taxed mercilessly. As ruler, Ptolemy took over ownership of all the country's land, which we can call "crown land," with the exception of temples and sacred precincts, and all were treated and taxed differently.[48] He leased out much of his crown land to peasant farmers of all nationalities, who paid annual rents and other taxes, but in addition, he provided the grain to be grown, which had to be paid for at a fixed percentage the following year. He probably devised the status of "cleruchies," which were designated plots of land (*kleroi*) throughout Egypt, which soldiers farmed, and which increased in number during the time of the later Ptolemies. By settling his soldiers on these lands, Ptolemy therefore saved money from maintaining a standing army. Some of these men moved to Egypt voluntarily, but others were drafted into the army, such as Perdiccas' troops in 320, whom Ptolemy was coaxing to his side from the time they entered Egypt, or the 8,000 soldiers after the battle of Gaza in 312, who were sent to live "in all the nomes."[49] These men had to farm and serve in the army when needed, and probably also were a check on any potential native revolt. As such, they paid less rent, and so were something of a privileged class compared to their Egyptian neighbors.[50]

Almost everything in Ptolemaic Egypt was taxed, often exorbitantly.[51] For example, there was a 10% tax on sales and a 33⅓% tax on vineyards, orchards, and gardens, as well as on profits even from selling pigeons. In addition to taxes, the Ptolemies enforced monopolies, a practice that may again have begun with Ptolemy I. There were monopolies on mines, quarries, and the production of salt, but perhaps the most famous was Ptolemy II's monopoly on oil production.[52] This controlled everything from sowing the plant to selling the oil at fixed prices. Ptolemy I was also responsible for imposing the same taxation rates and methods of collection on Egypt's overseas possessions.[53] The proliferation of taxes under the Ptolemies meant that there must have been

[48] Caroli 2007, pp. 238–248; Kehoe 2010; and especially Monson 2012.

[49] Diodorus 19.85.4.

[50] Lewis 1986, pp. 24–26; Manning 2010, pp. 161–163; Fischer-Bovet 2014, pp. 199–237; cf. Rostovtzeff 1941, vol. 1, pp. 284–287 and Pollard 2010, pp. 450–452, on the cleruchies.

[51] On taxes, see Tarn and Griffith 1952, pp. 193–194; Walbank 1993, pp. 110–112.

[52] Austin, no. 236, pp. 400–407, with, for example, Rostovtzeff 1941, vol. 1, pp. 302–305; Tarn and Griffith 1952, pp. 190–192.

[53] In detail, Bagnall 1976; see too Rostovtzeff 1941, vol. 1, pp. 332–351, 381–385.

an enormous civil service in Alexandria keeping all manner of records and accounts.

Ptolemy also introduced a new bronze coinage, as well as a lighter standard of Egyptian coins—gold, copper, and especially silver—as part of a monetization of the economy and to replace what had largely been business by barter.[54] Whether he or Cleomenes was responsible for building a mint at Alexandria is unknown. However, the mint there allowed Ptolemy to start striking currency in his capital, and so was a major step in turning Egypt into a sovereign state as every coin was issued in his name.

One of Ptolemy's greatest achievements was to turn Egypt into a "closed currency system."[55] He banned the use of any coinage in Egypt other than Egyptian—any foreign currency that traders or others brought with them to Egypt had to be handed over on arrival, and was reminted according to his new standard. His measure added more revenue to the state coffers: because all trade was conducted on the lighter standard, foreign coins that were heavier generated Ptolemy additional income when they were reminted. In particular, the imposition of a unified monetary system between Egypt and Cyrenaica, Cyprus, and Coele-Syria, from where he imported most of his grain, timber, and metals, highlights both his dependency on these areas and his astute economic move to maintain his influence over them. Only Ptolemaic currency could be used in them, and hence they were shut off from effectively trading with other countries.

We have an edict, dating to 304, which ordered payment of fines to the state in silver drachmas.[56] This is perhaps part of a series of new laws that Ptolemy introduced after he became king in 306, which ensured that fines were paid in a timely fashion and using accepted coinage. Since these coins still bore Alexander's portrait on them and were issued twenty years after his death, as well as after Ptolemy had become king in his own right, the edict also provides an interesting glimpse into Ptolemy's continued association with the late king.

Ptolemy deserves praise for his economic policy, which greatly benefited Egypt, and shows a side of him that is often overlooked. However, by deliberately favoring Greeks and Macedonians at the higher levels of his bureaucracy, and by making the language of that bureaucracy Greek, he shut out many Egyptians from positions of governance.[57] In this he was no different

---

[54] Rostovtzeff 1941, vol. 1, pp. 263–264, 398–404; Lianou 2014, pp. 391–399; cf. Bingen 2007, pp. 216–217; Manning 2010, pp. 1301–1338. See also Robinson 1941; Stewart 1993, pp. 229–243.

[55] Lianou 2014, pp. 399–409.

[56] Hagerdorn 1986; Rigsby 1988.

[57] Cf. Peremans 1983, pp. 268–273; Clarysse 1985.

from the other Successors, who likewise heavily taxed and marginalized their native subjects.[58] Nor would the Egyptians turn a blind eye to the fact that his measures made him and his dynasty fabulously wealthy at their very real expense. It is hardly a surprise that over the following decades native discontent turned into opposition, as seen in the concessions Ptolemy IV was forced to make to the priests, and Ptolemy V being crowned Pharaoh in Memphis and not Alexandria to try to appease the native people.

Religion

The priests were a powerful element in Egyptian society, and Ptolemy set out to win them over as soon as he arrived in Egypt. He assured them that he would do nothing against the native religions, and he lived up to his word.[59] In fact, as a sign of his open-mindedness, he continued with the traditional payment of taxes to the priests of Amun at Thebes.[60] Partly in response to the Egyptians' warm welcome and his desire to show they were not swapping one despotic king for another, he sacrificed to Apis. His action was a deliberate contrast to previous Persian rulers, such as Cambyses, who had killed the Egyptian sacred bulls. Ptolemy was also active in restoring and even adding to some of Egypt's most ancient temples, including part of the temple of Amun Re at Thebes (including the sanctuary of Akhmenu) and the great temple of Thoth at Hermopolis.[61]

At all times, though, Ptolemy's attitude toward Egyptian religion was pragmatic: to bolster his rule. In 311 he restored lands and income rights to the priests at Buto in the Nile delta, which the Persians had earlier seized for themselves. In gratitude they set up the so-called satrap stele, praising his action and his recognition of their status and rights (pp. 122–124). While he may well have earned their goodwill, his action ultimately was to help safeguard that area from a possible Antigonid invasion.

In 306 Ptolemy became Pharaoh, and received the formal titles of King of Upper and Lower Egypt, Son of Ra, and Beloved of Ammon (Amun).[62] We noted earlier that Ptolemy was careful to carry out the duties associated with

---

[58] Billows 1995, pp. 20–24, and passim, on taxes levied on the indigenous peoples by all the Successors.

[59] Bouché-Leclercq 1903, pp. 103–121; Bevan 1927, pp. 87–90, 177–188; Swinnen 1973; Caroli 2007, pp. 131–144; Müller 2009, pp. 172–175.

[60] Peremans 1976, pp. 222–223.

[61] Ladynin 2014.

[62] Burstein 1991; Caroli 2007, pp. 123–129.

the Pharaoh in order to maintain the loyalty of the Egyptians. However, he was faced with the dilemma of divinity. The Pharaoh, as Horus (son of Osiris and Isis, ruler of the land of the living), was also a god on earth, who after death was resurrected and assumed the attributes of Osiris (who ruled the land of the dead). But while Alexander likely saw himself as divine, Ptolemy certainly did not.[63] He was content with the Rhodians and the League of the Cycladic Islands having a cult to him, but none of Egypt's population was allowed to follow suit. As Pharaoh, Ptolemy was technically a god to the Egyptians, and as Pharaohs all of the Ptolemies were the high priests of the gods and were depicted on temple walls making offerings to the Egyptian gods. However, Ptolemy's adoption of the title was a political move: it placated the natives, but did not cause the same adverse reaction as the Macedonians and Greeks had felt for Alexander.

As Pharaohs, Ptolemy and his successors were responsible for financing new buildings, especially temples, which in turn had their images on them, and so promoted their rule.[64] Thus Ptolemy was responsible for the construction of temples to Hathor in the delta and to Amun in Naucratis, as well as in the age-old city of Memphis, for example. After he moved the capital of Egypt to Alexandria, Memphis continued to be an important religious center, and was so recognized by all the Ptolemies. It was there that the sacred Apis bulls were buried, and Ptolemy was careful not to interfere with its priests.[65] He may have funded an avenue of Egyptian sphinxes to connect the temple of Anubis (the god of mummification) to the Sarapeum, a temple in honor of Ptolemy's new god Sarapis.

In these early actions Ptolemy was clearly emulating Alexander, who, for example, had likewise sacrificed a bull to Apis. But after receiving the various titles reserved for the Pharaohs, Alexander had left Egypt, never to return. Ptolemy intended to stay, and while he was content to allow the Egyptians, Greeks, and Macedonians the freedom to worship their own gods, he saw in religion the means to create harmony. To this end, and in consultation with two advisers, Timotheus and Manetho, he likely created a new patron deity for his subjects: Sarapis.[66] This god was a combination of the Greek gods Zeus and Pluto with the Egyptian sacred bull Apis, who after death was identified with

---

[63] Here I disagree with Hölbl 2001, pp. 92–94, that Ptolemy associated himself with Alexander to establish his own divinity.

[64] See Hölbl 2001, pp. 83–90, citing bibliography.

[65] Crawford 1980.

[66] Austin, no. 261, pp. 438–440, with Bouché-Leclercq 1903, pp. 113–121; Bevan 1927, pp. 41–48; Seibert 1983, pp. 227–232; Bowman 1986, pp. 175–176; Ellis 1994, pp. 30–32; Hölbl 2001, pp. 99–101; Caroli 2007, pp. 309–354; Fassa 2013, noting Sarapis' long connection to kingship, which made the god a good choice (pp. 121–122).

Osiris. The coupling with Pluto, god of the underworld, was meant to offer assurance of life after death, for Egyptians believed that they would lead a happier life after they died. This concept was alien to Greeks, who did not equate happiness with an afterlife.

There is a tradition that Ptolemy had a dream in which the god ordered him to take his image from Sinope on the Black Sea to Egypt, and in doing so help unite the native and Egyptian people. This may have been a rumor put out to help explain why he foisted a new god on all his people.[67] There was a cult of Sarapis in Alexander's time, but Ptolemy's pragmatic innovation was to spread the worship of the god as a way of bringing his people together.[68] Ptolemy ordered the construction of temples to the god in all the nomes, as well as sacred precincts to him throughout Egypt. The largest Sarapeum (temple), unsurprisingly, was at Alexandria. Here apparently the god's followers could sleep overnight in the temple and be cured of various illnesses, making Sarapis a savior god of sorts. The temple was said to have housed an image of Sarapis as a bearded Zeus, crowned by the modius (the corn measure of Egypt), and with Pluto's three-headed dog Cerberus at his feet. Again, the meshing together of Greek and Egyptian beliefs was obvious from the iconography of the statue. Although the cult of Sarapis survived until the late fourth century AD, when the emperor Theodosius banned it in favor of Christianity and a Christian mob smashed the Sarapeum at Alexandria, the Egyptians never really embraced Sarapis to the extent that Greeks and Macedonians in Egypt did.[69]

The cult of Sarapis is important for showing us Ptolemy's determination to unite his disparate people. It is even possible that to further the appeal of Sarapis he linked Alexander's name to the god, given the popular appeal of that king.[70] Ptolemy's successors likewise promoted Sarapis to support their own rules, using reverance of the god as a stepping stone to ruler cult.[71] Eventually Sarapis was worshipped outside Egypt; temples to the god were built at Delos and Ephesus, and many of the Hellenistic kings recognized the value of adopting the god to help forge unity in their realms.[72]

---

[67] Tacitus, *Histories* 4.83–84; Plutarch, *Moralia* 361f–362b. See too Stiehl 1963/64; Fraser 1972, vol. 1, pp. 246–276 (against even the belief that Ptolemy created the god). Burstein 2012 acepts Tacitus' version, and argues that it was based on the Egyptian Bentresh Stela (Louvre C 284).

[68] Earlier worship and temple of Sarapis: Bosworth 1988, pp. 167–170, for example.

[69] For example, Fassa 2013.

[70] Cf. Arrian 7.26.2, with Ellis 1994, p. 86 (n. 24).

[71] Stambaugh 1972; Samuel 1989, pp. 67–81; Caroli 2007, pp. 188–193; Pfeiffer 2008, pp. 387–408; Vandorpe 2010, pp. 163–164.

[72] Fraser 1960.

   Despite Ptolemy's many challenges, we may see in his administration of Egypt a genuine attempt to recognize the rights, customs, laws, and religion of the different peoples, and to promote unity between Macedonians, Greeks, native Egyptians, and others. For example, he did not simply confiscate land and expel the native people from it in order to settle his newly arriving Greek and Macedonian population, knowing the discontent this measure would cause. Instead, he scattered the immigrants throughout the countryside, especially the Fayum where Egyptian settlement was less dense, to live side by side with the native population. Nevertheless, at the heart of all of his administrative, economic, and other measures was the continuation of Ptolemaic rule of Egypt. In this he was successful, for just as his administrative and economic innovations lasted for centuries under his successors, so too did that rule.

The End—and Beyond

After his final involvement in Greece in the mid-280s, Ptolemy's power was at its greatest, and Lysimachus and Seleucus were no longer a threat to him. Now old and most likely in declining health, Ptolemy prepared to live out his days in the city he had made so great, Alexandria. He had already taken steps to create a dynasty by naming his successor, and it is a tribute to his careful eye to the future that the aftermath of his death witnessed none of the chaos, uncertainty, and even insurrection that had occurred when Alexander had died in 323. In ensuring the continuation of Ptolemaic rule, Ptolemy had more in common with Philip II, whose death in 336 likewise saw the smooth transition of his son Alexander to the throne.

Ptolemy's fellow dynasts were not so lucky. Lysimachus' likely heir, his eldest son Agathocles, had been put to death for treason, as we have seen, and when Lysimachus was killed at the battle of Corupedion in 281, Ptolemy Ceraunus seized his throne, intent also on capturing Greece and Macedonia. Although this Ptolemy was unsuccessful, Thracian stability had been badly disrupted. Seleucus seems to have taken a leaf out of Ptolemy's book by making a son, Antiochus (from his marriage to Apame), co-ruler with him. This was in 291, and a decade later Antiochus became sole king after Ptolemy Ceraunus murdered his father, who had crossed into Thrace to seize Greece for himself. Antiochus was faced by a revolt in Syria, and in 278 an invasion by the Gauls; worse was that to maintain his throne, he had had to make peace with Ceraunus and give up his father's claims to Greece and Macedonia.

Ptolemy's Successor

In 287, Berenice, Ptolemy's fourth wife, secured the elevation of her son Ptolemy as heir over his older half-brother Ptolemy Ceraunus (born to Ptolemy and his third wife Eurydice).[1] Her move was reminiscent of Olympias' maneuvers to

---

[1] Memnon, *BNJ* 434 F 8.2; Justin 17.2.6.

leapfrog her son Alexander over his older half-brother Arrhidaeus as heir to the Macedonian throne. Demetrius of Phalerum had apparently urged Ptolemy to choose Ceraunus, but to no avail.[2] Intellectuals, though, should not meddle in politics—remembering what Demetrius had told his father, Ptolemy II had him arrested and put to death in 280—by the bite of an asp, it was said.[3]

Setting aside the eldest son was, however, going against the norm, and Ptolemy had to explain to his subjects why he had made his younger one next in line so that they would accept him.[4] Although Ceraunus tried to reach an agreement with his half-brother, even apparently offering to give up any claim to Egypt, he was ignored.[5] At that point, he and Eurydice left Alexandria for the court of Lysimachus and later Seleucus, who apparently promised "to restore him to Egypt, his paternal kingdom, if his father should die."[6] That never happened.

Why did Ptolemy set aside Ceraunus, who was then about 32 years old, in favor of the younger Ptolemy, who was about 22 years old? Possibly it was because of Berenice's entreaties, since it was said that she had the greatest influence over him.[7] But Ptolemy was a pragmatist. He had ruled Egypt for nearly 40 years, during turbulent times to say the least, and he wanted to ensure the continuation of Ptolemaic rule. He does not strike us as the sort of person who would succumb to his wife's charms in making decisions—how different would history have been if Caesar and Antony had had the willpower to resist Cleopatra's apparent charisma! Since Ptolemy's marriages to Thais, Eurydice, and Berenice had produced several sons, and he did not consider one of them in place of Ceraunus until now, there must be another reason that he selected his younger son to replace him.

Ceraunus, we are told, was "young and inexperienced in the business of war, and [was] by nature rash and impetuous, exercising no prudence or foresight."[8] This inexperience and unstable personality later led to his death in battle against invading Gauls in 279. If that side of Ceraunus was manifesting itself by the early 280s, then someone as sensible, balanced, and with the military experience of Ptolemy would consider Ceraunus' traits and lack of leadership skills dangerous for a monarch. Given that relations between Egypt and Syria

---

[2] Diogenes Laertius 5.78–79.

[3] Diogenes Laertius 5.79, with Fraser 1972, vol. 1, pp. 322–323; Green 1990, pp. 87–88; Ellis 1994, pp. 59–60.

[4] Justin 16.2.7–8, with Ogden 1999, p. 71.

[5] Justin 17.2.9–10, with Bouché-Leclercq 1903, pp. 95–100.

[6] Memnon, BNJ 434 F 8.2; see further Heinen 1972, pp. 3–20; Hazzard 1987, p. 149.

[7] Plutarch, Pyrrhus 4.4, with Bevan 1927, p. 53.

[8] Diodorus 22.3.1.

were deteriorating, Ptolemy may have thought that Ceraunus' impulsive personality could harm Egypt's future if he were king.

Possibly also the younger Ptolemy was more of an intellectual than Ceraunus, given that the poet Straton of Lampsacus and Zenodotus of Ephesus, the first librarian at Alexandria, had been his private tutors. Ptolemy may have wanted not only a strong successor but also someone more scholarly to oversee the Library and the Museum.[9] Obviously Ptolemy selected his younger son as successor because he saw him as the best choice. And he was proved right. Although Ptolemy II was not a military man like his father, Egypt prospered under his long reign (283–246); the kingdom remained an imperial power, the Library and the Museum made their greatest intellectual strides forward, and the lighthouse at Pharos was completed.[10]

Ptolemy's Death

Little is known of the last years of Ptolemy's life.[11] In 285, probably due to age and perhaps failing health, he made his heir Ptolemy joint-king of Egypt.[12] There is a belief that the idea of the co-regency was something Ptolemy II later invented against the claims of Ceraunus; however, this is unlikely.[13] So too is the assertion that before Ptolemy died he abdicated in favor of Ptolemy II.[14]

Because Ptolemy used two different chronologies for his rule, we do not know exactly when he died. Most likely it was sometime after January and before the summer of 283.[15] He was about 82 years old, and he died peacefully in Alexandria, with "a glorious record of achievements to his credit."[16] He was the only one of the first generation of Alexander's Successors to die a natural death, which was no mean feat in that day and age, and he would have been buried close to the *sema* housing Alexander's body. Then in the reign of

[9] Ellis 1994, p. 59, rightly says that we know of Ptolemy II's tutors probably because he became the next king; therefore it does not follow that Ceraunus was less educated than him.

[10] On Ptolemy II see, for example, Bouché-Leclercq 1903, pp. 141–243; Bevan 1927, pp. 56–78; Elgood 1938, pp. 41–74; Green 1990, pp. 145–147; Hölbl 2001, pp. 35–46. See also the papers in McKechnie and Guillaume 2008.

[11] Bouché-Leclercq 1903, pp. 93–101.

[12] Porphyry, *BNJ* 260 F 2.2, with Samuel 1962, pp. 25–28; Grzybek 1990, pp. 131, 171, 175; Caroli 2007, pp. 356–359. Hazzard 1987, pp. 140–158, argues for 284.

[13] Hazzard 1987, pp. 148–152.

[14] Pausanias 1.6.8; Justin 16.2.7, with Hazzard 1987, pp. 150 and 151. Pausanias errs on Ptolemaic matters: see p. 131 (the transfer of Alexander's body to Alexandria).

[15] Josephus, *Jewish Antiquities* 12.2, with Samuel 1962, pp. 28–30; Grzybek 1990, pp. 97–99 (November); but see Hazzard 1987, pp. 140, 146–147, 149–150, for spring 322.

[16] Justin 16.2.7.

Ptolemy IV (221–204) his body was moved to the new dynastic mausoleum, which became the resting place of the Ptolemaic rulers.[17]

On his father's death, Ptolemy II held funeral games and sacrifices.[18] Piety meshed with politics as his motive was both to honor his father and to win over his friends and advisers. He may also have united his parents as *theoi soteres* ("savior gods"), thus elevating Berenice over all of Ptolemy's other wives. When he deified his father as *theos soter*, he established a dynastic cult of the Ptolemies, which had its origins with the cult of Alexander that Ptolemy had instituted in Alexandria.[19]

From Ptolemy to Cleopatra

Ptolemy II became sole ruler on his father's death, and was probably crowned Pharaoh on January 7, 282.[20] Even though his father had made sure he was the next king, Ptolemy II's succession may not have been a smooth one.[21] Apparently one of Eurydice's sons stirred up a rebellion in Cyprus,[22] Arsinoe I (the king's first wife) was accused of plotting against her husband, and yet another conspiracy was hatched by the daughter of his half-sister Theoxene and Agathocles of Syracuse.[23] There was also the danger of a challenge from Ceraunus, and finally, Ptolemy II had his brother Argaeus executed for treason, which indicates that he may have been involved in some intrigue against the new king.[24] Ptolemy II thus had his hands full, but nevertheless he quickly and easily overcame all obstacles.

Ptolemy II was very different from his father.[25] Among other things, he enjoyed exorbitant parties and excessive animal hunts, especially of elephants.[26] Where Ptolemy I was frugal and conservative, the son was the reverse. Early in his

---

[17] Zenobius, *Proverb* 3.94; on this tomb, see Chapter 8, p. 132.

[18] Theocritus 17.121–125, *SIG*³ 390.27–56.

[19] Bevan 1927, pp. 127–131; Walbank 1984a, pp. 97–98; cf. Vandorpe 2010, pp. 163–164. It has been argued that the promotion was later, perhaps even in 263: Hazzard 2000, pp. 3–24; see too Caroli 2007, pp. 196–197, 360–362; Hauben 2010, on the cult of Ptolemy on Rhodes and in the Cyclades preceding the imperial cult.

[20] Grzybek 1990, pp. 81–86.

[21] Hazzard 1987, pp. 148–152.

[22] Pausanias 1.7.1.

[23] Scholion to Theocritus 17.128.

[24] van Oppen de Ruiter 2013 argues that Argaeus was the illegitimate son of Alexander the Great and Thais, whom Ptolemy raised, and because he posed a threat as Alexander's son, Ptolemy II had him executed.

[25] See the succinct comparison of the two of them at Hazzard 2000, pp. 103–110.

[26] Austin, no. 278, pp. 458–459 (= Diodorus 3.36.3–5, 37.7–8).

reign he held an enormously ostentatious and expensive propaganda procession around the streets of Alexandria, which included hundreds of people in different guises and a vast array of animals and birds, from elephants, zebras, ostriches, buffalos, caged lions, tigers, and panthers, to even a rhinoceros.[27] Where Ptolemy I had not accepted a cult to himself in Egypt, Ptolemy II established one to himself and his sister-wife Queen Arsinoe II as *theoi adelphoi* (brother/sister gods) in 272, which in turn promoted the practice of ruler cult in the Hellenistic world.[28]

Ptolemy II also preferred diplomacy to military conflict, and as a result the monarchy changed under him from the military one of Ptolemy I to a more cultural, civilian one. The change also impacted the queens of the Ptolemaic line. In my Introduction I asked the question, "How did a dynasty that began with male rulers who had queens at their beck and call evolve into one with queens as rulers, especially queens as powerful and charismatic as Cleopatra?" This transformation had nothing to do with Ptolemy I, who ensured that his wives were always subordinate to him, but with Ptolemy II. His marriage to his sister Arsinoe (II), sometime before 274, brought her into political prominence, as she ruled Egypt with him and was one of the biggest schemers in Egyptian and even Greek politics (Figure 12.1).[29] Future queens (Cleopatras II, III, and the famous VII) likewise asserted themselves over their husbands.

Ptolemy II's marriage to his sister also set an incestuous trend, which was not only the preserve of adult Ptolemies—in 51, the 18-year old Cleopatra VII married her 10-year old brother Ptolemy XIII. Ptolemy II and Arsinoe II had no children.[30] However, a generation later the marriage of Ptolemy IV (r. 221–203) to his sister Arsinoe III produced a son, Ptolemy V. This inbreeding was not sexual, but political, in the sense that the Ptolemies exploited it as a sign of their singularity and power.[31]

And there is no question that the Ptolemaic dynasty *was* powerful, although as the centuries progressed that power decreased.[32] The reign of Ptolemy III Euergetes ("Benefactor"), from 246 to 221, saw military intervention in Syria and an expansion of Egyptian influence in eastern Syria, the Aegean, and Thrace, as well as an alliance with Sparta. But that was the zenith of the Egyptian Empire. Egypt fared badly under Ptolemy IV Philopator, "son of a beloved

---

[27] Austin, no. 219, pp. 361–362 (= Athenaeus 5.201b–f, 202f–203e), with Rice 1983; Stewart 1993, pp. 252–260; Hazzard 2000, pp. 59–79.

[28] See the works cited in Chapter 9 n. 97.

[29] Marriage: Pausanias 1.7.1; see further, Longega 1968; Burstein 1982; Hazzard 2000, pp. 81–100; Carney 2013 (with pp. 70–105 on her marriage to Ptolemy II).

[30] Pausanias 1.7.3.

[31] Ager 2005, also arguing that the Ptolemies did not suffer from any negative genetic effects, as is often believed; see too Buraselis 2008.

[32] On Ptolemaic Egypt, see the works cited in Chapter 1 n. 8.

Figure 12.1 Portrait of Ptolemy II and his sister wife Arsinoe II. © The Trustees of the British Museum / Art Resource, New York

father" (r. 221–203), during whose reign Antiochus III ("the Great") of Syria seized lower Syria and Palestine in 219 and prepared to invade Egypt before a Ptolemaic army defeated him at Raphia in 217. Because Ptolemy IV had been forced to use a large number of Egyptians in his army, the native peoples began to demand better treatment, and the influence of the priests in society rose.

Ptolemy V Epiphanes (r. 203–181) also faced problems from Syria. In 202 Antiochus III, still thirsty for revenge for his defeat at Raphia, captured Coele Syria, and even defeated an Egyptian army at the battle of Panium (on the Lebanon–Palestine border), before winning over Ptolemaic possessions in Aisa Minor. Fortunately, in 195 Ptolemy married Antiochus' daughter Cleopatra (I), and so made peace between the two kingdoms. Ptolemy V also faced increasing discontent at home, so in 196, aged twelve, he was crowned Pharaoh not in Alexandria but significantly in Memphis to appease the people.[33] He made large grants to the native temples, and so forceful a role did

[33] His coronation was recorded on an inscription of March 27, 196, which listed his titles, family tree, and his various gifts to the temple and priests. Almost two millennia later, in 1799,

the priests play in society after this time that even after Octavian, the future emperor Augustus, captured Egypt in 30, he took care to win their support before becoming Pharaoh.[34]

Ptolemy V's successor was Ptolemy VI Philometor, "he who loves his mother" (r. 181–145). This ruler faced Antiochus IV's invasion of Egypt, which included the capture of Pelusium and Memphis and siege of Alexandria itself in 168. Ptolemy desperately sought assistance from Rome, which forced Antiochus to withdraw, but thus brought Roman involvement in Egyptian affairs.[35] Friendly relations with Rome accounted for its lack of involvement in Egypt until Cleopatra VII (r. 51–30). After Ptolemy VI and before Cleopatra VII came a series of exploitive Ptolemaic rulers, whose actions infuriated the Egyptians further. Included among them was the loathsome Ptolemy VIII (r. 145–116), who married his sister and daughter (Cleopatra II and III). After he was forced to flee in 130, an angry mob burst into his palace and smashed statues of him; he blamed his wife Cleopatra, whom he had left behind in his scramble to flee, and so killed their young son, sending his dismembered body in a box to the mother as a birthday present.

But the spread of Roman rule was inexorable. It is a great tribute to the famous Cleopatra, with whom this book began, that she was able to play off Rome for as long as she did, thereby maintaining Egypt's independence against the tide of Roman imperialism.[36] She seduced Julius Caesar in 48, moving to Rome in 46 with their child to be with him. Always hated by the Roman people, who scornfully called her "the Egyptian," she fled back to Egypt after Caesar's assassination on the Ides of March 44. Still, she had kept Rome out of Egypt's affairs when it had already swallowed up Greece, Macedonia, and Syria into its empire. Rome was now ripped apart by civil war until 42, when Mark Antony and Octavian divided up the world between them, Octavian taking Italy and the West, and Antony the East. Intent on keeping Egypt free from Rome, from 41 Cleopatra was first Antony's lover, then his wife. She might rule Egypt with him, but she never saw the country as anything but hers. Yet once Octavian had declared Antony an enemy of the Republic in 34, the writing was on the wall;

Napoleon's soldiers discovered the inscription at Rosetta (on the Nile's west bank), and in 1801 (following Napoleon's defeat by the British) the Rosetta Stone, as it became commonly known, was moved to the British Museum in London. The inscription is in three scripts, hieroglyphics at the top, Egyptian demotic in the middle, and Greek at the bottom, which allowed the French scholar and philologist Jean-François Champollion to decipher hieroglyphics in 1822. For a Greek translation of the stone, see Austin, no. 227, pp. 374–378.

[34] Herklotz 2012.
[35] Lampela 1998.
[36] Bingen 2007, pp. 63–79.

the end came for Antony and Cleopatra at the decisive battle of Actium in 31. The following year, they committed suicide.

Like Philip II, the architect of the Macedonian Empire, and his son Alexander, its master builder, Ptolemy I left his son the building blocks of the Egyptian Empire: a stable Egypt; a functioning administrative structure; wealth; a formidable army and fleet; and dominion over a large number of geographic areas—Cyrenaica, Cyprus, Phoenicia, Palestine, Coele-Syria, various parts of Asia Minor, and numerous Greek islands.[37] As has been rightly said, "the first fifty years of Ptolemaic rule in Egypt can be characterized only through the actions of [Ptolemy]."[38] It is a fitting tribute to the founder of the Ptolemaic dynasty that over 250 years after his death, the country he molded was seen as one of the most dangerous by the greatest imperial power of antiquity, Rome.

The Greatest Successor?

Ptolemy's achievement was all the more remarkable when we consider that his rule was based on military conquest, not constitutional legitimacy. Strictly speaking, "military conquest" misrepresents the basis of his power. Alexander absorbed Egypt into the Macedonian Empire in 331 largely because of the Egyptians' hatred of their Persian masters at that time. He did not need to fight the Egyptians and conquer them, nor did they ever revolt during his reign. Even when he died in 323, Egypt did not shrug off Macedonian rule, all of which allowed Ptolemy to move seamlessly into a position of power. His rule of Egypt was of course anchored in his military might, and he saw the country as his spear-won territory, as we have noted throughout the book, but at no point did he face any insurrection. One reason for his popularity was that he seems to have been a genuinely kind and generous man, as Diodorus makes plain, part of an image he carefully cultivated to help legitimize his monarchy. At the same time, he could be utterly ruthless, as the people of Cyrene or the wretched Cleomenes, for example, discovered. As with Philip II and Alexander, kindness and diplomacy worked only to a point.

Ptolemy's success is also remarkable when we consider his background and rise to power. He was not a general under Alexander, nor did Alexander apparently ever see him as one. He fought with the king in his battles and sieges, and he was a tough and loyal soldier. Yet Alexander gave his trusted boyhood

[37] Vandorpe 2010, pp. 169–171.
[38] Turner 1984, p. 122.

friend only a handful of commands during his campaign, of which the one to take Bessus into custody in 328 marked a turning point. But Ptolemy's other commands, even if he set out to sensationalize them in his *History*, were essentially reconnoitering and mopping-up types. His promotion to the royal bodyguard in 328 was indeed a coup for him, and a sign of the trust that Alexander had in him. Still, other contemporaries, as well as the king's boyhood friends, leapfrogged over Ptolemy into far more powerful posts, such as Perdiccas, who became *chiliarch*.

Yet Ptolemy's career in Egypt, especially his defeats of Perdiccas there in 320, of Demetrius at Gaza in 312, and of Demetrius and Antigonus by Egypt in 306, showed him to be anything but a man who was good only for capturing or killing enemy stragglers. While Demetrius, Antigonus, and Pyrrhus were the best generals of this period, we cannot forget that Ptolemy defeated Demetrius and Antigonus, as well as forged a close alliance with Pyrrhus. He was, then, a highly successful military strategist and leader, who, like any Macedonian king, led from the front to exhort his men, as we saw when he was fighting Perdiccas at the Fort of the Camels in 320, or at the battle at Gaza in 312, or even when he marched into Coele-Syria in 302. His army respected him, and it was not difficult for him to coax enemy troops over to him to increase his manpower.

Alexander seems to have overlooked Ptolemy's potential, and why we do not know. Perhaps it was because others in his retinue were more forceful in their personalities and views, like Perdiccas or Craterus, or had more authority because of their seniority, like Parmenion and Cleitus. Ptolemy may simply not have been seen as made of "the right stuff" for generalship. Yet in many respects his position on the periphery of Alexander's senior staff worked to his advantage. As a bodyguard he was presumably not viewed with the same suspicion and distrust as the generals and satraps had for each other.

Clearly Ptolemy was not prepared to remain in the wings after Alexander's death at Babylon in 323. His defiance of Perdiccas' plan and his radical proposal to administer the empire immediately set him apart from the man that the others had served with under Alexander. Nor was his proposal something that was spur of the moment. When Alexander died and the succession issue became as critical as it did, Ptolemy saw the chance to position himself where he would be the equal of the others, hence his push for a ruling council. He may have known that his idea would not be accepted, but it got him what he wanted: serious attention, and power. He deserves praise for elevating himself from bodyguard to satrap of Egypt within the space of a few days. And the way he conducted himself in Egypt and in his relations with the other Successors is evidenced by the territories bestowed on him at Triparadeisus in 320 and

in the settlement of 311, and by Seleucus fleeing to him in 315 for help against
Antigonus.

Ptolemy knew from personal experience that the differing personalities and
greed of the other protagonists of the Babylon settlement would never allow
uninterrupted peace between them, and he was right. That was why he wisely
chose Egypt because of its location: away from the major hot spots of the early
Hellenistic period, and with abundant natural defenses, Ptolemy could consolidate his rule and increase his resources and fighting strength, while the
other Successors waged war and did away with each other. Far from someone
who was intent only on separating Egypt from the rest of the world or pursuing a purely defensive policy, as has often been assumed, Ptolemy was no
different from the others in wanting his share of empire, as even our ancient
writers saw.[39]

We have charted Ptolemy's ambition beginning with his speech at Babylon
in 323; his execution of Cleomenes in 322; his hijacking of Alexander's corpse
in 321; the roles he played in all five Wars of the Successors; and especially his
bid on Greece and Macedonia in 308. Although he did not operate on as many
fronts at the same time as, say, Antigonus, Ptolemy followed a strategic policy
of protecting Egypt and expanding it, especially to his north and east. Ptolemy
II inherited an Egypt that controlled Cyrenaica, Cyprus, Rhodes, Coele-Syria,
Phoenicia, and the Cycladic Islands, not to mention ruled the waves throughout the eastern Mediterranean and Aegean. His father's thalassocracy facili-
tated Egyptian trade and aided the country's prosperity, as well as protected
it from hostile forces.[40] Although Ptolemy lost his naval ascendancy at times,
most notably in 306 after his crippling defeat off Cyprus, he bounced back
within a few short years, usually to a stronger position than before. Thanks
to a strong economic policy and bureaucratic innovations, Ptolemy really did
bring Egypt out of being part of Asia and into the Greek world.[41] As has been
rightly said, an assessment of his achievements needs to be based on events in
Egypt and in his kingdom throughout his reign, not on a few "unfortunate and
isolated incidents."[42]

In the same year as his loss off Cyprus, Ptolemy became king, making him
truly equal with the most influential rulers of the time: Antigonus, Demetrius,
Lysimachus, Seleucus, and Cassander. That he continued to outfox them
(and outlive most of them) while adding to his territories made him first

[39] Diodorus 20.37.4; see too Hauben 2014 and Meeus 2014.
[40] On the nature of Ptolemy's foreign policy and possessions, see Bagnall 1976, pp. 224–229;
cf. Caroli 2007, pp. 70–71 and 99–104.
[41] Lloyd 2010a.
[42] Hölbl 2001, pp. 27–28.

among equals. However, one prize always eluded him—as it did many of the Successors—control of Greece and Macedonia. In his attempt on the latter in 308, we see him for what he really was: an imperialist, who used anyone, including Alexander's sister Cleopatra, or any means, including putting out the rumor that he was Philip II's illegitimate son and circulating Alexander's dummy will, to achieve his goals. When his plan collapsed, we still find him involving himself in events on the mainland—backing Pyrrhus' bid to reclaim the throne of Epirus in 297, and supporting Athens in 288.

We know less about Ptolemy's activities in Egypt and relations with his people because of the paucity of our sources. That there was no native revolt on his death shows that the Egyptians had come to accept Ptolemaic rule. Even though his administration favored the natives less than Macedonians and Greeks, and was ultimately geared to increasing revenue to support his army, Ptolemy respected native deities, allowed the Egyptians their own social and religious customs, and made a real attempt to foster good relations with all his subject population. Perhaps here he was influenced by his experiences with Alexander. Ptolemy's piety was evident from the time he arrived in Egypt, and the erection of the satrap stele in 311 by the priests of Buto to commemorate his restoration of their lands (and revenues) in the northwest delta seems to have been inspired by genuine feeling on their part. Then there was Sarapis, the introduction of which god was a master stroke on Ptolemy's part, as it was meant to bring together Greek and Egyptian in common worship. Not even Alexander the Great had attempted something so enterprising.

Ptolemy was always quick to exploit Alexander's name for the edge this gave him in the Wars of the Successors, and from his plush palace he came to rule an exotic and affluent country. But in his lifestyle he was more the traditional Macedonian than Alexander had turned out to be. Where Alexander had given in to the influence of Persian luxury, from clothing to perfumes, and even had pretensions to personal divinity, Ptolemy remained one of the old school. Like the Macedonians back home, he ate plain food, drank rustic wine, dressed like an ordinary person, generally avoided ostentation, and did not allow himself to be distracted from his goals by any of the finer things in life. He took great pains to avoid any pretense to divinity, except for the godhead that was part of his persona as Pharaoh, and which in any case was meant only for his Egyptian subjects.

Ptolemy, then, really did seem to have his people's interests at heart, even allowing for the way he took advantage of the Egyptians and foisted Greek language and culture on them. He could easily have moved Egypt's capital from Memphis to Alexandria merely for economic and security reasons, as well as its association with Alexander, and left it at that. Instead he went further, founding the great Library and the Museum, which served him twofold: it gave him something that his rivals did not have, and it made his Egypt the intellectual center of the world. Antigonus never treated his subjects with respect; Alexander the Great never fully grasped his subjects' social and religious customs, and even ignored their own culture, causing their resentment. But Ptoemy really did endear himself to his people by understanding them.

The son of a minor Macedonian living in the rural parts of that kingdom, Ptolemy rose to be one of Alexander the Great's trusted friends and a personal bodyguard; as one of Alexander's first-generation Successors he became satrap and then King of Egypt, amassing for himself and his country considerable wealth and power, and founding the longest of the Hellenistic dynasties. What he did, how he went about it, and the stellar results of his actions arguably make him the greatest of those Successors. Ptolemy deserves to be seen in this light; he was a sterling example of a king, commander, statesman, and intellectual.

It might be overkill to describe Ptolemy as someone who "decisively influenced world history,"[43] but there is no question that he helped to shape not only Egypt's history but also that of the early Hellenistic world to a far greater extent than has often been thought.

---

[43] Hölbl 2001, p. 14.

Appendix 1

PTOLEMY'S HISTORY OF ALEXANDER

Wherever Ptolemy son of Lagus and Aristobulus son of Aristobulus have both given the same accounts of Alexander son of Philip, it is my practice to record what they say as completely true, but where they differ, to select the version I regard as more trustworthy and also better worth telling. In fact other writers have given a variety of accounts of Alexander, nor is there any other figure of whom there are more historians who are more contradictory of each other, but in my view Ptolemy and Aristobulus are more trustworthy in their narrative, since Aristobulus took part in king Alexander's expedition, and Ptolemy not only did the same, but as he himself was a king, mendacity would have been more dishonourable for him than for anyone else.[1]

Thus writes Arrian in the *Preface* to his *History (Anabasis) of Alexander*. Arrian is commonly viewed as the most reliable of the later narrative sources for Alexander's reign, even though writing several centuries after the king, because, as he tells us, he largely used Ptolemy's history of Alexander's life and career and that of another contemporary, Aristobulus of Cassandreia, both of whom accompanied Alexander on his campaigns.[2] It is certainly true, as Arrian says, that no other historical figure, at least up to his time, had been the subject of more contradictory accounts of his life and career. However, while we can see the value of using writers who had marched with Alexander, Arrian's explanation that Ptolemy's account is even more trustworthy because

---

[1] Arrian, *Preface* 1–2, trans. Brunt 1976, *ad loc.*

[2] Bosworth 1988, pp. 40, 61–64, 79–83; cf. Lane Fox 2014, pp. 165–168. For the sources of our other narrative writers on Alexander, likewise writing centuries later, Diodorus, Curtius, Justin, and the biographer Plutarch, see Hammond 1983 and 1993b; Bosworth 1988 and 1996; Baynham 1998; cf. Habicht 2006c. On the sources, see Appendix 2.

he was a king, and therefore less likely to falsify facts, is to us naïve. As we have seen, Ptolemy, like his rivals, was not afraid of using deception and pursuing his own agenda. Why, therefore, should Ptolemy be trustworthy in his account of Alexander?

Ptolemy's *History* in fact causes all sorts of problems.[3] To begin with, we do not have it in its entirety, but only extracts (usually referred to as "fragments") quoted or paraphrased in later writers, especially Arrian.[4] In fact, we have no idea how lengthy the *History* was—Arrian included the most fragments from it, and even then, there are only thirty-five of varying length. Second, why Ptolemy really wrote it is impossible to decide, and the information in it is suspect.[5] It was once argued that Arrian followed Ptolemy without any thought of originality throughout his entire account, but few would agree with that conclusion anymore.[6] Ptolemy was biased in favor of himself and against many of his contemporaries, principally Perdiccas, thereby making his *History* dangerously subjective.

I have said that I believe that Ptolemy was present at the events he describes, and I have used his *History* for his role in Alexander's invasion, paying attention to those episodes and his projection of people in them with whom he interacts. Although there is no need to rehearse all his embellishments or biases here, a few words must still be said about some of them by way of illustration.

Ptolemy likely exaggerated his role in the battle at the Persian Gates in 331 (pp. 38–39) and in taking Bessus into custody in 328 (pp. 45–46).[7] As far as the latter goes, no other ancient writer tells us that the villagers reneged on their previous agreement and refused to surrender Bessus, forcing Ptolemy to resort to diplomacy and military threat before they relented. In fact, Arrian states that according to Aristobulus, Spitamenes and Dataphernes did surrender Bessus. Likewise, Ptolemy's deadly fight with the Aspasian chieftain in India in 326 (pp. 54–55), has a Homeric feel to it, and perhaps deliberately so, to emulate the sort of combat in which Alexander delighted.

While what Ptolemy claims he did is important, so too is what he does not tells us. For example, he has nothing to say about the fierce argument between Alexander and Cleitus in 328 that led to the king murdering his old general in

---

[3] In addition to the works cited in the preceding note, see Bouché-Leclercq 1903, pp. 134–138; Welles 1963; Seibert 1969, especially pp. 64–83; Errington 1969; Roisman 1984; Ellis 1994, pp. 18–22; Bosworth 1996, pp. 41–53; Bingen 2007, pp. 20–24; Howe 2008; cf. Schepens 1983.

[4] The fragments are collected together at *FGrH* 138; they are currently being re-edited and translated with a critical commentary by T. Howe as *BNJ* 138; there is a translation of them in Robinson 1953, pp. 183–205.

[5] Roisman 1984, p. 385; see too Rosen 1979, pp. 462–472.

[6] Kornemann 1935.

[7] Battle: Arrian 3.18.9; Bessus: Ptolemy, *FGrH* 138 F 14 = Arrian 3.29.6–30.5; see too Welles 1963, pp. 107–108 (the battle episode) and pp. 109–110 (Bessus).

cold blood (pp. 48–49). Ptolemy might well have wanted to keep Alexander's contemptible and unheroic reaction to Cleitus hidden to the readers of his *History*, as has been suggested.[8] But he may also have left out the incident because of the damage it did to his own reputation: he was a royal bodyguard, and although he had initially broken up the fight, even bundling Cleitus out of the room, he had not prevented him from returning, at which point Cleitus might have attacked the king. It was better for Ptolemy's image, then, to omit the whole thing.

The same may well be true for Ptolemy's alleged actions at the siege of Malli in India (pp. 61–62). Arrian and Curtius claim that Ptolemy was with Alexander, helped to save his life, and for that the king rewarded him with the epithet *soter* ("savior"), but Ptolemy himself denied all this.[9] Again, his dissent may be to mask the fact that he had not given the king sufficient protection as a bodyguard, and thus had not done his job properly.

Ptolemy also displays animosity toward individuals, especially Perdiccas.[10] His *History* begins with Perdiccas' alleged impetuosity in attacking Thebes in 335, which led to a brutal military engagement in which a number of Macedonian troops were killed and wounded (pp. 24–26).[11] It is worth noting that Arrian is our only source for Perdiccas acting as he did, and that Diodorus claims that he followed Alexander's orders loyally.[12] At another time, Diodorus and Curtius tell us that Perdiccas was among several senior personnel wounded at the battle of Gaugamela in 331, but Arrian does not include Perdiccas in his account, which might mean that Ptolemy had omitted it.[13] Ptolemy may well have resented seeing Perdiccas, one of his fellow bodyguards, rise so quickly to influence, especially after Alexander's death, and of course relations between the two of them were forever soured when Perdiccas tried to wrest Egypt from

[8] Seibert 1969, p. 19; cf. Errington 1969, pp. 238–239; but note Roisman 1984, pp. 377–378.

[9] Arrian 7.11.8; Curtius 10.5.21 (from Ptolemy, *FGrH* 138 F 26a), with Welles 1963, pp. 114–115; Errington 1969, p. 239; Roisman 1984, p. 382; Bosworth 1988, pp. 76–77 and 79–83. A later writer such as Timagenes may have added Ptolemy and his epithet to the story, mistakenly believing an earlier account, perhaps by Cleitarchus, that had Ptolemy saving Alexander's life; cf. Bosworth 1988, pp. 80–81; Muccioli 2012, pp. 81–94; Prandi's commentary on Cleitarchus, *BNJ* 137 F 24.

[10] For details of Ptolemy's treatment of other individuals, especially Antigonus and the bodyguard Aristonous, whom Ptolemy may have ignored because of his bravery and especially for his prominence in the Babylon negotiations of 323, see Errington 1969, pp. 234–235; but against Errington's view, note Roisman 1984, pp. 381–382.

[11] Ptolemy, *FGrH* 138 F 3 = Arrian 1.8.

[12] Diodorus 17.12.3. Since the first two books of Curtius are lost, we have no idea how (if at all) he treated this episode.

[13] Diodorus 17.61.3; Arrian 3.15.2; Curtius 4.16.32; though see Strasburger 1934, p. 35, and Roisman 1984, p. 376, for Arrian using a difference source.

him. Thus Ptolemy did not want to show Perdiccas' bravery at Gaugamela, and Perdiccas' costly impetuosity at Thebes may be far from the truth. However, it is going too far to claim that Ptolemy intended his account to make Perdiccas responsible for Thebes' destruction, or even that the entire *History* was written against Perdiccas.[14]

Added to the problem of veracity is that we do not know why or when Ptolemy wrote his *History*. Arian goes on to say in his *Preface* that "[Ptolemy and Aristobulus] wrote when Alexander was dead and neither was under any constraint or hope of gain to make him set down anything but what happened."[15] It is all but certain that Ptolemy composed his account after Alexander's death, but its date of composition may have nothing to do with why he wrote it.[16] There is a belief that the work was intended to be an objective and accurate account of Alexander's reign, mainly because of its lack of sensationalism (in contrast to other, contemporary Alexander historians), and that Ptolemy wrote it later in his reign.[17] That view has been challenged. In its place is Ptolemy writing earlier in the Wars of the Successors for propagandist reasons, and in doing so selecting events and structuring his *History* to give him an edge over the other Successors, especially Perdiccas.[18] He might also have intended it to help win the loyalty of Alexander's veterans by embellishing his role in Alexander's invasion of Asia and by depicting himself as more of a confidant to the king than he was.

Here, I propose a third option: Ptolemy's *History* was simply part of the "movement" of historical writing during his reign, which included Hecataeus of Abdera's history of Egypt (the most important Hellenistic account of Egypt) and Cleitarchus' history of Alexander (the most popular ancient biography of the king, in which Ptolemy played a significant part). After all, Ptolemy associated himself with Egyptian intellectuals, including the priest and historian Manetho, whose *Aegyptiaca* (*History of Egypt*) was presumably in the planning stage at this time. And as he wrote his version of Alexander's invasion he seized the opportunity to project himself more into it.

First, let us consider the early and late contexts of the *History*. It is hard to imagine that given the chaotic and fast-moving events of the years immediately

[14] Errington 1969, pp. 236–241; this view is far-fetched: Roisman 1984, pp. 374–376; Ellis 1994, pp. 20–21.

[15] Arrian, *Preface* 2, trans. Brunt 1976, *ad loc.*

[16] Note the caution of Roisman 1984, pp. 373–374, on the assumption that the date and reason are interlinked.

[17] Strasburger 1934, pp. 15–16; Welles 1963, pp. 101–116; Seibert 1969, pp. 1–26; Ellis 1994, pp. 20–22, especially p. 21.

[18] Strasburger 1934, pp. 53–54; Errington 1969, pp. 233–242; Bosworth 1980a, pp. 22–23; Howe 2008; but Roisman 1984, pp. 373–385, queries this assumption.

following Alexander's death that Ptolemy had time to start, let alone complete, a polished account of the king down to his death. Ptolemy may well have been suspicious of Perdiccas' attitude to him from the beginning, especially when he foisted Cleomenes on him as a likely spy, but Ptolemy was too busy establishing himself in Egypt and invading Cyrenaica to think about writing anything. It therefore seems unlikely that his work was intended to give him leverage over Perdiccas, as has been argued.[19] Moreover, the schism between the two men really only occurred when Ptolemy stole Alexander's body in 321, forcing Perdiccas to invade Egypt the following year.

After the First War of the Successors (321–320) and the Triparadeisus settlement (320), Ptolemy was in a far stronger position in Egypt than he had been in the two or three years after the Babylon settlement (323). The murder of the last Antigonid king, Alexander IV, in 310, moved the Successors from satraps to kings *ex officio*, even if they did not take this formal title until 306. Even though Ptolemy suffered defeat and the loss of Cyprus at the hands of Demetrius Poliorcetes in the same year, he was still king and had faced down a serious invasion threat from the Antigonids. Five years later, in 301, Antigonus was killed in the battle of Ipsus, marking the end of the Fourth War of the Successors (307–301); although Demetrius still proved to be a formidable enemy to the remaining Successors, Ptolemy was far less involved in their machinations than before.

In other words, by the time Ptolemy was established as King of Egypt in 306, and given his role in events after that year, he had no need to write about Alexander for propagandist reasons, and Perdiccas was long dead. Thus if we try to find a context for his *History*, we have to consider dates either before 306, say, or much later in his reign. As far as the former is concerned, I have argued that as part of his bid on the Macedonian throne in 308, Ptolemy fabricated Alexander's will, put out the rumor that he was an illegitimate son of Philip II, and arranged his marriage to Cleopatra, Alexander's sister (pp. 151–154). Ptolemy may well have been planning his attempt to seize Macedonia and Greece from as early as 310, when Alexander IV was put to death and Ptolemy began a series of campaigns in Cilicia, Lycia, Caria, and Cos. His aim was to become the dominant power in the eastern Mediterranean and parts of the Aegean at the expense of the Antigonids, who were also vying for kingship of Macedonia. Perhaps, then, he thought that a propagandist history of Alexander, with Ptolemy as the king's confidant, would strengthen his chances of acceptance by the Macedonian people. But this is surely too short a time

---

[19] Errington 1969, pp. 236–241; *contra* Roisman 1984.

frame—310 to 308—to write a history of this sort, especially as he was on active campaign overseas in each of those years.

That is why we should look later in his reign, and in doing so a case for linking date and purpose may still be made. We cannot rule out that Ptolemy simply wanted to add his voice to the growing number of histories being composed at this time, for he was certainly not writing in a vacuum. As the founder of the Museum and the Library at Alexandria, he was himself an intellectual, and, given that he fought alongside Alexander who was already becoming the stuff of legend, he had every reason to want to write his own version of marching with that king. In doing so, we cannot rule out that he zealously wrote badly of his rivals because they were his bitter enemies while vainly elevating his own role. The comment of one modern scholar is very apt here: "Perhaps it would be better to leave the riddle of Ptolemy's aims unsolved as long as his work exists in its present fragmentary form. For all we know, Ptolemy could have written his history simply for the sake of writing history. If so, the time of its composition was of little political relevance."[20]

I agree, though I find the comment a tad pessimistic. As we have seen, Ptolemy propelled himself to the forefront of events whenever he could, something that even our ancient writers noticed—thus Curtius' statement that he was "truly no detractor from his own glory."[21] What emerges from the fragments we have—and the information that is and is not given—is a history of Alexander from a military perspective by someone who has not styled himself as a peripheral character, who did not point out his own faults, and who downplayed or ignored certain individuals. It therefore ought to surprise us that Ptolemy says nothing of his role in the aftermath of Alexander's death in Babylon; his defeats of Perdiccas and the Antigonids; the move to Alexandria and the impetus he gave it as a cultural and intellectual center; the establishment of an Egyptian empire; being named savior; and of course becoming King of Egypt. For someone who was no "detractor from his own glory," the silence of Ptolemy's very real achievements in Egypt, where he had no need to embellish, omit, or change anything, is surely significant. Indeed, Ptolemy's contact at his court with Manetho, who planned his own history of Egypt, ought to have motivated Ptolemy to want to write about Alexander and his own Egypt. Yet he did not.

Ptolemy's failure to discuss both his extensive role in the Wars of the Successors and his exceptional rule of Egypt suggests that he began his *History* late in life, and had not started on events after Alexander's death by the time

---

[20] Roisman 1984, p. 385, who doubts a political purpose to the *History*.
[21] Curtius 9.5.21.

Ptolemy died in 283. Perhaps he started to dictate his account to a scribe in 285, when he had all but retired from public and military life, and his son was sharing the throne with him. If so, he may well have made mistakes because his "memory or imagination [had] run away with him" or because of the "mists of forty years."[22]

What we can say for sure is that had Ptolemy intended to write about his rule of Egypt, we would doubtless have had to put up with more personal embellishments and denigrations of opponents. At the same time, we would have had a vastly far-reaching contemporary picture of the turbulent years of the Wars of the Successors, which we cannot glean from our few fragments of Arrian's *Events after Alexander.*

---

[22] Welles 1963, p. 110 (on Ptolemy at the Persian Gates and on his securing Bessus).

Appendix 2

THE SOURCES OF INFORMATION

Ptolemy's life spans the late Classical and early Hellenistic periods, from the era of Macedonian greatness under Philip II and Alexander the Great, through the disintegration of the Macedonian Empire, and the formation of the great Hellenistic dynasties. The ancient writers on these periods are very uneven in terms of number and reliability, principally because they lived and worked considerably later than the events of this book. Many focused more on Alexander because of his superhuman feats in Asia, and after his death, none treated the long and complex Wars of the Successors in the same depth. Hence the gaps in our knowledge of the early Hellenistic age throw many aspects of Ptolemy's life and actions into darkness. On the sources for him, see especially Seibert 1969, pp. 52–83; cf. Habicht 2006c.

For the reigns of Philip and Alexander, we have four major narrative sources: Diodorus Siculus (of Sicily), who in late republican Roman times wrote a *Universal History* from the mythical era to Julius Caesar's campaigns in Gaul in 54 (only fifteen of the forty books survive); Arrian (Lucius Flavius Arrianus Xenophon), who in the second century AD wrote a history of Alexander; Quintus Curtius Rufus, whose history of Alexander was written in the mid- to later-first century AD (only eight of the ten books survive); and Justin (Marcus Junianus Justinus), who in the second to fourth centuries AD wrote an epitome (précis) of a first-century BC work by Gnaeus Pompeius Trogus. To these we can add other writers, such as the biographer Plutarch, who in the first to second centuries AD composed a series of lives of prominent Greeks and Romans (including Alexander) to the end of the Roman Republic. Then we have the geographers Strabo (first century BC–first century AD) and Pausanias (second century AD), who provide descriptions of many areas and cities, together with historical events, as well as scattered mentions of our period in, for example, Polybius (second century BC) and Livy (first century BC).

These later ancient writers used a number of earlier works, which were written contemporaneously with the events of this book; all are lost to us, apart from quotations and paraphrases in the later writers. Among the more important contemporary acounts were those by Ptolemy (see Appendix 1); Aristobulus of Cassandreia; Duris of Samos; Callisthenes of Olynthus; and Cleitarchus of Colophon (in Asia Minor). In addition, we have the *Ephemerides*, or royal journal, perhaps compiled by Eumenes of Cardia, which recorded Alexander's actions in his final days and his death.

All the later writers have problems, not least being how carefully they used their earlier sources, and whether they were influenced by Roman attitudes to kingship and generalship, and so styled their accounts accordingly. In addition, the information in Plutarch's biographies is often suspect, as he was more interested in the personalities and morality of his subjects than with historical accuracy. Historical veracity likewise was not Pausanias' primary aim, and he gives contradictory or erroneous information at times. For a discussion of the ancient sources on Philip II and Alexander, see the appendix in Worthington 2014, pp. 311–319, citing bibliography.

When it comes to the Hellenistic period, we are less well served by literary writers, but we do have important archaeological material; cf. Rostovtzeff 1941, vol. 1, pp. 255–261; Seibert 1969, pp. 52–83, and 1983, pp. 1–69; Walbank 1984b; Shipley 2000, pp. 5–32, 196–201; and Habicht 2006c.

Arrian also wrote a history of the Successors, but we have only fragments of it (*FGrH* 156): Goralski 1989. Curtius deals with events after Alexander's death to the Babylon settlement of 323 in cursory fashion at the tail end of book 10. Diodorus (books 18–21) provides us with the most information on the complex years following Alexander's death down to 311, even if at times what he says is suspect and his chronology is at fault; cf. Anson 2014a, pp. 116–121 and 157–162. After the settlement of 311, however, Diodorus is more selective about what he includes, and becomes more interested in Sicilian, Carthaginian, and Roman affairs. Our fullest account is that of Justin (books 13–15), and even though his work is an epitome of an earlier history, he is regarded as a reliable source.

We also have Plutarch's biographies of Demetrius Poliorcetes, Eumenes, and Pyrrhus, but as noted earlier, historical reliability is not one of Plutarch's fortes. Then we have mention of Ptolemy in other writers, such as Pausanias and Strabo, whose description of Hellenistic Alexandria is the only one we have (Strabo 17.1.6–10).

Contemporary accounts of this period (as with Alexander) are lost or fragmentary. To those cited earlier, we may add Hieronymus of Cardia (a supporter of Eumenes before his death in 316; afterward, Hieronymus moved to the Antigonid camp). Hieronymus wrote an account of the Wars of the

Successors down to Pyrrhus' death in 272, which was used by Arrian for his *Events after Alexander*, and by Diodorus and Justin in their accounts, as well as by Plutarch in his biographies.

Other important sources include the *Parian Marble* or *Parian Chronicle* (*BNJ* 239). This records chronology down to 299/8, though it is often flawed; cf. Anson, 2014a, pp. 116–121, 157–162, and 184–186, and Sickinger, *BNJ* 239. Then we have the so-called satrap stele, set up by the priests of Buto in 311, thanking Ptolemy for restoring lands to them previously taken by the Persians. The stele is our only hieroglyphic evidence for Ptolemy, and also tells us that he had moved to Alexandria by 311: see Goedicke 1985.

Coins are highly important contemporary evidence, though they are limited when it comes to Ptolemy's rule. He, like the other Successors, continued to mint coins with Alexander's head on them for propaganda purposes, even when he was issuing coinage in the name of Philip III and Alexander IV. Later he minted coinage with his own head on them, but even after he became king in 306 he still used a silver coin with Alexander's portrait on it.

Finally, of great importance is contemporary papyri, of which we have an abundance (tens of thousands in fact) for Ptolemaic Egypt, containing all manner of information—leases, contracts, relations with temples, petitions— to do with administration and daily life. Almost all of the papyri were written in Greek (though some are in demotic, a written everyday form of Egyptian), and although what we have date from the time of Ptolemy II and his successors, they still cast light on Ptolemy I's reign, who likely introduced or adapted for his use many administrative measures: Rostovtzeff 1941, vol. 1, pp. 256–259; Turner 1984, pp. 118–119; Shipley 2000, pp. 196–201.

TIMELINE

367 (?) Birth of Ptolemy.

359–336 Reign of Philip II of Macedonia, father of Alexander the Great.

353 (?) Ptolemy begins serving as a royal page (?) in Pella.

338 Battle of Chaeronea; Ptolemy likely fought in the battle; Philip becomes master of Greece.

337 League of Corinth assures Macedonian hegemony of Greece; Philip announces invasion of Asia; Pixodarus affair sees banishment of Ptolemy and other friends of Alexander.

336 Assassination of Philip (July); Alexander III ("the Great") becomes king.

335 Alexander campaigns against the Triballi and Illyrians; revolt of Thebes; Ptolemy likely to have taken part in these campaigns.

334 Alexander invades Asia (summer); Battle of the Granicus River; sieges of Miletus and Halicarnassus; Ptolemy likely to have been present at all.

333 Alexander conquers coastal Asia Minor; "unties" the Gordian knot; Alexander almost dies at Tarsus; Battle of Issus, with Ptolemy present.

332 Alexander besieges Tyre and Gaza; conquest of the Levant; Alexander enters Egypt and receives its surrender; Ptolemy likely to have been present at all.

331 Alexander founds Alexandria; Ptolemy accompanies him to the Oracle of Zeus Ammon at Siwah; Battle of Gaugamela, with Ptolemy fighting in it; Alexander takes control of Babylon and Susa; Battle at the Persian Gates; Ptolemy tasked with mopping up Persian survivors from the battle.

330 Ptolemy promoted to a royal bodyguard (*somatophylax*).

329 Revolt of Bactria and Sogdiana.

328 Ptolemy tasked with taking the disgraced Bessus into custody; Ptolemy in command of troops operating in Sogdiana; end of revolt of Bactria and Sogdiana.

327 Siege of the Rock of Chorienes, involves Ptolemy in charge of night time operations; Pages' Conspiracy allegedly betrayed to Ptolemy; Alexander marches to India; his men including Ptolemy involved in deadly clash with Aspasians, with Ptolemy apparently killing their chieftain in combat; siege of the Rock of Aornus, in which Ptolemy plays a vital role.

326 Battle of the Hydaspes River, in which Ptolemy would have fought; mutiny at the Hyphasis River (Ptolemy's position not known).

325 Ptolemy and others suffer near-fatal wounds at Harmatelia from arrows dipped in snake venom; Alexander, with Ptolemy, sails down the Indus into the Indian Ocean; leaves India, which revolts; disastrous march through the Gedrosian Desert, with Ptolemy likely with him.

324 Ptolemy arranges funeral pyre for the Brahman philosopher Calanus' suicide by self-immolation; mass marriage at Susa, with Ptolemy marrying Artacama, daughter of Artabazus (second wife); after Hephaestion's death, the Cossaean campaign involves Ptolemy.

323 Alexander dies (June 11) in Babylon; the Babylon Settlement: Philip III and Alexander IV proclaimed kings (Perdiccas as regent), and Alexander's empire divided up; Ptolemy becomes satrap of Egypt; Ptolemy moves to Egypt this year or following one.

322 Ptolemy executes Cleomenes; makes alliances with Cypriot kings; conquers Cyrenaica.

321 Ptolemy hijacks Alexander's corpse; Perdiccas declares war on Ptolemy; start of the First War of the Successors (321–320).

320 Ptolemy marries Eurydice (third wife); Perdiccas unsuccessfully invades Egypt; Ptolemy makes amends with Philip III and Alexander IV, and is offered the regency (refuses); end of the First War of the Successors; Triparadeisus settlement; Ptolemy reconfirmed as satrap of Egypt, and Antipater as regent of the two kings; Ptolemy annexes Coele-Syria and Phoenicia; further intervention in Cyrene.

319 Death of Antipater; Polyperchon his successor; Antipater's son Cassander forms an alliance with Ptolemy, Antigonus Monophthalmus, and Lysimachus, against Polyperchon; start of the Second War of the Successors (319–316).

317 Murder of Philip III Arrhidaeus; Cassander in control of Macedonia and Greece; start of regime of Demetrius of Phalerum in Athens (317–307); Ptolemy marries Berenice (fourth wife).

316 Death of Eumenes; end of the Second War of the Successors.

315 Seleucus flees to Ptolemy; Ptolemy makes alliance with Lysimachus and Cassander against Antigonus; start of the Third War of the Successors (315–311).

314 Ptolemy issues an edict proclaiming freedom of the Greeks to counteract that of Antigonus, but has little effect; possibly in this year Ptolemy moves to Alexandria as his capital.

312 Ptolemy wins control of Cyprus; campaigns in Syria and Cilicia; Demetrius (Poliorcetes) invades Egypt; battle of Gaza results in Ptolemy defeating Demetrius.

311 The "satrap stele" honors Ptolemy; Ptolemy's troops support Seleucus' return to Babylon; official start of the Seleucid dynasty (311–65); end of the Third War of the Successors.

310 Murder of Alexander IV and his mother Roxane; end of the Argead dynasty of Macedonia; Ptolemy sends his general Leonides to seize cities from Antigonus in Cilicia as part of campaign against Antigonus.

309 Ptolemy campaigns in Lycia and Caria; takes over Cos; remains there for the winter, during which time Berenice gives birth to Ptolemy (II) on Cos; unsuccessfully besieges Halicarnasssus; Ptolemy now dominant in the eastern Mediterranean and parts of the Aegean.

308 Ptolemy sails to Greece; intends to seize control of Greece and Macedonia; circulates Alexander's will; perhaps now circulates rumor he is an illegitimate son of Philip II; proposed marriage to Cleopatra, sister of the late Alexander the Great, collapses when Antigonus murders her; Ptolemy ends his Greek campaign, makes peace with Cassander, returns to Egypt; revolt of Cyrenaica (until 300).

307 Antigonus and Demetrius seize Athens and expel Demetrius of Phalerum; start of the Fourth War of the Successors: Ptolemy, Lysimachus, Cassander, and Seleucus versus Antigonus and Demetrius (307–301).

306 Demetrius wins control of Cyprus after defeating Ptolemy at Salamis (Cyprus), crippling his naval power for the next few years; Antigonus and Demetrius assume the kingship; Lysimachus, Seleucus, Cassander, and Ptolemy also become kings; Demetrius and Antigonus unsuccessfully invade Egypt; Egyptians (?) bestow title *soter* ("savior") on Ptolemy.

305–304 Demetrius' epic (but unsuccessful) siege of Rhodes; Rhodians establish a cult to Ptolemy.

301 Battle of Ipsus; defeat of the Antigonids and death of Antigonus; Ptolemy occupies Coele-Syria; end of the Fourth War of the Successors.

300–299 End of revolt of Cyrenaica; Magas, Ptolemy's stepson, appointed governor; Ptolemy makes alliance with Lysimachus of Thrace.

297 Death of Cassander; Ptolemy supports Pyrrhus' bid to reclaim the throne of Epirus; Demetrius of Phalerum arrives in Alexandria; Museum and Library take shape; work begins (or continues) on lighthouse of Pharos.

295 Demetrius makes another bid for Greece; Ptolemy sends a fleet to Greece, but it is ineffectual; Demetrius captures Athens and becomes master of Greece.

294 Ptolemy recaptures Cyprus; takes over (?) from Demetrius the League of the Cycladic Islands; league members establish a cult to Ptolemy; Demetrius becomes King of Macedonia; Ptolemy remains in Egypt the next few years.

288–287 Ptolemy's last campaign; Demetrius' plan to invade Asia leads to coalition of Ptolemy, Lysimachus, Seleucus, and Pyrrhus against him; start of the Fifth War of the Successors; Ptolemy sails to Greece, Pyrrhus and Lysimachus invade Macedonia; Ptolemy sends aid and military support to Athens; Berenice's son Ptolemy becomes heir to Egyptian throne (287).

285 Ptolemy makes his son and heir Ptolemy (II) co-ruler with him.

283 January/February: death of Ptolemy I, aged about 82; Ptolemy II becomes king; buries his father in Alexandria; names his parents *theoi soteres* ("savior gods"); deification of Ptolemy I, and cult to him.

BIBLIOGRAPHY

Abel, F. M., "La Syrie et la Palestine au temps de Ptolémée Soter," *Revue Biblique* 44 (1935), pp. 559–581.

Adams, W. L., "The Hellenistic Kingdoms," in G. R. Bugh (ed.), *The Cambridge Companion to the Hellenistic World* (Cambridge: 2007), pp. 28–51.

Adams, W. L., "Alexander's Successors to 221 BC," in J. Roisman and Ian Worthington (eds.), *A Companion to Ancient Macedonia* (Malden, MA: 2010), pp. 208–224.

Ager, S., "Familiarity Breeds: Incest and the Ptolemaic Dynasty," *JHS* 125 (2005), pp. 1–34.

Andronikos, M., "Art during the Archaic and Classical Periods," in M. B. Sakellariou (ed.), *Macedonia, 4000 Years of Greek History and Civilization* (Athens: 1983), pp. 92–110.

Anson, E. M., "Diodorus and the Date of Triparadeisus," *AJPh* 107 (1986), pp. 208–217.

Anson, E. M., "Antigonus, the Satrap of Greater Phrygia," *Historia* 37 (1988), pp. 471–477.

Anson, E. M., "The Dating of Perdiccas' Death and the Assembly at Triparadeisus," *GRBS* 43 (2003), pp. 373–390.

Anson, E. M., *Eumenes of Cardia: A Greek among Macedonians* (Leiden: 2004).

Anson, E. M., "The Chronology of the Third Diadoch War," *Phoenix* 60 (2006), pp. 226–235.

Anson, E. M., *Alexander's Heirs: The Age of the Successors* (Malden, MA: 2014a).

Anson, E. M., "Discrimination and Eumenes of Kardia Revisited," in H. Hauben and A. Meeus (eds.), *The Age of the Successors and the Creation of the Hellenistic Kingdoms (323–276 B.C)* (Leuven: 2014b), pp. 539–558.

Antela-Bernárdez, B., "Simply the Best: Alexander's Last Words and the Macedonian Kingship," *Eirene* 47 (2011), pp. 118–126.

Archibald, Z., *The Odrysian Kingdom of Thrace: Orpheus Unmasked* (Oxford: 1998).

Ashton, N. G., "Craterus from 324 to 321 B.C.," *Ancient Macedonia* 5 (Thessaloniki: 1991), pp. 125–131.

Ashton, S.-A., *Cleopatra and Egypt* (Malden, MA: 2008).

Ashton, S.-A., "Ptolemaic and Romano-Egyptian Sculpture," in A. B. Lloyd (ed.), *A Companion to Ancient Egypt* 2 (Malden, MA: 2010), pp. 970–989.

Austin, M. M., *The Hellenistic World from Alexander to the Roman Conquest: A Selection of Ancient Sources in Translation* (Cambridge: 1981).

Austin, M. M., "The Seleukids and Asia," in A. Erskine (ed.), *A Companion to the Hellenistic World* (Malden, MA: 2003), pp. 121–133.

Badian, E., "A King's Notebooks," *HSCPh* 72 (1967), pp. 183–204.

Badian, E., "Agis III Revisited," in Ian Worthington (ed.), *Ventures into Greek History: Essays in Honour of N. G. L. Hammond* (Oxford: 1994), pp. 258–292.

Bagnall, R. S., *The Administration of the Ptolemaic Possessions Outside Egypt* (Leiden: 1976).

Bagnall, R. S., "The Date of the Foundation of Alexandria," *AJAH* 4 (1979), pp. 46–49.

Bagnall, R. S. and P. Derow, *Greek Historical Documents: The Hellenistic Period* (Chico, CA: 1981).

Barker, E. A., "Alexandrian Literature," in S. A. Cook, F. E. Adcock, and M. P. Charlesworth (eds.), *Cambridge Ancient History*, vol. 7 (Cambridge: 1954), pp. 249–283.

Bartson, L. J., "Cyrenaica in Antiquity," unpub. Ph.D. diss. (Ann Arbor, MI: 1982).

Baynham, E., "Antipater: Manager of Kings," in Ian Worthington (ed.), *Ventures into Greek History: Essays in Honour of N. G. L. Hammond* (Oxford: 1994), pp. 331–356.

Baynham, E., *The Unique History of Quintus Curtius Rufus* (Ann Arbor, MI: 1998).

Baynham, E., "Cleomenes of Naucratis, Villain or Victim?" in T. Howe, E. E. Garvan, and G. Wrightson (eds.), *Greece, Macedon and Persia: Studies in Social, Political and Military History in Honour of W. Heckel* (Haverton: 2015), pp. 127–134.

Bell, H. I., "Alexandria ad Aegyptum," *JRS* 36 (1946), pp. 130–132.

Bengtson, H., *Die Diadochen: Die Nachfolger Alexanders (323–281 v. Chr.)* (Munich: 1987).

Bennett, B. and M. Roberts, *The Wars of Alexander's Successors, 323–281 BC*, vol. 1 (Barnsley: 2008) and vol. 2 (Barnsley: 2009).

Bernand, A., *Alexandrie des Ptolemées* (Paris: 1995).

Berthold, R. M., *Rhodes in the Hellenistic Age* (London: 1984).

Berti, M. and V. Costa, *La Biblioteca di Alessandria* (Rome: 2010).

Bevan, E. R., *The House of Seleucus* (London: 1902).

Bevan, E. R., *The House of Ptolemy: A History of Egypt under the Ptolemaic Dynasty* (London: 1927).

Bhandare, S., "Not Just a Pretty-Face: Interpretations of Alexander's Numismatic Legacy in the Hellenistic East," in H. P. Ray and D. T. Potts (eds.), *Memory as History: The Legacy of Alexander in Asia* (New Delhi: 2007), pp. 208–256.

Bikerman, E., *Institutions des Séleucides* (Paris: 1938).

Billows, R., *Antigonus the One-Eyed and the Creation of the Hellenistic State* (Berkeley, CA: 1990).

Billows, R., *Kings and Colonists: Aspects of Macedonian Imperialism* (Leiden: 1995).

Billows, R., "Cities," in A. Erskine (ed.), *A Companion to the Hellenistic World* (Malden, MA: 2003), pp. 196–215.

Bingen, J., *Hellenistic Egypt: Monarchy Society, Economy, Culture* (Edinburgh: 2007).

Boiy, T., *Between High and Low: A Chronology of the Early Hellenistic Period* (Bonn: 2007).

Bosworth, A. B., "The Death of Alexander the Great: Rumour and Propaganda," *CQ²* 21 (1971), pp. 112–136.

Bosworth, A. B., *A Historical Commentary on Arrian's History of Alexander* 1 (Oxford: 1980a).

Bosworth, A. B., "Alexander and the Iranians," *JHS* 100 (1980b), pp. 1–21.

Bosworth, A. B., "A Missing Year in the History of Alexander the Great," *JHS* 101 (1981), pp. 17–39.

Bosworth, A. B., "Alexander the Great and the Decline of Macedon," *JHS* 106 (1986), pp. 1–12.

Bosworth, A. B., *From Arrian to Alexander* (Oxford: 1988).

Bosworth, A. B., "Philip III Arrhidaeus and the Chronology of the Successors," *Chiron* 22 (1992), pp. 55–81.

Bosworth, A. B., "Perdiccas and the Kings," *CQ²* 43 (1993), pp. 420–427.

Bosworth, A. B., *Alexander and the East: The Tragedy of Triumph* (Oxford: 1996).

Bosworth, A. B., "Ptolemy and the Will of Alexander," in A. B. Bosworth and E. J. Baynham (eds.), *Alexander the Great in Fact and Fiction* (Oxford: 2000), pp. 207–241.

Bosworth, A. B., *The Legacy of Alexander: Politics, Warfare and Propaganda under the Successors* (Oxford: 2002).

Bosworth, A. B., "Alexander the Great and the Creation of the Hellenistic Age," in G. R. Bugh (ed.), *The Cambridge Companion to the Hellenistic World* (Cambridge: 2007), pp. 9–27.

Bouché-Leclercq, A., *Histoire des Lagides*, 4 vols. (Paris: 1903–1907).

Bouché-Leclercq, A., *Histoire des Séleucides (323–64 avant J.-C.)*, 2 vols. (Paris: 1914).

Bowden, H., "Alexander in Egypt: Considering the Egyptian Evidence," in P. Bosman (ed.), *Alexander in Africa* (Pretoria: 2014), pp. 38–55.

Bowman, A. K., *Egypt after the Pharaohs: 332 BC to AD 642: From Alexander to the Arab Conquest* (London: 1986).

Braund, D., "After Alexander: The Emergence of the Hellenistic World, 323–281," in A. Erskine (ed.), *A Companion to the Hellenistic World* (Malden, MA: 2003), pp. 19–34.

Briant, P., "D'Alexandre le Grand aux Diadoques: Le cas d'Eumène de Kardia," *REA* 74 (1972), pp. 32–73, and 75 (1973), pp. 43–81.

Briant, P., *From Cyrus to Alexander: A History of the Persian Empire*, trans. P. T. Daniels (Winona Lake, IN: 2002).

Briant, P., *Alexander the Great and His Empire*, trans. A. Kuhrt (Princeton, NJ: 2010).

Brunt, P. A., "Alexander, Barsine, and Heracles," *Rivista di Filologia* 103 (1975), pp. 22–34.

Brunt, P. A., *Arrian, History of Alexander*, Loeb Classical Library, vol. 1 (Cambridge, MA: 1976).

Bugh, G. R., "Introduction," in G. R. Bugh (ed.), *The Cambridge Companion to the Hellenistic World* (Cambridge: 2006), pp. 1–8.

Buraselis, K., "The Problem of the Ptolemaic Sibling Marriage: A Case of Dynastic Acculturation?" in P. McKechnie and P. Guillaume (eds.), *Ptolemy II Philadelphus and His World* (Leiden: 2008), pp. 291–302.

Burn, A. R., "The Generalship of Alexander," *G&R*² 12 (1965), pp. 140–154.

Burstein, S. M., "Arsinoë II Philadelphos: A Revisionist View," in W. L. Adams and E. N. Borza (eds.), *Philip II, Alexander the Great, and the Macedonian Heritage* (Lanham, MD: 1982), pp. 197–212.

Burstein, S. M., *The Hellenistic Age from the Battle of Ipsos to the Death of Kleopatra VII* (Cambridge: 1985).

Burstein, S. M., "Pharaoh Alexander: A Scholarly Myth," *Anc. Society* 22 (1991), pp. 139–145.

Burstein, S. M., *The Reign of Cleopatra* (Westport, CT: 2004).

Burstein, S. M., "Alexander's Organization of Egypt: A Note on the Career of Cleomenes of Naucratis," in T. Howe and J. Reams (eds.), *Macedonian Legacies: Studies in Ancient Macedonian History and Culture in Honor of E. N. Borza* (Claremont, CA: 2008a), pp. 183–194.

Burstein, S. M., "Elephants for Ptolemy II: Ptolemaic Policy in Nubia in the Third Century BC," in P. McKechnie and P. Guillaume (eds.), *Ptolemy II Philadelphus and His World* (Leiden: 2008b), pp. 135–147.

Burstein, S. M., "An Egyptian Source of Tacitus' Sarapis Narrative (*Histories* 4.84)," *ZPE* 183 (2012), pp. 37–38.

Burstein, S. M., "The Satrap Stela and the Struggle for Lower Nubia," in J. R. Anderson and D. A. Welsby (eds.), *The Fourth Cataract and Beyond: Proceedings of the 12th Conference for Nubian Studies* (Leuven: 2014), pp. 573–576.

Burstein, S. M., "Alexander's Unintended Legacy: Borders," in T. Howe, E. E. Garvan, and G. Wrightson (eds.), *Greece, Macedon and Persia: Studies in Social, Political and Military History in Honour of W. Heckel* (Haverton: 2015), pp. 118–126.

Canfora, L., *The Vanished Library: A Wonder of the Ancient World* (Berkeley, CA: 1990).

Carney, E. D., *Women and Monarchy in Macedonia* (Norman, OK: 2000).

Carney, E. D., "The Trouble with Philip Arrhidaeus," *AHB* 15 (2001), pp. 63–89.

Carney, E. D., "The Role of the *Basilikoi Paides* at the Argead Court," in T. Howe and J. Reames (eds.), *Macedonian Legacies: Studies in Ancient Macedonian History and Culture in Honor of Eugene N. Borza* (Claremont, CA: 2008), pp. 145–164.

Carney, E. D., *Arsinoe of Egypt and Macedon: A Royal Life* (New York, NY: 2013).

Caroli, C. A., *Ptolemaios I. Soter—Herrscher zweier Kulturen* (Konstanz: 2007).

Cartledge, P., *Alexander the Great: The Hunt for a New Past* (London: 2003).

Cawkwell, G. L., *Philip of Macedon* (London: 1978).

Champion, J., *Pyrrhus of Epirus* (Barnsley: 2012).

Champion, J., *Antigonus the One-Eyed: Greatest of the Successors* (Barnsley: 2014).

Chaniotis, A., "The Divinity of Hellenistic Rulers," in A. Erskine (ed.), *A Companion to the Hellenistic World* (Malden, MA: 2003), pp. 431–445.

Chaniotis, A., *War in the Hellenistic World: A Social and Cultural History* (Malden, MA: 2005).

Clarysse, W., "Greeks and Egyptians in the Ptolemaic Army and Administration," *Aegyptus* 65 (1985), pp. 57–76.

Clayton, P. A., "The Pharos at Alexandria," in P. A. Clayton and M. J. Price (eds.), *The Seven Wonders of the Ancient World* (London: 1988), pp. 138–157.

Cloché, P., *Le Dislocation d'un Empire: Les Premiers successeurs d'Alexandre le Grand (323–281/ 280 avant J.-C.)* (Paris: 1959).

Cohen, G. M., "The Diadochoi and the New Monarchies," *Athenaeum* 52 (1974), pp. 177–179.

Collins, A. W., "The Office of Chiliarch under Alexander and his Successors," *Phoenix* 55 (2001), pp. 259–283.

Collins, A. W., "Alexander the Great and the Office of *Edeatros*," *Historia* 61 (2013), pp. 414–420.

Collins, A. W., "Alexander's Visit to Siwah: A New Analysis," *Phoenix* 68 (2014), pp. 62–77.

Collins, N. L., "The Various Fathers of Ptolemy I," *Mnemosyne* 50⁴ (1997), pp. 436–476.

Crawford, D. J., "Ptolemy, Ptah and Apis in Hellenistic Memphis," *Studia Hellenistica* 24 (1980), pp. 1–42.

Criscuolo, L., "Considerazioni generali sull' epiteto *PHILADELPHOS* nelle dinastie ellenistiche e sulla sua applicazione nella titolatura degli ultimi seleucidi," *Historia* 43 (1994), pp. 402–422.

Cruz-Uribe, E., "Social Structure and Daily Life: Graeco-Roman," in A. B. Lloyd (ed.), *A Companion to Ancient Egypt*, vol. 1 (Malden, MA: 2010), pp. 491–506.

Dahmen, K., *The Legend of Alexander the Great on Greek and Roman Coins* (London: 2007).

Daszewski, W. A., "Nicocles and Ptolemy: Remarks on the Early History of Nea Paphos," *RDAC* (1987), pp. 171–175.

Davies, J. K., "The Interpenetration of Hellenistic Sovereignties," in D. Ogden (ed.), *The Hellenistic World: New Perspectives* (London: 2002), pp. 1–21.

Davis, N. and C. M. Kraay, *The Hellenistic Kingdoms: Portrait Coins and History* (London: 1973).

Delev, P., "Lysimachus, the Getae, and Archaeology," *CQ²* 50 (2000), pp. 384–418.

Depuydt, L., "The Time of Death of Alexander the Great: 11 June 323 B.C., ca. 4.00–5.00 p.m.," *Die Welt des Orients* 28 (1997), pp. 117–135.

Develin, R. and W. Heckel, *Justin: Epitome of the Philippic History of Pompeius Trogus* (Atlanta, GA: 1994).

Devine, A. M., "Diodorus' Account of the Battle of Gaza," *Acta Classica* 27 (1984), pp. 31–40.

Devine, A. M., "A Pawn-Sacrifice at the Battle of the Granicus: The Origins of a Favorite Stratagem of Alexander the Great," *Anc. World* 18 (1988), pp. 3–20.

Devine, A. M., "Alexander the Great," in J. Hackett (ed.), *Warfare in the Ancient World* (New York, NY: 1989a), pp. 104–129.

Devine, A. M., "The Generalship of Ptolemy I and Demetrius Poliorcetes at the Battle of Gaza (312 B.C.)," *Anc. World* 20 (1989b), pp. 29–38.

Dixon, M., "Corinth, Greek Freedom, and the Diadochoi, 323-301 B.C.," in W. Heckel, L. Tritle, and P. Wheatley (eds.), *Alexander's Empire: Formulation to Decay* (Claremont, CA: 2007), pp. 151–178.

Dmitriev, S., *The Greek Slogan of Freedom and Early Roman Politics in Greece* (Oxford: 2011).

Doherty, P., *The Death of Alexander the Great* (New York, NY: 2004).

Dreyer, B., "Athen und Demetrios Poliorketes nach der Schlact von Ipsos (301 v. Chr.)," *Historia* 49 (2000), pp. 54–66.

Droysen, J. G., *Geschichte der Diadochen* (Leipzig: 1877).

Eckstein, A. M., *Mediterranean Anarchy, Interstate War, and the Rise of Rome* (Berkeley, CA: 2006).

Eggermont, P. H. L., *Alexander's Campaigns in Sind and Baluchistan and the Siege of the Brahmin Town of Harmatelia* (Leuven: 1975).

Elgood, P. G., *The Ptolemies of Egypt* (London: 1938).

Ellis, J. R., *Philip II and Macedonian Imperialism* (London: 1976).

Ellis, W. M., *Ptolemy of Egypt* (London: 1994).

Emmons, B., "The Overstruck Coinage of Ptolemy I," *ANSMN* 6 (1954), pp. 69–84.

Errington, R. M., "Bias in Ptolemy's History of Alexander," *CQ*² 19 (1969), pp. 233–242.

Errington, R. M., "From Babylon to Triparadeisos," *JHS* 90 (1970), pp. 49–77.

Errington, R. M., *The Dawn of Empire: Rome's Rise to World Power* (London 1971).

Errington, R. M., "Diodorus Siculus and the Chronology of the Early Diadochoi, 320–311 B.C.," *Hermes* 105 (1977), pp. 478–504.

Errington, R. M., "The Nature of the Macedonian State under the Monarchy," *Chiron* 8 (1978), pp. 77–133.

Errington, R. M., *A History of the Hellenistic World: 323–30 BC* (Malden, MA: 2008).

Erskine, A., "Culture and Power in Ptolemaic Egypt: The Museum and Library of Alexandria," *G&R*² 42 (1995), pp. 38–48.

Erskine, A., "Life after Death: Alexandria and the Body of Alexander," *G&R* 49 (2002), pp. 167–179.

Erskine, A., "Ruler Cult and the Early Hellenistic City," in H. Hauben and A. Meeus (eds.), *The Age of the Successors and the Creation of the Hellenistic Kingdoms (323–276 B.C)* (Leuven: 2014), pp. 579–597.

Falivene, M. R., "Government, Management, Literacy. Aspects of Ptolemaic Administration in the Early Hellenistic Period," *Anc. Society* 22 (1991), pp. 203–227.

Fassa, E., "Shifting Conceptions of the Divine: Sarapis as Part of Ptolemaic Egypt's Social Imaginaries," in E. Stavrianopoulou (ed.), *Shifting Social Imaginaries in the Hellenistic Period* (Leiden: 2013), pp. 115–139.

Ferguson, W. S., *Hellenistic Athens: An Historical Essay* (New York, NY: 1911).

Ferguson, W. S., "Demetrius Poliorcetes and the Hellenic League," *Hesperia* 17 (1948), pp. 112–136.

Fischer-Bovet, C., "Counting the Greeks in Egypt: Immigration in the First Century of Ptolemaic Rule," in C. Holeran and A. Pudsey (eds.), *Demography in the Graeco-Roman World: New Insights and Approaches* (Oxford: 2011), pp. 135–154.

Fischer-Bovet, C., "Egyptian Warriors: The *machimoi* of Herodotus and the Ptolemaic Army," *CQ*² 63 (2013), pp. 209–236.

Fischer-Bovet, C., *Army and Society in Ptolemaic Egypt* (Cambridge: 2014).

Fischer-Bovet, C., "Les Égyptiens dans les forces armées de terre et de mer sous les trois premiers Lagides," in T. Derda and A. Łajtar (eds.), *Proceedings of the 27th International Congress of Papyrology* (Warsaw: 2016), pp. 1669–1678.

Fletcher, J., *Cleopatra the Great: The Woman behind the Legend* (New York, NY: 2011).

Fraser, P., "Two Studies on the Cult of Sarapis in the Hellenistic World," *Opuscula Atheniensia* 3 (1960), pp. 1–54.

Fraser, P., *Ptolemaic Alexandria*, 3 vols. (Oxford: 1972).

Fraser, P., *Cities of Alexander the Great* (Oxford: 1996).

Fredricksmeyer, E. A., "Alexander, Midas, and the Oracle at Gordium," *CPh* 56 (1961), pp. 160–168.

Fredricksmeyer, E. A., "Alexander the Great and the Kingship of Asia," in A. B. Bosworth and E. J. Baynham (eds.), *Alexander the Great in Fact and Fiction* (Oxford: 2000), pp. 136–166.

Fuller, J. F. C., *The Generalship of Alexander the Great* (repr. New Brunswick, NJ: 1960).

Gabbart, J., *Antigonos II Gonatas: A Political Biography* (London: 1997).

Gabriel, R. A., *Philip II of Macedon: Greater Than Alexander* (Washington, DC: 2010).

Gambetti, S., *The Alexandrian Riots of 38 CE and the Persecution of the Jews: A Historical Reconstruction* (Leiden: 2009).

Gambetti, S., Satyrus, *BNJ* 631 (Leiden).

Garlan, Y., "Alliance entre les Iasiens et Ptolémée Ier," *ZPE* 18 (1975), pp. 193–198.

Garoufalias, P. E., *Pyrrhus, King of Epirus* (London: 1979).

Geer, R. M., *Diodorus Siculus 18 and 19.1–65*, Loeb Classical Library, vol. 9 (Cambridge, MA: 1947).

Geer, R. M., *Diodorus Siculus 19.66–110 and 20*, Loeb Classical Library, vol. 10 (Cambridge, MA: 1954).

Gesche, H., "Nikokles von Paphos und Nikokreon von Salamis," *Chiron* 4 (1974), pp. 103–125.

Gilley, D. L. and Ian Worthington, "Alexander the Great, Macedonia and Asia," in J. Roisman and Ian Worthington (eds.), A *Companion to Ancient Macedonia* (Malden, MA: 2010), pp. 186–207.

Giovannini, A., "Le traité entre Iasos et Ptolémée Ier (IK 28,1, 2-3) et les relations entre les cités grecques d'Asie Mineure et les souverains hellénistiques," *Epig. Anat* 37 (2004), pp. 69–87.

Goedicke, H., "Comments on the Satrap Stela," *BES* 6 (1985), pp. 33–54.

Golan, D., "The Fate of a Court Historian: Callisthenes," *Athenaeum* 66 (1988), pp. 99–120.

Goralski, W. J., "Arrian's *Events after Alexander*: Summary of Photius and Selected Fragments," *Anc. World* 19 (1989), pp. 81–108.

Grabowski, T., "Ptolemy's Military and Political Operations in Greece 314–308 BC," in E. Dabrowa, *Studies on the Greek and Roman Military History* (Krakow: 2008), pp. 33–36.

Graham, D., G. Shipley, and M. H. Hansen, "The Polis and Federalism," in G. R. Bugh (ed.), *The Cambridge Companion to the Hellenistic World* (Cambridge: 2006), pp. 52–72.

Grainger, J. D., *Seleukos Nikator: Constructing a Hellenistic Kingdom* (London: 1999).

Grainger, J. D., *The Rise of the Seleukid Empire (323–223 BC): Seleukos I to Seleukos III* (Barnsley: 2014).

Grant, M., *From Alexander to Cleopatra* (New York, NY: 1982).

Green, P., *Alexander to Actium: The Historical Evolution of the Hellenistic Age* (Berkeley, CA: 1990).

Greenwalt, W. S., "The Search for Arrhidaeus," *Anc. World* 10 (1985), pp. 69–77.

Greenwalt, W. S., "Argaeus, Ptolemy II, and Alexander's Corpse," *AHB* 2 (1988), pp. 39–41.

Greenwalt, W. S., "Polygamy and Succession in Argead Macedonia," *Arethusa* 22 (1989), pp. 19–45.

Grimm, G., *Alexandria, Die erste Königsstadt der hellenistichen Welt* (Mainz: 1998).

Gruen, E. S., *The Hellenistic World and the Coming of Rome*, 2 vols. (Berkeley, CA: 1984).

Gruen, E. S., "The Coronation of the Diadochoi," in J. Eadie and J. Ober (eds.), *The Craft of the Ancient Historian: Essays in Honor of Chester G. Starr* (Lanham, MD: 1985), pp. 253–271.

Grzybek, E., *Du calendrier macédonien au calendrier ptolémaïque: Problemes de chronologie hellénistique* (Basel: 1990).

Habicht, C., *Gottmenschentum und griechishe Städte*[2] (Munich: 1970).

Habicht, C., *Athens from Alexander to Antony*, trans. D.L. Schneider (Cambridge, MA: 1997).

Habicht, C., "Argaeus, Ptolemy II, and Alexander's Corpse," in C. Habicht (ed.), *The Hellenistic Monarchies: Selected Papers* (Ann Arbor, MI: 2006a), pp. 153–154.

Habicht, C., "The Ruling Class in the Hellenistic Monarchies," in C. Habicht (ed.), *The Hellenistic Monarchies: Selected Papers* (Ann Arbor, MI: 2006b), pp. 26–40.

Habicht, C., "The Literary and Epigraphic Evidence for the History of Alexander and His First Successors," in C. Habicht (ed.), *The Hellenistic Monarchies: Selected Papers* (Ann Arbor, MI: 2006c), pp. 74–84.

Hagerdorn, D., "Ein Erlass Ptolemaios' I. Soter," *ZPE* 66 (1986), pp. 65–70.

Hammond, N. G. L., "The Victory of Macedon at Chaeronea," in N. G. L. Hammond, *Studies in Greek History* (Oxford: 1973), pp. 534–557.

Hammond, N. G. L., *Three Historians of Alexander the Great* (Cambridge: 1983).

Hammond, N. G. L., *Alexander the Great: King, Commander, and Statesman*[2] (Bristol: 1989a).

Hammond, N. G. L., "Casualties and Reinforcements of Citizen Soldiers in Greece and Macedon," *JHS* 109 (1989b), pp. 56–68.

Hammond, N. G. L., "Royal Pages, Personal Pages, and Boys Trained in the Macedonian Manner during the Period of the Temenid Monarchy," *Historia* 39 (1990), pp. 261–290.

Hammond, N. G. L., "The Macedonian Imprint on the Hellenistic World," in P. Green (ed.), *Hellenistic History and Culture* (Berkeley, CA: 1993a), pp. 12–23.

Hammond, N. G. L., *Sources for Alexander the Great* (Cambridge: 1993b).

Hammond, N. G. L., *Philip of Macedon* (London: 1994).

Hammond, N. G. L., "Alexander's Non-European Troops and Ptolemy I's Use of Such Troops," *BASP* 33 (1996), pp. 99–109.

Hammond, N. G. L., "The Continuity of Macedonian Institutions and the Macedonian Kingdoms of the Hellenistic Era," *Historia* 49 (2000), pp. 141–160.

Hammond, N. G. L. and G. T. Griffith, *A History of Macedonia*, vol. 2 (Oxford: 1979).

Hammond, N. G. L. and F. W. Walbank, *A History of Macedonia*, vol. 3 (Oxford: 1988).

Hansen, E. V., *The Attalids of Pergamum*² (Ithaca, NY: 1971).

Hardiman, C. L., "Classical Art to 221 BC," in J. Roisman and Ian Worthington (eds.), *A Companion to Ancient Macedonia* (Malden, MA: 2010), pp. 505–521.

Harding, P. E., *From the End of the Peloponnesian War to the Battle of Ipsus* (Cambridge: 1985).

Hatzopoulos, M. B., "Succession and Regency in Classical Macedonia," in *Ancient Macedonia*, vol. 4 (Institute for Balkan Studies, Thessaloniki: 1986), pp. 279–292.

Hauben, H., "On the Chronology of the Years 313–311 B.C.," *AJPh* 94 (1973), pp. 256–267.

Hauben, H., "Antigonos' Invasion Plan for His Attack on Egypt in 306 B.C," *Orientalia Lovaniensia Periodica* 6/7 (1975/76), pp. 267–271.

Hauben, H., "Fleet Strength at the Battle of Salamis, 306 BC," *Chiron* 6 (1976), pp. 1–5.

Hauben, H., "Sur la stratégie et la politique ètrangère du premier Ptolémée," *RPh* 103 (1977a), pp. 265–266.

Hauben, H., "The First War of the Successors (321 B.C.): Chronological and Historical Problems," *Anc. Society* 8 (1977b), pp. 85–120.

Hauben, H., "Rhodes, Alexander, and the Diadochoi from 333/332 to 304 BC," *Historia* 26 (1977c), pp. 307–339.

Hauben, H., "Cyprus and the Ptolemaic Navy," *RDAC* (1987a), pp. 213–226.

Hauben, H., "Philocles, King of the Sidonians and General of the Ptolemies," *Studia Phoenicia* 5 (Leuven: 1987b), pp. 413–427.

Hauben, H., "Rhodes, the League of the Islanders, and the Cult of Ptolemy I Soter," in A. Tamis, C. J. Mackie, and S. G. Byrne (eds.), *Philathenaios: Studies in Honour of Michael J. Osborne* (Athens: 2010), pp. 103–121.

Hauben, H., "Ptolemy's Grand Tour," in H. Hauben and A. Meeus (eds.), *The Age of the Successors and the Creation of the Hellenistic Kingdoms (323–276 B.C)* (Leuven: 2014), pp. 235–261.

Hauben, H. and A. Meeus (eds.), *The Age of the Successors and the Creation of the Hellenistic Kingdoms (323–276 B.C.)* (Louvain: 2014).

Hazzard, R. A., "The Regnal Years of Ptolemy II Philadelphus," *Phoenix* 41 (1987), pp. 140–158.

Hazzard, R. A., "Did Ptolemy I Get His Surname from the Rhodians?" *ZPE* 93 (1992), pp. 52–56.

Hazzard, R. A., *Imagination of a Monarchy: Studies in Ptolemaic Propaganda* (Toronto: 2000).

Heckel, W., "The *Somatophylakes* of Alexander the Great: Some Thoughts," *Historia* 27 (1978), pp. 224–228.

Heckel, W., "*Somatophylakia*: A Macedonian *cursus honorum*," *Phoenix* 40 (1986), pp. 279–294.

Heckel, W., *The Marshals of Alexander's Empire* (London: 1992).

Heckel, W., "The Politics of Distrust: Alexander and His Successors," in D. Ogden (ed.), *The Hellenistic World: New Perspectives* (London: 2002), pp. 81–95.

Heckel, W., "Kings and Companions: Observations on the Nature of Power in the Reign of Alexander," in J. Roisman (ed.), *Brill's Companion to Alexander the Great* (Leiden: 2003a), pp. 197–225.

Heckel, W., "Alexander the Great and the 'Limits of the Civilised World'," in W. Heckel and L. A. Tritle (eds.), *Crossroads of History: The Age of Alexander* (Claremont, CA: 2003b), pp. 147–174.

Heckel, W., "A King and His Army," in W. Heckel and L. Tritle (eds.), *Alexander the Great: A New History* (Malden, MA: 2009), pp. 69–82.

Heckel, W. and J. Yardley, *Alexander the Great: Historical Sources in Translation* (Malden, MA: 2003).

Heinen, H., *Untersuchungen zur hellenistischen Geschichte des 3. Jh. v. Chr. Zur Geschichte der Zeit des Ptolemaios Keraunos und zum Chremonideischen Krieg* (Wiesbaden: 1972).

Herklotz, F., "*Aegypto Capta*: Augustus and the Annexation of Egypt," in C. Riggs (ed.), *The Oxford Handbook of Roman Egypt* (Oxford: 2012), pp. 11–21.

Heuss, A., "Antigonos Monophthalmos und die griechischen Städte," *Hermes* 73 (1938), pp. 133–194.

Higgins, R., "The Colossus at Rhodes," in P. A. Clayton and M. J. Price (eds.), *The Seven Wonders of the Ancient World* (London: 1988), pp. 124–137.

Hinge, G. and J. A. Krasilnikoff (eds.), *Alexandria: A Cultural and Religious Melting Pot* (Aarhus: 2009).

Hölbl, G., *A History of the Ptolemaic Empire*, trans T. Saavedra (London: 2001).

Holt, F., *Alexander the Great and the Mystery of the Elephant Medallions* (Berkeley, CA: 2003).

Horat Zuffa, G., "Tolemeo I in Grecia," *Atti Venezia* 130 (1971/1972), pp. 99–112.

Howe, T., "Alexander in India: Ptolemy as Near Eastern Historiographer," in T. Howe and J. Reams (eds.), *Macedonian Legacies: Studies in Ancient Macedonian History and Culture in Honor of E. N. Borza* (Claremont, CA: 2008), pp. 215–234.

Howe, T., "Founding Alexandria: Alexander the Great and the Politics of Memory," in P. Bosman (ed.), *Alexander in Africa* (Pretoria: 2014), pp. 72–91.

Huss, W., *Ägypten in hellenistischer Zeit, 323-30 v. Chr.* (Munich: 2001).

Johnson, C., "Ptolemy I's Epiklesis *Soter*: Origin and Definition," *AHB* 14 (2000), pp. 102–106.

Jones, A., "On the Reconstructed Macedonian and Egyptian Lunar Calendars," *ZPE* 119 (1997), pp. 157–166.

Kasher, A., *The Jews in Hellenistic and Roman Egypt* (Tübingen: 1985).

Kehoe, D., "The Economy: Graeco-Roman," in A. B. Lloyd (ed.), *A Companion to Ancient Egypt*, vol. 1 (Malden: 2010), pp. 309–325.

Kertész, I., "Ptolemy I and the Battle of Gaza," *Studia Aegyptiaca*, vol. 1, *Recueil d'études dédiées à V. Wessetzky à l'occasion de son 65 anniversaire* (Budapest: 1974), pp. 231–241.

King, C. J., "Kingship and Other Political Institutions," in J. Roisman and Ian Worthington (eds.), *A Companion to Ancient Macedonia* (Malden, MA: 2010), pp. 374–391.

Kolbe, W., "Die griechische Politik der ersten Ptolemäer," *Hermes* 51 (1916), pp. 530–553.

Koenen, L., "Die Adaptation Ägyptischer Königsideologie am Ptolemäerhof," in E. Van 'T Dack, P. van Dessel, and W. van Gucht (eds.), *Egypt and the Hellenistic World* (Louvain: 1983), pp. 143–190.

Koenen, L., "The Ptolemaic King as a Religious Figure," in A. Bulloch et al. (eds.), *Images and Ideologies: Self-definition in the Hellenistic World* (Berkeley, CA: 1993), pp. 25–115.

Kornemann, E., *Die Alexandergeschichte des Königs Ptolemaios I von Aegypten* (Leipzig: 1935).

Ladynin, I. A., "The Argeadai Building Program in Egypt in the Framework of Dynasties' XXIX–XXX Temple Building," in K. Nawotka and A. Wojciechowska (eds.), *Alexander the Great and Egypt: History, Art, Tradition* (Wiesbaden: 2014), pp. 221–240.

Lampela, A., *Rome and the Ptolemies of Egypt: The Development of Their Political Relations, 273-80 BC* (Helsinki: 1998).

Landucci Gattinoni, F., *Lisimaco di Tracia: Un sovrano nella prospettiva del primo ellenismo* (Milan: 1992).

Landucci Gattinoni, F., "Cassander and the Legacy of Philip II and Alexander III in Diodorus' Library," in E. Carney and D. Ogden (eds.), *Philip II and Alexander the Great: Lives and Afterlives* (Oxford: 2010), pp. 113–121.

Landucci Gattinoni, F., "Diodorus XVIII 39.1-7 and Antipatros' Settlement at Triparadeisos," in H. Hauben and A. Meeus (eds.), *The Age of the Successors and the Creation of the Hellenistic Kingdoms (323-276 B.C)* (Leuven: 2014), pp. 33–48.

Lane Fox, R. (ed.), *Brill's Companion to Ancient Macedon* (Leiden: 2011).

Lane Fox, R., "King Ptolemy: Centre and Periphery," in E. Baynham and P. Wheatley (eds.), *East and West in the World Empire of Alexander: Essays in Honour of Brian Bosworth* (Oxford: 2014), pp. 163–195.

Laronde, M. A., "Observations sur la politique d'Ophellas à Cyrène," *RH* 245 (1971), pp. 297–336.

Laronde, M. A., "La date du diagramma de Ptolémée," *REG* 100 (1987), pp. 85–128.

Larsen, J. A. O., "Notes on the Constitutional Inscription from Cyrene," *CPh* 24 (1929), pp. 351–368.

Lehmann, G. A., "Der 'lamische Krieg' und die 'Freiheit der hellenen.' Überlegungen zur hieronymianischen Tradition," *ZPE* 73 (1988a), pp. 121–149.

Lehmann, G. A., "Das neue Kölner Historiker-Fragment (P. Köln Nr. 247) und die *chronike suntaxis* des Zenon von Rhodos (FGrHist. 523)," *ZPE* 72 (1988b), pp. 1–17.

Le Rider, G., "Cléomène de Naucratis," *BCH* 121 (1997), pp. 71–93.

Lévèque, P., *Pyrrhos* (Paris: 1957).

Lewis, N., *Greeks in Ptolemaic Egypt: Case Studies in the Social History of the Hellenistic World* (Oxford: 1986).

Lianou, M., "The Role of the Argeadai in the Legitimation of the Ptolemaic Dynasty: Rhetoric and Practice," in E. Carney and D. Ogden (eds.), *Philip II and Alexander the Great: Lives and Afterlives* (Oxford: 2010), pp. 123–133.

Lianou, M., "Ptolemy I and the Economics of Consolidation," in H. Hauben and A. Meeus (eds.), *The Age of the Successors and the Creation of the Hellenistic Kingdoms (323–276 B.C.)* (Leuven: 2014), pp. 379–411.

Lloyd, A. B., "The Egyptian Elite in the Early Ptolemaic Period: Some Hieroglyphic Evidence," in D. Ogden (ed.), *The Hellenistic World: New Perspectives* (London: 2002), pp. 117–136.

Lloyd, A. B., "From Satrapy to Hellenistic Kingdom: The Case of Egypt," in A. Erskine and L. Lewellyn-Jones (eds.), *Creating a Hellenistic World* (Swansea: 2010a), pp. 83–105.

Lloyd, A. B., "The Reception of Pharaonic Egypt in Classical Antiquity," in A. B. Lloyd (ed.), *A Companion to Ancient Egypt*, vol. 2 (Malden, MA: 2010b), pp. 1067–1085.

Lloyd, A. B. (ed.), *A Companion to Ancient Egypt*, 2 vols. (Malden, MA: 2010c).

Longega, G., *Arsinoë II* (Rome: 1968).

Lorber, C. C., "A Revised Chronology for the Coinage of Ptolemy I," *NC* 165 (2005), pp. 45–64.

Lorton, D., "The Names of Alexandria in the Text of the Satrap Stele," *GöttMisz* 96 (1987), pp. 65–70.

Łukaszewicz, A., "Sur les pas de Ptolémée Iᵉʳ. Quelques remarques concernant la ville d'Alexandrie," in H. Hauben and A. Meeus (eds.), *The Age of the Successors and the Creation of the Hellenistic Kingdoms (323–276 B.C)* (Leuven: 2014), pp. 189–205.

Lund, H. S., *Lysimachus: A Study in Early Hellenistic Kingship* (London: 1994).

Ma, J., "Kings," in A. Erskine (ed.), *A Companion to the Hellenistic World* (Malden, MA: 2003), pp. 177–195.

Ma, J., "Chaironeia 338: Topographies of Commemoration," *JHS* 128 (2008), pp. 172–191.

MacLeod, R. (ed.), *The Library of Alexandria: Centre of Learning in the Ancient World* (London: 2000).

Mahaffy, J. P., *The Empire of the Ptolemies* (London: 1895).

Mahaffy, J. P., *A History of Egypt under the Ptolemies* (London: 1898).

Manni, E., *Demetrio Poliorcete* (Rome: 1951).

Manning, J., *Land and Power in Ptolemaic Egypt: The Structure of Land Tenure* (Cambridge: 2003).

Manning, J., *The Last Pharaohs: Egypt under the Ptolemies, 305–30 BC* (Princeton, NJ: 2010).

Mansuelli, G. A., "Contributo a Deinokrates," in N. Bonacasu and A. Di Vita (eds.), *Alesandria eil mondo ellenistico-romano. Studi in onere di A. Adrian* 1 (Rome: 1983), pp. 79–80.

Marasco, G., "Sui problemi dell'approvvigionamento di cereali in Atene nell'età dei Diadochi," *Athenaeum* 62 (1984), pp. 286–294.

Marsden, F. W., *Greek and Roman Artillery: Technical Treatises* (Oxford: 1971).

Martin, T. R., "Quintus Curtius' Presentation of Philip Arrhidaeus and Josephus' Accounts of the Accession of Claudius," *AJAH* 8 (1983 [1987]), pp. 161–190.

McKechnie, P. and P. Guillaume (eds.), *Ptolemy II Philadelphus and His World* (Leiden: 2008).

Meeus, A., "The Power Struggle of the Diadochoi in Babylonia, 323 BC," *Anc. Society* 38 (2008), pp. 39–82.

Meeus, A., "Some Institutional Problems Concerning the Succession to Alexander the Great: 'Prostasia' and Chiliarchy," *Historia* 58 (2009a), pp. 302–310.

Meeus, A., "Alexander's Image in the Age of the Successors," in W. Heckel and L. Tritle (eds.), *Alexander the Great: A New History* (Malden, MA: 2009b), pp. 235–250.

Meeus, A., "Kleopatra and the Diadochoi," in P. van Nuffelen (ed.), *Faces of Hellenism: Studies in the History of the Eastern Mediterranean (4th Century B.C.–5th Century A.D.)* (Leuven: 2009c), pp. 63–92.

Meeus, A., "Diodorus and the Chronology of the Third Diadoch War," *Phoenix* 66 (2012), pp. 74–96.

Meeus, A., "The Territorial Ambitions of Ptolemy I," in H. Hauben and A. Meeus (eds.), *The Age of the Successors and the Creation of the Hellenistic Kingdoms (323–276 B.C)* (Leuven: 2014), pp. 262–306.

Meeus, A., "The Career of Sostratos of Knidos: Politics, Diplomacy and the Alexandrian Building Programme in the Early Hellenistic Period," in T. Howe, E. E. Garvan, and G. Wrightson (eds.), *Greece, Macedon and Persia: Studies in Social, Political and Military History in Honour of W. Heckel* (Haverton: 2015), pp. 143–171.

Mehl, A., *Seleukos Nikator und sein Reich* (Louvain: 1986).

Mélèze Modrzejewski, J., "The Judicial System in Theory and Practice. 10.1. Ptolemaic Justice," in J. G. Keenan, J. G. Manning, and U. Yiftach-Firanko (eds.), *Law and Legal Practice in Egypt from Alexandria to the Arab Conquest* (Cambridge: 2014), pp. 471–477.

Merker, I. L., "The Ptolemaic Officials and the League of the Islanders," *Historia* 19 (1970), pp. 141–160.

Mitford, T. B., "The Character of Ptolemaic Rule in Cyprus," *Aegyptus* 33 (1953), pp. 80–90.

Monson, A., *From the Ptolemies to the Romans: Political and Economic Change in Egypt* (Cambridge: 2012).

Mooren, L., "The Nature of the Hellenistic Monarchy," in E. Van 'T Dack, P. van Dessel, and W. van Gucht (eds.), *Egypt and the Hellenistic World* (Louvain: 1983), pp. 205–240.

Mooren, L., "Foreigners in the Hellenistic World: Hellenic Immigrants in Ptolemaic Egypt," in A. Tamis, C. J. Mackie, and S. G. Byrne (eds.), *Philathenaios: Studies in Honour of Michael J. Osborne* (Athens: 2010), pp. 123–137.

Mørkholm, O., "Cyrene and Ptolemy I: Some Numismatic Comments," *Chiron* 10 (1980), pp. 145–159.

Morrison, A. D., "Greek Literature in Egypt," in A. B. Lloyd (ed.), *A Companion to Ancient Egypt*, vol. 2 (Malden, MA: 2010), pp. 755–778.

Mossé, C., *Athens in Decline, 404–86 B.C.*, trans. J. Stewart (London: 1973).

Muccioli, F., *Gli epiteti ufficiali dei re ellenistici* (Stuttgart: 2012).

Mueller, K., *Settlements of the Ptolemies: City Foundations and New Settlement in the Hellenistic World* (Leuven: 2006).

Müller, S., *Das hellenistische Königspaarin der medialen Repräsentation* (Berlin: 2009).

Müller, S., "Philip II," in J. Roisman and Ian Worthington (eds.), *A Companion to Ancient Macedonia* (Malden, MA: 2010), pp. 166–185.

Murray, W. M., *The Age of Titans: The Rise and Fall of the Great Hellenistic Navies* (Oxford: 2012).

Ogden, D., *Polygamy, Prostitutes and Death: The Hellenistic Dynasties* (London: 1999).

Ogden, D., *Alexander the Great: Myth, Genesis and Sexuality* (Exeter: 2011).

Oliver, G., *War, Food, and Politics in Early Hellenistic Athens* (Oxford: 2007).

Osborne, M. J., "Kallias, Phaidros, and the Revolt of Athens in 287 BC," *ZPE* 35 (1979), pp. 181–194.

O'Sullivan, L., *The Regime of Demetrius of Phalerum in Athens, 317–307 BCE* (Leiden: 2009).

Parsons, E. A., *The Alexandrian Library* (Amsterdam: 1952).

Perdu, O., "Saites and Persians (664–332)," in A. B. Lloyd (ed.), *A Companion to Ancient Egypt*, vol. 1 (Malden, MA: 2010), pp. 140–158.

Peremans, W., "Egyptiens et étrangers dans le milieu d'Alexandrie au temps des Lagides," *Anc. Society* 7 (1976), pp. 167–176.

Peremans, W., "Les indigènes Egyptiens dans l'armée de terre des Lagides," *Anc. Society* 9 (1978), pp. 83–100.

Peremans, W., "Étrangers et égyptiens en Égypte sous le règne de Ptolémée Ier," *Anc. Society* 11/12 (1980/81), pp. 222–223.

Peremans, W, "Le Bilinguisme dans les Relations Gréco-Égyptiennes sous les Lagides," in E. Van 'T Dack, P. van Dessel, and W. van Gucht (eds.), *Egypt and the Hellenistic World* (Louvain: 1983), pp. 253–280.

Pfeiffer, R., *History of Classical Scholarship* (Oxford: 1968).

Pfeiffer, S., "The God Serapis, His Cult and the Beginnings of the Ruler Cult in Ptolemaic Egypt," in P. McKechnie and P. Guillaume (eds.), *Ptolemy II Philadelphus and His World* (Leiden: 2008), pp. 387–408.

Pimouguet-Pédarros, I., *La Cité à l'épreuve des rois: Le siège de Rhodes par Démétrios Poliorcète, 305–304 av. J.-C* (Rennes: 2001).

Pollard, N., "Military Institutions and Warfare: Graeco-Roman," in A. B. Lloyd (ed.), *A Companion to Ancient Egypt*, vol. 1 (Malden, MA: 2010), pp. 446–465.

Pollard, N. and H. Reid, *The Rise and Fall of Alexandria: Birthplace of the Modern World* (London: 2009).

Prandi, L., Kleitarchos, *BNJ* 137 (Leiden).

Préaux, C., *L'économie royale des Lagides* (Brussels: 1939).

Rathmann, M., *Perdikkas zwischen 322 und 320: Nachlassverwalter des Alexanderreiches oder Autokrat?* (Vienna: 2005).

Rice, E. E., *The Grand Procession of Ptolemy II Philadelphus* (Oxford: 1983).

Rice, E. E., *Cleopatra* (Ann Arbor, MI: 1999).

Rigsby, K. J., "An Edict of Ptolemy I," *ZPE* 72 (1988), pp. 273–274.

Rihll, T. E., "Science and Technology: Alexandrian," in A. B. Lloyd (ed.), *A Companion to Ancient Egypt*, vol. 1 (Malden, MA: 2010), pp. 409–424.

Ritner, R. K., "The Satrap Stela," in W. K. Simpson, R. K. Ritner, and V. A. Tobin (eds.), *Literature of Ancient Egypt: An Anthology of Stories, Instructions, Stelae, Autobiographies, and Poetry* (New Haven, CT: 2003), pp. 392–397.

Robinson, C. A., *The History of Alexander the Great*, 2 vols. (Providence, RI: 1953).

Robinson, D. and A. Wilson (eds.), *Alexandria and the North-Western Delta* (Oxford: 2010).

Robinson, E. S. G., "The Coin Standards of Ptolemy I," in M. I. Rostovtzeff, *The Social and Economic History of the Hellenistic World*, vol. 3 (Oxford: 1941), pp. 1635–1639.

Rodriguez, P., "Les Égyptiens dans l'armée de terre ptolémaïque (Diodore, XIX, 80, 4)," *REG* 117 (2004), pp. 104–124.

Roisman, J., "Ptolemy and His Rivals in His History of Alexander the Great," *CQ* 34 (1984), pp. 373–385.

Roisman, J., "Honor in Alexander's Campaign," in J. Roisman (ed.), *Brill's Companion to Alexander the Great* (Leiden: 2003), pp. 279–321.

Roisman, J., *Alexander's Veterans and the Early Wars of the Successors* (Austin, TX: 2012).

Roisman, J., "Perdikkas's Invasion of Egypt," in H. Hauben and A. Meeus (eds.), *The Age of the Successors and the Creation of the Hellenistic Kingdoms (323–276 B.C.)* (Leuven: 2014), pp. 455–474.

Roisman, J., "Opposition to Macedonian Kings: Riots for Rewards and Verbal Protests," in T. Howe, E. E. Garvan, and G. Wrightson (eds.), *Greece, Macedon and Persia: Studies in Social, Political and Military History in Honour of W. Heckel* (Haverton: 2015), pp. 77–86.

Roisman, J. and Ian Worthington (eds.), *A Companion to Ancient Macedonia* (Malden, MA: 2010).

Roller, D., *Cleopatra: A Biography* (Oxford: 2010).

Romm, J., *Ghost on the Throne: The Death of Alexander the Great and the War for Crown and Empire* (New York: 2011).

Rosen, K., "Die Reichsordnung von Babylon (323 v. Chr.)," *Acta Classica* 10 (1967), pp. 95–110.

Rosen, K., "Die Bündnisformen der Diadochen und der Zerfall des Alexanderreiches," *Ant. Class.* 11 (1968), pp. 182–210.

Rosen, K., "Politische Ziele in der frühen hellenistischen Geschichtsschreibung," *Hermes* 107 (1979), pp. 460–477.

Rostovtzeff, M. I., *The Social and Economic History of the Hellenistic World*, 3 vols. (Oxford: 1941).

Rostovtzeff, M. I., "Ptolemaic Egypt," in S. A. Cook, F. E. Adcock, and M. P. Charlesworth (eds.), *Cambridge Ancient History*, vol. 7 (Cambridge: 1954), pp. 109–154.

Rowlandson, J., "Town and Country in Ptolemaic Egypt," in A. Erskine (ed.), *A Companion to the Hellenistic World* (Malden, MA: 2003), pp. 249–263.

Rowlandson, J., "Administration and Law: Graeco-Roman," in A. B. Lloyd (ed.), *A Companion to Ancient Egypt*, vol. 1 (Malden, MA: 2010), pp. 237–254.

Samuel, A. E., *Ptolemaic Chronology* (Munich: 1962).

Samuel, A. E., *The Shifting Sands of History: Interpretations of Ptolemaic Egypt* (Lanham, MD: 1989).

Samuel, A. E., "The Ptolemies and the Ideology of Kingship," in P. Green (ed.), *Hellenistic History and Culture* (Berkeley, CA: 1993), pp. 168–192.

Schäfer, C., *Eumenes von Kardia und der Kampf um die Macht im Alexanderreich* (Frankfurt: 2002).

Schäfer, D., "Nachfolge und Legitimierung in Ägypten im Zeitalter der Diaochen," in H. Hauben and A. Meeus (eds.), *The Age of the Successors and the Creation of the Hellenistic Kingdoms (323–276 B.C)* (Leuven: 2014), pp. 441–452.

Schepens, G., "Les Rois Ptolémaïques et l'historiographie. Réflexions sur la transformation de l'histoire politique," in E. Van 'T Dack, P. van Dessel, and W. van Gucht (eds.), *Egypt and the Hellenistic World* (Louvain: 1983), pp. 351–368.

Schiff, S., *Cleopatra: A Life* (New York, NY: 2010).

Schmitt, O., *Der Lamische Krieg* (Bonn: 1992).

Schmitthenner, W., "Über eine Formveränderung der Monarchie set Alexander d. Gr.," *Saeculum* 19 (1968), pp. 31–46.

Schur, W., "Das Alexanderreich nach Alexanders Tode," *RhM* 83 (1934), pp. 129–156.

Seibert, J., *Untersuchungen zur Geschichte Ptolemaios' I* (Munich: 1969).

Seibert, J., "Philokles, Sohn des Apollodoros, König der Sidonier," *Historia* 19 (1970), pp. 337–351.

Seibert, J., "Ptolemaios I. und Milet," *Chiron* 1 (1971), pp. 159–166.

Seibert, J., "Nochmals zu Kleomenes von Naukratis," *Chiron* 2 (1979), pp. 99–102.

Seibert, J., *Das Zeitalter der Diadochen* (Darmstadt: 1983).

Sekunda, N. V., "The Macedonian Army," in J. Roisman and Ian Worthington (eds.), *A Companion to Ancient Macedonia* (Malden, MA: 2010), pp. 446–471.

Sethe, K., *Hieroglyphische Urkunden der griechisch-römischen Zeit* 2 (Leipzig: 1916).

Shear, T. L., *Kallias of Sphettos and the Revolt of Athens in 286 B.C.* (Princeton, NJ: 1978).

Shipley, G., *The Greek World after Alexander 323–30 BC* (London: 2000).

Shipley, G., "Between Macedonia and Rome: Political Landscapes and Social Changes in Southern Greece in the Early Hellenistic Period," *BSA* 100 (2005), pp. 315–330.

Sickinger, J., *Marmor Parium, BNJ* 239 (Leiden).

Simpson, R. H., "The Historical Circumstances of the Peace of 311," *JHS* 74 (1954), pp. 25–31.

Simpson, R. H., "Antigonus, Polyperchon and the Macedonian Regency," *Historia* 6 (1957), pp. 371–373.

Simpson, R. H., "Antigonus the One-Eyed and the Greeks," *Historia* 8 (1959), pp. 385–409.

Skeat, T. C., *The Reigns of the Ptolemies* (Munich: 1954).

Smith, H. S., "A Satrap at Memphis," in J. Baines et al. (eds.), *Pyramid Studies and Other Essays Presented to I. E. S. Edwards* (London: 1988), pp. 184–186.

Squillace, S., "The Comparison between Alexander and Philip: Use and Metamorphosis of an Ideological Theme," in T. Howe, E. E. Garvan, and G. Wrightson (eds.), *Greece,*

Macedon and Persia: Studies in Social, Political and Military History in Honour of W. Heckel (Haverton: 2015), pp. 107–113.

Stambaugh, J. E., *Sarapis under the Early Ptolemies* (Leiden: 1972).

Stewart, A., *Faces of Power: Alexander's Image and Hellenistic Politics* (Berkeley, CA: 1993).

Stewart, A., "Alexander in Greek and Roman Art," in J. Roisman (ed.), *Brill's Companion to Alexander the Great* (Leiden: 2003), pp. 31–66.

Stiehl, R., "The Origin of the Cult of Sarapis," *History of Religions* 3 (1963/64), pp. 21–36.

Stoneman, R., "The Alexander Romance: From History to Fiction," in J. R. Morgan and R. Stoneman (eds.), *Greek Fiction: The Greek Novel in Context* (London: 1994), pp. 117–129.

Strasburger, H., *Ptolemaios und Alexander* (Leipzig: 1934).

Strootman, R., "Men to Whose Rapacity Neither Sea Nor Mountain Sets a Limit: The Aims of the Diadochs," in H. Hauben and A. Meeus (eds.), *The Age of the Successors and the Creation of the Hellenistic Kingdoms (323–276 B.C.)* (Leuven: 2014a), pp. 307–322.

Strootman, R., *Courts and Elites in the Hellenistic Empires: The Near East after the Achaemenids, c. 330–30 BCE* (Edinburgh: 2014b).

Strauss, B., "Alexander: The Military Campaign," in J. Roisman (ed.), *Brill's Companion to Alexander the Great* (Leiden: 2003), pp. 133–156.

Swinnen, W., "Sur la politique religieuse de Ptolémée Ier," in *Les syncrétismes dans les religions Grecque et Romaine* (Paris: 1973), pp. 115–133.

Tarn, W. W., *Antigonus Gonatas* (Oxford: 1913).

Tarn, W. W., "Heracles, Son of Barsine," *JHS* 41 (1921), pp. 18–28.

Tarn, W. W. and G. T. Griffith, *Hellenistic Civilisation* (London: 1952).

Taylor, L. R., "The Cult of Alexander at Alexandria," *CPh* 22 (1927), pp. 162–169.

Thompson, D. J., *Memphis under the Ptolemies* (Princeton, NJ: 1988).

Thompson, D. J., "Language and Literacy in Early Hellenistic Egypt," in P. Bilde, T. Engberg-Pedersen, L. Hannestad, and J. Zahle (eds.), *Ethnicity in Hellenistic Egypt* (Aarhus: 1992), pp. 39–52.

Thompson, D. J., "Hellenistic Hellenes: The Case of Ptolemaic Egypt," in I. Malkin (ed.), *Ancient Perceptions of Greek Ethnicity* (Cambridge: 2001), pp. 301–322.

Thompson, D. J., "The Ptolemies and Egypt," in A. Erskine (ed.), *A Companion to the Hellenistic World* (Malden, MA: 2003), pp. 105–120.

Touratsoglou, J., "Art in the Hellenistic Period," in M. B. Sakellariou (ed.), *Macedonia: 4000 Years of Greek History and Civilization* (Athens: 1983), pp. 170–191.

Tracy, S. V., *Athenian Democracy in Transition: Attic Letter-cutters of 340 to 290 BC* (Berkeley, CA: 1995).

Turner, E., "Ptolemaic Egypt," in F. W. Walbank, A. E. Astin, M. W. Frederiksen, and R.M. Ogilvie (eds.), *Cambridge Ancient History*, vol. 7² (Cambridge: 1984), pp. 118–174.

van der Spek, R. J., "Seleukos, Self-appointed General (*Strategos*) of Asia (311–305 B.C.) and the Satrapy of Babylonia," in H. Hauben and A. Meeus (eds.), *The Age of the Successors and the Creation of the Hellenistic Kingdoms (323–276 B.C.)* (Leuven: 2014), pp. 232–342.

Vandorpe, K., "The Ptolemaic Period," in A. B Lloyd (ed.), *A Companion to Ancient Egypt*, vol. 1 (Malden, MA: 2010), pp. 159–179.

van Oppen de Ruiter, B. F., "The Marriage of Ptolemy I and Berenice I," *Anc Society* 41 (2011), pp. 83–92.

van Oppen de Ruiter, B. F., "Argaeus: An Illegitimate Son of Alexander the Great?" *ZPE* 187 (2013), pp. 206–210.

van 'T Dack, E., P. van Dessel, and W. van Gucht (eds.), *Egypt and the Hellenistic World* (Louvain: 1983).

Vogt, J., "Kleomenes von Naukratis—Herr von Aegypten," *Chiron* 1 (1971), pp. 153–157.

Walbank, F. W., "Monarchies and Monarchic Ideas," in F. W. Walbank, A. E. Astin, M. W. Frederiksen, and R. M. Ogilvie (eds.), *Cambridge Ancient History*, vol. 7² (Cambridge: 1984a), pp. 62–100.

Walbank, F. W., "Sources for the Period," in F. W. Walbank, A. E. Astin, M. W. Frederiksen, and R. M. Ogilvie (eds.), *Cambridge Ancient History*, vol. 7² (Cambridge: 1984b), pp. 1–22.

Walbank, F. W., *The Hellenistic World* (Cambridge: 1993).

Walbank, F. W., A. E. Astin, M. W. Frederiksen, and R. M. Ogilvie (eds.), *Cambridge Ancient History*, vol. 7² (Cambridge: 1984).

Walker, S. and P. Higgs, *Cleopatra of Egypt: From History to Myth* (Princeton, NJ: 2001).

Walton, F. R., *Diodorus Siculus 21–32*, Loeb Classical Library, vol. 11 (Cambridge, MA: 1957).

Waterfield, R., *Dividing the Spoils: The War for Alexander the Great's Empire* (Oxford: 2011).

Waterfield, R., *Taken at the Flood: The Roman Conquest of Greece* (New York: 2014).

Waters, M., *Ancient Persia: A Concise History of the Achaemenid Empire, 550–330 BCE* (Cambridge: 2014).

Weber, G., "The Court of Alexander the Great as Social System," in W. Heckel and L. Tritle (eds.), *Alexander the Great: A New History* (Malden, MA: 2009), pp. 83–98.

Welles, C. B., "The Discovery of Sarapis and the Foundation of Alexandria," *Historia* 11 (1962), pp. 271–298.

Welles, C. B., "The Reliability of Ptolemy as an Historian," *Miscellanea di Studi Alessandrini in Memoria di A. Rostagni* (Turin: 1963), pp. 101–116.

Westlake, H. D., "Eumenes of Cardia," in H. D. Westlake (ed.), *Essays on the Greek Historians and Greek History* (Manchester: 1969), pp. 313–330.

Wheatley, P., "Ptolemy Soter's Annexation of Syria, 320 B.C.," *CQ²* 45 (1995), pp. 433–440.

Wheatley, P., "The Chronology of the Third Diadoch War, 315–311 B.C.," *Phoenix* 52 (1998), pp. 257–281.

Wheatley, P., "Antigonus Monophthalmus in Babylonia, 310–308 B.C.," *JNES* 61 (2002), pp. 39–47.

Wheatley, P., "Demetrius the Besieger on the Nile," in P. Bosman (ed.), *Alexander in Africa* (Pretoria: 2014), pp. 92–108.

Whitehouse, H., "Mosaics and Painting in Graeco-Roman Egypt," in A. B. Lloyd (ed.), *A Companion to Ancient Egypt*, vol. 2 (Malden, MA: 2010), pp. 1008–1031.

Will, E., "La Cyrénaïque et les partages successifs de l'empire d'Alexandre," *Ant. Class.* 29 (1960), pp. 269–290.

Will, E., "Ophellas, Ptolémée, Cassandre et la chronologie," *REA* 66 (1964), pp. 320–333.

Will, E., *Histoire politique du monde hellénistique (323–30 av. J.-C.)*, vol. 1 (Nancy: 1966).

Will, E., "The Succession to Alexander," in F. W. Walbank, A. E. Astin, M. W. Frederiksen, and R. M. Ogilvie (eds.), *Cambridge Ancient History*, vol. 7² (Cambridge: 1984a), pp. 23–61.

Will, E., "The Adventures of Demetrius Poliorcetes (301–286)," in F. W. Walbank, A. E. Astin, M. W. Frederiksen, and R. M. Ogilvie (eds.), *Cambridge Ancient History*, vol. 7² (Cambridge: 1984b), pp. 101–109.

Wirth, G., "Zur Politik des Perdikkas 323," *Helion* 7 (1967), pp. 281–322.

Wörrle, M., "Epigraphische Forschungen zur Geschichte Lykiens, 1: Ptolemaios I. und Limyra," *Chiron* 7 (1977), pp. 43–66.

Wörrle, M., "Epigraphische Forschungen zur Geschichte Lykiens, 2: Ptolemaios II. und Telmessos," *Chiron* 8 (1978), pp. 83–111.

Worthington, Ian, "The Harpalus Affair and the Greek Response to the Macedonian Hegemony," in Ian Worthington (ed.), *Ventures into Greek History: Essays in Honour of N. G. L. Hammond* (Oxford: 1994), pp. 307–330.

Worthington, Ian, *Philip II of Macedonia* (London: 2008).

Worthington, Ian, "Alexander the Great, Nation-building, and the Creation and Maintenance of Empire," in V. D. Hanson (ed.), *Makers of Ancient Strategy: From the Persian Wars to the Fall of Rome* (Princeton, NJ: 2010), pp. 118–137.

Worthington, Ian, *Demosthenes of Athens and the Fall of Classical Greece* (New York, NY: 2013).

Worthington, Ian, *By the Spear: Philip II, Alexander the Great, and the Rise and Fall of the Macedonian Empire* (New York, NY: 2014).

Worthington, Ian, "Ptolemy I as *Soter*: The Silence of Epigraphy and the Case for Egypt," *ZPE* 198 (2016), pp. 128–130.

Yardley, J., *Quintus Curtius Rufus: The History of Alexander*, Penguin Classics (Harmondsworth: 1984).

Yardley, J. and W. Heckel, *Justin: Epitome of the Philippic History of Pompeius Trogus 1, Books 11–12: Alexander the Great* (Oxford: 1997).

Yardley, J., P. Wheatley, and W. Heckel, *Justin: Epitome of the Philippic History of Pompeius Trogus 2, Books 13–15: The Successors to Alexander the Great* (Oxford: 2011).

INDEX

Printed in the USA/Agawam, MA
September 2, 2022

797976.005